WATERCRAFT ON WORLD COINS

"In the realm of coins there are two major hobbyists, the collector and the numismatist. The former merely amasses coins for the pleasure of having them while the latter goes much further. The numismatist strives to uncover the history including every fascinating detail associated with each coin. Mr. Yossi Dotan is definitely a numismatist and in the field of coins depicting watercraft is one of its foremost authorities. In fact it is highly doubtful that any person exceeds his knowledge of SHIP COINS. His book shares this learning of many decades; it is a most needed tool for collectors, numismatists, and historians."

Dr. Lloryel W. Antoine, Ed.D, CPO USN (retired), of Florida, USA wrote a monthly column on "ship coins" in *World Coin News* for five years in the 1990s, and is the author of the book *Nautical Numismatics*

"Yossi Dotan's *Watercraft on World Coins: Volume I – Europe 1800–2005* will long be the standard of numismatic topical descriptions. His research is richly detailed and the narratives of ships – particularly fighting ships, but also cargo carriers – of the last two centuries is not only amazingly accurate but also extremely interesting reading for all students of naval warfare, shipping, and of course, numismatics. I highly recommend this book for the library of any numismatist as well as anyone interested in naval history."

Mr. Charles R. Hosch of Georgia, USA is the author of *Heraldic Coats of Arms on Coins of the World, 1700–1998: Complete Descriptions* (1998) and *World Gold Proof Sets Since 1900 – Complete Descriptions* (2002)

"Thanks to Yossi Dotan's research journey, the *Watercraft on World Coins* series is unique. These coins form the basis for exciting and intriguing tales."

Cees van Romburgh, Maritime Historian, Amsterdam, The Netherlands

"With thoughtful story-lines, excellent research and superb illustrations, this book is an exciting literary journey to hundreds of distant and exotic shores. This comprehensive study of watercraft depicted on coins will be of interest not only to maritime history enthusiasts, but also to coin collectors and numismatists."

Cecilia Meir, Curator of the Kadman Numismatic Pavilion, Eretz Israel Museum, Tel Aviv, Israel

"This volume, with its presentation of comprehensive data for each ship, fills a long-existing gap. The book raises high expectations for the next two volumes and may even give rise to a sequel that will narrate coins (and perhaps even tokens) of the 17th and 18th centuries."

Harm-Henning Kuhlmann, editor of *Numisnautik*, Hamburg, Germany

WATERCRAFT ON WORLD COINS

Volume I

EUROPE, 1800–2005

YOSSI DOTAN

THE *Alpha* PRESS

BRIGHTON • PORTLAND

2 4 6 8 10 9 7 5 3 1

First published 2007 in Great Britain by
THE ALPHA PRESS
PO Box 139
Eastbourne BN24 9BP

and in the United States of America by
THE ALPHA PRESS
920 NE 58th Avenue, Suite 300
Portland, Oregon 97213-3786

British Library Cataloguing in Publication Data
A CIP catalogue record for this book is available from the British Library.

Library of Congress Cataloging-in-Publication Data
Dotan, Yossi.
Watercraft on world coins / by Yossi Dotan.
p. cm.
Includes bibliographical references and index.
ISBN 978-1-898595-49-6 (v. 1 : pbk. : alk. paper)
1. Ships in numismatics. 2. Coins—Catalogs. 3. Ships—History—Miscellanea.
4. Navigation—History—Miscellanea. 5. Naval history—Miscellanea. I. Title.

CJ161.S5D68 2007
737.4–dc22 2006038343

Typeset and designed by The Alpha Press, Brighton & Eastbourne.
Printed by TJ International, Padstow, Cornwall.
This book is printed on acid-free paper.

To Channa,
to our children and children-in-law,
and to our lovely grandchildren

Volume I: Europe, 1800–2005
Volume II: America and Asia, 1800–2008
Volume III: Africa and Oceania, 1800–2011

CONTENTS

PREFACE

"Ships on Coins" is a popular collecting theme. The design of such coins is attractive and the stories of the engravings tell of adventure, battles, circumnavigations of the world, discoveries, exploration, foreign countries and many other exciting historical subjects.

Collectors of "ship coins," as other thematical collectors, make their own rules. For this book, any coin qualifies that depicts watercraft, even if the coin depicts only part of the watercraft—such as the railing of a deck, masts or sails, and even where the watercraft is barely distinguishable. The watercraft range from ocean liners to canoes and rafts, and from battle ships and cargo vessels to fishing craft and sport and leisure craft. Symbols such as anchors and rudders, lighthouses, fish, and designs that depict the sea are outside the scope of the book. Volume I: Europe aims to list all legal tender coins issued from the year 1800 arranged by issuing country. The other volumes in preparation are Volume II: America and Asia, and Volume III: Africa and Oceania.

The Numbering System

The coins are listed by the KM-numbers assigned in the *Standard Catalog of World Coins* published by KP Books. Coins with a common watercraft design are grouped together. If their KM-numbers are not sequential, they are referenced to the T-number (T for Topical design) under which they are listed at the end of the country. T-numbers are also used as temporary numbers for coins for which KM-numbers are not yet available.

The Narratives

For each design a description is given of the side of the coin that depicts the watercraft, followed by information on the vessel, those individuals identified with the vessel, the historical background, and other aspects relating to the coin. This information falls short of the complete descriptions of obverse and reverse found in standard numismatic publications. Design elements which are not described in this volume include the name of the sovereign depicted, the coat-of-arms, and inscriptions such as the name of the issuing country or authority and the denomination, because they are of no special interest to the topical collector. The diameter is only stated when the coin is exceptionally large.

Tonnage, length, beam and depth are stated as found in the sources consulted. Tonnage of merchant vessels usually relates to their cargo-carrying capacity, which may be calculated in different ways. For warships, tonnage mostly means their weight measured by the volume of water displaced when afloat, but no single method is generally accepted. Major reconstruction of a ship during her life may cause a change in her tonnage. The length of a vessel is often the overall length from the tip of the bow sprit to the stern rudder, but other authors give the length of the keel or the main deck, or the length at waterline. The data in the book may therefore differ from that found elsewhere and should be considered as only a general indication of the size of the vessel. Information provided on the watercraft does not include details of the rig, engines and armament.

The narratives presented in this volume are rather more historical vignettes than complete descriptions as would be found in a standard numismatic book or book on watercraft.

Abbreviations and References

Where first and last dates are given for a coin, coins were not necessarily struck in each of the intervening years. Where coins have been issued in more than one metal composition, the dates relate to any of these types of issue.

BCE — Before Christian Era
CE — Christian Era (Western date)
mm — Millimeters (coin diameter)
ND — No date; undated

References in the present volume to coins of countries outside Europe relate to coins that will be listed in Volumes II and III.

A Personal Note

Collecting ship coins, researching the narratives and writing this volume has given me much pleasure. I am grateful to many people who assisted me in diverse ways, and these individuals are named under Acknowledgments below. But I take this opportunity to give special thanks to:

- My wife, Channa, who started my interest in coins when she suggested, in the early 1970s, that I buy an album for our children to collect the circulation coins that I brought home from business travel abroad. (The children were not interested, but I was bitten by the world coin collecting bug.)
- The Dutch ship mortgage bank Nederlandse Scheepshypotheekbank (now DVB-Bank) that used images of ship coins to illustrate the cover of its annual report for 1975. This caused me to focus my collecting endeavors on this fascinating theme.
- The late Herr Wolf Mueller-Reichau of Germany who presented so many interesting facts about ship coins in his quarterly *Flaschenpost* (Bottle Mail), his book *Naves in Nummis* and other publications. He encouraged me to share my interest with other

collectors by writing a short article about particular coins with interesting stories. The first narratives for this book were written using research notes for these articles.

I hope that you the reader will enjoy this book. Any comments and corrections will be greatly appreciated. Please write me at yosdotan@bezeqint.net, also if you are willing to contribute to the research of the ship coins of North and South America in Spanish-language sources, which will be presented in Volume II.

ACKNOWLEDGMENTS

Special thanks are due to my wife, Channa, for her support during the years of writing of this volume and for her constructive criticism, particularly concerning the coin images included herein.

A major authority on ship coins, who answered my questions, read the manuscript and provided invigorating criticism, was the late Dr. Lloryel W. Antoine of Florida, who regretfully passed away just before the publication on this volume. Our correspondence since he began writing a column on ship coins in *World Coin News* in the 1990s had developed into a close friendship which I cherished very much. His assistance and his contribution to this book have been extremely valuable.

Mr. Charles R. Hosch of Georgia has been so kind to read the manuscript and made numerous helpful comments, corrections and suggestions for which I am most grateful.

Others who have provided me with information or have assisted me in other ways are listed below in alphabetical order. I appreciate and acknowledge their assistance with thanks.

Yuri Barshay
Szilvia Böröcz
Gerard Borst
Jane L. Colvard
Geoff Corkish
Gideon S. Dotan
Menahem M. Dotan
Pamela Fuchs
Barbara J. Gregory
Werner Kahle
Mordechai Kleinberg
Marcel Kroon
Julie A. Levy
Dr. Dennis G. Rainey
Dragana Lucija Ratkovic
Yana Reznikov
Cees van Romburgh
Julie H. Seijffers
Tuukka Talvio
Amber N. Thompson
Spyros Vretos
Michael de Vries
Argyro Xenou.

Finally, the author and publisher wish to thank the following for their kind permission to reproduce coin images on the pages indicated:

The Central Bank of the Russian Federation (Bank of Russia) 209–12, 217–19, 220 (first image), 222–23, 226 (first image), 231, 232 (second image), 235 (second image), 236–37, 238 (first image),
Deutsches Münzen Magazin (www.muenzenmagazin.de) 58 (second image), 61, 74, 113, 116, 129, 130 (first image), 151, 165, 170 (first image), 189 (second and third images), 193, 196 (first image), 204–05, 226 (second image), 229, 235 (first image), 247, 259, 267,
Professor Michael Stadler 41 (first image),
and UBS AG 13 (first image), 41 (second image).

ALBANIA

The Republic of Albania in the Balkans on the Adriatic Sea gained its independence from the Ottoman Empire in 1912.

Circulation Coin

KM-6 • 1 frang ar • 1927–28 .835 silver

The reverse features the prow of an ancient Roman war galley with a three-pronged ram. The obverse depicts Mercury, the winged-helmeted messenger of the Roman gods. Present-day Albania was part of the Roman province of Illyricum that was established along the Adriatic east coast in 167 BCE to bring an end to raids by Illyrian pirates. The denomination, frang ar, means gold franc. The coin was issued during the reign of President Ahmed Bey Zogu (1895–1961; president 1925–1928, King Zog I from 1928, deposed by Mussolini 1939).

Durres Harbor

KM-57 • 5 lekë • 1987 copper-nickel, issued also in .900 gold
KM-58 • 50 lekë • 1987 .925 silver, 65 mm, issued also in .999 gold
KM-59 • 100 lekë • 1987 .900 gold

KM-58
50 lekë
1987 .925 silver, 65 mm

The reverse depicts a polacca (polacre in French), a 17th-century three-masted cargo vessel used on Mediterranean long-distance routes, approaching the walls of the Adriatic seaport of Durres. A typical polacca was about 115 ft (35 m) in length, with a beam of about 20 ft (6.1 m) and a draft of some 9 ft (2.7 m). It measured about 110 tons and had a complement of 20–30 men. The city of Durres (Durazzo in Italian) was founded in 625 BCE by Greek colonists.

Olympic Games 1992 Barcelona

KM-68 • 10 lekë • 1991 .925 silver

KM-68
10 lekë
1991 .925 silver, 39 mm

The obverse presents an allegorical scene – a reclining woman holding the Olympic torch in the foreground at left, a sailing ship at sea at right, and a lighthouse in the center in the background. The reverse features a horse with rider heading right. The reverse is concave and has an incuse design. It forms a pair with KM-69, the reverse of which is convex and has a raised design. KM-69 features Albania's coat-of-arms on the obverse and a horse with rider heading left on the reverse. The two coins together form a double thickness (piedfort) coin with the ship design of KM-68 as the reverse and the coat-of-arms of KM-69 as the obverse; the equestrians are on the inside. Such pairing of coins appears to be unique. The legends of KM-68 are in Spanish to honor the host city of the 1992 Olympic Games; those of KM-69 are in Albanian. In the Coin of the Year[1] contest for 1991 the coins were selected as the best in both "the best silver coin" and "the most innovative coinage" categories.

Circulation Coin

KM-78 • 20 lekë • 1996 brass

KM-78
20 lekë
1996 brass, 22.5 mm

The obverse features a liburnia and a dolphin. The liburnia, originally a vessel used by the pirates of Liburnia (a region on the eastern coast of the Adriatic Sea), was a fast and very handy bireme (galley with two banks of oars) with the ability to deliver heavily armed men to quickly board and subdue passing craft. The liburnia was first used on a large scale by the Romans in the battle by Octavian against Mark Antony and Cleopatra VII at Actium in 31 BCE. It is estimated that the liburnia had a length of 75–100 ft (23–30 m), a beam including the outriggers of 13–16 ft (4–5 m) and a draft of 2 ft (60 cm). A galley with a length of 75 ft (23 m) is likely to have had a rowing crew of 36 and a sail of 450 sq ft (42 m^2). The speed and maneuverability of this war galley brought about a radical change in Roman tactics which had previously relied on the quality of skill in close combat of the soldiers of their legions. The liburnian galley formed the backbone of Roman naval strength for some four centuries.

ALDERNEY

Alderney is the most northerly of the Channel Islands, lying 8 miles (13 km) from the Cherbourg Peninsula, France. Politically it is a part of the Bailiwick of Guernsey which is ruled by the British crown.

40th Anniversary of the Accession of Queen Elizabeth II

KM-3 • 2 pounds • 1992 copper-nickel, issued also in .925 silver and .917 gold

The reverse depicts the *Mora*, the flagship of the fleet of Duke William of Normandy (1027–1087) in which he crossed the Channel

1 The Coin of the Year awards are bestowed annually by the periodical *World Coin News* (Krause Publications, Iola, Wisconsin, USA). A number of coins listed in this work have been selected as the best coin in one or more of the different categories.

KM-3
2 pounds
1992 copper-nickel, 38.6 mm

in 1066 to claim the crown of England. The *Mora* is shown as a longship with square-rigged sails and a fearful carved figure-head of a lion at the prow, following the tradition of William's Norman (Viking) ancestors. A brilliant lantern hangs atop the mast of the vessel, to serve in the darkness as a rallying point for the ships in the fleet. The ship is shown as depicted on the Bayeux Tapestry that was embroidered by William's wife and the ladies of her court to mark William's conquest of England. The tapestry shows the Norman invasion fleet and tells the story of William who set sail from St. Valéry at the mouth of the Somme in Normandy, crossed the Channel in darkness, landed at Pevensey, and invaded England with 400–500 vessels that eventually ferried 7,000 men and their 2,000 mounts. The ships are similar to those of the Vikings and are steered by a large paddle fastened to the starboard gunwale. They have a single square sail set on a mast which can be unstepped. Both bow and stern posts are raised. Most of the vessels are decorated with dragon heads. Those ships transporting warriors show shields carried on the gunwales. William's invasion followed the acceptance of the throne of England by Harold, the son of the Saxon earl of Essex, because William thought he was entitled to the throne. Harold fell in the battle against William near Hastings on the southeast coast of England on 14 October 1066. William the Conqueror was crowned as king of England on Christmas Day, 1066. The crowned wreathed monogram E II R on the reverse denotes Elizabeth II Regina (Queen).

50th Anniversary of the D-Day Landings

KM-7 ● 2 pounds ● 1994 copper-nickel, issued also in .925 silver
KM-11 ● 100 pounds ● 1994 .999 gold

The reverse shows a scene of the D-Day invasion – a composite design with assault landing craft, the light cruiser HMS *Ajax*, Allied troops and Spitfire fighter airplanes. The coin commemorates the landings of the Allied Forces on the German-held Normandy coast in France on D-Day, 6 June 1944. *Ajax* had a length of 554 ft (169 m), her beam was 56 ft (17 m), and she had a draft of 19 ft (5.8 m). She displaced 9,144 tons and her crew numbered 570. She could reach a speed of 32 knots. *Ajax* was built by Vickers-Armstrong, Barrow-in-Furness in 1935. She was named for one of the heroes of the 12th-century BCE Trojan War related in Homer's *Iliad*. On 3 September 1939, three hours after the outbreak of World War II, *Ajax* sank the German merchant ship *Olinda*, the first merchant casualty of the war. In December 1939 *Ajax*, the flagship of Commodore Harry Harwood's South America Division, engaged the German "pocket battleship" *Graf Spee* in the battle of the River Plate. In 1940 *Ajax* was transferred to the Mediterranean Sea and in 1941 she took part in the battle of Matapan, the evacuation of Greece and the battle for Crete. Later she took part in the D-Day landings, the landings in South France and operations in the Aegean Sea. After the war, *Ajax* was in command of a flotilla which pursued *Exodus 1947*, a former ferry boat bringing 4,554 Jewish survivors of the Holocaust from France to Palestine. *Ajax* rammed the unarmed vessel and forcibly boarded her off the Palestine coast, killing four and wounding 217. *Ajax* was scrapped in 1949.

50th Anniversary of the Return of the Islanders

KM-13 ● 2 pounds ● 1995 copper-nickel, issued also in .925 silver and .917 gold

The reverse features the 822-ton SS *Autocarrier* approaching Alderney in December 1945 with Islanders returning after their five years of exile during the occupation of Alderney by German forces. *Autocarrier* was built in 1931 by D. & W. Henderson, Glasgow for the Southern Railway Company for service between Dover, England and Calais, France. She was Britain's first purpose-built car ferry, and had a capacity of 26 cars and 307 passengers. The steamer's deck was 220 ft (67 m) long, her beam 36 ft (11 m) and she drew 14 ft (4.3 m) of water. Her maximum speed was 16 knots. In 1940 she was used as a naval vessel during the evacuation of the British army from Dunkirk, and was one of the more than twenty ships that took part in the evacuation of those women and children who wanted to leave the Channel Islands before the expected arrival of the German forces and the transportation of men of military age who would join the British forces. The Alderney islanders were evacuated to England on 23 June 1940, just prior to the arrival of the Germans in the Channel Islands a week later. Later *Autocarrier* was fitted out as a recreation ship for the Royal Navy. After the war she was refitted and served as a cargo ship and as a ferry. She was sold for scrap in 1954 by the British Transport Commission, of which the Southern Railway Company had become a part in 1948. The German forces in Alderney surrendered on 16 May 1945. After the removal of more than 30,000 land mines and rendering safe numerous buildings, the first of those exiled returned from mainland Britain on 2 December 1945 in the launch *Guillemont*, followed by the main party who arrived on 15 December 1945 on *Autocarrier*. The reverse inscription OUR DEAR CHANNEL ISLANDS ARE ALSO TO BE FREED is a quotation from the VE (Victory Europe) Day speech by Britain's prime minister Sir Winston Churchill (1874–1965) on 8 May 1945 in which he announced Germany's unconditional surrender and added, "I should not forget to mention that our dear Channel Islands, the only part of His Majesty's Dominions that has been in the hands of the German foe, are also to be freed today."

150th Anniversary of the Death of the Duke of Wellington

KM-29 ● 5 pounds ● 2002 copper-nickel, issued also in .925 silver and .917 gold
KM-30 ● 25 pounds ● 2002 .917 gold

The reverse depicts in the foreground a portrait of Arthur Wellesley, Duke of Wellington (1769–1852) at Walmer Castle in 1839, at left his coat-of-arms, and in the background Walmer Castle and to its left a sailing ship at sea. The portrait was taken from a painting by Benjamin Haydon. The duke of Wellington, a military leader and statesman, earned his place in history with his victory over Napoleon at the battle of Waterloo in June 1815. This victory marked the end of Napoleon's military adventures and brought peace to Europe for the next hundred years. After Waterloo, the duke was active in politics, even serving as Prime Minister (1828–1830). The silver issue shows Wellington's crest in the colors of red and yellow.

60th Anniversary of the D-Day Landings – Ships

KM-38 ● 5 pounds ● 2004 copper-nickel, issued also in .925 silver and .917 gold
KM-39 ● 25 pounds ● 2004 .917 gold

The reverse depicts HMS *Belfast* heavily laden with men and equipment, leading a flotilla of warships to the Normandy beaches on 6 June 1944, and at the bottom a poppy. The 11,553-ton cruiser was built in 1939 at the Harland and Wolff shipyard in Belfast, Northern Ireland at a cost of some £2 million. She is 614 ft (187 m) long, has a beam of 69 ft (21 m), and draws 20 ft (6 m) of water. She could make 32 knots and had a complement of 750. In 1939, early in World War II, *Belfast* passed over a magnetic mine off Scotland that exploded under the ship. Casualties were light but the damage to the ship was so severe that repairs took almost three years. She became the flagship of the Tenth Cruiser Squadron, responsible for providing close range heavy cover for the Arctic convoys taking supplies to the Soviet Union. On D-Day, *Belfast* was the flagship of Bombardment Force E, which was part of the Eastern Naval Task Force that supported the British and Canadian assaults on Gold and Juno beaches. Bombardment Force E included five battleships, two monitors, 20 cruisers and 65 destroyers—part of the force of 2,700 seagoing vessels and 1,900 smaller craft that were deployed in support of Operation Neptune, the naval side of the Normandy landings. In 1950–1952 *Belfast* saw action in the Korean War. She was paid off in 1963 but was saved from the scrapyard and brought to London where she has been open to visitors since 1971. The poppy on the reverse is the symbol of Britain's war heroes. On the silver coin the poppy is colored red.

60th Anniversary of the D-Day Landings – Normandy Beach

KM-40 • 50 pounds • 2004 .925 silver, 100 mm, 1000 gr
KM-41 • 1000 pounds • 2004 .917 gold, 100 mm, 1000 gr

The reverse depicts Allied troops attacking German hedgehogs and other fortifications on a Normandy beach; the bow of a ship approaching the beach (near the rim at 9 o'clock); an outline map of Normandy and Alderney (in the upper half); and three barrage balloons (at the top). The hedgehogs were steel posts set in concrete in a manner that would rip out the bottoms of landing craft. The barrage balloons were aimed at preventing Allied planes from swooping down for strafing runs on the German troops. The Germans spent some four years preparing these devices but the Allied troops succeeded in overcoming them in a very short time. In the annual Coin of the Year contest the 50-pound coin was named best contemporary event coin for coins issued in 2004.

The History of the Royal Navy – *Mary Rose*

KM-44 • 5 pounds • 2003 – *see* T-1

The History of the Royal Navy – Alfred the Great

KM-45 • 5 pounds • 2003 copper-nickel, issued also in .925 silver and .917 gold

The reverse depicts King Alfred of the West Saxons (849–899, king from 871) standing on the deck of his rowing galley and in the background Viking longships (*see* Isle of Man KM-24). In 897 Alfred organized a defense against the Danish Vikings whose fast mobile armies—numbering thousands of men embarked in shallow draft longships—had raided the coasts and inland waters of England for plunder since the 790s. Alfred had a navy built of a few fast ships to repulse the attacks by the Vikings. It is for his valiant defense of his kingdom against a strong enemy that Alfred, alone among the English monarchs, is known as "the Great." The ensign of the Royal Navy appears in color on the silver coin only.

The History of the Royal Navy – *Mary Rose*

KM-46 • 25 pounds • 2003 – see T-1

T-1 The History of the Royal Navy – *Mary Rose*

KM-44 • 5 pounds • 2003 copper-nickel, issued also in .925 silver
KM-46 • 25 pounds • 2003 .917 gold

The reverse depicts the 727-ton four-masted carrack *Mary Rose* built in 1510 by the royal dockyard at Portsmouth for King Henry VIII of

England. She was the flagship of his navy. *Mary Rose* was named for the king's sister Mary and the Tudor emblem—the rose. Her length was 148 ft (45 m), she was 38 ft (12 m) in beam and she had a draft of 15 ft (4.6 m). Her crew numbered 415. In 1535 she was rebuilt with a modern system of armament numbering approximately 91 guns. *Mary Rose* is the earliest known ship to have mounted guns within the hull firing through gunports in the vessel's side. She capsized in 1545 just off Portsmouth in a battle with a French force that threatened to land on the Isle of Wight. The king himself watched the battle from the shore. She foundered apparently for much the same reasons as the *Vasa* (*see* Sweden KM-875) did in 1628—too much weight on board and open gunports too close to the water. *Mary Rose* was rediscovered in 1979 buried in the silt that preserved most of one side of the ship, her bottom, and her lower stern. The remains of the ship were raised in one piece in 1982 and placed in a covered dock in the Portsmouth dockyard for treatment and exhibition. The ensign of the Royal Navy appears in color on the silver coin only.

T-2 The History of the Royal Navy – HMS *Warspite*

KM-? ● 5 pounds ● 2005 copper-nickel

The reverse depicts the British battleship HMS *Warspite*. She was built in 1915 and participated in both world wars (*see* Gibraltar KM-117).

KM-?
5 pounds
2005 copper-nickel, 38.6 mm

T-3 The History of the Royal Navy – HMS *Revenge*

KM-? ● 5 pounds ● 2005 copper-nickel, issued also in .925 silver
KM-? ● 25 pounds ● 2005 gold

The reverse depicts HMS *Revenge* in a scene of the battle at the Azores in 1591. The 46-gun galleon of 457 tons was built in 1577. In 1588 she was the flagship of Sir Francis Drake (*see* Great Britain KM-844) during battles with the Spanish armada. *Revenge* sunk in 1591 after a 15-hour battle with Spanish warships off the Azores. The ensign of the Royal Navy appears in color on the silver coin only.

T-4 The History of the Royal Navy – Samuel Hood

KM-? ● 5 pounds ● 2005 copper-nickel, issued also in .925 silver and .917 gold

The reverse depicts the British Vice Admiral Samuel Hood (1724–1816) on his flagship HMS *Barfleur* after the battle off The Saintes in 1782. The three-masted *Barfleur* was a second-rate ship-of-the-line of 90 guns, built in 1768 at Chatham Dockyard according to a design by Sir Thomas Slade. She was 177 ft (54 m) long, had a beam of 50 ft (15 m), and drew 21 ft (6.4 m) of water. She had a tonnage of 1,935 and a complement of 750. She was named for the Anglo-Dutch victory over the French at Cape Barfleur in 1692. In 1780 *Barfleur* was made flagship of Hood, second-in-command to Admiral George Rodney. In 1782 Rodney and Hood had to prevent the French fleet under Comte François de Grasse from joining a force of French and Spanish ships at Haiti and to forestall a French invasion of Jamaica. The fleets met off The Saintes and, after a day-long battle, de Grasse in *Ville de Paris* surrendered to Hood in *Barfleur*. *Barfleur* also saw action in the Wars of the French Revolution. She was broken up in 1819. Hood was made viscount in 1796 and became Lord of the Admiralty in 1798. The ensign of the Royal Navy appears in color on the silver coin only.

T-5 200th Anniversary of the Battle of Trafalgar

KM-? ● 50 pounds ● 2005 .999 silver, 100 mm, 1000 gr

The reverse depicts the first ships in the British line at the battle of Trafalgar (*see* Gibraltar KM-12) opposite a burning ship of the combined French–Spanish fleet, and the portraits of Vice Admiral Lord Horatio Nelson and Nelson's second-in-command, Vice Admiral Cuthbert Collingwood (1750–1810). The British fleet entered the battle sailing in two columns, Nelson in HMS *Victory* commanding one and Collingwood in HMS *Royal Sovereign* the other. Both flagships were 100-gun first-rate ships-of-the-line. The 2,175-ton three-masted *Royal Sovereign* was 184 ft (56 m) long and had a beam of 52 ft (16 m). She was built at Devonport Dockyard in Plymouth in 1787 and had a complement of 850. In 1825 she was renamed *Captain*. She survived until 1849. At Trafalgar, Collingwood was first into battle, closing with the 112-gun *Santa Ana*, Vice Admiral Ignacio de Alava y Navarrete's flagship. After Nelson's death, Collingwood assumed command of the British ships. He was raised to the peerage as Baron Collingwood of Coldburne and Heathpool, awarded a pension of £2,000 a year, and appointed as Nelson's successor to the command of the Mediterranean fleet. Colllingwood was buried in St. Paul's Cathedral alongside Nelson.

ANDORRA

The Principality of Andorra lies in the Pyrenees Mountains between France and Spain. The heads of state are the president of France and the bishop of Urgel, Spain, as co-princes of Andorra. This political structure is based on an agreement signed in 1278. Since then Andorra has been autonomous from both France and Spain. The language of the principality is Catalan. Its currency is the Andorran diner but diner-denominated coins do not circulate. Instead, today, the euro is used (and prior to the introduction of the euro – French and Spanish money).

Olympic Games 1992 Barcelona and Albertville

KM-46 ● 2 diners ● 1987 copper-nickel, varieties exist

The reverse depicts a kayak racer and a cross-country skier. The kayaker alludes to the Summer Olympic Games of 1992 in Barcelona, Spain. The skier refers to the Winter Olympic Games of that year in Albertville, France.

KM-46
2 diners
1987 copper-nickel, 32 mm

Olympic Games 1992 Barcelona – Windsurfer

KM-54 ● 20 diners ● 1989 .925 silver

The reverse shows a windsurfer in the harbor of Barcelona against the skyline of that city dominated by the Columbus column.

Olympic Games 1992 Barcelona – Kayaker

KM-57 ● 20 diners ● 1989 .925 silver

KM-57
20 diners
1989 .925 silver, 35 mm

The reverse depicts a kayaker near the cathedral of La Seu d'Urgell, Spain. The kayaker passes through a gate that consists of two striped poles hanging just above the water from a wire strung over the slalom racing course. The slalom made its Olympic debut at the 1972 Olympic Games in Munich. Because of the costs associated with building the courses it didn't return until the Games in Barcelona that are marked by this coin. La Seu d'Urgell was the host city of the Olympic events of the wildwater canoe-kayak slalom at these Games. The city is the Spanish gateway to Andorra, and the official seat of the episcopal co-prince of the Principality of Andorra. The Santa Maria d'Urgell Cathedral (12th century) is its most emblematic building and is the only Romanesque cathedral preserved in Catalonia, having been restored in the 20th century.

500th Anniversary of the Discovery of America – Issue of 1992

KM-78 ● 10 diners ● 1992 .925 silver

The reverse features the 100-ton three-masted sailing ship *Santa Maria*, the flagship of Christopher Columbus (1451–1506) on his discovery voyage of 1492. The vessel is shown superimposed on a globe. *Santa Maria* was some 85 ft (26 m) long and about 23 ft (7 m) in the beam, and drew approximately 10 ft (3 m) of water. Columbus was born in Genoa, Italy. In 1486 he approached the Spanish monarchs King Ferdinand and Queen Isabella with a plan to reach the Indies in the east by sailing westward. Under their patronage he set sail from Los Palos de la Frontera, Spain, on 3 August 1492 in the nao *Santa Maria*, a merchant ship from Spanish Galicia. Her owner, Juan de la Cosa, came on the voyage as sailing master. (Nao means ship. The term was used by Columbus to indicate that the *Santa Maria* was a square-rigged vessel larger than a caravel. She was a carrack, whereas the other two vessels of his fleet, the 50-ton *Pinta* and the 90-ton *Niña*, were caravels.) On 12 October 1492 Columbus unknowingly discovered the Western Hemisphere. Some sources state that he landed on Samana Cay in the Bahamas; others name as his landing place San Salvador Island, until 1926 named Watling Island, also in the Bahamas. (San Salvador is the name Columbus originally gave to the island.) On 27 October Columbus discovered Cuba and, in December of 1492, he visited the island he named La Isla Española, now Hispaniola. At midnight on Christmas Day, *Santa Maria* grounded on a coral reef. There were no fatalities but the ship was immovable. Everything that could be salvaged was removed. Her timbers were taken to build a fort, La Navidad, as the two remaining vessels were too small to hold all the men. Some of the crew volunteered to remain until another ship could come for them from Spain but none survived to greet their rescuers. On his return to Palos in the *Niña* on 15 March 1493 Columbus was greatly honored. He made three more voyages to seek a passage to the Indies, in 1493–1496, 1498–1500 and 1502–1504. From his fourth voyage Columbus returned ill, dying not long afterwards in Valladolid, Spain. He never realized the true nature of his discoveries. In 1542 his remains were taken to Hispaniola and buried in Santo Domingo. The reverse inscription is A LA DESCOBERTA DEL NOU MON (On the Discovery of The New World).

KM-78
10 diners
1992 .925 silver, 38.6 mm

500th Anniversary of the Discovery of America – Issue of 1994

KM-98 • 10 diners • 1994 .925 silver

The reverse depicts the *Santa Maria*, the flagship of Christopher Columbus on his discovery voyage of 1492 (*see* KM-78). The reverse inscription is A LA DESCOBERTA D'UN NOU MON (On the Discovery of A New World.)

Sailing Ship

KM-120 ● 10 diners ● 1996 .925 silver

KM-120
10 diners
1996 .925 silver, 38.6 mm

A three-masted sailing ship of the Age of Exploration is featured on the reverse. The vessel is most likely a Spanish nao, representing Christopher Columbus' *Santa Maria* (*see* KM-78).

Antonio Vivaldi

KM-133 ● 10 diners ● 1997 .925 silver

The reverse features a portrait of the Venetian composer and violinist Antonio Vivaldi (1678–1741) with a violin, and in the background at left a gondola approaching the Rialto bridge in Venice, Italy. A gondola is a sweep-powered flat-bottomed passenger boat peculiar to the canals and lagoon of Venice (*see* Italy KM-141). Vivaldi was one of the most influential composers of the baroque period.

Holy Year 2000

KM-163 ● 10 diners ● 1999 .925 silver

The reverse depicts Jesus standing on a boat on the Sea of Galilee. The coin marks the 2,000th anniversary of Jesus' birthday, and the Holy Year 2000 which began on 24 December 1999 when Pope John Paul II opened the Holy Gate in St. Peter's Cathedral in Rome.

ARMENIA

The Republic of Armenia is bordered by Georgia, Azerbaijan, Turkey and Iran. It gained its independence in 1991, after it had been ruled by the Turks for centuries and had become a part of the USSR in 1920. The country forms the eastern part of the historic area inhabited by the Armenians.

T-1 Coat-of-Arms

KM-56 ● 5 dram ● 1994 aluminum
KM-58 ● 10 dram ● 1994 aluminum
KM-69 ● 100 dram ● 1996 copper-nickel, 32nd Chess Olympiad
The coins listed are just a sample of the coins issued.

The obverses of all coins of the Republic of Armenia feature the country's coat-of-arms that carries a shield depicting the two peaks of Mount Ararat with Noah's Ark resting on top of the mountain. As told in the Bible book of Genesis, Noah and his wife, and their three sons Shem, Cham and Japhet and their wives, were the only humans whom God considered worthy of being saved from the flood. God instructed Noah to build an ark for his family and for male and female representatives of each animal species, to be preserved after the flood subsided. Noah made the ark of *gopher* wood caulked with pitch inside and out. It had lower, middle and upper decks, a window on top for ventilation, and a loading door in the side of the hull. Its dimensions are stated in the Bible in cubits. Assuming a cubit of 1.6 ft (50 cm), the ark was 480 ft (150 m) long, 80 ft (25 m) wide and 48 ft (15 m) high. It had the shape of a box. Accordingly, the ark had usable space of approximately 115,000 sq ft (11,000 m^2) and a volume for its animal cargo of approximately 1.8 million cubic ft (56,000 m^3). After 40 days of rain the waters had risen to above the top of the highest mountain. Water covered the earth for 150 days and then had receded to such an extent that the ark grounded on the Ararat mountains. Noah knew that the waters had abated when, four months later, the dove he let out came back with a fresh olive leaf in its beak. The flood destroyed all of mankind because of their wickedness, those in the ark being the sole survivors. Noah became the ancestor of the present human race. The dove with the olive leaf in its beak has become a symbol of peace. According to the Jewish calendar, which counts from the creation of the world, the world was created in six days in 3761 BCE (2000 CE corresponds with the Jewish Era year 5761). Counting from this year of the creation and using the genealogical data stated in the Bible, Noah lived in the years 2704–1754 BCE and the flood occurred in 2104 BCE. Some geologists believe that the Biblical story of the flood finds its origin in the water from the Mediterranean Sea that inundated the Black Sea area when the land bridge between Europe and Asia in what is now Turkey burst and became the Bosporus strait. Mount Ararat, 16,959 ft (5,172 m) high, has become the symbol of Armenia. It is now in eastern Turkey but in the past it was in Armenia.

AUSTRIA

The Republic of Austria is situated in central Europe. Until becoming a republic in 1918 it was the center of the Austrian Empire (from 1867 the Dual Monarchy of Austria–Hungary) which for many centuries was ruled by emperors of the Habsburg family.

Completion of the Southern Railway Line

KM-2246 • 2 vereinsthaler • 1857 .900 silver, varieties exist

KM-2246
2 vereinsthaler
1857 .900 silver, 41 mm

The reverse depicts a two-masted sailing / paddle wheel steam vessel at top right, a steam engine at top left, in the middle the lighthouse of the port of Trieste, and at lower left and right the arms of Vienna and Trieste. The coin commemorates the completion of the railway line between the capital Vienna and the empire's principal port, Trieste, on the Gulf of Trieste at the head of the Adriatic Sea. (Austria is landlocked since the end of World War I but for some 600 years it had a connection to the sea through Trieste, now in Italy.) The section of the line that crosses the Semmering pass, with 15 tunnels and 16 viaducts, was the first mountain railway in the world. The obverse features Emperor Franz Joseph I (1830–1916, emperor from 1848). The vereinsthaler (German for "Union taler") was struck to the specifications set forth in the coin convention of 1857 between Austria and the German states that had joined the German Customs Union (*see* German States / Frankfurt KM-326). Under this convention, 30 talers were to contain 500 grams (16.075 oz.) of pure silver and the talers were to be struck in .900 silver.

100th Anniversary of Steamboat Shipping on Lake Constance

KM-2967 • 500 schilling • 1984 .925 silver

KM-2967
500 schilling
1984 .925 silver, 37 mm

The reverse depicts the motor ship *Vorarlberg* above the coat-of-arms of Vorarlberg province for which she is named. The 392-ton passenger ship was built in 1965 at the Korneuburg shipyard and is capable of carrying 1,000 people. She is 203 ft (62 m) long and 40 ft (12 m) in beam, draws 5 ft (1.5 m) of water, and makes 28 knots. Lake Constance (Bodensee in German) is a large fresh-water lake bordered by Austria, Germany and Switzerland through which the Rhine River flows. Austria controls only a relatively small section of the shoreline of the lake. Austria's main lake port is Bregenz in Vorarlberg province. The coin commemorates the inauguration of steamboat shipping on Lake Constance by Emperor Franz Joseph I in 1884. The reverse legend translates to "100 Years of Shipping on Lake Constance." The obverse has a circular pattern of ten coats-of-arms. The top one is the republican eagle of Austria, followed clockwise by the shields of the nine federal provinces: Burgenland, Carinthia, Lower Austria, Upper Austria, Salzburg, Styria, Tirol, Vorarlberg and Vienna.

Austria and Its People – Hallstatt in the Lakes Region

KM-3011 ● 500 schilling ● 1993 .925 silver

The reverse depicts a boat on Lake Hallstatt (Hallstätter See in German) in Upper Austria carrying the Blessed Sacrament in the annual Corpus Christi procession to a chapel across the lake. The boat is decorated by an arch with church banners and flowers, and is propelled by rowers as a token of respect. Other boats decorated with flowers and carrying musicians and local groups circle around the boat with the sacrament. While in other towns the Corpus Christi procession takes place in the streets, in Hallstatt it is held on the lake because the town's streets are too narrow and too steep for the magnificent procession to pass. This tradition goes back to 1623. The obverse features a modernistic view of the picturesque town at the base of a precipitous cliff, crammed along the shore of its mountain lake with its two churches and closely built houses. Hallstatt means "Salt Mine Town." Excavations conducted in the years 1846–1899 have found a prehistoric salt mine and near to it more than 2,000 graves. The implements that accompanied the deceased on their journey to the afterlife and parts of clothing in the graves have been preserved because of the salinity of the soil. These were the first objects that were identified as characteristic of the Early Iron Age (800–500 BCE). Due to this find, the name Hallstatt now denotes generally the Celtic Late Bronze and Early Iron Age cultures in central and western Europe. The United Nations Educational, Scientific and Cultural Organization (UNESCO) has declared the region a world cultural heritage site. In the annual Coin of the Year contest the coin was chosen as most artistic coin for 1993.

The Era of Emperor Franz Joseph I

KM-3019 ● 100 schilling ● 1994 .900 silver

The reverse shows in the foreground a side-wheel steamship on the Danube River at right and a steam locomotive at left, and behind these a factory at right, an Art Nouveau subway pavilion at left, and the Vienna city hall in the background. The steamer is generic, it does not depict a particular vessel. The designer employed several pictures of different ships for his model. Although paddle steamers were also employed in the Adriatic Sea, this type of ship is typical of the paddle steamers used on the rivers and lakes of the Monarchy—especially on the Danube—between 1875 and 1890. The ship and locomotive represent the impact of steam on transportation by water and rail and the resulting prosperity during the reign of Emperor Franz Joseph I; the buildings represent industrialization and achievements in art and architecture during his reign. The subway pavilion is the Otto Wagner pavilion at the Karlsplatz

(Charles Square) in Vienna. The coin commemorates Emperor Franz Joseph I, who was born in 1830, acceded to the throne during the Revolution of 1848 and died in 1916. He is shown on the obverse in uniform and military overcoat, with at left the crowns of Austria and Hungary. The crowns symbolize the "compromise" of 1867 that changed the Habsburg Empire into the Dual Monarchy of Austria–Hungary. Franz Joseph I was Emperor of Austria and King of Hungary. The Habsburg family took its name from the Habichtsburg at Aargau in what is now Switzerland.

Tragedies in the House of Habsburg - Emperor Maximilian of Mexico

KM-3046
100 schilling
1997 .900 silver, 34 mm

KM 3046 ● 100 schilling ● 1997 .900 silver

The reverse features at right SMS[2] *Novara* (*see* KM-3112) and at left Miramar castle near Trieste. The obverse depicts Ferdinand Maximilian Joseph (1832–1867), Archduke of Austria, a brother of Emperor Franz Joseph I. In 1854 the archduke became rear admiral and supreme commander of the Austrian fleet. In 1863 he was offered the imperial crown of Mexico by an assembly of Mexican notables in exile who met under French auspices and adopted an imperial form of government—the Second Mexican Empire. The offer was supposed to be from a representative majority of the Mexican people. After obtaining a pledge of military support from the French emperor, Napoleon III, Maximilian accepted the crown by signing the Miramar Treaty. Four days later he left Miramar castle and embarked with his wife Charlotte on *Novara*, in April 1864. Only after his arrival in Mexico Maximilian did learn that his presence was not wanted by most of the Mexican people and that the throne was safe only because of the presence of French troops. With the aid of these French troops he drove Benito Juárez over the northern frontier. After the end of the American civil war the US government—under the Monroe doctrine—demanded the withdrawal of the French army. Napoleon III withdrew his troops from Mexico, breaking his pledge to Maximilian and thus sealing the fate of the Mexican empire. Maximilian decided not to leave the country. Juárez returned and besieged Maximilian at Querétaro where he was captured by republican troops, condemned to death by court-martial and shot by firing squad on 19 June 1867. His remains were returned to Europe on *Novara* later that year, arriving in Trieste in 1868. He was buried in Vienna. Miramar castle, west of Trieste, was built by Maximilian in the middle of the 19th century. His study in the castle was a copy of the cabin of the *Novara*. In the annual Coin of the Year contest the coin was selected as the best silver coin for 1997.

2 SMS is the abbreviation of Seiner Majestät Schiff, His Majesty's Ship.

Tragedies in the House of Habsburg – Empress Elizabeth

KM-3052 ● 1000 schilling ● 1998 .995 gold

The reverse features the paddle wheel steamer *Genève* (Geneva) on Lake Geneva against the background of the city of Geneva, Switzerland, and two ladies on the quay in the foreground. Built in 1896 by Sulzer Brothers at Winterthur, Switzerland, the 334-ton *Genève* is 208 ft (63 m) long and 46 ft (14 m) in the beam, and draws 6 ft (1.8 m) of water. In 1934 she became the first vessel in Europe with diesel–electric drive. She plied Lake Geneva until 1973 and is still used as an accommodation ship at Geneva, retaining her ability to move under her own power when required. The city of Geneva was first named in the writings of Julius Caesar, who passed through the walled town in 58 BCE. The ladies depicted on the reverse are Elizabeth ("Sisi"), Empress of Austria and Queen of Hungary (1837–1898), the wife of Emperor Franz Joseph I, traveling incognito under the name of Countess of Hohenembs, and her court-lady, the countess Irma Sztáray. They hurry to catch the steamer back to the health resort Territet, at which they were staying. The coin captures the moment before Elizabeth's assassination on 10 September 1898, the empress raising her left hand in a defensive gesture to ward off the attack by her murderer, the anarchist Luigi Luccheni. He had come to Geneva to murder the French Duke of Orleans but when he learned that the duke had departed from Geneva he decided to murder another celebrity who happened to be within reach, so that the newspapers would report the murder. Fate determined this person to be Elizabeth. She was stabbed with an improvised dagger and died on the *Genève*. The obverse features Elizabeth wearing gala evening dress at the Vienna imperial court as queen of Hungary.

Austria through the Ages – The Romans

KM-3069 ● 100 schilling ● 2000 .900 silver

KM-3069
100 schilling
2000 .900 silver, 34 mm

The obverse depicts a detachment of Roman legionnaires led by a centurion crossing the Danube River over a pontoon bridge. The Danube was the northern border of the Roman empire for hundreds of years. For security reasons the Romans preferred to use easily movable pontoon bridges across the river rather than fixed bridges. Pontoons—that could be preassembled and floated into position—were also often used in military campaigns. Scenes similar to the one on the obverse are depicted on Trajan's column in Rome and on some of the coins of the Roman emperor Marcus Aurelius (ruled 161–180). Roman rule in Austria began when Tiberius and Drusus, on behalf of Emperor Augustus, took over the kingdom of Noricum in 15 BCE; it ended in

488 CE. During this period the Romans constructed along the south bank of the Danube the *limes*, a defensive line of forts, watchtowers and posts to defend the border. The reverse depicts a portrait of Marcus Aurelius. In 175–180 he campaigned from present-day Austria against Germanic tribes across the Danube in an effort to re-establish a secure border. It is believed that the emperor died at Vindobona, an outlying fortress of the large military and civilian settlement at Carnuntum, the capital of the Roman province Pannonia Superior. The fortress developed into Vienna, the capital of Austria.

First Global Circumnavigation by an Austrian Ship

KM-3112 ● 20 euro ● 2004 .900 silver

KM-3112
20 euro
2004 .900 silver, 34 mm

The obverse depicts the 52-gun sailing frigate SMS *Novara* and in the background a junk in Chinese waters in 1858, during the *Novara*'s circumnavigation of the globe. *Novara*'s keel was laid in 1843 at the Riparto Novissimetta dockyard in Venice as *Minerva*. (At that time Venice, now Italian, was Austrian-held.) The Venetians, who proclaimed their independence in 1848, continued her construction as *Italia*. After the capitulation of Venice the following year, the ship's name was changed to *Novara* to commemorate the victory of the Austrian army under Field Marshal Joseph Radetzky over the Piedmontese troops in 1849 near the city of Novara, 28 miles (45 km) west of Milan. Construction was completed and the ship launched in 1850. The three-master displaced 2,107 tons, had a length of 171 ft (52 m), was 47 ft (14 m) in beam and drew 19 ft (5.9 m) of water. Her sail area was 19,687 sq ft (1,829 m^2) and she had a complement of 403. She made 13 knots. In 1857–1859 *Novara* circumnavigated the world on a scientific expedition sent by Archduke Ferdinand Maximilian, Commander-in-Chief of the Imperial and Royal Navy, returning to Trieste with some 30,000 scientific objects. This was the first circumnavigation of the globe by an Austrian ship. *Novara* was the last ship-of-the-line to circumnavigate the world solely under sail. Her commander on this voyage was Commodore (later Vice Admiral) Bernhard von Wüllerstorf-Urbair (1816–1883). The frigate was converted to steam in 1862, for which her length was increased by 51 ft (15 m), her tonnage to 2,650, and her complement to 538. She then became the flagship of the Austrian navy. In 1864 she took Archduke Ferdinand Maximilian to Mexico to become Emperor Maximilian and three years later she returned his remains to Europe (*see* KM-3046). In 1866 *Novara* took part in the battle of Lissa against the Italian Navy. In her later years she served as an artillery school ship, until being broken up in 1898. The inscription at the top of the obverse is WELTUMSEGLUNG DER S.M.S. NOVARA 1857–1859 (SMS *Novara*'s Circumnavigation of the World in 1857–1859). The reverse features a double portrait of Archduke Ferdinand Maximilian and Commodore von Wüllerstorf standing behind a table on which a ship's globe, navigation instruments, documents and a microscope are shown to mark the scientific character of the circumnavigation.

Austria on the High Seas – SMS *Erzherzog Ferdinand Max*

KM-3114 • 20 euro • 2004 .900 silver

KM-3114
20 euro
2004 .900 silver, 34 mm

The obverse depicts the 5,130-ton armored frigate SMS *Erzherzog Ferdinand Max* (Archduke Ferdinand Max). She was 275 ft (84 m) long, had a beam of 52 ft (16 m), and drew 23 ft (7.1 m) of water; she could make 13 knots and had a complement of 511. Like all early steam vessels, the ironclad wooden battleship also had three masts and sails. The frigate was designed by Josef von Romako. Built in 1865 at Stabilimento Tecnico Triestino in Trieste, she was named for Archduke Ferdinand Maximilian Joseph (1832–1867), naval commander-in-chief and brother of the emperor, later Emperor Maximilian of Mexico (*see* KM-3046). In 1866 Rear Admiral Baron Wilhelm von Tegetthoff (1827–1871), commander of the Adriatic fleet, chose *Ferdinand Max* as his flagship. Commander of the ship was Captain Maximilian Freiherr von Daublebsky von Sterneck (who was naval commander-in-chief from 1883 to 1897). Two years later *Ferdinand Max* became the flagship of the fleet. In 1869 she accompanied Emperor Franz Joseph I to the opening of the Suez Canal. Taken out of service in 1885 and renamed SMS *Ferdinand Max*, she became a tender to a gunnery training ship and, from 1908, an accommodation ship. She was scrapped in 1916. The reverse depicts Von Tegetthoff according to a painting by Anton Romako. The admiral stands on the bridge of the ship during the battle of Lissa in 1866 and in the foreground four crew members struggle with the wheel to bring the ship into a ramming position. The battle took place between an Austrian fleet under Von Tegetthoff and an Italian fleet under Admiral Carlo Conte di Pesano that was sent to capture the Austrian-held island of Lissa (in Croatian, Vis) in the eastern Adriatic. The Austrians were seriously outnumbered in ships and guns; however, Von Tegetthoff ordered his seven ironclads to ram their opponents. *Ferdinand Max* rammed the *Rè d'Italia*, the flagship of the Italian fleet, amidships, tearing such a large hole in her side that she sank within two minutes. The Italians lost at Lissa two armored ships and 612 officers and men, while the Austrians lost 38 men and had only one wooden ship severely damaged. Because of Von Tegetthoff's tactics, thereafter, until the beginning of the 20th century, the battleships and heavy cruisers of all nations were built with a ram, even though the ram slowed them down and made them unwieldy. After Von Tegetthoff's success at Lissa, it was decreed that there should always be in the Austrian fleet an ironclad bearing his name. The obverse inscription is PANZERFREGATTE S.M.S. ERZHERZOG FERDINAND MAX (Armored Frigate HMS *Archduke Ferdinand Max*).

Austria on the High Seas – *Admiral Tegetthoff* Polar Expedition

KM-3126 ● 20 euro ● 2005 .900 silver

The obverse depicts the 220-ton three-masted schooner *Admiral Tegetthoff* in the Arctic during the Austrian–Hungarian polar expedition of 1872–1874. Built for the expedition by Tecklenborg & Beurmann in Bremerhaven, Germany in 1872, the ship was 126 ft (38 m) long and 23 ft (7 m) in beam. She was fitted with an auxiliary engine to enable her to proceed under sail or by steam. Her wooden hull was sheathed in iron. She was named for Rear Admiral Baron Wilhelm von Tegetthoff (*see* KM-3114) who had just died. The aim of the expedition was to locate the Northeast Passage from Europe to eastern Asia, and to explore the sea to the northeast of Novaya Zemlya. The expedition was organized and financed by private citizens. Commander of the ship was naval lieutenant Karl Weyprecht (1838–1881). Infantry lieutenant Julius von Payer (1842–1915) was leader of the land journeys. The crew was composed of 24 men, most of them members of the Austro–Hungarian navy in the Adriatic Sea. The language of command was Italian. *Admiral Tegetthoff* departed from Bremerhaven in June 1872 with provisions for three years. Soon after reaching Arctic waters she became icebound off Novaya Zemlya. She drifted in the pack-ice for over a year. In August 1873 the mountains and glaciers of Franz Josef Land were sighted. This group of 85 ice-covered islands is the northernmost group of islands in Asia. The previously unknown archipelago was named for the Austrian emperor. After exploring the islands up to 82° 5' N. latitude, it was decided to abandon the ship. The men took three of the ship's life boats with them, on sleds. After getting to the edge of the ice pack, the men took to the open boats. After 96 days without shelter they found at Novaya Zemlya a group of Russian Arctic coast dwellers headed by Feodor Voronin who took them on board the Russian schooner *Nikolay* to Vardø in Norway. The reverse depicts Weyprecht in front and Von Payer behind him, both in Arctic gear on Franz Josef Land against the background of the *Tegetthoff* frozen in the ice. The first to navigate the Northeast Passage was Adolf Erik Nordenskjöld in the steamship *Vega* in 1878/79.

Austria on the High Seas – SMS *Sankt Georg*

KM-3127 ● 20 euro ● 2005 .900 silver

The obverse features the 7,289-ton armored cruiser SMS *Sankt Georg* passing the Statue of Liberty in New York harbor in 1907. The reverse depicts the stern and propellers of the ship under construction, just prior to her launching at the Navy shipyard on Olive Island in the naval base of Pola, and in the foreground a steam launch used for transporting supplies and towing large ships in the naval base. The cruiser was built in 1905 for the Austro-Hungarian Navy. She was 408 ft (124 m) long, had a beam of 62 ft (19 m) and a draft of 22 ft (6.6 m), and could make 22 knots. Her wartime complement numbered 670. She was named for St. George, the legendary knight on horseback who killed a dragon with his lance and died as a martyr in Lydda, Palestine at the beginning of the 4th century CE. In 1907 *Sankt Georg* represented Austria in the United States at the celebration of the 300th anniversary of the founding of the British colony of Jamestown in Virginia. She anchored at Hampton Roads, Virginia, at the US Naval Academy in Annapolis, Maryland, and in New York. During World War I she was the flagship of Austria's 1st cruiser division and took part in various actions. At that time the Austro-Hungarian navy was the seventh largest maritime power in the world. After the end of the war the ship was ceded as war reparations to Great Britain, which sold her to Italy. *Sankt Georg* was scrapped in Genoa, Italy in 1920. Pola was the main base of the Austro-Hungarian navy from the middle of the 19th century. After World War I the city became part of Yugoslavia; now it is Pula in Croatia. The obverse inscription is PANZERKREUZER S.M.S. ST. GEORG (Armored Cruiser HMS *Saint George*). The reverse inscription reads SEEARSENAL POLA (Navy Yard Pola).

KM-3127
20 euro
2005 .900 silver, 34 mm

BAVARIA

The 19th-century ship coins of the Kingdom of Bavaria are listed under **German States**.

BELARUS

The Republic of Belarus in eastern Europe, north of the Ukraine, attained independence in 1991 upon the dissolution of the USSR.

Cities of Belarus – Polotsk

KM-19 ● 1 rouble ● 1998 copper-nickel
KM-28 ● 20 roubles ● 1998 .925 silver

The reverse gives a view of the walled city of Polotsk and depicts the city's shield that features a ship, alluding to the importance of the river waterways to its economy. Polotsk (pronounced Polatsak) in northern Belarus on the confluence of the Polota and Western Dvina Rivers, 120 miles (192 km) north–northeast of Minsk, is named for the Polota River. The city was founded by the Kryvicy tribe of the Eastern Slavs. First mentioned in chronicles of the year 862, it is the oldest city in Belarus. From that time until the 12th century it was the capital of the Principality of Polotsk.

BELGIUM

The Kingdom of Belgium is situated in western Europe on the North Sea between The Netherlands to the north and France to the South.

T-1 Enlargement of the European Union

KM-? ● 100 euro ● 2004 gold

The reverse depicts buildings, statues or nature monuments symbolic for the ten countries that became member states of the European Union on 1 May 2004. Malta is represented along the rim at 7 o'clock by buildings at the quay in the Grand Harbour in Valletta and a Maltese boat in front of them. Such boats are used for fishing by private persons, not commercial fishing. They are approximately 12 ft (3.7 m) long. The other sights on the reverse are the statue of the mermaid in Warsaw, Poland (at 1 o'clock), the Castle of Prague, Czech Republic (2 o'clock), the Gediminas tower in Vilnius, Lithuania (3 o'clock), the tower of St. Peter's church in Riga, Latvia (4 o'clock), Aphrodite's Rock near Paphos, Cyprus (5 o'clock), the Pikk Hermann tower in Tallinn, Estonia (8 o'clock), the Castle of Bratislava, Slovakia (9 o'clock), Parliament Building in Budapest, Hungary (10 o'clock), and Predjama Castle near Postojna, Slovenia (11 o'clock). The reverse inscription in Latin, AMPLIATA VNIO EVROPAEA, translates as "Enlargement of the European Union." The obverse features a map of the 25 countries that make up the enlarged European Union, and denotes the names of the new member states in their local languages. Coins of Belgium depict the country name in its three official languages—Dutch, French and

German. Together with the Latin reverse legend and the ten country names on the obverse the coin has inscriptions in 14 different languages.

BULGARIA

The Republic of Bulgaria is situated in the Balkans in southeastern Europe.

Canoeing World Championships

KM-178 ● 2 leva ● 1989 copper-nickel

The reverse depicts two contestants—in the center a kayaker and below him a canoe paddler. The coin was issued to mark the 22nd Canoeing World Championships that were held in 1989 in Plovdiv in southern Bulgaria.

KM-178
2 leva
1989 copper-nickel, 30 mm

Olympic Games 1992 Barcelona

KM-189 ● 25 leva ● 1989 .925 silver

The reverse depicts two competing canoe paddlers in stylized canoes.

Radetzky

KM-212 ● 100 leva ● 1992 .925 silver

KM-212
100 leva
1992 .925 silver, 38.6 mm

The reverse features the Austrian side-wheeler *Radetzky*. The steamer was built in 1851 and measured 180 ft (55 m) long with a beam of 23 ft (7 m) that increased to 43 ft (13.1 m) over the paddle wheel boxes. She was named for Field Marshal Joseph von Radetzky, commander of the Austrian army that crushed the revolution in Italy in 1849. In 1876, the year stated on the reverse, *Radetzky* was operated by the Danube Steam Navigation Company as a river transport. When she was making her usual run on the Danube River toward Vienna, Hristo Botev, a leader in the Bulgarian independence fighter movement against the Turks, who had ruled Bulgaria since 1396, boarded the vessel as a passenger at her stop at Giurgiu, Romania. At stops in other Romanian cities—Zimnicea, Turnu Măgurele and Corabia—another 204 Bulgarian independence fighters boarded the vessel, also as passengers. On 17 May 1876, Botev and the other Bulgarians forced *Radetzky*'s captain to stop at Kozlodoui in northwestern Bulgaria, an isolated area on the Bulgarian bank of the Danube, where they disembarked as a well-organized revolutionary detachment of volunteers. The independence fighters engaged and fought bravely against the Turks; however, all but eight of them were eventually killed or captured. Botev died in a skirmish on 20 May 1876.

Kaliakra

KM-220 ● 1000 leva ● 1996 .925 silver

The tall ship on the reverse is the steel barquentine *Kaliakra* that was built in 1984. The 247-ton vessel is 161 ft (49 m) long, has a beam of 26 ft (7.9 m), and draws 11 ft (3.4 m) of water. Her main mast extends above the main deck at 109 ft (33 m). She carries approximately 11,000 sq ft (1,000 m^2) of sail. She is named for Cape Kaliakra in northeastern Bulgaria on the Black Sea. *Kaliakra* is used in training naval cadets. She often participates in tall ship races.

KM-220
1000 leva
1996 .925 silver, 38.6 mm

CROATIA

The Republic of Croatia in southeastern Europe is situated on the Adriatic Sea. To the north of Croatia are Slovenia and Hungary, to the south and east is the Republic of Bosnia and Herzegovina. Croatia was part of the Austro-Hungarian Empire until the end of World War I, then became part of Yugoslavia, and declared independence in 1991.

Olympic Games 1996 Atlanta – Sailboat Racing

KM-41 ● 100 kuna ● 1996 .925 silver

The obverse shows a Mistral windsurfer, commemorating the Olympic Games held in Atlanta from 19 July to 4 August 1996. The Mistral form of sailing was introduced as an Olympic event at the Olympic Games of 1984 in Los Angeles. Sailboats at the Olympic Games are one-design class boats, meaning that they are built to precise specifications as to materials, methods used in construction, size and weight by builders who have been licensed by the International Sailing Federation. Because all Olympic boats in a class are identical, the best sailor will win a race, not the best boat.

More than 10,300 athletes participated in the Olympic Games at Atlanta. The reverse features a wheelbound javelin thrower, commemorating the Paralympic Games held in Atlanta from 16 to 25 August 1996. The Paralympic Games are Olympic-style games for athletes from different disability groups that are held in the same year and at the same venues as the Olympic Games. The first Paralympic Games were held in Rome in 1960. Some 3,200 athletes participated in the Paralympic Games at Atlanta.

Olympic Games 1996 Atlanta – Rowing

KM-42 • 100 kuna • 1996 .925 silver

The obverse depicts an Olympian rowing a rowboat in sweep-oared racing. In this form of rowing the rower has both hands on a single oar, and rows on one side of the boat only. There are sweep races for pairs, fours and eights. The reverse shows a water polo player. A water polo team has six field players and a goalie.

800th Anniversary of the City of Osijek

KM-56 • 150 kuna • 1996 .925 silver
KM-57 • 200 kuna • 1996 .925 silver
KM-58 • 500 kuna • 1996 .986 gold

The reverse depicts two riverboats on the Drava River in front of the city of Osijek. The city is the administrative and economic center of Eastern Croatia, known as Slavonia and Baranja. It is situated on the Drava's right bank 15 miles (25 km) from its confluence with the Danube and is the fourth largest city in Croatia. Until the 19th century it was the largest city in the country. Osijek was first mentioned in a document dated 1196 in which King Emerik conferred rights to the Cikador abbey to collect tolls on trade and transportation by ship.

Expo 1998 Lisbon

KM-63 • 25 kuna • 1998 brass core in copper-nickel ring, twelve-sided planchet

KM-63
25 kuna
1998 brass core in
copper-nickel ring, 31 mm

The reverse features a lateen-rigged falkuša at sea. The falkuša was a half-decked, one-mast Croatian fishing boat, already being mentioned in chronicles in the 11th century. Specially constructed for three-week sardine fishing around the island of Palagruža near the Italian coast, it was fitted with removable planks named *falci* ("dead sides") that ran from stem to stern and increased the height of the sides by 1.6 ft (50 cm), making it possible to cross the open Adriatic Sea after successful fishing, because the fully loaded boat had a deeper draft.

As boats under 28 ft (8.5 m) were forbidden to go to Palagruža, the falkuša was 28–31 ft (8.5–9 m) long and up to 9 ft (2.7 m) wide. The falkuša had a crew of five and was equipped with four oars. Its removable mast had a main and a small bow rig that carried 1,292 sq ft (120 m^2) of sails. It was used by the fishermen of Komiža, a small town on the island of Vis, who made the 48 miles (78 km) from Vis to Palagruža in 10–15 hours of rowing, or in 5 hours if the wind conditions were good. Seasonal fishing area rights were acquired and determined on the basis of who got there first in a race in which all falkušas left Komiža for Palagruža at the same time. The boats that arrived first got the most productive fishing spots. The sardines caught were salted in barrels and brought home to market when the falkuša was loaded up to capacity, which took twenty days. Sardine fishing around Palagruža ceased in 1936, after falkušas had caught more sardines than any other Adriatic boat of any type in the past millennium. The last surviving falkuša, named *Cicibela*, was restored in 1986 and became an exhibit in the Fishermen's Museum at Komiža. Using her specifications as a blueprint, a replica of a falkuša was built in 1997 at a shipyard in Trogir. This replica was exhibited as an example of Croatian nautical tradition at Expo '98, the world fair held in Lisbon, Portugal in 1998, to signify the maritime heritage shared by Komiža and Lisbon. The replica was named *Comeza-Lisboa*. The reverse inscription reads EXPO LISABON 1998. The obverse depicts the "25" of the 25-kuna denomination superimposed on a pine marten. The kuna takes its name from the Croatian word for marten, the little animal whose pelt served as a unit of barter in the Middle Ages.

CYPRUS

Cyprus, an island in the eastern Mediterranean Sea south of Turkey, attained its independence from Great Britain in 1960. The Republic of Cyprus, which occupies less than two-thirds of the island, is controlled by the Greek-Cypriot community, is internationally recognized, and is a member of the European Union since 2004. The Turkish Republic of Northern Cyprus occupies the remainder of the island and is recognized only by Turkey.

Ancient Galley

KM-37 • 100 mils • 1955–57 – see T-1
KM-39 • 5 mils • 1963–80 – see T-1

Death of Makarios III

KM-47 • 50 pounds • 1977 .917 gold

The obverse features a map of the island of Cyprus, with as ornamentation a ship of indiscernible type above the map and four dolphins below it. The reverse depicts Michael Mouskos (1913–1977), Archbishop Makarios III of the Orthodox Church of Cyprus (from 1950), who served as the country's first president (from independence in 1960).

Ancient Galley

KM-50 • 5 mils • 1981–82 – see T-1

T-1 Ancient Galley

KM-39
5 mils
1963 bronze, 21 mm

KM-37 • 100 mils • 1955–57 copper-nickel, issued under British rule
KM-39 • 5 mils • 1963–80 bronze, issued by the Republic
KM-50 • 5 mils • 1981–82 aluminum, varieties exist

The reverse depicts an ancient Phoenician galley (*see* Lebanon KM-4). The design of this merchant ship of approximately the 6th century BCE is based on a painting on a jug that was found in Cyprus and is representative of the island's trade. The steering oar can be seen near the stern. Cyprus was colonized by the Phoenicians about 750 BCE and became noted for its richly decorated vases which, along with other works of art, were shipped to cities and towns throughout the Mediterranean region.

CZECH REPUBLIC

The Czech Republic in central Europe was formed in 1993 when Czechoslovakia split up into its two component parts—the Czech Republic and the Slovak Republic.

400th Anniversary of the Death of Jakub Krčin

KM-70 • 200 korun • 2004 .900 silver, varieties exist

The upper half of the reverse depicts two fishermen punting a boat in a carp fish pond in front of a spread-out fishing net, while the

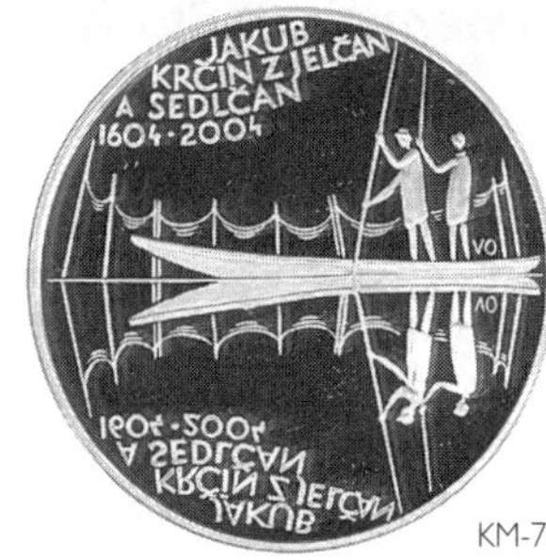

KM-70
200 korun
2004 .900 silver, 30.8 mm

lower half mirrors their image in the water. The design shows the harvesting of the fish: When the pond is emptied, the fish concentrate in the deepest part of the pond. Fishermen on the shore spread a long net between them and pull the net tight. After the fish are trapped in the net, fishermen in boats pull the larger carps out of the water one after another by hand, while the smaller fish are pulled out of the net mechanically and transferred into containers. The fish are harvested particularly toward Christmas, as carp is traditionally part of the Christmas Eve dinner menu in the Czech lands. The design relates to southern Bohemia, in which there are more than 7,600 carp fish ponds covering a surface area of 104 square miles (269 km^2). Most of the ponds were built in the 15th and 16th centuries under the Lords of Rožmberk (Rosenberg), the family that ruled southern Bohemia from 1366 until they sold the land to the Czech king at the beginning of the 17th century. The most famous pond builders were Stepanek Netolicky and his successor, Jakub Krčin of Jelčany and Sedlčany (1535–1604), who were regents for the Rosenbergs. To drain the marshy region, they designed a unique water regulation system of oval fish ponds where a river or canal supplies the pond with water, with the overflow supplying the next pond in the chain. The largest pond, Rožmberk, has a water area of 1.9 square miles (4.9 km^2). It was built by Krčin. The Trebon basin in the area, which contains hundreds of ponds, canals, rivers, meadows and forests, and covers 270 square miles (700 km^2), has been declared a UNESCO biosphere reserve. The first written accounts of carp fish pond construction—by monasteries—date back to the 11th century. The reverse inscription reads JAKUB KRČÍN Z JELČAN A SEDLČAN 1604–2004. The coat-of-arms on the obverse is mirrored, similar to the boat on the reverse.

CZECHOSLOVAKIA

The Republic of Czechoslovakia in central Europe was formed after World War I as a nation of Czechs and Slovaks of the former Austro-Hungarian Empire. After the collapse of the communist regime in 1989, it became the Czech Slovak Federal Republic that consisted of the Czech Republic and the Slovak Republic. In 1993 the country split into the Czech Republic and the Slovak Republic.

Bohemia's 150th Anniversary

KM-145 ● 50 korun ● 1991 .700 silver

KM-145
50 korun
1991 .700 silver, 27 mm

The reverse depicts the wooden side-paddle steamer *Bohemia*, the first passenger steamer in the Czech lands. Built in Prague in 1841 at John Joseph Ruston's Rustonka engineering plant for the shipping company of John Andrew, the vessel was 125 ft (38 m) long and had a beam of 15 ft (4.7 m). Ruston was her captain on her maiden voyage. *Bohemia* maintained a passenger service on the Elbe river to Dresden, the capital of the Kingdom of Saxony; however, she could reach Prague only when navigation conditions were very favorable. In 1851 she was transferred to the Elbe Steamship Navigation Company. The vessel was broken up in 1856. Steam river traffic between Prague and Dresden ceased in 1850 after the opening of the direct railway connection between the two cities. When resumed in 1857, it was for tourist purposes only.

DANZIG

Danzig was part of the Kingdom of Prussia, the leading state in Germany, from 1814 until World War I. Under the Treaty of Versailles signed after the war, Danzig became a "free city" under the protection of the League of Nations. Its name on the coins is Freie Stadt Danzig (Free City of Danzig). The city was overrun by German troops at the beginning of World War II whereafter it became part of Poland, and was renamed Gdańsk. The city is situated on the Bay of Gdańsk about 3 miles (4.8 km) from the Baltic Sea.

Circulation Coin

KM-144 ● $^1/_2$ gulden ● 1923–27 .750 silver

KM-144
$^1/_2$ gulden
1923 .750 silver, 19.4 mm

The stylized vessel on the reverse symbolizes the merchant ships of the Hanseatic League (Hansa), of which Danzig was a member. The city became the major international port on the Baltic. In its Golden Age it was the greatest grain exporter in Europe. The Hansa (a German word meaning Union) was an association for the protection of merchant ships on the high seas. At its peak, the Hansa included nearly 100 cities in Germany, the Low Countries and the Baltic countries. Its chief cities, besides Lübeck and Hamburg that founded the alliance in 1241, were Bremen, Danzig, London, Venice (Italy), Bruges (Flanders in present-day Belgium), Bergen (Norway), Visby (Sweden) and Novgorod (Russia). One of the Hansa's main tasks was to control the exchange of raw materials from the north and east for finished goods from the south and west. Another goal was to drive the pirates from European waters, in which the League succeeded by the 15th century. The Hansa built lighthouses to aid in safe navigation. It established codes of fair business practice which were binding on all Hanseatic merchants. Wherever necessary the League brought suit in foreign countries for damages suffered by its members. The discovery of the sea route around Africa to the Indies broke the power of the Hansa cities and the League gradually declined in importance after 1500.

Circulation Coins

KM-145 ● 1 gulden ● 1923 .750 silver
KM-146 ● 2 gulden ● 1923 .750 silver

The round ship on the obverse is a stylized cog, a North European merchant ship of the 13th, 14th and 15th centuries used by the Hansa. Remains of a cog dating back to circa 1380 were uncovered in 1962 in Bremen, Germany. The tonnage of a typical cog was 52 and it had a length of 60 ft (18 m), a beam of 25 ft (7.6 m) and a draft of 7 ft (2.1 m).

Circulation Coin

KM-155 ● 2 gulden ● 1932 – see T-1

Circulation Coin

KM-157 ● 5 gulden ● 1932 .500 silver

The obverse depicts a sailing vessel being loaded up from the Krantor (Crane Gate), Danzig's most famous building, which exists in its present form from 1440. Its towers served as part of the city's defenses. Between them there is a protruding wooden structure that served as an elevator for loads of up to 4 tons. Prisoners had to crawl into wheels with a diameter of 16 ft (5 m) to turn the wheels with the weight of their bodies, thereby hoisting the loads that were attached to ropes wound around the wheels. The Krantor was destroyed in World War II and rebuilt after the war in its original form.

Circulation Coin

KM-158 ● 5 gulden ● 1935 – see T-1

T-1 Circulation Coins

KM-155 ● 2 gulden ● 1932 .500 silver
KM-158 ● 5 gulden ● 1935 nickel

The obverse depicts a cog. The design is based on the city seal of 1399.

KM-158
5 gulden
1935 nickel, 29 mm

ESTONIA

The Republic of Estonia is situated on the Gulf of Finland and the Baltic Sea. Estonia attained independence in 1918 after centuries of Danish, Swedish, German and Russian rule but in 1940 it came once again under Russian rule. It regained sovereignty in 1991.

Circulation Coin

KM-16 ● 1 kroon ● 1934 aluminum-bronze

The vessel on the reverse is a 13th-century Viking ship (*see* Isle of Man KM-24).

KM-16
1 kroon 1934 aluminum-bronze, 25 mm

Olympic Games 1992 Barcelona

KM-25 ● 10 krooni ● 1992 .925 silver

The reverse features two sailing yachts.

FINLAND

The Republic of Finland is situated in northern Europe on the Gulf of Bothnia, the northern part of the Baltic Sea. Under Swedish rule from the 12th to the 19th centuries, Finland was an autonomous grand duchy of Russia from 1809, and attained independence in 1917.

Circulation Coin

KM-53 ● 5 markkaa ● 1972–78 aluminum-bronze

The obverse features the 5,000-ton icebreaker *Varma*. Built in 1968 according to a special design, with screws fore and aft, she is 281 ft (86 m) long, has a beam of 71 ft (22 m), and draws 23 ft (7 m) of water. Icebreakers are vessels with reinforced bow and forefoot that have powerful engines to break open channels through pack ice for other ships to follow. They work through a combination of power and weight, using their power to force their bows up onto the ice, and then crushing it with their weight. The icebreaking season in Finland lasts from November to May.

Circulation Coin

KM-57 ● 5 markkaa ● 1979–93 aluminum-bronze

The obverse features the 9,500-ton icebreaker *Urho* that was built in 1975. She has a length of 338 ft (103 m), a beam of 78 ft (24 m) and a draft of 25 ft (7.6 m). With her five diesel–electric engines and four screws, two fore and two aft, she allows year-round shipping to the ports in the northern Gulf of Bothnia.

KM-57
5 markkaa
1979 aluminum-bronze, 26 mm

750th Anniversary of the Founding of Turku

KM-58 ● 25 markkaa ● 1979 .500 silver

The stylized view of Turku on the reverse includes in the center the Aura River with a freight vessel and a crane at 3 o'clock, at upper left the late-Romanesque cathedral, at lower right the castle built in 1280, and various other buildings. Turku (Åbo in Swedish) is the oldest and third largest city of Finland. For centuries it was the country's administrative and cultural center and from 1809 to 1812 it was Finland's capital city. The obverse depicts a shoal of 25 Baltic herrings (*Clupea harengus membras*), their number alluding to the coin's denomination.

70th Anniversary of Finland's Sovereignty over the Åland Islands

KM-70 ● 100 markkaa ● 1991 .925 silver

The reverse shows a four-masted bark of the late 19th century. No specific vessel was intended by the designer, who may have been inspired by the fleet of famous sailing ships that was owned by the memorable Åland ship owner Gustav Erikson (1883–1947), which included the *Herzogin Cecilie* (*see* Congo-Brazzaville KM-15), *Pamir* (*see*

Liberia KM-647) and *Passat* (*see* Guinea-Bissau KM-34). He kept their names, took on young men from all over Europe who were proud to be crew members (and were even willing to pay for that privilege), and let the ships run in the Australian grain trade without insurance (except for insurance of the cargo they carried). Åland is an archipelago of some 6,500 islands between Finland and Sweden. Sweden lost the islands to Russia in 1809 along with Finland. The Åland population speak Swedish. The League of Nations granted Åland to Finland in 1921 with certain guarantees concerning its language and culture. Seafaring is one of Åland's major trades. The obverse features the coat-of-arms of the region.

50th Anniversary of the End of World War II

KM-79 • 2000 markkaa • 1995 .900 gold

The obverse features two elk boats. The somewhat mysterious comb-like motif is based on prehistoric Scandinavian and Karelian rock carvings dated to the later Stone Age. Some archaeologists believe that the carvings depict prehistoric boats with an elk head as a figurehead (probably made of wood); however, no remains of such boats have been found and the interpretation is conjectural. The reverse features a fishing net based on a prehistoric Finnish rock painting. The symbolism of the obverse and reverse designs is difficult to interpret and there is nothing on the coin to indicate that it was struck to mark the end of World War II. In Finland this war with Germany, the so-called Lapland War, ended on 25 April 1945.

250th Anniversary of the Suomenlinna Fortress

KM-88 • 100 markkaa • 1998 .925 silver

KM-88
100 markkaa
1998 .925 silver, 35 mm

The reverse depicts an 18th-century sailing ship near the entrance gate to the Suomenlinna fortress. The obverse features a stylized depiction of the fortress which was constructed in 1748 on six islands facing the coast of Helsinki as protection against the imminent danger of a Russian attack. Suomenlinna included a navy shipyard at which the first navy frigate was built in 1764, and had one of the biggest dry docks in the world. The construction of Suomenlinna was the most extensive building project in Finland during Swedish rule. For a certain period of time the fortress had more inhabitants than Helsinki. The fortress—which has been preserved intact because of its military use—was included in 1991 in UNESCO's world heritage list. Nowadays it is one of Finland's major tourist attractions as well as a suburb of Helsinki, with hundreds of people living in the renovated ramparts and barracks.

90th Birthday of Tove Jansson

KM-116 ● 10 euro ● 2004 .925 silver

The reverse features the Swedish-language Finnish artist and author of children's books Tove Jansson (1914–2001), and different images shown in whirlwind fashion—a strip of the sky with birds, a painter's pallet, a sailboat at 5 o'clock, and a half-moon. Jansson herself drew the illustrations for her books, which were translated into 35 languages. The obverse depicts three of Jansson's moomintrolls: the troll Moomin who looks somewhat like a hippopotamus, Snorkmaiden and Little My.

FRANCE

The French Republic is situated in western Europe.

French Arctic Territories

KM-1007 ● 5 francs ● 1992 .900 silver, reverse: albatrosses
KM-1010 ● 100 francs ● 1992 .900 silver, reverse: sea lions
KM-1011 ● 100 francs ● 1992 .900 silver, reverse: emperor penguins

KM-1010
100 francs
1992 .900 silver, 37 mm

The obverse depicts the French navy officer Jules-Sébastien-César Dumont d'Urville (1790–1842) with the corvette *Astrolabe* (ex *Coquille*) against the background of a polar landscape. *Astrolabe* was Dumont d'Urville's flagship on his expedition to the Pacific Ocean and Antarctica in 1837–1840 (*see* Vanuatu KM-37). She was accompanied by the corvette *Zélée* (*see* Vanuatu KM-36). In the course of the voyage, which was the first French expedition to explore south of the Antarctic Circle, Dumont d'Urville reached 73° S. latitude and discovered Adélie Land (now Adélie Coast), which he named for his wife. He also found the approximate position of the South Magnetic Pole. Twenty of his men died during the expedition. Earlier, Dumont d'Urville had become famous when, in 1820, he convinced the French government to purchase for 1,000 francs a newly excavated statue from the Greek isle of Milos that dates back to around 100 BCE, today known as the *Vénus de Milo* of the Louvre in Paris. He also led an expedition to the Pacific Ocean in 1826–1829 on the *Astrolabe* during which the remains were found of the ships of the Comte de la Pérouse who had disappeared in 1788 (*see* Samoa KM-102). On that expedition more than 120 islands in the Fiji archipelago were charted, and knowledge of the hydrography of the South Pacific was so greatly increased that the islands in the area were henceforth divided into the three distinct groups of Polynesia, Micronesia and Melanesia. Rear Admiral Dumont d'Urville, after surviving the hazards of three circumnavigations, disease, ice and storm, was killed in a railroad accident near Versailles in 1842—less than two years after his return from his expedition to the Antarctic. In 1950 the French established a permanent scientific base on the Adélie Coast which is named the Dumont d'Urville Station.

50th Anniversary of the D-Day Landings

KM-1014 • 1 franc • 1993 .900 silver
KM-1015 • 1 franc • 1993 .925 gold

The obverse shows Allied troops storming a beach and various naval vessels at sea in the background. The reverse depicts the crowned head of the Statue of Liberty (*see* United States KM-212), and the flags of France, Canada, the United Kingdom and the United States. The coin commemorates the D-Day landings by the Allied invasion force on 6 June 1944 at Utah, Omaha, Gold, Juno and Sword—the five Normandy beaches covering a 50-mile (80-km) front between Cherbourg and Le Havre.

World Cup 1998 France

KM-1167 • 10 francs • 1998 .900 silver

The reverse depicts the shields of the ten French cities that hosted the 1998 FIFA World Cup soccer matches around an image of the cup. The shield of Paris at 11 o'clock features a ship. Its origin goes back to the beginning of the municipal government of Paris in 1260, when St. Louis appointed leading men to administer the township. These men were members of the watermen's guild from whose shield the ship motif was incorporated in that of the city. In the 16th century the device was completed by the Latin motto FLUCTUAT NEC MERGITUR (She Is Buffetted by the Waves But Does Not Sink). The other shields are of Bordeaux, Lens, St. Etienne, Marseilles, St. Denis, Nantes, Montpellier, Lyon and Toulouse. FIFA is the acronym for Fédération Internationale de Football Association. The FIFA World Cup was designed by the Italian sculptor Silvio Gazzaniga. The cup is made of .750 gold and depicts two intertwined athletes celebrating their victory by holding a globe aloft on their outstretched arms. The cup is 14 inches (36 cm) high and has a weight of 14 pounds (6.2 kg). The world champion team gets the cup on loan for four years and receives a gold-plated replica to keep. The obverse shows the World Cup '98 logo. The 1998 Cup was won by the host country, France.

200th Anniversary of the Sale of Louisiana to the United States

KM-1336 • 1½ euro • 2003 – see T-1
KM-1337 • 20 euro • 2003 – see T-1

Traveling Around the World – *Normandie*

KM-1341 • 1½ euro • 2003 .900 silver
KM-1342 • 20 euro • 2003 .920 gold

KM-1341
1½ euro
2003 .900 silver, 37 mm

The reverse depicts the 79,280-ton French transatlantic liner SS *Normandie* arriving in New York. Built by Chantiers & Ateliers de St. Nazaire at St. Nazaire in 1935, *Normandie* was 1,029 ft (314 m) in length and had a beam of 118 ft (36 m) and a draft of 33 ft (10 m). Designed for the Compagnie Générale Transatlantique by naval architect Vladimir Yourkevich, she was the largest and most elegant liner of her day. She had accommodation for 1,952 passengers; her crew numbered 1,345. On her maiden voyage she captured the Blue Riband (*see* Isle of Man KM-231), which she lost in 1936 to the *Queen Mary* but recaptured in 1937 reaching a speed of 31 knots. In 1939 *Normandie* was in New York when World War II broke out and did not return to France. In 1941 she was seized by the US government. During the work to convert her for use as an American troop transport named USS *Lafayette* (AP 53) a spark from a welder's torch ignited a bundle of kapok life vests. Too much water was pumped into the ship to extinguish the fire and she capsized. She was subsequently refloated but did not return to service and was broken up in 1946. The style of the reverse design alludes to the art deco style in which *Normandie* was appointed. At the Mint Directors Conference held in 2004, the 20 euro coin received the Most Beautiful Commemorative Gold Proof award.

400th Anniversary of French Settlement in North America

KM-1372 • ¼ euro • 2004 .900 silver

KM-1372
¼ euro
2004 .900 silver, 37 mm

The reverse depicts *Don de Dieu* (Gift of God), the flagship in the expedition of Pierre du Gua, Sieur de Monts that in 1604 brought a group of French settlers to what is now Canada (*see* Canada KM-512). *Don de Dieu* also carried Samuel de Champlain, the king's geographer (*see* Cook Islands KM-104), who is featured on the obverse. These men were the first settlers in Acadia, the first French colony in North America.

Compagnie des Messageries Maritimes

KM-1378 • 1½ euro • 2004 silver – see T-2
KM-1379 • 1½ euro • 2004 gold – see T-2

T-1 200th Anniversary of the Sale of Louisiana to the United States

KM-1336 • 1 1/2 euro • 2003 .900 silver
KM-1337 • 20 euro • 2003 .920 gold
KM-? • 100 euro • 2003 .999 gold, 50 mm

The design elements of the reverse relate to the US state of Louisiana and include a paddle steamer riverboat, a neo-classical plantation house and the jazz trumpeter and singer Louis Armstrong (1900–1971). In 1682 the French explorer René-Robert Cavalier de la Salle reached the mouth of the Mississippi River after four years of exploring the length of the river. He claimed the entire Mississippi basin for his king, Louis XIV. The territory, named Louisiana, constituted a wide corridor from Canada to the Gulf of Mexico that stretched from west of the Mississippi River to the Rocky Mountains and covered 828,000 square miles (2,144,000 km^2). It was sold by France to the young United States on 30 April 1803 for 60 million francs following negotiations between the French emperor Napoleon Bonaparte and envoys of the US President Thomas Jefferson. Both leaders are depicted on the obverse along with a map of the United States that highlights the area transferred by France, which includes the present-day states of Louisiana, Missouri, Arkansas, Iowa, South Dakota, North Dakota, Nebraska, Oklahoma, Colorado, Wyoming, Montana and Minnesota, and part of Kansas. Napoleon used the money to re-equip his troops and finance his wars in Europe.

T-2 Compagnie des Messageries Maritimes

KM-1378 • 1 1/2 euro • 2004 .900 silver
KM-1379 • 1 1/2 euro • 2004 .920 gold
KM-? • 20 euro • 2004 .920 gold

The reverse depicts a generic ocean liner of the beginning of the 20th century heading toward the Far East, a sailing vessel, and a Japanese woman gazing out at the sea. The coin commemorates the "Compagnie des Messageries Maritimes" (Steam Navigation Company), often shortened to "MM." This company was founded in 1851 and started a regular service to Japan in 1865. It was merged into the Compagnie Générale Maritime in 1977.

T-3 100th Anniversary of the Death of Jules Verne

KM-? • 1/4 euro • 2005 copper-nickel
KM-? • 10 euro • 2005 .920 gold

The obverse features images representing nine novels by the French science fiction writer Jules Verne (1828–1905), including near the inscription at 9 o'clock a sailing ship alongside a balloon, in the center another sailing ship, and near the rim at 4 o'clock the fictitious submarine *Nautilus* (*see* Cuba KM-585). Six out of the nine novels represented by the images are the themes of coins to be issued to mark the 100th anniversary of Verne's death. They are: *Five Weeks in a Balloon* (1863), *Journey to the Center of the Earth* (1864), *From the Earth to the Moon* (1866), *Twenty Thousand Leagues Under the Sea* (1870 – *see* T-4), *Around The World In Eighty Days* (1873 – *see* T-5), and *Michael Strogoff: The Courier of the Czar* (1876). Drawing upon his interest in science and geography, Verne wrote more than fifty novels that combine scientific fantasy and adventure. He forecast with remarkable accuracy many scientific and technological achievements that were developed only after his death. These include flight into outer space, submarines, helicopters, air conditioning, guided missiles, and motion pictures. Verne's work has been published in nearly 150 different languages, making him the most popular novelist in history. The reverse features a portrait of the author, his tools (a pen and an inkwell) and the tools of an explorer (an astrolabe, a telescope, a caliper, a sextant, a sailor's cap, an anchor, and a ship's wheel). This reverse design is common to all the coins issued in 2005 to mark the 100th anniversary of Verne's death. The obverse inscription is LE MONDE FANTASTIQUE DE JULES VERNE (The Fantastic World of Jules Verne). The reverse inscription is PRÉCURSEUR DE LA SCIENCE FICTION (Creator of Science Fiction).

T-4 Jules Verne – *Twenty Thousand Leagues Under the Sea*

KM-? • 1 1/2 euro • 2005 .900 silver
KM-? • 10 euro • 2005 .920 gold
KM-? • 20 euro • 2005 .950 silver
KM-? • 100 euro • 2005 .999 gold, 50 mm

KM-?
1 1/2 euro 2005 .900 silver, 37 mm

The obverse depicts the fictional submarine *Nautilus* (*see* Cuba KM-585), the battle against the giant squid, the exploration of the lost city of Atlantis, and various marine life—including kelp beds, fish and Portuguese man-of-war. As denoted in the obverse inscription VINGT MILLE LIEUES SOUS LES MERS (*Twenty Thousand Leagues Under the Sea*), these images relate to the novel of that title published in 1870 by the French science fiction writer Jules Verne (1828–1905). The novel is narrated by Professor Aronnax who sets out to find an explanation for various incidents caused by an unknown sea creature and finds himself a captive of Captain Nemo in that sea creature, Nemo's electrically powered submarine *Nautilus*. The submarine travels to numerous places in the world's oceans before Arronax manages to escape. The story was written before modern submarines were a reality. The reverse is common to all the French coins issued in 2005 to mark the 100th anniversary of Verne's death (*see* T-3).

T-5 Jules Verne – *Around the World in Eighty Days*

KM-?
1 1/2 euro
2005 .900 silver, 37 mm

KM-? • 1 1/2 euro • 2005 .900 silver
KM-? • 10 euro • 2005 .920 gold
KM-? • 20 euro • 2005 .950 silver
KM-? • 100 euro • 2005 .999 gold, 50 mm

The obverse—the upper left half of which depicts a map of part of the globe and the upper right half a segment of a watch—also features different modes of transportation: a steamship at 6 o'clock, a railway engine at 8 o'clock, a dog sled at 11 o'clock, and an elephant at 4 o'clock. These design elements relate to the novel published by Jules Verne in 1873, the title of which is stated in the obverse inscription LE TOUR DU MONDE EN 80 JOURS (*Around the World in 80 Days*). The book's hero, Phileas Fogg, an English gentleman, bets that he can travel around the world in 80 days, a feat seemingly impossible at Verne's time. After adventures in many parts of the world, and the use of the four modes of transportation featured on the obverse, Fogg manages to win his bet—with ten minutes to spare. The reverse is common to all the French coins issued in 2005 to mark the 100th anniversary of Verne's death (*see* T-3).

FRANKFURT

The 19th-century ship coins of the Free City of Frankfurt are listed under **German States**.

GERMAN DEMOCRATIC REPUBLIC

The German Democratic Republic, also known as DDR (the initial letters of the country name in German) or East Germany, was formed after World War II in Soviet-occupied eastern Germany in the north of central Europe. After replacement of its Communist regime it was reunited with West Germany in 1990. It is now a part of the German Federal Republic (*see* **Germany**).

25th Anniversary of the National People's Army

KM-80 ● 10 mark ● 1981 copper-nickel

KM-80
10 mark
1981 copper-nickel, 31 mm

The reverse features at the top three MIG 23-U jet fighter aircraft, in the center a fast missile boat of the OSA 1 class marked "750," and at the bottom a T-55 tank, representing Soviet-manufactured equipment of the sea, air and land military forces. The OSA 1 patrol craft displaced 209 tons, had a length of 123 ft (37 m), a beam of 25 ft (7.6 m) and a draft of 12 ft (3.8 m), and could make 35 knots. Its complement numbered 26. The first boats of this class were added to the DDR navy in 1962. The reverse inscription NVA is the acronym of Nationale Volks-Armee (National People's Army). This military organization was established in 1956 to create a German identity to the occupying Soviet presence but was totally subservient to the Soviet armed forces.

Rostock Overseas Port

KM-121 ● 5 mark ● 1988 copper-nickel

KM-121
5 mark
1988 copper-nickel, 29 mm

The reverse features a semi-container ship of the Meridian type berthed at a pier in the harbor of Rostock, and in the foreground a tug boat. The ship on the coin is not a specific ship. Meridian ships were built around 1980 at the Warnow yard in Rostock–Warnemünde, including eleven ships that were delivered to the East German shipping company Deutfracht of Rostock. Most of the ships built at the Warnow yard (18 out of a total of 29 Meridian ships) were of the Meridian II type. Deutfracht's MS *Erfurt* was one of them. This 10,230-ton ship was 514 ft (157 m) long, had a beam of 72 ft (22 m) and a draft of 30 ft (9 m), and could make 18 knots. She had a crew of 31. The Baltic Sea city of Rostock, Mecklenburg was founded around 1200. Its present harbor was built in 1957–1960. The reverse inscription is ÜBERSEEHAFEN ROSTOCK (Rostock Overseas Port).

GERMAN STATES / BAVARIA

In the 19th century Bavaria in southern Germany was a kingdom. It is now one of the 16 states that comprise the Federal Republic of Germany.

Rhinegold Ducats with Two-Masted Vessel

KM-366 • (ducat) • 1821 .937 gold, King Maximilian I Joseph
KM-399 • (ducat) • 1830 .937 gold, King Ludwig I, Latin legend
KM-400 • (ducat) • 1830 .937 gold, King Ludwig I, German legend

The reverse depicts the Rhine River in front of the city of Speyer and on the river near the right bank a two-masted freight vessel. The main building shown in the city is the 11th-century Romanesque cathedral of Maria and St. Stephan which is now on UNESCO's world heritage list. The city of Speyer is a port on the left bank of the Rhine at the mouth of the Speyer River, south of Ludwigshafen. The legend in the exergue of the reverse—EX AVRO RHENI on the 1821 ducat and EX AURO RHENI on the issues of 1830—denotes that the coin was made of gold obtained from the Rhine. Other ducats struck by Bavaria in the same period, which do not feature ships, were made of gold from the Danube, Inn and Isar rivers. No denomination is stated on these ducats. The obverse legend—AVGVSTA NEMETVM on the 1821 ducat and AUGUSTA NEMETUM on the issues of 1830—translates as the Sublime (City of) Speyer. An ancient Celtic settlement, it arose about 100 BCE as a Roman military and trading town, Noviomagus, later named Nemetes after the local inhabitants (Nemetae, the Germanic tribe of the Nemetes). The name and title of the king on the obverse of the first two coins is in Latin—MAXIMILIANVS IOSEPHVS BAVARIAE REX on KM-366 and LUDOVICUS I BAVARIAE REX on KM-399; on the third coin, KM-400, it is in German—LUDWIG I KOENIG VON BAYERN.

Customs Union

KM-403 • 1 thaler • 1833 .833 silver

The reverse depicts Fortuna, the Roman goddess of fortune and good luck, standing between a prow at right and an anchor at left. The cornucopia in her left hand and the caduceus in her right are symbols for plenty and commerce (the caduceus is more widely known as a symbol of medicine). The reverse legend is ZOLLVEREIN MIT PREUSSEN, SACHSEN, HESSEN U. THÜRINGEN (Customs Union with Prussia, Saxony, Hesse and Thuringia). The coin marks the customs treaty concluded in 1833 by 18 German states with a total population of 23 million that created an economic union. Customs duties were levied by each state separately but according to uniform rules; duties collected were allotted to each state according to the number of its inhabitants.

Rhinegold Ducats with One-Masted Vessel

KM-433 • (ducat) • 1842–46 .937 gold, King Ludwig I

KM-462 ● (ducat) ● 1850–56 .937 gold, King Maximilian II
KM-477 ● (ducat) ● 1863 .937 gold, reduced size, King Maximilian II

The reverse is similar to that of KM-366; however, the freight vessel on the Rhine River has one mast only. The legend EX AURO RHENI at the top denotes the source of the metal—gold obtained from the Rhine.

KM-462
ducat
1850 .937 gold, 20 mm

GERMAN STATES / FRANKFURT

Frankfurt regained its independent status—which it lost in 1806—with the Treaty of Vienna in 1815. It remained one of Germany's four free cities ("Freie Stadt" in German) until 1866. In the Austro–Prussian war of 1866 Frankfurt chose Austria's side and Prussia occupied and then annexed the city, levying a 6 million florin fine in retaliation.

City View

KM-317 ● 1 kreuzer ● ND (1839) billon, 14 mm

The reverse features a view of the city of Frankfurt from the west toward the bridge over the River Main with a few vessels on the river; two sailboats at left and two river barges at right are discernible. The obverse legend reads FREIE STADT FRANKFURT (Free City of Frankfurt).

City View

KM-326 ● $3^1/_2$ gulden / 2 thaler ● 1840–44 .900 silver
KM-328 ● $3^1/_2$ gulden / 2 thaler ● ND (1838) .900 silver, "mule"

KM-326
$3^1/_2$ gulden / 2 thaler
1844 .900 silver , 40 mm

The obverse features a view of the city of Frankfurt from the west toward the bridge over the River Main; the foreground on the river shows a sailboat and a rowboat. The legend VEREINS-MUENZE (Union coin) at the top of the reverse denotes that the coin was struck to the rules of the coin convention of 1838 which introduced coins of uniform specifications in the states of the German Customs Union. "Union coins" were legal tender in all member states. The legend VII EINE F. MARK along the rim at the bottom of the reverse means that 7 (VII) coins had an actual silver weight of one (*Eine*) fine mark, the mark being the Cologne mark of about 7.5 oz. (233.855 g). The denomination of $3^1/_2$ (South German) gulden equaled 2 (North German) thalers. The thaler equivalent was stated on the coin to facilitate commerce with northern Germany.

KM-328 is an error coin: the obverse is that of KM-326, the reverse is the obverse of KM-329 that depicts the city's coat-of-arms. This error coin thus features the name of the city on both obverse and reverse but it lacks the denomination and year of issue.

City View

KM-350 ● 6 kreuzer ● 1852–56 .333 silver

The view of the city of Frankfurt on the obverse is similar to that of KM-317; however, on the river there are three vessels. The obverse legend reads F. ST. FRANKFURT (Free City of Frankfurt).

GERMANY

Germany is situated in north–central Europe. The coins of 1927 and 1931 were issued by the "Weimar Republic" established by the National Assembly in Weimar after World War I. The coin of 1976 was issued by the Federal Republic formed in West Germany after World War II. For coins of East Germany *see* **German Democratic Republic**.

100th Anniversary of Bremerhaven

KM-50 ● 3 reichsmark ● 1927 .500 silver
KM-51 ● 5 reichsmark ● 1927 .500 silver

KM-50
3 reichsmark
1927 .500 silver, 30 mm

The reverse features a three-masted bark flying the flag of Bremen that breaks through a chain and, at the bottom, the coat-of-arms of the City of Bremen. In the early 19th century the Weser River, Bremen's navigation artery, was becoming silted up. Bremen purchased a coastal strip at the mouth of the river from the Kingdom of Hanover, on which it started construction of Bremerhaven (Bremen's Harbor) in 1827. The ship breaking through a chain symbolizes the free navigation to the new harbor and the end of the dependence on the Weser. The edge inscription is NAVIGARE NECESSE EST (Navigation is Necessary).

300th Anniversary of the Rebuilding of Magdeburg

KM-72 ● 3 reichsmark ● 1931 .500 silver

The reverse depicts a view of the city of Magdeburg in north–central Germany on the Elbe River, on which a barge is seen above the bridge that spans the river. This design is similar to that of talers issued by the city in the 17th century. The coin marks the 300th anniversary of the day on which the city was put to fire in the Thirty Years' War (1618–1648), a religious conflict between Protestants and Catholics fought in central Europe. To forestall Catholic aggression against the German states the Swedish King Gustavus Adolphus sent Colonel Diedrich von Falkenburg with 2,400 soldiers to defend the Lutheran city of Magdeburg. The city was besieged by the 24,000-men army of the Catholic Habsburg emperor under Johann Tserclaes, Count of Tilly, who was commander-in-chief of the imperial army, and his subordinate General Count Gottfried zu Pappenheim. The city did not surrender. On 20 May 1631 the imperial troops and the forces of the Catholic League stormed the city and succeeded in entering. Enraged by the lengthy resistance put up by the Magdeburgers, they sacked and then burned the city, massacring 25,000 of the 30,000 residents and defenders. The others fled, leaving only a population of 400 in the city which was almost totally in ashes. The sack of Magdeburg was one of the bloodiest incidents in the war. After the end of the war Magdeburg was rebuilt. The city, which is first mentioned as Magadoburg in a record dated 805, is now the capital of the state of Sachsen-Anhalt. The reverse inscription is WIEDERGEBURT NACH ZWIETRACHT & NOT (Rebirth after Discord and Hardship).

300th Anniversary of the Death of Hans von Grimmelshausen

KM-144 ● 5 mark ● 1976 .625 silver

The reverse features a fabulous creature holding a book opened on a page on which there are strange symbols, including a ship. The creature—a combination of a man, a beast, a bird and a fish—stands on three masks. This design is adapted from the frontispiece of the first edition of *The Adventurous Simplicissimus*, a novel by the German novelist Hans Jacob Christoph von Grimmelshausen (1621–1676). *Simplicissimus* is perhaps the greatest 17th-century German novel, its first part being published in 1669. The strange creature is an allegorical rendition of the novel's hero. The satirical and partially autobiographical novel deals with the wanderings and adventures of a simple youth who becomes successively a soldier, jester, worker, robber, pilgrim, slave and hermit. The novel gives a realistic picture of the havoc wrought in Germany by the Thirty Years' War (1618–1648). Like the hero of his famous book, von Grimmelshausen led an adventurous life. He was kidnapped by Hessian soldiers at the age of ten and experienced military life with them during the Thirty Years' War. The edge inscription, DER ABENTHEUERLICHE SIMPLICISSIMUS, is the novel's title in German.

GIBRALTAR

Gibraltar, a dependency of the United Kingdom, is situated at the southern tip of Spain on the Strait of Gibraltar, the narrow strait linking the Mediterranean Sea with the Atlantic Ocean. It is British since its capture in 1704 during the War of Spanish Succession. Its name derives from the Arabic *Gebel el Tarik* (Tarik's Hill), for Tarik ibn Ziyad who fortified the peninsula in 711.

Ecu-denominated issues are not listed herein as they do not fit into the territory's monetary system.

175th Anniversary of the Death of Horatio Nelson

KM-12 • 1 crown • 1980 copper-nickel, issued also in .925 silver
KM-13 • 50 pounds • 1980 .917 gold

KM-12
1 crown
1980 .925 silver, 38.6 mm

The reverse features the square-rigged three-masted HMS *Victory* with a portrait of Admiral Lord Horatio Nelson (1758–1805). The *Victory* was a 100-gun first-rate ship-of-the-line designed by Sir Thomas Slade, the Senior Surveyor of the Navy. She displaces 3,500 tons, measures 227 ft (69 m) in length and 52 ft (16 m) in beam, and draws 24 ft (7.4 m) of water. Her complement numbered 850. *Victory* was built at Chatham Dockyard in 1765 at a cost of £63,175 (approximately £50 million today) and was laid up for 13 years. She was not put into commission until 1778, when France allied itself with the American colonists. She saw action in the American War of Independence (1775–1782), was the flagship of Admiral Lord Howe when the British raised the siege of Gibraltar in 1782, and took part in the Wars of the French Revolution (1792–1802). In 1803 Great Britain resumed the war against France and *Victory* became Nelson's flagship. In 1805 his task was to contain the French fleet at Toulon but Admiral Pierre Villeneuve managed to slip past the British. Villeneuve made Cádiz and remained there with the Spanish fleet. On 19 October, the combined French–Spanish fleet began to emerge from the anchorage and on the morning of 21 October, off Cape Trafalgar to the west of Gibraltar, the battle commenced with Nelson's signal "England expects that every man will do his duty." Britain did not lose a single ship but the battle resulted in the surrender of 18 ships of the French–Spanish coalition. Among the vessels defeated in this battle was the largest warship of the time, the *Santisima Trinidad*, which mounted 130 guns (*see* Cuba KM-118). During the battle *Victory* broke through the French line. Coming along the *Redoutable*, Nelson was fatally shot by a musketeer. After the battle *Victory* was towed to Gibraltar and repaired, and returned home with Nelson's body for a state funeral. In 1812 she was paid off but retained at the royal naval dockyard at Portsmouth as flagship of the commander-in-chief. In the 1920s she was restored to her former glory and she is now on display to the public in a special dry dock at Portsmouth—the oldest ship-of-the-line still in commission.

Circulation Coins

KM-21 • 2 pence • 1988–94 – see T-1
KM-21a • 2 pence • 1995–97 – see T-1

10th Wedding Anniversary of Prince Charles and Lady Diana

KM-86 • 1 crown • 1991 copper-nickel, issued also in .925 silver and .999 gold

The reverse features the royal yacht HMY *Britannia* (*see* Guernsey KM-52) departing Gibraltar with the British royal couple, Charles, Prince of Wales, and Lady Diana Spencer, on their honeymoon in 1981. The couple divorced in 1996. Diana was killed in a car crash in 1997.

500th Anniversary of the Discovery of America

KM-98 • 2 pounds • 1992 virenium[3], issued also in .925 silver, .917 gold and .950 platinum

The reverse depicts Christopher Columbus against the background of the *Santa Maria*, his flagship during his discovery voyage of 1492 (*see* Andorra KM-78).

Circulation Coin

KM-112 • 10 pence • 1992–97 – see T-2

Warships of World War II

KM-113 • 1 crown • 1993 USS *Philadelphia* – see T-3
KM-114 • 1 crown • 1993 USS *McLanahan* – see T-4
KM-115 • 1 crown • 1993 HNLMS *Isaac Sweers* – see T-5
KM-116 • 1 crown • 1993 USS *Weehawken* – see T-6
KM-117 • 1 crown • 1993 HMS *Warspite* – see T-7
KM-118 • 1 crown • 1993 HMS *Hood* – see T-8
KM-119 • 1 crown • 1993 HMS *Penelope* – see T-9
KM-120 • 1 crown • 1993 HMCS *Prescott* – see T-10

---

3 Virenium is an alloy of copper, zinc and nickel; it is named for Virena Pobjoy, the wife of the owner of the Pobjoy Mint™.

KM-121 • 1 crown • 1993 HMS *Ark Royal* – see T-11
KM-122 • 1 crown • 1993 USS *Gleaves* – see T-12
KM-123 • 1 crown • 1993 HMAS *Waterhen* – see T-13
KM-144 • 1 crown • 1993 FFS *Savorgnan de Brazza* – see T-14
KM-153 • 1/5 crown • 1993 USS *Philadelphia* – see T-3
KM-154 • 1/5 crown • 1993 USS *McLanahan* – see T-4
KM-155 • 1/5 crown • 1993 HNLMS *Isaac Sweers* – see T-5
KM-156 • 1/5 crown • 1993 USS *Weehawken* – see T-6
KM-157 • 1/5 crown • 1993 HMS *Warspite* – see T-7
KM-158 • 1/5 crown • 1993 HMS *Hood* – see T-8
KM-159 • 1/5 crown • 1993 HMS *Penelope* – see T-9
KM-160 • 1/5 crown • 1993 HMCS *Prescott* – see T-10
KM-161 • 1/5 crown • 1993 HMS *Ark Royal* – see T-11
KM-162 • 1/5 crown • 1993 USS *Gleaves* – see T-12
KM-163 • 1/5 crown • 1993 HMAS *Waterhen* – see T-13
KM-164 • 1/5 crown • 1993 FFS *Savorgnan de Brazza* – see T-14

Dependent Territories Conference

KM-199 • 1/5 crown • 1993 .999 gold
KM-200 • 1 crown • 1993 copper-nickel, issued also in .925 silver

The reverse features the shields of the countries that participated in 1993 in the Dependent Territories Conference in London: in the center the arms of Gibraltar (left) and of the Falkland Islands (right), and along the rim clockwise from the top the shields of Bermuda, the Cayman Islands, New Caledonia, the Isle of Man and the Netherlands Antilles. The arms of two of the territories feature ships (*see* Bermuda T-1 and Falkland Islands T-1).

World War II

KM-253 • 1/5 crown • 1994 Maltese convoy – see T-15
KM-255 • 1/5 crown • 1994 James Somerville – see T-16
KM-258 • 1/5 crown • 1994 Dwight Eisenhower – see T-17
KM-259 • 1 crown • 1994 Maltese convoy – see T-15
KM-261 • 1 crown • 1994 James Somerville – see T-16
KM-264 • 1 crown • 1994 Dwight Eisenhower – see T-17

25th Anniversary of the First Man on the Moon

KM-267 • 1/5 crown • 1994 .999 gold
KM-273 • 1 crown • 1994 copper-nickel, issued also in .925 silver

The reverse features the *Columbia* command module of *Apollo XI* splashing down in the Pacific Ocean, in the background USS *Hornet* and, in the sky, two HS-4 helicopters approaching the space capsule. *Hornet* (aircraft carrier CV 12) was built in 1943 by the Newport News Shipbuilding & Dry Dock Co. at Newport News, Virginia and had a complement of 3,448. For the last 16 months of World War II she was in the Pacific Ocean, supporting nearly every amphibious landing in that theater. She was under air attack 59 times but was never hit. Her aircraft destroyed 1,410 Japanese aircraft. For her service in World War II she earned nine battle stars. After a thorough modernization in 1953 she measured a length of 898 ft (274 m), a beam over flight deck and projections of 152 ft (46 m) and a draft of 28 ft (8.5 m), displaced 40,600 tons and made a speed of 32 knots. In 1958 *Hornet* was redesignated CVS 12 as an anti-submarine warfare support carrier. Eleven years later she was the primary recovery vessel for the historic mission of *Apollo XI*, carrying on board President Richard Nixon. The scene depicted on the reverse occurred on 24 July 1969, 400 miles (640 km) south–southwest of Wake Island and 15 miles (24 km) from *Hornet*. In the recovered space capsule were Neil Armstrong, Edwin Aldrin and Michael Collins who returned to Earth after Armstrong and Aldrin had become the first men to set foot on the Moon. In November 1969 the carrier participated in the recovery of the *Apollo XII* astronauts Charles Conrad, Richard Gordon and Alan Bean. *Hornet* was decommissioned in 1970 and was struck from the navy list in 1989. In 1991 she was designated a national historic landmark and is now a museum ship at Alameda Point on San Francisco Bay. The *Columbia* command module is in the National Air and Space Museum at Washington, DC.

100th Anniversary of the Return of Sherlock Holmes

KM-281 • 1/5 crown • 1994 .999 gold
KM-289 • 1 crown • 1994 copper-nickel, issued also in .925 silver

KM-289
1 crown
1994 copper-nickel, 38.6 mm

The reverse features *Mary Celeste* with a medallion portrait of Sherlock Holmes, the fictional master detective in the stories of Sir Arthur Conan Doyle (1859–1930). The 282-ton brigantine was launched in 1861 at Dewis shipyard, Spencer's Island, Nova Scotia, and named *Amazon*. She was 99 ft (30 m) long and had a beam of 25 ft (7.7 m) and a draft of 11 ft (3.4 m). After she was grounded in 1868 her wreck was sold to a Mr. Winchester of New York. She was refitted and renamed *Mary Celeste*. In 1872 she was found by Captain Morehouse of *Dei Gratia* floating just north of the Azores with no one aboard. *Mary Celeste* had set sail from New York to Genoa, Italy under the command of Captain Benjamin Briggs, on board with his wife Sarah, his two-year-old daughter Sophia, a crew of seven, and 1,701 barrels of pure alcohol. When found, the ship's only boat, a 17 ft (5.2 m) yawl, was gone, together with the chronometer, sextant and most of the vessel's papers. *Mary Celeste* was brought to Gibraltar by the crew of *Dei Gratia*. The inquiry found no obvious reason for the abandonment since the ship was in sound condition, and the crew of *Dei Gratia* was awarded the salvage money—$8,000. The mystery of the disappearance of the crew has never been solved. One theory is that a seaquake shook the vessel, causing the loosening of the stays of a few of the barrels of alcohol and the release of alcohol fumes. The fear that the fumes would explode may have caused the captain to abandon ship. The yawl may have sunk due to an aftershock of the seaquake. *Mary Celeste* was a commercial failure for the rest of her days, changing owners 16 times in 13 years, until she was wrecked on the Rochelois Reef off Haiti in 1885. The remains of the vessel were found in 2001. In 1884 Conan Doyle wrote a short story about the vessel, *Marie Celeste* [sic]. Three years later, Conan Doyle introduced Sherlock Holmes in *A Study in Scarlet* but later "killed him off" in *The Final Problem*. So compelling was Conan Doyle's portrayal that the fictional Holmes and his friend Dr. Watson were both treated as living persons. When the public demanded more of Holmes, the detective returned to 221B Baker Street in 1894 in *The Case of the Empty House*. The coins mark the 100th anniversary of this return.

50th Anniversary of the D-Day Landings

KM-309 • 5 pounds • 1994 virenium, issued also in .925 silver and .917 gold

The lower part of the reverse depicts a landing ship, a tank and airplanes, while the upper part features a sailor, a soldier and a pilot. The coin commemorates the landings of the Allied Forces on the German-held Normandy coast in France on D-Day, 6 June 1944.

40th Anniversary of Queen Elizabeth II's First Visit

KM-324 • 1 pound • 1994 nickel-brass
KM-325 • 2 pounds • 1994 virenium

The reverse depicts the royal yacht HMY *Britannia* (*see* Guernsey KM-52) against the background of the Rock of Gibraltar. The coins mark the first official visit to Gibraltar by Queen Elizabeth II, in 1954.

190th Anniversary of the Death of Horatio Nelson

KM-341 • 5 pounds • 1995 virenium, issued also in .925 silver and .917 gold

The reverse features a portrait of Admiral Lord Horatio Nelson (1758–1805) and at left HMS *Victory*, his flagship in the battle of Trafalgar (*see* KM-12).

Duke of Edinburgh Award Scheme

KM-431 • 1/5 crown • 1996 .999 gold
KM-432 • 1 crown • 1996 copper-nickel, issued also in .925 silver

The reverse depicts seven activities that are supported by the Duke of Edinburgh Award Scheme, among them sailing at 9 o'clock and kayaking at 11 o'clock. The logo of the Award Scheme is shown in the center of the reverse above the castle in Gibraltar's coat-of-arms. The Award Scheme is a program for development of young people founded by Prince Philip, Duke of Edinburgh, in 1956. The Scheme presents bronze, silver and gold awards to young people aged 14 to 25 for special achievements, such as humanitarian aid, research and courage. In this way varied talents are stimulated as well as many kinds of sports and leisure-time activities. The coins were issued to mark the 75th birthday of Prince Philip (born 1921), consort of Queen Elizabeth II.

The Seven Wonders of the Ancient World – The Pharos of Alexandria

KM-575 • 1 crown • 1997 .925 silver with .999 gold coin inset

The reverse features the lighthouse of Alexandria, Egypt at night with an ancient galley in the background, and a gold coin inset. The lighthouse was built on the rock island of Pharos in Alexandria and named for the island. A 4,900-ft (1,500-m)-long dike connected the island to the mainland. The Pharos was a stone tower 384 ft (117 m) high—the first recorded lighthouse and at its time the tallest building in the world. Its construction by the architect Sostratus took 17 years. The building, completed in 280 BCE, was composed of three stages on a foundation and had a white marble cover. The lowest stage of the tower was 183 ft (56 m) high, square and had a round core through which the fuel was lifted for the fire. The middle stage was octagonal and was 90 ft (27 m) high. The third stage was round and had a height of 24 ft (7.3 m). At night a wood fire was lit in the tower; by day sun rays were reflected by means of a mirror, guiding sailors into Alexandria's Great Harbor from a distance of 31 miles (50 km). The lighthouse, in operation for more than a thousand years, was destroyed by earthquakes in the 14th century. Fragments of the tower were found in the harbor of Alexandria in 1995. Pharos has become synonymous with "lighthouse"—for instance in the French "phare." The coin is part of a series depicting the supreme man-made structures known as the Seven Wonders of the Ancient World. In addition to the Pharos these Wonders are the Great Pyramid of Giza, the Hanging Gardens of Babylon, the Statue of Zeus at Olympia, the Temple of Artemis at Ephesus, the Mausoleum of Halicarnassus, and the Colossus of Rhodes (*see* KM-577). The gold coin inset on the reverse features

Queen Arsinoe, the wife of Ptolemy II Philadelphus (King of Egypt 287–246 BCE).

The Seven Wonders of the Ancient World – The Colossus of Rhodes

KM-577 • 1 crown • 1997 .925 silver with .999 gold coin inset

The reverse depicts an ancient galley to the left of the Colossus of Rhodes on the Mediterranean island of that name, and a gold coin inset. This colossal statue of the sun god Helios was about 108 ft (33 m) high. It was cast in bronze by the Rhodian sculptor Chares and stood on a white marble base. It stood near the entrance to one of the harbors of the city of Rhodes. Its construction took 12 years and was completed in 282 BCE. One of the Seven Wonders of the Ancient World (*see* KM-575), the Colossus was financed by the inhabitants of Rhodes from the sale of military equipment left behind by the Antagonids of Macedonia after their siege of the city of Rhodes in 304 BCE. The Colossus was broken at its knees by an earthquake in 226 BCE and its re-erection was forbidden by an oracle. The fragments of the broken Colossus were sold by the Arabs after their invasion of Rhodes in 654 CE. The gold inset on the reverse shows a coin of Greek origin that dates back to about 400 BCE.

200th Anniversary of the Arrival of Horatio Nelson

KM-605 • 5 pounds • 1997 virenium, issued also in .925 silver and .917 gold

The reverse features HMS *Captain* and a medallion portrait of her commander at the battle of St. Vincent in 1797, Commodore Horatio Nelson (1758–1805). The 1,632-ton *Captain* was a third-rate ship of 74 guns. She was built by Batson at Limehouse and launched in 1787. Her length was 170 ft (52 m), her beam 47 ft (14 m), and she had a draft of 21 ft (6.4 m). Her complement numbered 550. On 14 February 1797 she was one of the 15 ships-of-the-line in the squadron of the British Admiral Sir John Jervis that was sailing 25 miles (40 km) off Cape St. Vincent on the southwestern coast of Portugal. They encountered a Spanish fleet of 27 ships-of-the-line under Don José de Córdoba that was sailing in two sections. Nelson realized that the Spanish fleet was in danger of escape and, without waiting for orders, ordered Captain Ralph Miller in *Captain* to take his ship out of the line of battle and to attack the larger section of the Spanish with *Santisima Trinidad*, their flagship. He led boarding parties onto *San José* of 112 guns and *San Nicolás* of 84 guns, and captured both. By nightfall, four Spanish ships, including two first-rates, had been taken with 3,000 prisoners. The British did not lose a single vessel and incurred only 300 casualties. Jervis was made Earl St. Vincent for this victory. Nelson was promoted to rear admiral and was made a Knight of the Bath for his courage and skill in battle. In 1809 *Captain* became a receiving ship at Plymouth, providing accommodation for Navy personnel. (The Royal Navy did not build barracks for its seamen in homeports until the beginning of the 20th century.) In 1813 she was burned by accident and broken up. The coin marks Nelson's first great battle and his rise to fame. The most famous of his battles is that of Trafalgar, in which he was killed (*see* KM-12).

Britannia's Last Voyage

KM-607 ● 5 pounds ● 1997 virenium, issued also in .925 silver and .917 gold

The reverse shows the royal yacht HMY *Britannia* passing the Rock of Gibraltar on her last voyage before she was decommissioned after having served Britain's royal family for 43 years (*see* Guernsey KM-52).

KM-607
5 pounds
1997 virenium, 36 mm

Traders of the World – Francis Drake

KM-608 ● 1/25 crown ● 1997 .999 gold
KM-609 ● 1 crown ● 1997 .925 silver

The reverse features Sir Francis Drake (1540–1596) with *Golden Hind* (*see* Great Britain KM-844) and a tropical island with coco palms and coconut shells. *Golden Hind* was Drake's flagship on his circumnavigation of the world in 1577–1580.

Traders of the World – Romans

KM-610 ● 1/25 crown ● 1997 .999 gold
KM-611 ● 1 crown ● 1997 .925 silver

The reverse depicts a Roman corbita of the third century CE against the background of a map of the Mediterranean Sea from Tunisia and Sicily in the west to the eastern end of that sea and two lions in the foreground. The corbita was the merchant ship of imperial Rome. It could be of many sizes but always had two masts—one with a couple of triangular sails and a smaller one with a small square sail, the artemon sail. One or two helmsmen handled the two steering oars. Corbitas were capable of carrying as much as 400 tons of cargo. They plied the Mediterranean Sea but also made regular voyages between ports in the Red Sea across the Arabian Sea to the west coast of India. The lions refer to the exotic animals that were brought to Rome for the arena fights.

Traders of the World – Venetians

KM-612 ● 1/25 crown ● 1997 .999 gold
KM-613 ● 1 crown ● 1997 .925 silver

The reverse depicts a 14th-century Venetian galley in the center, a gondola in Venice's Grand Canal approaching the Rialto bridge in the background, and a pair of oysters with pearls in the foreground. The large Venetian galleys were about 160 ft (49 m) long and had a beam of about 33 ft (10 m). They had two or three masts and 150 or more oarsmen. Although their cargo capacity was limited, the combination of sail and oar made the galleys fast, reliable and reasonably secure from enemy attacks, and capable of long voyages. A gondola is a sweep-powered flat-bottomed passenger boat peculiar to the canals and lagoon of Venice (*see* Italy KM-141). In the 14th century Venice had become one of the most powerful trading states in the world with a fleet of merchant vessels plying the seas. The oysters with pearls refer to the city's wealth.

Traders of the World – Portuguese

KM-614 ● 1/25 crown ● 1997 .999 gold
KM-615 ● 1 crown ● 1997 .925 silver

The reverse depicts a 15th-century Portuguese nau (merchant ship) and, in the foreground, gold ingots. The exploration voyages of Portuguese navigators along the African coast in the 15th century led the way to the discovery of sea routes to India and farther to the east. Commerce with these areas brought much wealth to Portugal.

Traders of the World – Spanish

KM-616 ● 1/25 crown ● 1997 .999 gold
KM-617 ● 1 crown ● 1997 .925 silver

The reverse depicts a Spanish galleon, a map of the Americas, part of Europe and Africa, a gem, an ingot, and tobacco leaves. The galleons brought from America across the Atlantic Ocean tremendous amounts of precious metals as well as gems. The tobacco (*Nicotiana tabacam*) which the Spanish introduced in Europe was obtained from Mexico and South America.

Traders of the World – English

KM-618 ● 1/25 crown ● 1997 .999 gold
KM-619 ● 1 crown ● 1997 .925 silver

The reverse depicts the pursuit of a Spanish galleon by an English privateer and a medallion portrait of Elizabeth I, Queen of England (1533–1603). Spanish galleons bringing home the treasures of the New World proved an irresistible target for privateers, many of them sailing with the consent of Queen Elizabeth I who felt that England should share in this new-found wealth. Privateers were armed, privately owned vessels that performed piracy on the sea on behalf or with the consent of a government. One of the most famous of all privateers was Sir Francis Drake's *Golden Hind* (*see* Great Britain KM-844).

Traders of the World – William Bligh

KM-620 • 1/25 crown • 1997 .999 gold
KM-621 • 1 crown • 1997 .925 silver

The reverse features Captain William Bligh (1754–1817) with his ship HMAV *Bounty* (*see* Pitcairn KM-6) and two breadfruits in the foreground. After loading breadfruit plants at Tahiti and sailing for the West Indies in 1789, part of the ship's company mutinied against Bligh and set him with 18 loyal men adrift in the ship's launch.

Traders of the World – James Cook

KM-622 • 1/25 crown • 1997 .999 gold
KM-623 • 1 crown • 1997 .925 silver

The reverse depicts Captain James Cook (1728–1779) with HM Sloop *Resolution* and a beaver on a rock in the foreground. *Resolution* was Cook's flagship on his second and third circumnavigations of the world (1772–1775 and 1776–1779). She was built by Thomas Fishburn in Whitby in 1770 as a 462-ton collier (coal ship) named *Marquis of Granby*. She measured 111 ft (34 m) in length, with a beam of 31 ft (9.4 m) and a draft of 13 ft (4 m). In 1771 she was purchased by the British Admiralty for Cook's second voyage and renamed HM Sloop *Drake*, and later renamed again, *Resolution*, after Cook took charge of the ship. Her crew, marines and the scientists aboard numbered 110. This second voyage, on which *Resolution* was accompanied by HMS *Adventure* (*see* Cook Islands KM-9), was aimed at finding *Terra Australis* by circumnavigating the world. The northern coast of this great southern continent was expected to lie somewhere in the Pacific Ocean. In January 1773 Cook's ships became the first to cross the Antarctic Circle, and in January 1774 Cook attained the most southern point mankind had ever reached—71°10' S. latitude—where he was blocked by ice. In 1773/74 the expedition explored the Pacific Ocean, discovering New Caledonia, Norfolk Island, and other islands. On this voyage Cook disproved the existence of *Terra Australis*. On Cook's third voyage, *Resolution* was accompanied by HMS *Discovery* (*see* Russia Y-242). This voyage was aimed at exploring the west coast of North America to look for the Northwest Passage. The beaver on the reverse probably refers to Cook's landings on this coast. *Resolution* was captured in 1782 by the French *Sphinx* whilst serving as an armed transportation ship in the East Indies. She remained in French service until 1783.

Traders of the World – Phoenicians

KM-691 ● $^1/_{25}$ crown ● 1998 .999 gold
KM-692 ● 1 crown ● 1998 .925 silver

The reverse depicts a Phoenician galley (*see* Lebanon KM-4) and in the foreground mollusc shells. The Phoenicians lived on the coastal regions of what is now Lebanon and parts of Syria and Israel. They were leading traders of the ancient world and founded colonies throughout the Mediterranean region, the most famous of which is Carthage near present-day Tunis. The galley depicted is dated to the period 200 BCE – 600 CE. The shells allude to a major industry of the Phoenicians—the manufacture of Tyrian purple, a dye derived from the molluscs *purpura* and *murex*.

Traders of the World – Vikings

KM-693 ● $^1/_{25}$ crown ● 1998 .999 gold
KM-694 ● 1 crown ● 1998 .925 silver

The reverse depicts two Viking ships of about 900 CE (*see* Isle of Man KM-24) and, in the foreground, two walrus tusks and fish. The ship served not only for trading but also for hunting walrus and for fishing.

Traders of the World – Marco Polo

KM-695 ● $^1/_{25}$ crown ● 1998 .999 gold
KM-696 ● 1 crown ● 1998 .925 silver

The reverse depicts the Venetian merchant Marco Polo (1254–1324) with a North European cog and, in the foreground, noodles with chop sticks and pepper. (For more about Marco Polo *see* China / People's Republic Y-54). The reason for the cog design is unclear: Polo made his way to China overland and returned to Europe by a Chinese junk. The noodles with chop sticks refer to Chinese food and the way it is eaten. In Marco Polo's time, prior to the discovery of the sea way to the East at the end of the 15th century, pepper from the East was brought to Europe overland.

Traders of the World – Hanseatic League

KM-697 ● $^1/_{25}$ crown ● 1998 .999 gold
KM-698 ● 1 crown ● 1998 .925 silver

The reverse depicts a Hanseatic cog of about 1350 CE (*see* Danzig KM-145), a map of western Europe where the member cities of the Hanseatic League were located, and coins issued by those cities.

Traders of the World – Chinese

KM-699 ● $^{1}/_{25}$ crown ● 1998 .999 gold
KM-700 ● 1 crown ● 1998 .925 silver

The reverse depicts a Chinese junk against the background of a partial map of Asia, a silkworm and silk thread at left, and pottery at right. Silk had been produced in China thousands of years prior.

Traders of the World – Christopher Columbus

KM-701 ● $^{1}/_{25}$ crown ● 1998 .999 gold
KM-702 ● 1 crown ● 1998 .925 silver

The reverse depicts the flagship *Santa Maria* of Christopher Columbus (1451–1506) during his discovery voyage of 1492, and a portrait of Columbus (*see* Andorra KM-78).

Traders of the World – Walter Raleigh

KM-703 ● $^{1}/_{25}$ crown ● 1998 .999 gold
KM-704 ● 1 crown ● 1998 copper-nickel, issued also in .925 silver

KM-704
1 crown
1998 copper-nickel, 38.6 mm

The reverse depicts Sir Walter Raleigh (1552–1618) (*see* Cook Islands KM-188) in front of his ship and, in the foreground, potatoes and tobacco leaves. In 1584–1589 Raleigh, an English navigator and discoverer, attempted to found a colony on the coast of what is now North Carolina (*see* United States KM-186 for the story of the "lost colony" on Roanoke Island). He brought back from America the potato and tobacco plants.

Traders of the World – Boston Tea Party

KM-705 ● $^{1}/_{25}$ crown ● 1998 .999 gold
KM-706 ● 1 crown ● 1998 .925 silver

The reverse depicts the scene of the "Boston Tea Party" and, at the top, a tea leaf. The design shows two East Indiamen in the harbor of Boston from which American colonists dump tea chests into the water, encouraged by a crowd of Bostonians in the foreground. One of the ships is the 130-ton *Dartmouth*, a brig with a length of 79 ft (24 m). On 16 December 1773 a group of about 60 disgruntled colonists disguised as Mohawk Indians boarded three arriving ships in the harbor of Boston—*Dartmouth*, *Beaver* and *Eleanor*—and threw overboard 342 chests of tea valued at £18,000 that had been brought to America by the British East India Company. The colonists were protesting the Tea Act passed earlier that year by the British Parliament. The act imposed a tax on tea exported to Britain's colonies other than that supplied by the East India Company, enabling the company to sell tea at lower prices than anyone else. The colonists protested these measures as they did not elect members of the House of Commons ("taxation without representation"). The "Boston Tea Party" was the trigger for the American War of Independence.

National Wonders of the World – Niagara Falls

KM-737 ● 1 crown ● 1998 .925 silver with .999 gold coin inset

The reverse shows a *Maid of the Mist* sightseeing boat against the background of the Niagara Falls on the border of the United States and Canada (*see* Canada KM-230). The inset features a reproduction of the reverse of the 10 dollar 1795 gold coin of the United States (KM-21) which depicts an eagle.

Year of the Ocean

KM-744 ● 1/5 crown ● 1998 .999 gold

The reverse depicts the god of the wind and two boats on the stormy ocean.

Year of the Ocean

KM-748 ● 1 crown ● 1998 copper-nickel, issued also in .925 silver

The reverse depicts two windsurfers on the ocean.

Circulation Coins

KM-774 ● 2 pence ● 1998–2001 – see T-1
KM-776 ● 10 pence ● 1998–2001 – see T-2

Olympic Games 2000 Sydney – Sailing

KM-786 ● 1/5 crown ● 1999 .999 gold
KM-787 ● 1 crown ● 1999 copper-nickel, issued also in .925 silver

The reverse features three sailboats, design elements signifying Australia, and, near the rim at 8 o'clock, the Greenwich Meridian 2000 logo. The Australian design elements are Sydney's Opera House and the Sydney Harbor Bridge in the background and a duck-billed platypus in the foreground. The platypus (*Ornithorhynchus anatinus*) is an amphibious egg-laying mammal found in eastern Australia. The Olympic Games of 2000 were held in Sydney on Australia's east coast. The Greenwich Meridian 2000 logo marks the starting point for the third millennium at the Greenwich royal observatory in England, the site of the prime meridian (zero degrees longitude).

Olympic Games 2000 Sydney – Rowing

KM-790 ● $^1/_5$ crown ● 1999 .999 gold
KM-791 ● 1 crown ● 1999–2000 copper-nickel, issued also in .925 silver

The reverse depicts two oarsmen in a scull below two cockatoos and, near the rim at 2 o'clock, the Greenwich Meridian 2000 logo (*see* KM-786). Cockatoos are parrots of the genus *Kakatoe* and related genera that are indigenous to Australia.

The World at War – Operation Torch

KM-798 ● $^1/_5$ crown ● 1998 .999 gold
KM-799 ● 1 crown ● 1998 copper-nickel, issued also in .925 silver

The reverse shows the bust of Lieutenant General Dwight D Eisenhower (1890–1969, *see* T-17), in the background a map of the Iberian peninsula that denotes the location of Gibraltar, and, below the map, Allied soldiers exiting a landing watercraft heading for the African coast. Superimposed on the map is the inscription OPERATION TORCH, the name of the Anglo-American invasion of Vichy-held French North Africa in 1942. Eisenhower, commander of the operation, was based in Gibraltar.

The World at War – *Tirpitz*

KM-854 ● $^1/_5$ crown ● 1999 .999 gold
KM-855 ● 1 crown ● 1999 copper-nickel, issued also in .925 silver

KM-855
1 crown
1999 copper-nickel, 38.6 mm

The reverse depicts the German battleship *Tirpitz* and a sailor. The battleship was built at the Kriegsmarinewerft (Navy Shipyard) in Wilhelmshaven at a cost of 181 million reichsmarks and completed in 1941. Her length was 823 ft (251 m), her beam 118 ft (36 m) and her draft 35 ft (11 m). She displaced 45,226 tons standard (50,153 tons fully loaded) and had a complement of 2,608. She could make 31 knots. The ship was named for Grand Admiral Alfred von Tirpitz (1849–1930) whose efforts in building Germany's combat fleet in the years leading up to World War I had resulted in that country having the second largest navy in the world at that time. From January 1942 *Tirpitz* served in Norwegian waters and constituted a constant threat to Allied convoys bound for North Russia. In September 1943 she was badly damaged by mines planted under her keel by two British midget submarines, X-6 and X-7, and in April 1944 she suffered extreme damage from an attack by 40 bombers from British carriers. On both occasions she was put out of action but became operational again after repairs. These attacks on the battleship by midget submarines and carrier-based aircraft had only limited effect, because of her double layer of armor plate. Finally a special 12,030-

pound (5,457-kg) bomb was built for the job, the *Tall Boy*, designed by the British inventor Sir Barnes Wallis. In September 1944 this bomb, launched during an attack by 27 *Lancaster* bombers, caused so much damage that it was not practical to make the *Tirpitz* seaworthy again and she became a floating heavy artillery battery anchored off Haakøy Island in the Tromsø fjord. Her end came in November 1944 when she was attacked by *Lancaster* bombers of the British Royal Air Force. She was hit by at least two *Tall Boy* bombs and sank off Tromsø with a loss of 971 of her crew. The wreck of *Tirpitz* was broken up between 1948 and 1957.

The World at War – D-Day Landings

KM-860 ● 1/5 crown ● 1999 .999 gold
KM-861 ● 1 crown ● 1999 copper-nickel, issued also in .925 silver

The scene on the reverse of soldiers disembarking landing craft marks the landing of Allied troops on the coast of Normandy, France on D-Day, 6 June 1944 (*see* Great Britain KM-966).

100th Anniversary of the Founding of the Mediterranean Rowing Club

KM-867 ● 5 pounds ● 1999 virenium, issued also in .925 silver and .917 gold

KM-867
5 pounds
1999 virenium, 36.1 mm

The reverse depicts a rower in a single scull and a team of four members in a quadruple scull against the background of the Rock of Gibraltar, and the arms of the Mediterranean Rowing Club. There are two classes in the modern sport of rowing: sculling and sweep-oared rowing. In sculling, as shown on the reverse, the oarsman rows with two oars (also known as blades)—one on either side of the boat. (In sweep-oared rowing, the rower has both hands on a single oar, and rows on one side of the boat only; the oars are positioned alternately on opposite sides of the vessel.) A single scull is 27 ft (8.2 m) in length, a quadruple scull is 44 ft (13 m) long. The blade of a scull has an average length of 10 ft (3 m).

The 21st Century

KM-906 ● 1 crown ● 2001 copper-nickel, issued also in .999 silver (tri-colored: outer ring with black finish, inner ring gold-plated, core .999 silver) and in tri-metallic (tri-colored: outer ring .999 silver, inner ring .999 gold, core .999 platinum)
KM-907 ● 5 crowns ● 2001 tri-metallic (tri-colored: outer ring .999 silver, inner ring .999 gold, core .999 platinum)

KM-906
1 crown
2001 copper-nickel, 38.6 mm

The core of the reverse depicts a Celtic cross, representing the years 1-1000 CE. The design elements on the inner ring represent the discoveries by mankind in the years 1001-2000—a Viking ship (discovery of foreign lands), a microscope (scientific discovery), a telescope (discovery of the solar system) and a space probe (entry into space). The outer ring represents the mysteries of the third millennium—stars, planets, a comet and a space ship.

The Victorian Age - Diamond Jubilee

KM-913 • 1/5 crown • 2001 .999 gold, issued also with an embedded diamond
KM-914 • 1 crown • 2001 copper-nickel, issued also in .925 silver

The reverse depicts Royal Navy ships that took part in the naval review held in 1897 at Spithead and a medallion portrait of Queen Victoria (1819–1901). Spithead is a strait of the English Channel between the entrance to Portsmouth harbor on the mainland of England and the Isle of Wight. The naval review with 165 vessels of the Home Squadron celebrated the Diamond Jubilee, the 60th anniversary of the accession of Queen Victoria to the throne of Great Britain in 1837. Among the beflagged vessels of the Home Squadron were 21 battleships, 53 cruisers, 30 destroyers and 24 torpedo boats. The reverse inscriptions are SPITHEAD REVIEW and THE DIAMOND JUBILEE. Part of the gold coins were issued with a tiny diamond weighing 0.015 carat embedded in the coin at the top of the fourth mast.

The Victorian Age - Isambard Brunel

KM-919 • 1/5 crown • 2001 .999 gold
KM-920 • 1 crown • 2001 copper-nickel, issued also in .925 silver

The reverse features a portrait of the British engineer Isambard Kingdom Brunel (1806–1859) wearing a top hat along with examples of his work—a large ship and a steam engine crossing a bridge. Brunel is considered one of the most innovative and prolific engineers of his time. He designed three famous ships—*Great Western*, *Great Britain* and *Great Eastern*. The 1,320-ton PS *Great Western* (1837), the first purpose-built transatlantic steamship, was built for the Great Western Steam Ship Company by Patterson & Mercer in Bristol. She was wooden-hulled, 236 ft (72 m) long and 58 ft (18 m) in the beam. She drew 17 ft (5 m) of water and was propelled by steam-driven paddle wheels that were 29 ft (8.8 m) in diameter. Her top speed was 9 knots. Upon arrival on her maiden voyage in New York in 1838 *Great Western* had more than 40 tons of coal left, showing that steam was practicable for transatlantic voyages. She completed 45 transatlantic voyages for her original owners and was then sold to the Royal Mail Steam Packet Company for crossings to the West Indies and South America. In the Crimean war she was employed as a troop transport. She was broken up in 1856. Brunel's second large ship was the 3,443-ton *Great Britain* (1843) which revolutionized shipping with her iron hull and six-bladed propeller (*see* Falkland Islands KM-20). Brunel's third famous ship was the 18,915-ton, six-masted paddle wheel steamer *Leviathan* (1858), later renamed *Great Eastern*, that at the time of construction was six times larger than any previous ship in the world (*see* Liberia KM-658). Brunel also designed roads, 125 bridges, 25 railway lines with over 1,000 miles (1,600 km) of track, numerous docks and piers, and the first prefabricated military hospital.

The Victorian Age – Charles Darwin

KM-923 ● 1/5 crown ● 2001 .999 gold
KM-924 ● 1 crown ● 2001 copper-nickel, issued also in .925 silver

The reverse features a portrait of Charles Robert Darwin (1809–1882), HMS *Beagle* at sea and, in the foreground, a squatting precursor of modern man. The three-masted bark *Beagle* was designed by Sir Henry Peake and built in 1820 at Woolwich Dockyard. She displaced 235 tons and measured 90 ft (27 m) in length, with a beam of 24 ft (7.5 m). She drew 12 ft (3.8 m) of water and had a complement of 70. During her first voyage to South America (1826–1830), under the command of Captain Pringle Stokes, in company with the 330-ton HMS *Adventure* commanded by Captain Parker King, *Beagle* made the first comprehensive survey of the southwest coast of South America, the Strait of Magellan and Tierra del Fuego, leaving her name on the Beagle Channel south of Tierra del Fuego. Command was taken over by Lieutenant Robert FitzRoy after Captain Stokes, under the stress of arduous conditions in the waters around Tierra del Fuego, committed suicide. Between 1831 and 1836 the young Darwin was official naturalist for the *Beagle*'s second scientific expedition to the coast of South America under the command of FitzRoy. On this voyage Darwin collected specimens of various life forms, making minute observations about their similarity and differences. During his one-month stay on the Galápagos Islands some 600 miles (1,000 km) west of Ecuador, Darwin made the observations that brought him to the conclusion that, regardless of the species, it changes over time in a manner that best allows it to adapt to its environment. He began writing down his thoughts in what would eventually became his revolutionary treatise *On the Origin of Species by Means of Natural Selection*, published in 1859. On her third voyage (1837–1843) the *Beagle* under the command of Captain John Lord Stokes surveyed the coasts of Australia, where they named Port Darwin. In 1845 *Beagle* became a permanently moored anti-smuggling station on the Essex coast for the Preventive Service, *Beagle Watch Vessel*. She was renamed *W.V.7* in 1863 and broken up in 1870. The reverse inscriptions are THE VICTORIAN AGE and CHARLES DARWIN 1809–1887 THE THEORY OF EVOLUTION. Note the error in the second inscription: Darwin died in 1882, not in 1887.

200th Anniversary of *The Gibraltar Chronicle*

KM-953 • 5 pounds • 2001 virenium, issued also in .925 silver and .917 gold

The reverse depicts warships at the battle of Trafalgar in 1805 (*see* KM-12) against the background of a copy of *The Gibraltar Chronicle* that reported on the battle. The *Chronicle*, one of the world's oldest still existing newspapers, was first published in 1801. It is now Gibraltar's sole daily newspaper.

KM-953
5 pounds
2001 .925 silver, 36.1 mm

50th Anniversary of the Accession of Queen Elizabeth II

KM-999 • 1/5 crown • 2002 .375 gold, issued also in .999 gold
KM-1000 • 1 crown • 2002 copper-nickel, issued also in yellow brass and 24-carat-gold clad .925 silver

The reverse depicts the royal yacht HMY *Britannia* (*see* Guernsey KM-52) passing under the Tower Bridge in London after a voyage that included a visit to Gibraltar.

T-1 Circulation Coins

KM-21 • 2 pence • 1988–94 bronze, Queen's portrait by Raphael Makhlouf
KM-21a • 2 pence • 1995–97 bronze-plated steel
KM-774 • 2 pence • 1998–2001 bronze-plated steel, Queen's portrait by Ian Rank-Broadley

The reverse depicts a sailing ship at sea behind the lighthouse on Europa Point, the southernmost tip of the Rock of Gibraltar. The fully automated lighthouse belongs to the Trinity House Lighthouse Service, Britain's General Lighthouse Authority. The present lighthouse started operations in 1841. It stands 161 ft (49 m) above the high water mark and its loom can be seen over a distance of 17 miles (27 km).

T-2 Circulation Coins

KM-112 • 10 pence • 1992–97 copper-nickel, issued also in .925 silver, .917 gold and .950 platinum
KM-776 • 10 pence • 1998–2001 copper-nickel, Queen's portrait by Ian Rank-Broadley

The reverse features the office building of the Europort harbor against the background of the Rock of Gibraltar, and at sea in the foreground two indiscernible vessels. The 12 stars along the rim of the reverse allude to the European Economic Community (now the European Union).

T-3 Warships of World War II – USS *Philadelphia*

KM-113 ● 1 crown ● 1993 copper-nickel, issued also in .925 silver
KM-153 ● 1/5 crown ● 1993 .999 gold

The reverse depicts the American light cruiser USS *Philadelphia* (CL 41) against the background of the Rock of Gibraltar. She displaced 9,700 tons, her length was 608 ft (185 m), her beam 62 ft (19 m) and her draft 19 ft (5.9 m). She made 32 knots and her complement numbered 868. *Philadelphia* was built at the Philadelphia navy yard in 1937. She served in the European theater in World War II escorting convoys and providing gunfire support to landings in Morocco in 1942, and in Sicily and southern France in 1943. She earned five battle stars in the war. In 1951 *Philadelphia* was sold to the Brazilian navy and renamed *Barroso* (C 11). She served under the Brazilian flag until 1973. The twelve issues listed under T-3 through T-14 honor ships that saw action in the Mediterranean Sea in World War II. The war for the most part was fought on continents and the maintenance, servicing and operating of the fighting machines required a steady source of supplies, most of which went by sea in Allied convoys of cargo ships escorted by naval vessels. These convoys battled in the Mediterranean Sea through a non-stop gauntlet of air and sea attacks by enemy aircraft, submarines and surface raiders. The relatively confined waters of the Mediterranean Sea provided little room to maneuver and a heavy toll was paid in men and ships before the Allies were able to establish air, sea and land superiority and turn the tide of the war.

T-4 Warships of World War II – USS *McLanahan*

KM-114 ● 1 crown ● 1993 copper-nickel, issued also in .925 silver
KM-154 ● 1/5 crown ● 1993 .999 gold

The reverse features the American destroyer USS *McLanahan* (DD 615) against the background of the Rock of Gibraltar. *McLanahan* was built by Bethlehem, San Francisco and commissioned in 1942. She displaced 1,620 tons. Her length was 348 ft (106 m) with a beam of 36 ft (11 m) and a draft of 17 ft (5.3 m). She could make 37 knots. Her complement numbered 259. The vessel was named for Tenant McLanahan, a courageous midshipman who was killed in California in 1848. In World War II *McLanahan* patrolled the waters around Gibraltar as far as Casablanca to the south, served as escort to convoys in the Atlantic Ocean and the Mediterranean Sea, and lent support to the Allied troops advancing up the Italian coast—providing gunfire support and ensuring the even flow of supplies. She earned four battle stars for her service during the war. *McLanahan* was decommissioned in 1946, remained in reserve until 1969 and was scrapped in 1974.

T-5 Warships of World War II – HNLMS *Isaac Sweers*

KM-115 ● 1 crown ● 1993 copper-nickel, issued also in .925 silver
KM-155 ● 1/5 crown ● 1993 .999 gold

KM-115
1 crown
1993 copper-nickel, 38.6 mm

The reverse depicts the Dutch destroyer HNLMS (Her NetherLands Majesty's Ship) *Isaac Sweers* against the background of the Rock of Gibraltar. Her length was 349 ft (106 m), her beam 34 ft (10 m) and her draft 11 ft (3.5 m). She displaced 1,922 tons standard (2,228 tons fully loaded) and made 37 knots. She was named for the Dutch vice admiral of that name (1622–1673) who died in the battle of the Texel at which the Dutch fleet commanded by Admiral Michiel Adriaanszoon de Ruyter defeated the Allied English–French fleet in the Third English–Dutch War. *Isaac Sweers* was launched at the yard of the Royal De Schelde Company at Flushing in March 1940 and was towed to England by the tugboat *Zwarte Zee* on 11 May 1940, the day following the German invasion of the Netherlands. Construction was completed in 1941 at the yard of John I. Thornycroft & Co. at Southampton. Based in Gibraltar, she served in the Mediterannean as part of a British squadron, mostly engaged in escorting troop and supply convoys. She was torpedoed by the German submarine *U431* off Algiers in November 1942 during "Operation Torch" (*see* KM-798). British vessels saved 86 out of the 194 men on board. While the Dutch Navy prevented *Isaac Sweers* from falling into German hands, it was not as successful with regard to her sister destroyer, *Gerard Callenburgh*, which was under construction by the Rotterdam Drydock Company when Germany invaded Holland. On 15 May 1940 she was scuttled in the Nieuwe Waterweg near Rotterdam but in July 1940 she was salvaged and towed to Hamburg. Construction was completed at the German Blohm & Voss yard in 1942 and the destroyer was incorporated in the German Navy as *ZH1* (*ZH* is short for Zerstörer Holland, meaning "Dutch destroyer"). *ZH1* was scuttled by her own crew in June 1944 after she was hit by torpedoes and gunfire from British, Canadian and Polish destroyers in the English Channel when she tried to reach Cherbourg in France shortly after the D-Day landings. Of the 203 men on board, 36 lost their lives. Thus the sister ships met the same fate while fighting in opposing navies.

T-6 Warships of World War II – USS *Weehawken*

KM-116 ● 1 crown ● 1993 copper-nickel, issued also in .925 silver
KM-156 ● 1/5 crown ● 1993 .999 gold

The reverse depicts USS *Weehawken* against the background of the Rock of Gibraltar. She was built in 1920 by William Cramp & Son Ships and Engines Building Company at Philadelphia for the Florida East Coast Car Ferry Company as the car ferry SS *Estrada Palma*, named for Tomás Estrada Palma, Cuba's first president (1835–1908). In 1942 the ferry was requisitioned by the War Shipping Administration, acquired by the US Navy, renamed *Weehawken* after a township in New Jersey on the Hudson River, converted to a minelayer by the Bethlehem Steel Company at Hoboken, New Jersey and given the designator CM-12. *Weehawken* displaced 6,525 tons (fully loaded), was 350 ft (107 m) in length and 57 ft (17 m) at the beam, and drew 18 ft (5.3 m) of water. She could make 12 knots. Her complement numbered 290. She laid defensive minefields off Casablanca and Sicily, surviving German air attacks. Later assigned to the Pacific theater, she was sturdy enough to outlast kamikaze raids and two major typhoons, in November 1944 and September 1945; however, in typhoon Louise in October 1945 off Okinawa her luck ran out and she ran aground. Being beyond economical salvage, *Weehawken* was decommissioned in December 1945 and broken up. For her service in World War II she earned two battle stars.

T-7 Warships of World War II – HMS *Warspite*

KM-117 • 1 crown • 1993 copper-nickel, issued also in .925 silver
KM-157 • 1/5 crown • 1993 .999 gold

KM-117
1 crown
1993 copper-nickel, 38.6 mm

The reverse depicts the British battleship HMS *Warspite* against the background of the Rock of Gibraltar. She was the most famous and the oldest battleship of the Royal Navy in World War II. The super dreadnought was built by the Devonport Dockyard at Plymouth in 1915. After her modernization in 1938 she displaced 32,450 tons, was 646 ft (197 m) long, had a beam of 104 ft (32 m), and drew 29 ft (8.8 m) of water. Her speed was 23 knots and her complement numbered 1,190. In World War I she was hit 13 times at the battle of Jutland in 1916 but she survived thanks to her excellent construction. In April 1940, shortly after the invasion of neutral Norway by the Germans, *Warspite* was the flagship of Vice Admiral William Whitworth. He took her into Ofot Fjord and in what is known as the second battle of Narvik harried the German destroyers there to destruction. She was then ordered to the Mediterranean theater where she served as the flagship of Admiral Andrew B. Cunningham ("ABC"). In July 1940, at the battle of Calabria off Italy's southernmost region, she hit the Italian battleship *Giulio Cesare* at the amazing range of 13 miles (21 km). In March 1941 off Cape Matapan, the most southerly point of mainland Greece, *Warspite* together with her sister ships *Barham* and *Valiant* sank three Italian cruisers—*Fiume*, *Zara* and *Pola*. In September 1943, during the Salerno landings east of Naples, she was severely damaged by three German FX.1400 radio bombs. These 1,400-kg (3,086-pound) radio-controlled armor-piercing bombs were the world's first guided missiles. The old ship nearly sank and needed seven tugs to tow her sideways through the Strait of Messina but she made it home for repairs. She was used as part of the bombardment force covering the D-Day landings in

Normandy. *Warspite*, with 14 battle honors to her credit, was sold out of the Navy in 1946 and went aground in 1947 while en route to be scrapped.

T-8 Warships of World War II – HMS *Hood*

KM-118 ● 1 crown ● 1993 copper-nickel, issued also in .925 silver
KM-158 ● 1/5 crown ● 1993 .999 gold

The reverse depicts the British battle cruiser HMS *Hood* against the background of the Rock of Gibraltar. She was built at John Brown's Clydebank yard in 1918 at a cost of £6,025,000. She was 861 ft (262 m) long, had a beam of 104 ft (32 m), and drew 29 ft (8.9 m) of water. She displaced 42,462 tons standard (48,360 tons fully loaded). *Hood* was named for Viscount Samuel Hood (*see* Alderney T-4). At the time of her completion in 1920 until World War II she was the largest warship in the world and with a speed of 32 knots also one of the fastest. Throughout the interwar period she was regarded as a symbol of British seapower and was employed to show the British flag on various cruises, including a circumnavigation in 1923/24 of thirty thousand miles (nearly fifty thousand km). In 1940 *Hood* was the flagship of Force H at Gibraltar and took part in the destruction of the French fleet at Oran, Algeria. In May 1941 *Hood*, flying the flag of Vice Admiral Lancelot Holland, was ordered to sail for Iceland. Her mission was to stop the 50,900-ton German battleship *Bismarck* and the 19,040-ton heavy cruiser *Prinz Eugen* from breaking out from the Scandinavian waters into the Atlantic Ocean, where the German ships would wreak havoc on the convoys that were critical to British survival, and where it would be almost impossible to track them down. When *Bismarck* was sighted in the Denmark Strait between Greenland and Iceland *Hood* opened fire and three minutes later the German vessels replied. A shell from *Prinz Eugen* struck *Hood*, starting a fire that spread among the ready-use ammunition lockers carried on the shelter deck. Only eight minutes after the start of the action a salvo from *Bismarck* at a range of 8.2 miles (13 km) penetrated *Hood*'s deck, detonated her aft magazines and split the ship in half. The stern section sank almost immediately while the bow followed three minutes later. There were only three survivors; 1,415 were lost. It was the blackest moment of the whole war for the Royal Navy. *Hood*'s wreck was found in 2001, approximately 9,200 ft (2,800 m) below the surface of the Denmark Strait.

T-9 Warships of World War II – HMS *Penelope*

KM-119 ● 1 crown ● 1993 copper-nickel, issued also in .925 silver
KM-159 ● 1/5 crown ● 1993 .999 gold

The reverse features the British light cruiser HMS *Penelope* against the background of the Rock of Gibraltar. She was built by Harland &

Wolff at Belfast, Northern Ireland in 1936. She displaced 5,270 tons standard (6,715 tons fully loaded). Her length was 506 ft (154 m), her beam 51 ft (16 m) and her draft 14 ft (4.3 m). In November 1941 *Penelope* was part of a small group of British light cruisers and destroyers in the Mediterranean Sea known as Force K. The force twice intercepted Axis convoys bound from southern Europe to North Africa, resulting in the sinking of the Italian destroyer *Fulmine* and nine German and Italian transports. In December 1941 the force ran into an Italian minefield. Two British ships—the light cruiser HMS *Neptune* and the destroyer HMS *Kandahar*—sank while *Penelope* was badly damaged. While she was under repair in a Malta dockyard in March 1942 she came under a heavy air attack. Her sides were riddled with holes from near-miss bombs which earned her the nickname Pepperpot. She eventually sailed from Malta with her numerous splinter holes filled with wooden plugs. In February 1944 she was torpedoed by the German submarine *U410* while covering the Anzio beachhead between Rome and Naples and sank west of Naples with a loss of 415. There were 206 survivors.

T-10 Warships of World War II – HMCS *Prescott*

KM-120 • 1 crown • 1993 copper-nickel, issued also in .925 silver
KM-160 • 1/5 crown • 1993 .999 gold

The reverse depicts the 925-ton HMCS (His Majesty's Canadian Ship) *Prescott* against the background of the Rock of Gibraltar. The corvette was built by Kingston Shipbuilding Co. of Kingston, Ontario and commissioned in 1941 by the Royal Canadian Navy. She was named for the city of Prescott, Ontario. She supported the Royal Navy during the invasion of North Africa and served on convoy escort duties in the Mediterranean Sea. In March 1943 *Prescott* sank the German submarine *U163* in a precision depth-charge attack in the Bay of Biscay. *Prescott* was one of the 125 Canadian-built corvettes of the Gladiolus corvette class (the "flower class" corvettes) that entered service between 1940 and 1944. They were of very simple construction so that they could be constructed quickly in large numbers. Based on a Smiths Dock design for a whale-catcher, the final design called for a vessel with a displacement of 1,170 tons (fully loaded) and a speed of 16 knots. Their length was 205 ft (62 m), their beam 33 ft (10 m) and their draft 10 ft (3.1 m); the crew numbered 47. From mid-1940 the "flower class" corvettes were used in increasing numbers for ocean escort duty. They formed a substantial part of the escort force which prevented the German submarines, the U-boats, from gaining victory in the early years of the battle of the Atlantic when the United States had not yet entered the war. *Prescott* survived the war, ended her service in 1945 and was scrapped in 1951.

T-11 Warships of World War II – HMS *Ark Royal*

KM-121 ● 1 crown ● 1993 copper-nickel, issued also in .925 silver
KM-161 ● 1/5 crown ● 1993 .999 gold

KM-121
1 crown
1993 copper-nickel, 38.6 mm

The reverse features HMS *Ark Royal* against the background of the Rock of Gibraltar. She was the first large aircraft carrier to be purpose-built for the Royal Navy. Built by Cammell Laird at Birkenhead, she was commissioned in 1938. Her design met the limits of the Washington Treaty of 1922 concerning naval armament. She was the only modern British carrier at the outbreak of the war. Her displacement was 22,352 tons standard (28,143 tons fully loaded). Her length was 800 ft (244 m), her beam 95 ft (29 m) and her draft 28 ft (8.5 m). She made a speed of 31 knots. Her crew, including air crew, numbered 1,600. The hangars were built on two levels and could carry 72 aircraft. Aircraft landed from the stern and were launched from the two catapults fitted at the forward end of the deck. Three lifts were provided to ensure the rapid transfer of aircraft from the hangars to the flight deck. At the beginning of World War II *Ark Royal* was deployed in the northwestern approaches to the British Isles, operated in the Southern Atlantic and took part in the Norwegian campaign in April–May 1940. In June 1940 she joined Force H under Vice Admiral Sir James Somerville (*see* T-16) at Gibraltar. In 1940 and 1941 *Ark Royal* was constantly in action, mainly escorting Malta convoys (*see* T-15) and carrying out strikes against the Italian mainland. One of her aircraft was responsible for two torpedo hits on the German battleship *Bismarck*. One of these torpedoes disabled the *Bismarck*'s steering gear, slowing her enough for the British fleet to catch and destroy her in May 1941. While returning from flying off air reinforcements for Malta in November 1941 *Ark Royal* was torpedoed by the German submarine *U81*, 30 miles (48 km) from Gibraltar. She was taken in tow but capsized and sank 13 hours after she was torpedoed. Only one of her crew was lost. The Royal Navy's first *Ark Royal* was the flagship of Lord Howard of Effingham whose fleet opposed the Spanish armada sent in 1588 to conquer England.

T-12 Warships of World War II – USS *Gleaves*

KM-122 ● 1 crown ● 1993 copper-nickel, issued also in .925 silver
KM-162 ● 1/5 crown ● 1993 .999 gold

KM-122
1 crown
1993 copper-nickel, 38.6 mm

The reverse depicts the destroyer USS *Gleaves* (DD 423) against the background of the Rock of Gibraltar. She was constructed by the Bath Iron Works at Bath, Maine and was commissioned in 1940. She displaced 1,630 tons standard (2,515 tons fully loaded). Her length was 348 ft (106 m), her beam 36 ft (11 m) and her draft 17 ft (5.3 m). She could make 37 knots. Her complement numbered 276. She was named for Admiral Albert

Gleaves (1858–1937). The destroyer was assigned to convoy escort duty and took part in landings in Italy and France. In one battle off the coast of San Remo near Monaco *Gleaves* destroyed five explosive-laden German E-boats and captured a sixth. Two of the German crew were able to provide the Allies with valuable intelligence. *Gleaves* received five battle stars for her service in World War II. She was decommissioned in 1946, was stricken from the US Navy list in 1969 and sold for scrap in 1972.

T-13 Warships of World War II – HMAS *Waterhen*

KM-123 ● 1 crown ● 1993 copper-nickel, issued also in .925 silver
KM-163 ● $^1/_5$ crown ● 1993 .999 gold

The destroyer HMAS (His Majesty's Australian Ship) *Waterhen*, shown on the reverse against the background of the Rock of Gibraltar, was built for the British Royal Navy by Palmers Shipbuilding & Iron Co. in Jarrow-on-Tyne in 1918. She displaced 1,100 tons standard (1,345 tons fully loaded), was 312 ft (95 m) long, had a beam of 30 ft (9 m), and drew 10 ft (2.9 m) of water. Her speed was 34 knots and her complement numbered 127. In 1933 she was leased to the Royal Australian Navy. Following the start of World War II in 1939 she was ordered to the Mediterranean Sea for escort and patrol duties. After the entry of Italy into the war and the collapse of French resistance in June 1940 all Mediterranean coasts except those of Gibraltar in the west, Malta in the center and Egypt, Palestine and Cyprus in the east were closed to the Royal Navy, and a bitter struggle for control of the Mediterranean Sea ensued. *Waterhen* escorted convoys, carried out bombardments of enemy positions, protected supply ships and water carriers, and participated in evacuation of Allied troops from Greece and Crete. In 1941 she was used to transport troops to Tobruk, Libya. Tobruk had been fortified by the Italians during their colonization of Libya. It had the best harbor in Libya. In January 1941, British troops advancing out of Egypt swept the Italians from the Western Desert and took Tobruk. Three months later, the offensive by the German General Erwin Rommel forced the British forces to retreat to Egypt; however, the Australian garrison at Tobruk held out and defended itself throughout 1941. Supplies and reinforcements were brought in by sea to the besieged garrison. *Waterhen* made 13 runs on the "Tobruk Ferry" until she was attacked in June 1941 en route from Alexandria to Tobruk by German *Junkers Ju87* Stukas (Stuka is short for *Sturzkampfflugzeug*, dive bomber). Off Sollum on the border of Egypt and Libya she was holed by near misses and immobilized. Her company and embarked troops could be saved but the ship sank after a few hours. She was the first Australian warship to be lost by enemy action in World War II.

T-14 Warships of World War II – FFS *Savorgnan de Brazza*

KM-144
1 crown
1993 copper-nickel, 38.6 mm

KM-144 ● 1 crown ● 1993 copper-nickel, issued also in .925 silver
KM-164 ● 1/5 crown ● 1993 .999 gold

The reverse depicts the FFS (Free French Ship) *Savorgnan de Brazza* against the background of the Rock of Gibraltar. The anti-aircraft sloop, classed as a colonial aviso, was built by Ateliers et Chantiers Maritimes du Sud-Ouest (the South–West shipyard) at Bordeaux in 1931. She was 340 ft (104 m) long, had a beam of 42 ft (13 m), and drew 15 ft (4.5 m) of water. She displaced 1,969 tons standard (2,600 tons fully loaded) and made 16 knots. Her wartime complement numbered 194. The vessel was named for the Italian count Pietro di Brazza Savorgnani (1852–1905) who joined the French navy and became a French national, changing his name to Pierre Savorgnan de Brazza. He explored Gabon and founded the colony of French Congo (now the Republic of the Congo). De Brazza founded Brazzaville in 1884 and was governor of the colony in the years 1886–1897. In 1940 *Savorgnan de Brazza* participated in the evacuation of Dunkirk, flying the flag of Rear Admiral Marcel Landriau who was in command of the approximately 200 French vessels assigned to this operation. *Savorgnan de Brazza* also took part in the evacuation of other French ports. Later that year she was sequestered in England and became part of the naval forces of the Free French resistance that was led by General Charles de Gaulle from London. In November 1940 she sank the French sloop *Bougainville* that served in the navy of Vichy France. In 1941 *Savorgnan de Brazza* took part in the blockade of Djibouti. For the remainder of World War II she served in the Far East. In 1946 she took part in the war in French Indochina (now Vietnam). *Savorgnan de Brazza* was broken up in 1957.

T-15 World War II – Maltese Convoy

KM-253 ● 1/5 crown ● 1994 .999 gold
KM-259 ● 1 crown ● 1994 copper-nickel, issued also in .925 silver

The reverse shows a convoy on its way to Malta, the strategically important British colony 55 miles (90 km) south of the Italian island of Sicily. Malta's position in the center of the Mediterranean Sea made it a staging point for convoys making for Egyptian and other North African ports with supplies, troops and munitions, and also a platform for strikes against Axis supply routes to North Africa. The convoys to supply and reinforce Malta setting out from Gibraltar were under surveillance from enemy reconnaissance aircraft stationed in Sardinia and had to cope with air and submarine attacks for most of their voyage, incurring heavy losses.

T-16 World War II – James Somerville

KM-255 ● $^{1}/_{5}$ crown ● 1994 .999 gold
KM-261 ● 1 crown ● 1994 copper-nickel, issued also in .925 silver

The reverse features the British Rear Admiral James Somerville (1882–1949) with one of his ships against the background of the Rock of Gibraltar. The ship may be the British aircraft carrier HMS *Ark Royal* (*see* T-11). Somerville was the commander of Force H which was based at Gibraltar and initially included the battle cruiser HMS *Hood* (*see* T-8), *Ark Royal*, battleships, cruisers and destroyers. The main duty of Force H was to escort convoys that transferred men, food and munitions throughout the Mediterranean Sea and the Atlantic Ocean.

T-17 World War II – Dwight Eisenhower

KM-258 ● $^{1}/_{5}$ crown ● 1994 .999 gold
KM-264 ● 1 crown ● 1994 copper-nickel, issued also in .925 silver

The reverse features General Dwight D. Eisenhower (1890–1969) with landing craft in the background. The reverse inscription names him as Supreme Allied Commander. In June 1942 Eisenhower was appointed Commanding General of the American troops in the European Theater, even though he had never served in combat, had small experience with troops, and little background in directing the efforts of large units of men and equipment; however, he had proven himself as a superb staff officer. In November 1942 the combined chiefs of staff appointed Lieutenant General Eisenhower Commander-in-Chief of the Allied Forces for the invasion of North Africa ("Operation Torch"). This operation—part of a strategy to tighten the ring around Germany—was extremely complex as it involved the three armed services of two nations, Great Britain and the United States, in a campaign launched on hostile soil by amphibious landings. After Italy's capitulation at the end of 1943, following the landings in Sicily and mainland Italy, the combined chiefs of staff named Eisenhower Supreme Commander of the Allied Expeditionary Force for the invasion of Europe. (About this invasion, on D-Day, 6 June 1944, *see* Great Britain KM-966.) The war in Europe ended on 7 May 1945 when Eisenhower received the unconditional surrender from German General Alfred Jodl at the Supreme Headquarters, Allied Expeditionary Force (SHAEF), in Rheims, France. Eisenhower became army chief of staff in 1945, commander-in-chief of NATO forces in 1950, and president of the United States in 1953.

T-18 200th Anniversary of the Battle of Trafalgar – Breaking the Line

KM-? ● 1 crown ● 2005 copper-nickel

The reverse depicts three warships breaking the line during the battle of Trafalgar (*see* KM-12).

KM-?
1 crown
2005 copper-nickel, 39 mm

T-19 200th Anniversary of Battle of Trafalgar – First Shots

KM-? ● 1 crown ● 2005 copper-nickel

The reverse depicts vessels of the British fleet at the start of the battle of Trafalgar (*see* KM-12). They are lead by HMS *Victory*, flagship of Admiral Lord Horatio Nelson.

KM-?
1 crown
2005 copper-nickel, 39 mm

GREAT BRITAIN

The United Kingdom of Great Britain and Northern Ireland—commonly referred to as Great Britain or the United Kingdom—is situated in western Europe northwest of France, between the Atlantic Ocean and the North Sea. Great Britain includes England, Scotland and Wales; Northern Ireland refers to the six northern counties in Ireland that remained part of the United Kingdom after the partition of Ireland in 1921.

Circulation Coins – King George III

KM-661 ● 1 farthing ● 1806–07 copper, 20 mm, issued also in bronzed copper and gilt copper
KM-662 ● 1/2 penny ● 1806–07 copper, 29 mm, issued also in bronzed copper
KM-663 ● 1 penny ● 1806–07 copper, 35 mm, issued also in bronzed copper and gilt copper

The reverse depicts Britannia seated on a rock holding a leafy branch, with a shield by her side and a three-masted sailing ship on the horizon. Britannia is the female personification of Great Britain. Her name was the ancient Roman name for the British island. The ship symbolizes Britain's maritime interests or its concern for naval supremacy and the importance of the Royal Navy in the Napoleonic Wars (1799–1815). The shield bears the Union Jack, the United Kingdom's national flag—a composite design including the crosses of England, Scotland and Ireland. The first coin on which Britannia is depicted as a seated woman with a shield is a *sestertius* issued in 119 CE by the Roman emperor Hadrian (117–138) who ruled over the southern part of England. She last appeared on Roman currency during the reign of Carausius (286/7–293) and reappeared on the reverse of halfpennies and farthings minted in 1671 by King Charles II (1660–1685). Since then she is featured regularly on British coinage. The coins have no stated denomination. The farthing is one-fourth of a penny. In the ancient monetary system used in Britain until decimalization in 1971 there were 12 pennies in the shilling and 20 shillings in the pound.

Circulation Coins - Queen Victoria

KM-747 ● 1 farthing ● 1860–73 bronze, sub-types not separately listed herein
KM-748 ● 1/2 penny ● 1860–74 bronze, sub-types not separately listed herein
KM-749 ● 1 penny ● 1860–74 bronze, sub-types not separately listed herein
KM-753 ● 1 farthing ● 1874–95 bronze, more mature bust of the queen
KM-754 ● 1/2 penny ● 1874–94 bronze, more mature bust of the queen
KM-755 ● 1 penny ● 1874–94 bronze, more mature bust of the queen

The reverse depicts Britannia seated on a rock wielding the trident of the Greek god of the sea, Poseidon (to the Romans, Neptune), an indiscernible vessel near her feet at right and a representation of the Eddystone Lighthouse at far left. The trident symbolizes Britain's maritime power. Queen Victoria's rule also extended over Britain's colonies around the world and it was claimed "the sun never sets on the British Empire." Eddystone is a group of rocks 14 miles (23 km) out at sea south-southwest of Plymouth. Already in 1698 a wooden tower with a fire was erected on the rocks by Henry Winstanley to render them safe to shipping. In 1703 this structure with its occupants was washed away in a storm. The second tower, constructed by John Rudyerd, was also made of wood and completed in 1709. It was destroyed by fire in 1755. The tower depicted on the reverse was Eddystone's third lighthouse. It was built of stone by John Smeaton in 1759, based on the shape of an English oak tree for strength. Its light of 24 candles shone 70 ft (21 m) above the rocks. In the 1870s cracks appeared in the rock on which the lighthouse stood. The tower was dismantled and re-erected on Plymouth Hoe as a monument, where it still stands today. The present Eddystone Lighthouse was completed in 1882. The station became automated and unmanned in 1982. The portrait of the queen on the obverse of the first three coins is often referred to as the bun head type. The bronze alloy of these coins was devised in France for the making of chuch bells. This "French bronze," which is composed of 95 percent copper, 4 percent tin and one percent zinc, is harder than either of its constituents and thus more resistant to wear.

Circulation Coin – King Edward VII

KM-801 • 1 florin / 2 shillings • 1902–10 .925 silver

The reverse depicts Britannia wielding a trident and holding a shield, standing on the prow of a galley.

Circulation Coins – *Golden Hind*

KM-844 • ½ penny • 1937–48 bronze, George VI, obverse legend Ind: Imp:
KM-868 • ½ penny • 1949–52 bronze, George VI, without Ind: Imp:
KM-892 • ½ penny • 1953 bronze, Elizabeth II, obverse legend Britt: Omn:
KM-896 • ½ penny • 1954–70 bronze, Elizabeth II, without Britt: Omn:

KM-868
½ penny
1952 bronze, 25 mm

The reverse depicts *Golden Hind*, a 100-ton bark-rigged galleon built in 1560 as *Pelican*. She was 102 ft (31 m) long, had a beam of 20 ft (6.1 m), drew 9 ft (2.7 m) of water, and had a crew of 70. The vessel carried some 18 guns and was the flagship of the English navigator, pirate, privateer and admiral Francis Drake (1540–1596) on his global circumnavigation in 1577–1580. During the voyage Drake renamed the ship *Golden Hind* in honor of his major financial backer, Sir Christopher Hatton, whose crest was a golden deer. Drake's other four ships on this voyage were *Elizabeth*, *Marigold*, *Swan* and *Christopher*. The aim of the voyage—with the consent of Queen Elizabeth I—was to disrupt the world trade monopoly of Spain and Portugal. After negotiating the Strait of Magellan, the first Englishman to do so, Drake sailed up the west coast of South America. En route he raided Valparaiso and captured the Spanish treasure ship *Cacafuego* off Callao, Peru. Drake expected the Spanish to wait for him if he returned to the Atlantic Ocean by way of the Strait of Magellan. He therefore returned home via the Cape of Good Hope. The voyage produced a profit of 4,700 percent on his backers' investment. Upon Drake's return in 1580, Queen Elizabeth bestowed a knighthood upon him aboard *Golden Hind*. The ship was placed in a special dock and became a museum piece but fell into disrepair and had to be dismantled in 1662. Today, a life-sized replica of the ship can be seen in Brixham, Devon, England. Prior to his circumnavigation Drake had been sailing in the slave trade to the Spanish Main (the lands of the Caribbean Basin—Mexico, Central America, the northern countries of South America, and the Caribbean islands). In 1568, while taking refuge for repairs to hurricane damage at San Juan de Ulúa near Veracruz, Mexico, Drake and his cousin John Hawkins (*see* Cook Islands KM-171) were attacked by the Spanish, only just escaping with their lives. From this day on Drake sought to avenge San Juan de Ulúa by harassing, plundering or destroying everything Spanish. He helped to defeat the Spanish armada in 1588. More than 1.4 billion coins with this beautiful design were struck. The obverse legend in abbreviated Latin IND: IMP: (Emperor of India) was deleted in 1949 after India became an independent republic, while the legend in abbreviated Latin BRITT: OMN: (All British Possessions) was deleted from the coinage in 1954 due to the changing status of many British Commonwealth nations.

50th Anniversary of the D-Day Landings

KM-966 ● 50 pence ● 1994 copper-nickel, seven-sided planchet, issued also in .925 silver and .917 gold

The reverse features stylized Allied towplanes and transport gliders above a flotilla of landing craft. The design illustrates the D-Day landings on 6 June 1944 by the Allied Expeditionary Force over a front of 50 miles (80 km) on the German-held coast of Normandy, France between Cherbourg and Le Havre. The five Normandy beaches were code-named—from west to east—Utah, Omaha, Gold, Juno and Sword. Utah and Omaha were assigned to the American troops, Gold and Sword to the British, and Juno to the Canadians. The code name of the invasion was "Operation Overlord." It was the largest amphibious landing ever undertaken in the history of warfare. The commander-in-chief was the US General Dwight D. Eisenhower (1890–1969, *see* Gibraltar T-17). Commander of the fleet that carried the assaulting force to Normandy was the British Admiral Sir Bertram Ramsay (1883–1945). The fleet included 4,126 landing ships and craft. In the evening of 6 June, 155,000 soldiers and 20,000 vehicles had landed. The soldiers were principally American, British and Canadian but also men from France, Belgium, Czechoslovakia, Greece, Luxembourg, Norway and Poland in Europe, and from Australia and New Zealand. Allied casualties totaled 11,000 (including 2,500 dead), far less than had been feared. The invasion gave the Allies a vital foothold on the mainland of Europe and was the essential starting point on the road to victory. The coin won the Coin of the Year honors for coinage dated 1994, after having been voted best contemporary event coin and most popular coin in the first round of balloting.

200th Anniversary of the Battle of Trafalgar

KM-1053 ● 5 pounds ● 2005 copper-nickel, issued also in .925 silver and .917 gold

KM-1053
5 pounds
2005 copper-nickel, 38.6 mm

The reverse depicts HMS *Victory* and HMS *Téméraire* (Bold) at the battle of Trafalgar in 1805 as viewed through a telescope from the French lines (*see* Gibraltar KM-12 about the *Victory* and the battle). The 98-gun second-rate ship-of-the-line *Téméraire* was built at Chatham in 1798. She was 185 ft (56 m) long, had a beam of 51 ft (16 m), and drew 22 ft (6.6 m) of water. She measured 2,121 tons. Her complement numbered some 750. She was named for the 74-gun French ship of that name that had been captured at Lagos in 1759 and had served in the Royal Navy under her original name until sold in 1784. At Trafalgar, under the command of Captain Eliab Harvey, *Téméraire* was the second in the line of battle behind Admiral Lord Horatio Nelson's *Victory*. When the French ship *Redoutable* attempted to board *Victory*, *Téméraire* saved her by a broadside from her port battery that destroyed the boarding party of roughly 200 men that had assembled on *Redoutable*. Falling masts and yards from *Redoutable* and *Téméraire* locked the two ships together in a tangle of rigging but *Téméraire* got a party aboard *Redoutable* and took possession of her. When *Fougueux* came to assist *Redoutable*, *Téméraire*'s starboard guns caused her to surrender within ten minutes and *Fougueux* was tied up on *Téméraire*'s starboard. *Téméraire* had 123 casualties at Trafalgar, of whom 47 were killed. She remained in service until she was broken up in 1838. The reverse design was inspired by the 1905 painting *A Panorama of the Battle of Trafalgar* by William Lionel Wyllie (1851–1931), now in the Royal Naval Museum in Portsmouth. The signal sent by Nelson ahead of the battle, ENGLAND EXPECTS THAT EVERY MAN WILL DO HIS DUTY, is inscribed on the edge of the gold version of the coin.

Trade Dollar

KM-T5 ● Trade dollar ● 1895–1935 .900 silver, restrikes exist in gold

The obverse depicts a standing Britannia holding a trident in her right hand and a shield with the Union Jack in her left, in the background at left a three-masted bark-rigged sailing ship symbolizing commerce, and, at the top, ONE DOLLAR. This denomination is stated on the reverse in Chinese characters and in Malay script. These dollars were legal tender in Hong Kong until 1937, and until 1904/05 also in the Straits Settlements and in Labuan off north-western Borneo. The coins were issued by the British government to facilitate British commerce in the Far East because of a lack of Mexican pesos at the time due to a fall in the price of silver. Their size and weight were similar to the Spanish–American dollars of 8 Spanish reales. The coins were distributed through banks in Hong Kong, Singapore, Penang in the Straits Settlements and Shanghai in China. Most of the 274 million coins issued were struck in Bombay (mintmark B on the middle prong of the trident) where the manufacturing costs were lower than in England. Minting of the coin ceased in 1935, when China introduced paper money.

Bank of England Token Issue

KM-Tn1 ● Bank of England 5 shillings / 1 dollar ● 1804 .903 silver, issued also in copper

The design element on the reverse to the left of Britannia's feet, near the edge of the medallion at 8 o'clock, has been identified as a ship. Actually it is a beehive symbolizing industry.

GREECE

Greece occupies the southern part of the Balkans in southeastern Europe and about 2,000 islands in the Ionian Sea to the west of the Balkans and the Aegean Sea to the east. The country attained independence from the Ottoman Empire after a prolonged struggle in the 1820s, becoming a kingdom. The monarchy was formally abolished in 1974. The country's official name is now the Hellenic Republic.

Ancient Galley

KM-73 ● 20 drachmai ● 1930 .500 silver

The obverse features the prow of an ancient galley. The galley's ram identifies it as a warship. The reverse features the bearded head of Poseidon, the Greek god of the sea. The obverse and reverse designs are both patterned after a tetradrachm of Antigonos Doson, King of Macedonia (229–221 BCE), but the Greek god Apollo, who is sitting on the prow of the galley on the ancient coin, has been excluded from the modern obverse design. The Macedonian coin is attributed as SNG Berry 365 and SNG Oxford 3264. It was probably issued to mark a naval victory by the Macedonians.

KM-73
20 drachmai
1930 .500 silver, 28.5 mm

100th Anniversary of the Royal Greek Dynasty

KM-86 ● 30 drachmai ● 1963 .835 silver

The reverse depicts a map of mainland Greece and its island groups, and an ancient sailing ship as a decoration on the map near the rim at 8 o'clock. The parts of the country named on the reverse are, reading clockwise from the top: ΜΑΚΕΔΟΝΙΑ (Macedonia), ΘΡΑΚΗ (Thrace), ΝΗΣΟΙ ΑΙΓΑΙΟΥ (Aegean Islands), ΔΩΔΕΚΑΝΗΣΟΣ (Dodecanese), ΚΡΗΤΗ (Crete), ΕΠΤΑΝΗΣΟΣ (Heptanesos), ΗΠΕΙΡΟΣ (Epirus) and ΘΕΣΣΑΛΙΑ (Thessaly). The obverse features medallion portraits of the five kings of the House of Schleswig-Holstein-Sonderburg-Glücksburg: George I (reigned

1863–1913), Constantine I (1913–1917 and 1920–1922), Alexander I (1917–1920), George II (1922/23 and 1935–1947) and Paul I (1947–1964). Greece was a republic from 1924 to 1935. The edge inscription is ΙΣΧΥΣ ΜΟΥ Η ΑΓΑΠΗ ΤΟΥ ΛΑΟΥ (The People's Love is My Strength).

Circulation Coin – Konstantinos Kanáris

KM-116 ● 1 drachma ● 1976–86 nickel-brass

The obverse depicts a merchant sailing ship of the first half of the 19th century. The reverse depicts the naval hero and statesman Konstantinos Kanáris (1790–1877). In the War of Greek Independence (1821–1832) against the Ottoman Empire, Kanáris contributed his own ship to the fleet of the Greek navy. (The obverse may purport to depict his ship.) Kanáris made good use of fire ships. In 1822 he blew up the Turkish admiral's flagship and so harassed the Turkish fleet that it retreated to the Dardanelles. He made additional attacks on the Turks from 1822 to 1825. In later years Kanáris served several terms as prime minister.

Circulation Coin

KM-147 ● 50 drachmes ● 1986–2000 nickel-brass

KM-147
50 drachmes
1986 nickel-brass, 27 mm

An ancient warship—a galley under sail—is depicted on the obverse. The reverse features the bust of the poet Homer (approximately 800 BCE) who is credited with the authorship of the *Iliad*, the narrative of the Trojan War which took place around 1200 BCE, and the *Odyssey* which relates the adventures of Odysseus, King of Ithaca, during his voyage home from that war. These epics are based on an oral tradition carried on by generations of bards. Types of ships described by Homer include small 20-oar galleys (10 per side) used for transportation, exploration or dispatch duties; the 50-oared pentecontor used as a troop carrier; and 100-oared vessels, some 90 ft (27 m) in length and about 20 ft (6.1 m) in width amidships, that served as heavy transports. These ships were long and narrow, with gently rounded hulls. They had a low draft, so that they could be hauled ashore at night or in bad weather. They had one mast with a square sail but could also be maneuvered by oarsmen. The crew consisted of the oarsmen, the captain-helmsman, the bow lookout and the time beater who paced the rowers. The most famous ship found in Homer was *Argo* (Swift) that had 50 or 60 oars. She was probably built at Pagasses near Mount Pelion some time before the Trojan War and must have been some 75 ft (23 m) long. Her travelers, the Argonauts, made an expedition—probably to Colchis at the end of the Black Sea—to retrieve the Golden Fleece. The coin's denomination is ΔΡΑΧΜΕΣ (drachmes) instead of the ΔΡΑΧΜΑΙ (drachmai) denomination on older coins. The change follows the adoption in 1976 of *dhimotiki* (the people's language) as the country's official language. It replaced a *katharevusa* (pure language) form of Greek which became the official language when the country attained independence and was used on coins until 1982. Both languages have their origin in ancient Greek. *Katharevusa* was derived from literary Greek without regard to *dhimotiki* that is spoken by the majority of the people. The coin was selected as best trade coin for 1986 in the annual Coin of the Year contest.

Circulation Coin

KM-150 ● 1 drachma ● 1988–2000 – see T-1

Euro Circulation Coin

KM-181 ● 1 cent-lepton ● 2002–05 copper-plated steel

KM-181
1 cent-lepton
2002 copper-plated steel, 16.2 mm

The obverse depicts a trireme of Attica from the time of Kimon (510–450 BCE). The design is based on a model exhibited in the Maritime Museum in Athens of an ancient oar-driven warship with a battering ram at the prow. A trireme (meaning "three-er" for the three superimposed banks of oars) measured some 22 tons, was about 123 ft (37 m) in length and 19 ft (5.8 m) at the beam, and had a draft of slightly more than 4 ft (1.2 m). It had one mast with a square sail and could be propelled by sail or by oars. Under oars the trireme was propelled by three rows of 30 oarsmen on each side of the ship. They provided speed and power for ramming. The trireme cruised up to 18 hours at a steady 7 to 8 knots. Its longest oars measured about 14 ft (4.2 m). The two bottom tiers of oarsmen rowed blind. Guidance came from the top level of rowers, who could see when the oars were overlapping. The crew included 20 to 30 archers and javelin throwers who fought to repel an attack. The trireme was the predominant warship of the Greeks in their wars against Persia and in the Peloponnesian War between Athens and Sparta in the 5th century BCE. For more than 200 years it was the largest warship afloat. A reconstruction of an Athenian trireme of the 5th century BCE was built in Greece and commissioned into the Hellenic Navy in 1987. Named *Olympias*, she is manned by 170 oarsmen arranged in three tiers. As no remains of oar-driven ancient warships have ever been found, the design of the reconstruction made by John Coates used ideas from vase paintings, coins, classical writings, excavations at ancient ship sheds, and inventories of the Piraeus dockyards that have been inscribed in stone. The building process took two years and cost about $700,000. It was the first trireme to sail the Mediterranean Sea in over 1,500 years. The ships on this coin and on the 2 and 5 euro-cent coins (KM-182 and KM-183) highlight

Greek maritime power over the centuries. The reverse design with two rows of six stars connected by lines and a globe, symbolizing the unity of the European Union and Europe's place in the world as a whole, is common to the 1, 2 and 5 cent coins of all twelve countries that in 2002 exchanged their national currencies for the euro. The obverse of the euro-denominated coins is the national side but those of Greece do not state the country's name. Instead, these coins are recognized as Greek coins by the double denomination—cent and lepton (λεπτο).

Euro Circulation Coin

KM-182 ● 2 cents-lepta ● 2002–05 – *see* T-1

Euro Circulation Coin

KM-183 ● 5 cents-lepta ● 2002–05 copper-plated steel

The obverse depicts a modern supertanker signifying the importance of shipping in modern Greece. The tanker is a generic ship, not a specific one.

The Last Drachma

KM-189 ● 1 drachma ● 2000 gold – *see* T-1

T-1 Circulation Coins

KM-150 ● 1 drachma ● 1988–2000 copper, Bouboulina
KM-182 ● 2 cents-lepta ● 2002–05 copper-plated steel, Euro circulation coin
KM-189 ● 1 drachma ● 2000 .917 gold, "The last drachma"

KM-150
1 drachma
1988 copper, 18 mm

The ship on the obverse is a polacca (polacre in French)—a three-masted sail ship used by the Greeks in their War of Independence against the Ottoman Empire between 1821 and 1832. The ship shown is generic, not a specific one. The reverse of KM-150 features the portrait of heroine Bouboulina, born Laskarina Pinotzis (1771–1825). She was married twice, the second time with Dimitrios Bouboulis. Both her husbands were captains who died at sea in battles with Barbary pirates raiding the Greek coasts. Their inheritances made her a rich woman. She owned shipyards, was a partner in several vessels, and built three vessels of her own. One of the three was her flagship, the 246-ft (75-m)-long corvette *Agamemnon* armed with 18 heavy cannons that she had built on Spetses Island in 1820 in preparation for the independence struggle. *Agamemnon* was the first and the largest fighting ship of the war in 1821. During the war, Bouboulina at the head of her squadron took part in the sieges of Monemvasia, Nafplion and Tripolitsa and in other naval operations, and spent a large portion of her inheritance maintaining the ships and her own small private army. Ultimately she was shot in a quarrel with members of another family following her son's seduction of a daughter of that family. After Bouboulina's death Russia conferred on her the honorary title of admiral, a unique honor for a woman. Her heirs gave the *Agamemnon* to the newly established Greek state. The ship was renamed *Spetses* and became the flagship of Greece's navy. In the civil war she was burned by the Greek Admiral Andreas Vokos Miaoulis at the naval base of Poros, in 1831. KM-189 is a gold issue of the old 1 drachma coin to commemorate the drachma currency that was replaced by the euro in 2002.

GUERNSEY

The Bailiwick of Guernsey, including mainly the islands of Guernsey, Alderney and Sark, is situated in Western Europe in the Channel between England and northwestern France, some 30 miles (48 km) west of Normandy, France. The bailiwicks of Guernsey and Jersey represent the last remnants of the medieval Duchy of Normandy. Ever since William the Conqueror, Duke of Normandy, became King William I of England in 1066 (*see* Alderney KM-3), the Channel Islands are British crown dependencies. The king or queen of England, who also is duke of Normandy, is their head of state.

HMS *Crescent*

KM-39 ● 1 pound ● 1983 nickel-brass

The reverse depicts the three-masted frigate HMS *Crescent*, an 869-ton fifth-rate vessel of 36 guns. She measured 137 ft (42 m) in length, had a beam of 38 ft (12 m), and drew 13 ft (4 m) of water. She was launched by Calhoun at Bursledon in 1784. In 1793 *Crescent*, under the command of Guernseyman Captain James de Saumarez, commander of the Channel Islands Squadron, later Admiral Lord Saumarez (1757–1836), became victorious in an engagement off the west coast of Guernsey with the French frigate *La Réunion*. After a close action lasting more than two hours *Réunion* surrendered to Saumarez. *Réunion*'s casualties numbered 33 killed and 48 severely wounded out of a crew of 300. *Crescent* had one seaman wounded out of her crew of 260. Saumarez's capture of *Réunion* earned him a knighthood. In 1794 Saumarez encountered a French squadron a few miles from Guernsey while sailing with *Euridice* and *Druid* with the charge to keep the seas around Guernsey free of the French fleet. In view of the superior strength of the French Saumarez could only try to bring his ships into safety. He ordered his other two ships to make for Guernsey with all speed while *Crescent* engaged the French fleet. An experienced Guernseyman who happened to be on board, Jean Le Breton, found a way for *Crescent* among the narrow channels and reefs of Guernsey's coastline that had never been navigated by a ship of that size. The dangerous maneuver brought *Crescent* outside the reach of the enemy. *Crescent* was wrecked on the coast of Jutland in 1808 on a voyage from Great Yarmouth to the Baltic. Of the 288 people on board only 62 survived. The wreck has been found and excavated. The obverse depicts the coat-of-arms of Guernsey which is based on a 13th-century royal seal and has the Latin legend S. BALLIVIE INSVLE DE GERNEREVE (Seal of the Bailiwick of the Island of Guernsey).

Circulation Coins

KM-42.1 • 5 pence • 1985–90 – see T-1
KM-42.2 • 5 pence • 1990–97 – see T-1

Royal Visit

KM-52 • 2 pounds • 1989 copper-nickel, issued also in .925 silver

The reverse depicts the 5,769-ton three-masted royal yacht HMY *Britannia* and the crest of the Bailiwick of Guernsey at the top. The yacht is 412 ft (126 m) long and 55 ft (17 m) in the beam, and has a draft of 16 ft (4.7 m). The main mast is 139 ft (42 m) from the waterline. She could make a speed of 21 knots. *Britannia* was built in 1954 by John Brown & Co. (Clydebank) Ltd. at a cost of £2,100,000—the 83rd royal yacht in a line which goes back to 1660. She was designed to be used as a hospital ship in time of war. Her captain had the rank of commodore. When members of the royal family were on board or when the ship embarked on a long ocean voyage the crew numbered 19 officers and 217 royal yachtsmen, and a Royal Navy band of 26. No shouted orders were given on the upper deck—hand signals and written orders took the place of a broadcast system. *Britannia* was equipped with the 40-ft (12-m)-long royal barge that was built in 1964 and could make 19 knots, and two 34-ft (10-m)-long speedboats that were used as escorts for the royal barge. For 44 years *Britannia* served as an official and private residence for the queen, her consort and other members of the royal family but she was also used to support Britain by undertaking many diplomatic, representational and commercial duties overseas. She steamed more than 1,000,000 nautical miles and carried out 696 visits abroad. She was decommissioned in 1997 because of her high operating costs. She made her last voyage to the Mediterranean Sea, Arabian Gulf, Indian Ocean, and Far East for the handover of Hong Kong. She has not been replaced by another royal yacht. *Britannia*, which is her official name since decommissioning, is now a floating museum in Leith, the port of Edinburgh, Scotland. The coin marks the visit by Queen Elizabeth II and Prince Philip, the Duke of Edinburgh, to St. Peter Port, Guernsey's capital, in May 1989 on board *Britannia*.

50th Anniversary of the D-Day Landings – Winston Churchill

KM-56 ● 2 pounds ● 1994 – see T-2

50th Anniversary of the D-Day Landings – Dwight Eisenhower

KM-58 ● 25 pounds ● 1994 .999 gold

The reverse features Supreme Allied Commander General Dwight D. Eisenhower (1890–1969, *see* Gibraltar T-17) watching Allied troops disembark from invasion ships depicted in the background. The ships are too small to identify. The design is probably based on a news photo of a landing on a Normandy beach on D-Day, 6 June 1944 (*see* Great Britain KM-966). The Normandy landings, even though very close to Guernsey and the rest of the Channel Islands, did not mean immediate freedom for the Islands, which were the only British soil occupied by German troops in World War II. The Islands remained under German occupation until V-E Day, after the surrender of the German forces in Europe. The Normandy landings and the Allied advance on the continent cut off all communications and supplies to the Channel Islands. Food rations had to be reduced drastically and there were practically no medical stores or soap, causing both the Bailiff of Jersey and the German authorities to appeal to the International Committee of the Red Cross for assistance. The first food supplies to the civilian population of the Islands were made by the Red Cross only in December 1944 (*see* KM-63).

50th Anniversaries

KM-60 ● 100 pounds ● 1994 D-Day landings – Winston Churchill – see T-2
KM-61 ● 2 pounds ● 1995 Liberation – Landing ship tank – see T-3

50th Anniversary of the Liberation – SS *Vega*

KM-63 ● 25 pounds ● 1995 .999 gold

KM-63
25 pounds
1995 .999 gold, 22 mm

The reverse features a sailor unloading Red Cross food packages from SS *Vega*, a relief ship of the International Red Cross, tied to a pier. The 1,640-ton steamer was 225 ft (69 m) long and 35 ft (11 m) wide, and had a draft of 15 ft (4.6 m). She had two masts, a black funnel and one deck. The hull was painted grey. Her speed was six knots. She was built in 1913 by Lindholmens Verkstads AB at Göteborg for Stockholms Rederi AB Svea of Stockholm, Sweden. In the winter of 1939/40 *Vega* was chartered by the International Committee of the Red Cross of Geneva for the transportation of aid for prisoners of war and civilian internees. She showed the signs agreed between the Red Cross and the parties at war to identify her as a Red Cross ship—the inscription C. INTERNATIONAL ("C." for Comité) on both sides of the hull and the Red Cross emblem on both sides and on the hatchways, all with maximum dimensions. These Red Cross signs were partly illuminated at night. A large Red Cross flag was placed on the bridge and the national flag of neutral Sweden flew from the masts and the stern. *Vega*'s skipper from June 1940 until July 1945 was Captain Gösta Wideberg (1899–?). After *Vega* had made 38 voyages between Lisbon and Marseilles—carrying on each voyage an average of 782 tons of prisoner of war packages—she was chosen to bring relief to the civilian population of the Channel Islands. Her choice took into account her fully loaded draft of only 15 ft (4.6 m) and the fact that at low water the entrance to the harbor at St. Helier, Jersey is only 10 ft (3 m). From December 1944 until May 1945 *Vega* made six voyages from Lisbon to the Islands, unloading first at Guernsey, then at Jersey. On each of these voyages she carried an average of 920 tons of supplies—Red Cross food packages, soap, salt, medical and surgical supplies, cigarettes, and some children's clothing and layettes for newborns. This aid undoubtedly saved many lives, for at that time the situation of the 61,551 civilian inhabitants on Jersey, Guernsey and Sark was desperate—lack of food, fuel, medical supplies and the bare essentials, with the population surviving on 1,137 calories a day compared with 2,200 calories needed by an adult to avoid malnutrition. On her voyages to and from the Islands, *Vega* also carried mail from the internment camps in Germany to which some 2,000 Islanders had been deported in 1942 and 1943, prisoner of war mail and Red Cross messages. After the war *Vega* was returned to her Swedish owners. She was broken up in 1954.

50th Anniversary of the Liberation – Surrender

KM-64 ● 50 pounds ● 1995 .999 gold

The reverse shows Generalmajor Siegfried Heine, the German commander of Guernsey, signing the surrender documents and in the background the British destroyer HMS *Beagle*, marked by her pennant number H30 (*see* Jersey KM-64). The surrender documents were signed on 9 May 1945 at 7:14 a.m. on a rum cask on the quarter-deck of HMS *Bulldog*. This destroyer was built by Swan, Hunter & Wigham Richardson Ltd., Wallsend-on-Tyne in 1931 and was modified in World War II for escort work. Her displacement was 1,360 tons. Her length was 323 ft (98 m), her beam 32 ft (9.8 m) and her draft 8.5 ft (2.6 m). She could make a speed of 35 knots and had a crew of 138. Between 1941 and 1945 *Bulldog* served on the Northern Atlantic, Russian and Channel convoy routes. In May 1941 *Bulldog* and two other destroyers escorting a convoy south of Iceland attacked the German submarine *U110* when it attacked the convoy. The submarine was blown to the surface by a depth charge. When the German crew abandoned their damaged submarine a boarding party from *Bulldog* led by Sub-Lieutenant David Balme got on board and recovered a working Enigma machine, its cipher keys, keybooks and other cryptological records. These were passed to the British government code and cypher school at Bletchley Park (between Oxford and Cambridge) which was the intelligence bureau responsible for interception and decryption of foreign transmissions. In June 1944 *Bulldog* sank the German submarine *U719* northwest of Ireland. *Bulldog* was broken up in 1946. The unconditional surrender of all German forces was signed at Reims, France on 7 May 1945 at 2:41 a.m. Hostilities were to cease at midnight on 8 May. The British sent *Bulldog* and *Beagle* to the Channel Islands on 8 May where they rendezvoused with a German trawler. The German lieutenant who embarked from a rubber dinghy pointed out that as the general cease-fire would not take effect until a minute after midnight on 9 May, the British destroyers should withdraw from the rendezvous area, or the powerful coastal guns would open fire. The British naval force commander, Rear Admiral C. G. Stuart in HMS *Bulldog*, decided to withdraw to a safe distance. It was then arranged that the commander of Guernsey would arrive at the same rendezvous at midnight. He arrived on board after midnight, whereupon he surrendered to Brigadier General Alfred E. Snow as depicted on the reverse.

KM-64
50 pounds
1995 .999 gold, 27 mm

50th Anniversary of the Liberation – Landing Ship Tank

KM-65 • 100 pounds • 1995 – see T-3

Castle Cornet

KM-74 • 5 pounds • 1997 copper-nickel, issued also in .925 silver

The reverse depicts sailboats in front of Castle Cornet. The castle is a fortress on Cornet Rock outside the anchorage of St. Peter Port, Guernsey's capital. The first castle was built in the 13th century as an English stronghold to help to protect the anchorage after the king of France conquered the mainland of Normandy, while

Guernsey remained linked to the English Crown. The castle was partly rebuilt and several additions were made over the centuries to keep up with technological advances in warfare. It was continually in use as a prison. It is now a museum.

70th Birthday of Queen Elizabeth II

KM-79 ● 5 pounds ● 1996 copper-nickel, issued also in .925 silver

The reverse depicts Queen Elizabeth II and Castle Cornet (*see* KM-74) in front of which a sailboat is shown. The design recalls the queen's visit to the castle in 1989.

Circulation Coin

KM-97 ● 5 pence ● 1999–2003 – *see* T-1

60th Anniversary of the D-Day Landings

KM-150 ● 5 pounds ● 2004 copper-nickel, colored
KM-151 ● 10 pounds ● 2004 .925 silver, 65 mm
KM-153 ● 50 pounds ● 2004 .925 silver, 100 mm, 1000 gr

The reverse depicts British troops storming a Normandy beach on D-Day, 6 June 1944, in the background various types of naval vessels, the sky filled with planes and airships, and at the bottom a poppy. The poppy is the logo of the Royal British Legion, the leading charity for British service veterans and those currently serving in Britain's armed forces, and their dependants. On the copper-nickel coin the poppy is colored red.

The History of the Royal Navy – *Golden Hind*

KM-158 ● 5 pounds ● 2003 copper-nickel

The coin depicts *Golden Hind*, Sir Francis Drake's flagship on his circumnavigation of the world in 1577–1580 (*see* Great Britain KM-844).

KM-158
5 pounds 2003 copper-nickel, 38.6 mm

The History of the Royal Navy – King Henry VIII

KM-166 ● 5 pounds ● 2004 copper-nickel

The reverse depicts King Henry VIII (1491–1547) and one of his warships, probably *Mary Rose* (*see* Alderney T-1).

The History of the Royal Navy – John Jellicoe

KM-167 ● 5 pounds ● 2005 copper-nickel

The reverse depicts Admiral Sir John Jellicoe (1859–1935), the commander-in-chief of Britain's Grand Fleet in World War I, and the

British battle cruiser HMS *Invincible*. The 19,940-ton ship was built by Sir W. G. Armstrong, Whitworth & Co. Ltd. at Newcastle-on-Tyne, England in 1908 at a cost of £1,770,000. She was 567 ft (173 m) long, had a beam of 79 ft (24 m), and drew 27 ft (8.1 m) of water. Her speed was 25 knots. She took part in the battle of the Falklands at the end of 1914 in which Admiral Maximilian Graf (Count) von Spee's cruiser squadron was destroyed, including the armored cruisers *Scharnhorst* and *Gneisenau*. *Invincible* blew up and sank at the battle of Jutland in 1916 after a hit from the German battle cruiser *Lützow*, with a loss of 1,026 men and only six survivors.

T-1 Circulation Coins

KM-42.1 • 5 pence • 1985–90 copper-nickel, 23.6 mm, Queen's portrait by Raphael Makhlouf
KM-42.2 • 5 pence • 1990–97 copper-nickel, 18 mm
KM-97 • 5 pence • 1999–2003 copper-nickel, Queen's portrait by Ian Rank-Broadley

The reverse depicts two sailboats symbolizing the island's tourist industry.

T-2 50th Anniversary of the D-Day Landings – Winston Churchill

KM-56 • 2 pounds • 1994 copper-nickel, issued also in .925 silver
KM-60 • 100 pounds • 1994 .999 gold

The reverse depicts British troops disembarking from an amphibious landing craft assault (LCA) and wading ashore onto a Normandy beach, and, at the top, a medallion portrait of Sir Winston Churchill (1874–1965). A landing craft is a type of boat used to convey troops and vehicles during an assault from sea to an enemy-held beach. Many of the landing craft used on D-Day were flat-bottomed and had a flat front rather than a normal bow, which made them very difficult to control. The LCA was intended to be transported by a larger vessel and then lowered into the water off the target beach. A typical LCA was capable of carrying one small tank or 100 troops. Because of fuel limitations an LCA was not capable of making a voyage longer than about six hours. Churchill was Britain's First Lord of the Admiralty in the years 1911–1915. He was Prime Minister and Minister of Defense during World War II (1940–1945) and is noted for his leadership in the war. He was once again Prime Minister in 1951–1955.

T-3 50th Anniversary of the Liberation – Landing Ship Tank

KM-61 • 2 pounds • 1995 copper-nickel, issued also in .925 silver
KM-65 • 100 pounds • 1995 .999 gold

The reverse depicts British liberation forces being welcomed by the population and in the background a vehicle with supplies leaving an amphibious LST (Landing Ship Tank). The LST was designed to transport troops, vehicles and supplies and to disgorge its cargo directly onto the beach, without the use of dock facilities. While at sea, a ballast system gave the LST enough draft to maintain stability. The ballast was pumped from the tanks to convert it to a shallow draft vessel that was capable of landing its cargo on most gradually sloped beaches. A typical LST was 328 ft (100 m) long and capable of carrying 2,100 tons of cargo. The heaviest vehicles were stored on the lower deck, which could accommodate up to 20 Sherman tanks. Maximum speed was 11 knots. American shipyards built 1,051 LSTs during World War II, of which 113 were supplied to Britain.

KM-65
100 pounds 1995 .999 gold, 32.7 mm

T-4 60th Anniversary of the Liberation

KM-? ● 5 pounds ● 2005 gold

The reverse depicts a crowd welcoming members of the crew of the International Red Cross ship SS *Vega* (*see* KM-63), in the background the ship and at the bottom the logo of the commemoration events of the 60th anniversary of the end of World War II. *Vega* was one of the first vessels to enter Guernsey after the end of the war. A ceremony was held to honor the captain and crew of "the good ship, the food ship, that brought relief to Jersey and Guernsey in 1944/45." The reverse inscriptions are 60th ANNIVERSARY OF LIBERATION – 9TH MAY 1945 and "OUR DEAR CHANNEL ISLANDS ARE ALSO TO BE FREED TODAY." The quotation is from Britain's prime minister Sir Winston Churchill's announcement of Germany's unconditional surrender on 8 May 1945. His complete sentence was "Hostilities will end officially at one minute after midnight tonight, Tuesday, 8th May, but in the interests of saving lives the 'Cease Fire' began yesterday to be sounded all along the fronts, and I should not forget to mention that our dear Channel Islands, the only part of His Majesty's Dominions that has been in the hands of the German foe, are also to be freed today."

HUNGARY

The Republic of Hungary is situated in central Europe. Until the end of World War I, Hungary was part of the Austro–Hungarian Empire.

Old Danube Ships – *Árpád*

KM-702 ● 500 forint ● 1993 .925 silver

KM-702
500 forint 1993 .925 silver,
38.6 mm

The reverse depicts the river side-wheel steamer *Árpád*, built in 1836 at a dockyard near Óbuda for the First Danube Steam Shipping Company. Her engine was bought from James Watt. She had accommodation for 400 passengers. She took her name from the dynasty founded by the 9th-century Khan Árpád of the Magyars. In 1837 *Árpád* made her maiden voyage. She was one of the first steamers to trade up and down the Danube, plying regularly between Pest and Vienna. (Budapest, Hungary's capital, was formed in 1873 by the union of Buda and Óbuda on the Danube's right bank with Pest on its left bank.) The construction of both the dockyard and the steamer was initiated by the reformer Count István Széchenyi as a step toward Hungarian national development. The reverse inscription is RÉGI DUNAI HAJÓK (Old Danube Ships).

Expo '96

KM-705 ● 500 forint ● 1993 .925 silver

The reverse depicts a sailing ship on a sea of words under a sky with lettered clouds. The sea is formed by the words ÍROTT SZAVAK TENGERE / BETÜKTENGER / SZÓTENGER / VÉGTELEN / ISMERET / TENG[ER] (Sea of Written Words ... Sea of Letters ... Word Sea ... Never Ending ... Knowledge ... Sea). The inscription in the cloud reads KOMMUNIKÁCIÓ EGY JOBB VILÁGÉRT (Communication for a Better World). The coin was issued to mark Expo '96, a world fair in Budapest planned for 1996 to commemorate Hungary's 1,100th anniversary; however, the exposition was never actually held. "Communication for a Better World" was the motto of the planned fair. Its logo is featured on the obverse.

Old Danube Ships – *Carolina*

KM-708 ● 500 forint ● 1994 .925 silver

The reverse depicts the side-wheel paddle steamer *Carolina*, the first Hungarian steamer on the Danube River. She was named for the wife of the Austrian–Hungarian emperor Francis I. Originally built as a tug by Antal Bernhard at Sellye on the Drava River in 1818, she was refitted into an excursion/passenger ship for use on the Danube. The reverse inscription is RÉGI DUNAI HAJÓK (Old Danube Ships).

Old Danube Ships – *Hableany*

KM-714 ● 1000 forint ● 1995 .925 silver

The reverse depicts the Danube steam freighter *Hableany* (Mermaid) on her maiden voyage to the World Exhibition in Paris in 1867. She was 66 ft (20 m) long, had a beam of 8 ft (2.4 m), and drew 2 ft (0.6 m) of water. She was built in Buda in 1866 and was one of the first ships completely built in Hungary. The reverse inscription is RÉGI DUNAI HAJÓK (Old Danube Ships).

KM-714
1000 forint
1995 .925 silver, 38 mm

Old Ships on Lake Balaton – *Helka* and *Kelén*

KM-722 • 2000 forint • 1997 .925 silver

The reverse depicts the twin steamers *Helka* and *Kelén*, the first passenger steamboats on Lake Balaton. The obverse gives a view of the lake with a number of sailboats. *Helka* and *Kelén* were built in 1891 at Budapest by Schoenichen & Hartmann. They are 115 ft (35 m) long and have a beam of 16 ft (4.9 m). Their engines were converted to diesel. The vessels take their names from a well known 19th-century novel about the boy Kelén and the girl Helka who lived on the Tihany Peninsula on the northern shore of Lake Balaton. *Helka* is preserved in Balatonfüred on the northern shore of Lake Balaton as an exhibit of the Hungarian Transport Museum. *Kelén* still operates as a passenger vessel for tourist excursions. Lake Balaton in western Hungary is the largest lake in central Europe. It is 48 miles (78 km) long and has a surface of 230 square miles (596 km^2). In the 19th century the lake became popular as a recreation region. Vessels like *Helka* and *Kelén* contributed to the opening up of the region.

KM-722
2000 forint
1997 .925 silver, 38 mm

Old Ships on Lake Balaton – *Phoenix*

KM-731 • 2000 forint • 1998 .925 silver

The reverse depicts the sailing vessel *Phoenix* that was built in 1797 at the Fenékpuszta shipyard of Count György Festetics in Keszthely at the western end of Lake Balaton for use as a transportation vessel on the lake. The obverse shows present-day leisure-time sailing yachts on the lake. *Phoenix* had a length of about 100 ft (30 m) and a beam of some 26 ft (7.9 m), and was propelled by 24 oarsmen. She was the largest sailing vessel ever to ply the lake. Her image is part of the coat-of-arms of Keszthely. Festetics also established in 1797 the Georgikon, Europe's first agricultural academy.

Children's Literature – János Arany

KM-756 • 200 forint • 2001 brass

The reverse depicts a knight kicking a boat off the shore, recalling an episode from the trilogy written about Miklós Toldi by the Hungarian poet János Arany (1817-1882). This epic poem—consisting of *Toldi* (published in 1847), *Toldi's Love* (1848-1879) and *Toldi's Evening* (1854)— is included in the Hungarian school curriculum.

ICELAND

Iceland, an island between the Greenland Sea and the Northern Atlantic Ocean, became a virtually independent kingdom under the Danish crown in 1918. Its political status was to be reviewed 25 years later, in 1943. At that time Denmark was occupied by Germany and Iceland by Allied forces. As the review between the two countries was impossible, a referendum was held in which 97 percent of the voters favored the immediate declaration of a republic. The republic was established on 17 June 1944 at Thingvellir, the site of Althing, the ancient Icelandic parliament.

1,100th Aniversary of the First Viking Settlement

KM-22 ● 10,000 krónur ● 1974 .900 gold

KM-22
10,000 krónur
1974 .900 gold, 28 mm

The reverse depicts the Viking chief Ingolf (Ingolfur) Arnarson standing in his Viking ship throwing into the sea the decorated pillars of his high seat at home. (The high seat is the chief's place of honor. Its pillars were adorned by carvings and dedicated to the god Thor.) Ingolf, of Firdafylke in Norway, lived at the time of the unification of Norway under Harald Haarfagr (Fairhair) (850–933). King Harald ruled the country with such a heavy hand that many fled to Iceland, Ingolf among them. According to ancient custom, upon approaching Iceland Ingolf threw the pillars of his high seat into the sea, vowing that he would make his permanent home at the spot where his god allowed the current to carry the pillars ashore. He built his house in 874 at the spot where the pillars were found. This constitutes the founding of Reykjavík (Smoke Harbor), Iceland's capital. The name refers to the steam of a geyser. The obverse shows a stylized representation of Iceland's four "guardian spirits"—a vulture, a dragon, a bull and a giant—who are the bearers of the country's coat-of-arms.

100th Anniversary of Icelandic Bank Notes

KM-30 ● 500 krónur ● 1986 .500 silver, issued also in .925 silver

The obverse depicts an open fishing boat under sail, typical of the boats used in the 1880s. The design illustrates Iceland's main industry, fishing. The reverse depicts Fjallkonan, the allegorical Woman of the Mountains who is shown as the personification of the country since the 19th century. She appeared on the back of the 50 krónur bank note issued in 1886 by Landssjod Íslands (Iceland's Treasury) which was the first issue of bank notes in Iceland. This note is attributed as Pick-3 in the *Standard Catalog of World Paper Money*.

IRELAND

The Republic of Ireland in western Europe attained independence in 1921. It occupies five-sixths of the island of Ireland in the Northern Atlantic Ocean, west of England and Wales.

Millennium

KM-31 ● 1 punt ● 2000 copper-nickel

KM-31
1 punt
2000 copper-nickel, 31 mm

The reverse features a stylized representation of the "Broighter Boat," a miniature in gold of a large ocean going vessel dating from the 1st century BCE. The miniature is approximately 3.9 inches (10 cm) long. It has seven cross-benches for rowers, a steering oar, and a mast with a yard. It was probably made of skin. This is the first proof of the use of the sail in northern Europe and is considered to testify to overseas trade relations that existed between Ireland and the Iberian peninsula two thousand years ago. The miniature was found in 1896 in County Derry as part of the Broighter Hoard. All items in the hoard—necklaces, torcs, a collar, and the boat—were made of gold in the ornamental Celtic art style known as "La Tène" after the Swiss valley where a large amount of Celtic artifacts were found. The boat is on display at the National Museum in Dublin.

ISLE OF MAN

The Isle of Man is one of the British Isles. It is situated in the Irish Sea, roughly equidistant between England, Ireland, Scotland and Wales. It is not a part of the United Kingdom but a British crown dependency that is self-governing in its internal affairs. The chief of state is the "Lord of Mann" who is the British queen or king. The island was purchased by the British parliament in 1765.

Ecu- and euro-denominated issues are not listed herein as they do not fit into the territory's monetary system which corresponds to Great Britain's pound-denominated currency.

Circulation Coin

KM-24 ● 50 new pence ● 1971–75 copper-nickel, seven-sided planchet, issued also in .925 silver and .950 platinum

The reverse depicts a Viking longship under full sail. Such ships were 75–100 ft (23–30 m) in length and 15–20 ft (4.6–6.1 m) in the beam, and drew less than 3 ft (0.9 m) of water. They had ports to accommodate 40–80 oars. Under sail with a following wind they could make 11 knots. They had one mast that measured some 30 ft (9.1 m) to carry a single large square woolen sail up to 40–50 ft (12–15 m) across. Longships were double-ended, constructed of oak, had no decks and were steered with a long oar on the starboard side of the hull. The prows were carved as snake's or dragon's heads, meant to drive away evil spirits and to scare the enemy. Longships carried up to 200 men when used as a raider or some 20 tons of cargo when used for trading. They are documented on 12th- and 13th-century seals. The Vikings came from Denmark, Norway and Sweden, and other lands bordering on the Baltic. They flourished from the late 700s until about 1100. Wherever they sailed along the coasts of Great Britain and continental Europe they looted the coastlines but they also settled in various parts of northern and western Europe. In 911, Charles II, King of Western France (893–922), signed a treaty with the Viking leader Rollo by which the lower valley of the Seine was ceded to the Vikings, who were called Normans (North-men) by the French. This district is still known as Normandy. The Vikings conquered the Isle of Man around 800 CE. Their kingdom of "Man and the Isles," which embraced the western isles of Scotland in addition to the Isle of Man, owed allegiance to the king of Norway until it was sold to the Scottish crown in 1266. It came under English control in 1341. The word "new" in the "new pence" denomination relates to one-hundredth of a pound, distinguishing this penny (plural: pence) from the pre-decimal denomination of the same name that constituted 1/240 part of a pound. Until the change to a decimal monetary system one pound equaled 20 shillings, and one shilling equaled 12 pence.

KM-24
50 new pence
1971 copper-nickel, 30 mm

Viking Ship Privy Mark

KM-26(v) ● 1/2 sovereign ● 1980 .917 gold with Viking ship privy mark
KM-27(v) ● 1 sovereign ● 1980 .917 gold with Viking ship privy mark

The privy mark on the reverse of a number of 1980-dated sovereigns and half-sovereigns depicts a Viking ship. It marks the Viking exhibition held in New York in 1980. The main reverse design of these coins, which were issued from 1973 until 1982, is a Viking on a horse brandishing his sword. Obviously this design was inspired by the famous design by Benedetto Pistrucci (1784–1855) of England's patron, St. George, on horseback slaying a dragon. The Pistrucci design has been used by Great Britain on sovereigns from 1817. The coins have no stated denomination. A sovereign valued at 20 shillings was first issued in the 16th century. Under Britain's pre-decimal monetary system 20 shillings equaled 1 pound. Thus the half-sovereign is considered a half-pound coin and the sovereign a pound coin.

Circulation Coin

KM-39 ● 50 pence ● 1976–79 copper-nickel, seven-sided planchet, issued also in .925 silver and .950 platinum

The reverse depicts a Viking longship (*see* KM-24) superimposed on a map of the Isle of Man. The depiction of the ship is based on a reconstruction in the Manx Museum. The Viking longship design continues that of the 50 new pence circulation coins of 1971–1975 (KM-24). The word "new" in the denomination was omitted after the population had got used to the decimal monetary system that was introduced in 1971.

1,000th Anniversary of Tynwald - Viking Longship

KM-46
1 crown
1979 copper-nickel, 38.6 mm

KM-46 ● 1 crown ● 1979 copper-nickel, issued also in .925 silver, .917 gold and .950 platinum

The reverse depicts King Godred Crovan (*see* T-26) standing in a Viking longship (*see* KM-24), in the background another longship and, at the top, Tynwald Hill depicted in a medallion. Godred, son of Harold the Black of the royal family of Norway, was appointed king of Man by the Norse King Harold the Imperious. He came with a fleet and an army and took possession of his kingdom in 1066. He ruled until 1087. Tynwald Hill is an artificially constructed mound consisting of three tiers in St. John's between Douglas and Peel. The hill measures 80 ft (24 m) in diameter and is 12 ft (3.7 m) high. Each year on 5 July, Tynwald Day, the island's national holiday which is Midsummer's Day by the old calendar, the lieutenant governor and members of both branches of the parliament, the House of Keys and the Legislative Council, assemble on Tynwald Hill to read the titles and a brief description of the new laws that have been enacted during the past year. The reading is done both in English and in Manx Gaelic. The assembly ends with a formal meeting of Tynwald, the Manx parliament, continuing the Norse tradition of an open-air assembly that dates back to the founding of Tynwald on Midsummerday in the year 979. (The word "Tynwald" is derived from the Norse thingvöllur, assembly field.) Tynwald claims to be the oldest parliament in the world in continuous existence. (Iceland's parliament, Althing, was founded earlier, in 930, but did not have a continuous existence.) A crown is one quarter of a pound. This denomination, then valued at five shillings, was introduced in England in 1526.

1,000th Anniversary of Tynwald - English Cog

KM-47 • 1 crown • 1979 copper-nickel, issued also in .925 silver, .917 gold and .950 platinum

The reverse depicts an English 14th-century cog in front of Castle Rushen. The castle in the town center of Castletown in the south of the island is one of the best examples in the British Isles of a medieval castle. It was built around 1200 and served as the residence of the last Norse king of Man, who died in 1266.

KM-47
1 crown
1979 copper-nickel, 38.6 mm

1,000th Anniversary of Tynwald - Flemish Carrack

KM-48 • 1 crown • 1979 copper-nickel, issued also in .925 silver, .917 gold and .950 platinum

The reverse depicts a Flemish carrack from the end of the 15th century riding at anchor in front of St. Michael's Isle. The isle forms the northernmost point of the Langness Peninsula near Castletown in the south of the Isle of Man. Once detached at high tide it is now connected to Langness by a causeway built in the 18th century. The isle has been a bird sanctuary since 1936.

1,000th Anniversary of Tynwald - English Man-of-War

KM-49 • 1 crown • 1979 copper-nickel, issued also in .925 silver, .917 gold and .950 platinum

The reverse depicts a royalist Manx soldier and an English man-of-war of the Civil War period (1642–1651). The war was a conflict between Charles I, King of England, and Parliament over their prerogatives. It led to the execution of the king in 1649 and the establishment of Oliver Cromwell's Protectorate in 1653.

1,000th Anniversary of Tynwald - Lifeboat

KM-50 • 1 crown • 1979 copper-nickel, issued also in .925 silver, .917 gold and .950 platinum

The reverse features the Greathead lifeboat of Sir William Hillary (1771–1847) being rowed to a ship in distress and, at the top, Hillary's portrait in a medallion. The introduction of the coastal lifeboat in the United Kingdom was triggered by the loss of the Newcastle ship *Adventure* that foundered with all hands at the mouth of the River Tyne in 1789 while a large crowd watching were unable to help. A group of Newcastle shipowners and businessmen offered a prize of two guineas (£2.10) for the best lifeboat design. Half of the prize was awarded to William Wouldhave and applying features of his design the shipwright Henry Greathead constructed in 1790 the first purpose-built lifeboat—*The Original*. She was 28 ft (8.4 m) long and 9 ft (2.7 m) in the beam, and had a draft of 2.5 ft (75 cm). The hull was fitted with cork both internally and externally for added buoyancy and was double-ended so that the boat could be rowed in either direction by its crew of 12 oarsmen. *The Original* served for 40 years until she was driven on to the rocks and split apart in 1830. In 1824 Hillary, who was a crew member of the lifeboat at Douglas on the Isle of Man, initiated the founding of a national organization which today is known as the Royal National Lifeboat Institution (RNLI). Since its founding in 1824 the RNLI has saved more than 130,000 lives. It has more than 200 lifeboat stations manned by highly trained volunteer crews and a fleet of some 300 lifeboats with lengths ranging from 16 ft (4.9 m) to 56 ft (17 m).

Miscellaneous

KM-51 • 50 pence • 1979 Royal visit – see T-1
KM-53 • 50 pence • 1979 Circulation coin – see T-1
KM-57 • 50 pence • 1980 Error coin – see T-2

Olympic Games 1980 Moscow – Scull

KM-66 • 1 crown • 1980 copper-nickel, issued also in .925 silver, .917 gold and .950 platinum

The triskeles of the Island's coat-of-arms in the center of the reverse is surrounded by Olympians competing in various disciplines, including at the top a javelin thrower and at 7 o'clock a rower in a scull (*see* Gibraltar KM-867).

Olympic Games 1980 Moscow – Kayak

KM-67 • 1 crown • 1980 copper-nickel, issued also in .925 silver, .917 gold and .950 platinum

The triskeles of the Island's coat-of-arms in the center of the reverse is surrounded by Olympians competing in various disciplines, including at the top a judo match and at 9 o'clock a paddling kayaker.

Viking Exhibition New York

KM-69 • 50 pence • 1980 – see T-1

Circulation Coin

KM-70 • 50 pence • 1980–84 copper-nickel, seven-sided planchet, issued also in .500 silver, .925 silver, .917 gold and .950 platinum

The reverse provides a starboard broadside view of a Viking longship (*see* KM-24). The ship is a warship with a large checkered sail. The design is based on an 8th-century picture stone found in Riddare in the parish of Hejum on the Swedish Baltic Sea island of Gotland. This is one of more than 300 picture stones—limestone memorials raised in honor of fallen Viking warriors—found on the island. Ships are depicted on 92 of the stones, possibly symbolizing the passage of the warrior's soul.

150th Anniversary of the Founding of the Isle of Man Steam Packet Company

KM-71 ● 50 pence ● 1980 – *see* T-2

Duke of Edinburgh Award Scheme

KM-76 ● 1 crown ● 1981 copper-nickel, issued also in .925 silver, .374 gold, .917 gold and .950 platinum

The reverse depicts a yachtsman in a sailboat at right, a motorcyclist at the top and a rock climber at left. The coin was issued to mark the 60th birthday of Prince Philip, Duke of Edinburgh and consort of Queen Elizabeth II, and the 25th anniversary of the Duke of Edinburgh Award Scheme (*see* Gibraltar KM-431).

International Year of the Disabled

KM-80 ● 1 crown ● 1981 copper-nickel, issued also in .925 silver, .374 gold, .917 gold and .950 platinum

The reverse depicts Sir Francis Chichester (1901–1972) and his sailing yacht *Gipsy Moth IV*. In this 18-ton ketch the 65-year-old Chichester single-handedly sailed around the world in 1966/67 in 274 days, with one stop of 48 days in Sydney. Making an average of 131 miles (211 km) per day, this was the fastest solo circumnavigation in a small vessel ever made. *Gipsy Moth IV* was designed by John Illingworth and Angus Primrose specially for the solo circumnavigation and was built of mahogany wood in 1966 by Camper & Nicholsons (Yachting) Ltd. at Gosport, Hampshire, England at a cost of £35,000. She is 53 ft (16 m) long, 11 ft (3.2 m) in beam and 7.6 ft (2.3 m) in draft, and has a sail area of 854 sq ft (79 m^2). When Chichester sailed his yacht up the Thames River to Greenwich he was knighted by Queen Elizabeth II—who used the sword that Queen Elizabeth I gave to Sir Francis Drake in 1581 after the completion of his circumnavigation (*see* Great Britain KM-844). *Gipsy Moth IV* has been preserved and can be seen in dry dock at Greenwich, England next to the *Cutty Sark* (*see* Maldive Islands KM-87). In 1929, after a mere five months' training, Chichester piloted his biplane *Gypsy Moth* from Croydon, London to Sydney, becoming the second man to fly solo from England to Australia, and in 1931 he became the first person to fly solo across the Tasman Sea from east to west in this airplane which was fitted with floats and converted into a seaplane. Chichester named all of his yachts *Gipsy Moth* for the airplane but spelled differently. In 1953–1957 he took part in 16 ocean races in *Gipsy Moth II*. In 1960 he won the first single-handed transatlantic yacht race in the 39-ft (12-m)-long sloop *Gipsy Moth III*, 16 days less than the previous record. In 1970, sailing in *Gipsy Moth V*, Chichester attempted to sail 4,000 miles (7,000 km) in 20 days but he fell short of his goal by one day. As denoted by the reverse legend, the coin marks the International Year of the Disabled. Chichester was honored to personify this theme because he continued sailing in spite of his disabilities. He entered the transatlantic race in 1960 to "complete his cure" from lung cancer and in 1972 he started the fourth single-handed transatlantic race even though he required regular blood transfusions because of a cancerous tumor. Chichester is remembered at Westminster Abbey in the Navigators Memorial plaque that features the vessels and routes of three great English circumnavigators: Francis Drake, James Cook and Francis Chichester.

Fisherman's Year

KM-84 ● 50 pence ● 1981 copper-nickel, seven-sided planchet, issued also in .925 silver, .917 gold and .950 platinum

KM-84
50 pence
1981 copper-nickel, 30 mm

The reverse depicts Nickey boats under full sail leaving the harbor of Peel against the background of Peel Hill at left and the 13th-century St. German's cathedral at right. The reverse portrays a 19th-century scene of Nickeys setting out for fishing on St. Stephen's day, the day after Christmas. Their mastheads are decorated with garlands of evergreens and ribbons, a Manx Yuletide tradition. The "nickey" rig—two masts with large rhomboidal sails—was used on Cornish boats that came to the Isle of Man about 1850 and when introduced on the Island it was named for the Cornish fishermen, many of whom were named Nicholas or Nickey. Nickeys were about 48 ft (15 m) long on the keel and had a crew of seven. In the 19th century mackerel and herring fishing was a major industry, with 200 fishing boats registered at Peel.

Medieval Norse History

KM-90 ● 20 pence ● 1982–83 copper-nickel, seven-sided planchet, issued also in .925 silver, .917 gold and .950 platinum

The reverse features a montage of Hiberno-Norse weapons and armor dating from the 9th to the 13th centuries. They include a winged helmet, a breast plate, broad swords, spears, battle axes, daggers, and a shield. The emblem on the shield is a lumphad (or lymphad)—a small galley with one mast that was rowed by up to 12 oarsmen. The lumphad emblem is an ancient Manx device that predates the triskeles emblem.

Manx Maritime Heritage - *Mayflower*

KM-96 • 1 crown • 1982 copper-nickel, issued also in .925 silver, .374 gold, .917 gold and .950 platinum

KM-96
1 crown
1982 copper-nickel, 38.6 mm

The reverse depicts the *Mayflower* (*see* United States KM-147) with a medallion portrait of Captain Myles Standish (1584–1656). Standish, a descendant of an ancient Manx family, was captain of marines on *Mayflower*'s voyage in 1620 on which she took the Pilgrim Fathers to Massachusetts. He was a professional soldier who was hired as military leader for the Massachusetts Bay Colony and later became a member of their community and one of its leaders.

Manx Maritime Heritage - HMAV *Bounty*

KM-97 • 1 crown • 1982 copper-nickel, issued also in .925 silver, .374 gold, .917 gold and .950 platinum

The reverse features HMAV *Bounty* (*see* Pitcairn KM-4) with a medallion portrait of Manxman Fletcher Christian, the master's mate on her voyage of 1787. Christian was the leader of the mutineers who set the ship's captain, William Bligh, and 18 loyal members of his crew adrift in the ship's longboat.

Manx Maritime Heritage - HMS *Victory*

KM-98 • 1 crown • 1982 copper-nickel, issued also in .925 silver, .374 gold, .917 gold and .950 platinum

The reverse depicts HMS *Victory* at the battle of Trafalgar (*see* Gibraltar KM-12) and a medallion portrait of Captain John Quilliam (1771–1829) who is perhaps the most famous of all Manx seamen. Quilliam was one of the more than 3,000 Manxmen—out of a population of less than 28,000—who served in the Royal Navy in the Revolutionary and Napoleonic Wars. Quilliam rose through the ranks and was commissioned lieutenant at the battle of Camperdown in 1797. At the battle of Copenhagen in 1801 he served in the frigate *Amazon* which suffered such heavy fire that all her senior officers were killed and he was left in command. This brought him to the notice of Lord Nelson who transferred him to *Victory*. At the battle of Trafalgar, when the ship's wheel was badly damaged making it impossible to steer, First Lieutenant Quilliam devised a mechanism to work the tiller in the gun room and remained there to control it during the battle. He became known as the man who steered *Victory* at Trafalgar. Quilliam's cool handling of this emergency kept the ship in action and gained him promotion to captain. His last command was *Crescent* that captured the American privateer *Elbridge Gerry* in 1813. Quilliam retired from the navy after the end of the Napoleonic War in 1815. He was elected to the House of Keys, the lower branch of the Tynwald, on a number of occasions.

Manx Maritime Heritage – PS *Mona's Queen II*

KM-99 ● 1 crown ● 1982 copper-nickel, issued also in .925 silver, .374 gold, .917 gold and .950 platinum

KM-99
1 crown
1982 copper-nickel, 38.6 mm

The reverse depicts the 1,564-ton paddle wheel steamer PS *Mona's Queen (II)*, at right an object that appears to represent a German U-boat (submarine) and at left the medallion portrait of *Mona's Queen*'s captain, William Cain. *Mona's Queen* was built in 1885 by the Barrow Shipbuilding Company. She measured 320 ft (98 m) in length and 38 ft (12 m) in the beam. She drew 14 ft (4.4 m) of water and made 19 knots. She served as a ferry for passengers and goods, making daily trips between the Isle of Man and Liverpool for the Isle of Man Steam Packet Company (originally named the Mona's Isle Company). In World War I, many of the company's ships were chartered by the admiralty and employed as coastal auxiliaries and troop transports. *Mona's Queen* served as a troop ship ferrying soldiers between Southampton and France, carrying some 500,000 troops in the years 1915–1919. *Mona's Queen* was engaged on 6 February 1917 in carrying 1,000 troops across the English Channel. As reported by her captain, she was attacked by a German submarine. The torpedo missed, and the steamer rammed the U-boat at full speed. A few seconds later *Mona's Queen*'s port paddle wheel crashed down, holing and sinking the submarine. This exploit is shown on the reverse; however, the story is probably an exaggeration. The U-boat involved was *UC-26* built by Vulkan at Hamburg in 1916. This 417-ton mine-laying submarine was 162 ft (49 m) long, had a beam of 17 ft (5.2 m), drew 12 ft (3.7 m) of water, and had a complement of 14. She was heavily damaged but returned to her base reporting that she had collided with a paddle wheeler. On the date of the collision no U-boat is listed as lost. *Mona's Queen* continued in service until 1929. She was the last paddle ship of the Isle of Man Steam Packet Company.

100th Anniversary of the Incorporation of Peel

KM-109 ● 1 pound ● 1983 nickel-brass, issued also in .925 silver, .374 gold, .917 gold and .950 platinum

The reverse features the coat-of-arms of the town of Peel that depicts two sailing ships in the harbor against the background of the medieval Peel Castle, enclosed in an oval formed by a heraldic sword-belt with thereon the inscription PEEL TOWN COMMISSIONERS 1883. Peel, on the west coast of the Isle of Man, is the center of the Manx fishing industry. Town commissioners for Peel were appointed in 1881. In 1883 the town was granted its charter of incorporation.

Miscellaneous

KM-110 ● 1 noble ● 1983–84 Platinum bullion issue – see T-3
KM-125 ● 50 pence ● 1984 Circulation coin – see T-4
KM-136 ● 1 pound ● 1986 Douglas coat-of-arms – see T-5
KM-137 ● 1/10 noble ● 1984 Platinum bullion issue – see T-3
KM-148 ● 50 pence ● 1985–87 Circulation coin – see T-4
KM-153 ● 1/10 noble ● 1985–87 Platinum bullion issue – see T-3
KM-154 ● 1 noble ● 1985–87 Platinum bullion issue – see T-3

Viking Ship Privy Mark

KM-167(vw) ● 2 pounds ● 1986 virenium

The privy mark on the reverse of some of the circulation coins dated 1986 depicts a Viking ship in a wreath to mark the Manx Heritage Year. The main reverse design is the Tower of Refuge, a fortress-like building with three towers on Conister Rock in Douglas Bay. The rock near the entrance to the harbor of Douglas is covered at high tide and was notorious as a place of shipwreck. The tower was built in 1832 at a cost of £255 to indicate the presence of the dangerous rock and to provide shelter for the crews of the many vessels that were wrecked on the reef. The idea to build the tower was conceived by Sir William Hillary (*see* KM-50), one of the founders of the Royal National Lifeboat Institution (RNLI), after he had taken part, as a member of the Douglas lifeboat crew, in the rescue of all 22 persons on board *St. George* in 1830, in the course of which he himself was washed overboard and injured. Hillary paid 30 percent of the cost of construction of the tower, the remainder was financed by public subscriptions. The tower is owned by the RNLI.

Miscellaneous

KM-168 ● 1/4 noble ● 1986–87 Platinum bullion issue – see T-3
KM-169 ● 1/2 noble ● 1986–87 Platinum bullion issue – see T-3
KM-170 ● 5 noble ● 1986–88 Platinum bullion issue – see T-3
KM-171 ● 10 noble ● 1986–88 Platinum bullion issue – see T-3
KM-175 ● 1 pound ● 1986 Douglas coat-of-arms – see T-5
KM-179 ● 1 crown ● 1987 America's Cup – sailboats and map – see T-6
KM-180 ● 5 crowns ● 1987 America's Cup and sailboats – see T-7

KM-181 ● 10 crowns ● 1987 America's Cup and Statue of Liberty – see T-8
KM-183 ● 1 crown ● 1987 America's Cup and sailboats – see T-7
KM-184 ● 1 crown ● 1987 America's Cup and Statue of Liberty – see T-8

America's Cup – George Steers and *America*

KM-185 ● 1 crown ● 1987 copper-nickel, issued also in .925 silver and .999 palladium

The reverse features the American 180-ton racing schooner *America* and a bust of her designer, the maritime architect George Steers (1819–1856). *America* was built in 1851 at William H. Brown's shipyard in New York for a syndicate of American yachtsmen at a cost of $20,000. She was 101 ft (31 m) long and 23 ft (7 m) in beam, and drew 11 ft (3.4 m) of water. Her canvas spread measured 5,263 sq ft (489 m^2) on two masts. She had a crew of 25. In a race around the Isle of Wight in 1851 she won a contest with 14 English vessels and was presented a silver cup that eventually became known as the America's Cup (*see* Bahamas KM-100). *America* was sold and remained in Britain for several years. Renamed *Camilla* she was owned by Lord Templetown. In 1858 she was sold to Henry Sotheby Pitcher, a shipbuilder, who rebuilt her at his yard near Gravesend on the Thames. He then sold her to Henry Edward Decie, who took her to America. In 1861 *Camilla* was sold to the Confederate government. Because of her speed she was used as a blockade runner in the Civil War. She may have been renamed *Memphis*. The vessel was scuttled in the St. John's River, Florida in 1862 when Jacksonville was taken by Union troops. A Union Navy lieutenant had her raised and she was outfitted for service in the US Navy as USS *America*. In 1863 she was ordered to Newport to serve as a training ship for midshipmen at the US Naval Academy. Three years later the navy laid her up at Annapolis. Admiral David Porter, a former superintendent of the Naval Academy, had *America* recommissioned in 1870 at a cost of $819,000 to the government, so that the schooner could participate in the first race for the America's Cup. She took fourth place. *America* was subsequently sold to the Butler family and raced for almost 30 years more, making her final appearance in 1901. When the Butlers decided to sell her, funds were collected so that she would stay in the United States. In 1921 she was donated to the US Naval Academy in Annapolis for preservation as a relic. In World War II she was stored in a shed but her hull split when the structure's roof caved in during a snowstorm in 1942. What was left of her was scrapped in 1945.

America's Cup – Thomas Lipton

KM-186 ● 1 crown ● 1987 copper-nickel, issued also in .925 silver and .999 palladium

The reverse depicts the bust of Sir Thomas J. Lipton (1850–1931) and two competing sailboats. Lipton built and raced five vessels that participated in America's Cup races for the Royal Ulster Yacht Club of Northern Ireland—*Shamrock (I)* in 1899, *Shamrock II* in 1901, *Shamrock III* in 1903, *Shamrock IV* in 1920 and *Shamrock V* in 1930. The shamrock, a three-leaved clover, is an Irish national symbol. All five vessels challenged American defenders of the cup, none defeated the defender. The 134-ton sloop *Shamrock V* was designed and built in 1930 by Camper and Nicholson's in Gosport, England. Her length is 119 ft (36 m), her beam 20 ft (6.1 m) and her draft 15 ft (4.5 m). Her mast reaches 160 ft (49 m) above the water. She can make 12 knots. *Shamrock V* was rebuilt and refitted several times for different owners. By 1980 she had an Italian owner and was named *Quadrifoglio*. In 1986 she was purchased by the Lipton Tea Company, donated to the Museum of Yachting at Newport, Rhode Island and restored to her original name of *Shamrock V*. Since 1998 she is privately owned. The American defender against *Shamrock V* was Harold Vanderbilt's 128-ton *Enterprise*, built in 1930; she was 121 ft (37 m) long, had a beam of 23 ft (7 m), and drew 14 ft (4.4 m) of water. Lipton, born in Glasgow of Irish descent, built up a worldwide tea company—introducing tea bags and creating the famous Lipton tea brand. He used his challenges to the America's Cup as a public relations campaign for his tea.

Gold Bullion Issue with Junk

KM-191 • 1 angel • 1987 .917 gold

The reverse depicts the archangel Michael, a junk, and the inscriptions HONG KONG and CELESTIAL JOY AND HAPPINESS in Chinese. The archangel design is that of KM-141, 1 angel 1985–1987, to which the junk and the Chinese characters have been added to mark the 6th Hong Kong International Coin Exposition that was held in September 1987. The archangel is shown with a halo, holding a shield and standing over a dragon with a lance in his hand. The image is based on the verse in the New Testament, "And there was war in heaven, Michael and his angels fought against the dragon" (Revelation 12:7). Gold bullion coins denominated in angels, multiple angels and subdivisions of an angel have been issued by the Isle of Man since 1984. The first English angel was introduced in 1465. It showed an angel seated with his feet placed on a dragon.

HMS *Sirius* Privy Mark

KM-195(ss) • $^1/_4$ angel • 1988 .917 gold with Viking ship privy mark
KM-197(ss) • 1 angel • 1988 .917 gold with Viking ship privy mark

The privy mark on the reverse of part of the 1988-dated $^1/_4$ and 1 angel coins depicts HMS *Sirius* to mark the Australian International

Coin Fair held in Sydney in March 1988. *Sirius* was the flagship of the "First Fleet" that brought the first convicts to Australia in 1788 to found a penal colony (*see* Australia KM-655). The main reverse design is the archangel Michael (*see* KM-191).

Miscellaneous

KM-202 ● 1/10 noble ● 1988–89 Platinum bullion issue – *see* T-3
KM-203 ● 1/4 noble ● 1988–90 Platinum bullion issue – *see* T-3
KM-204 ● 1/2 noble ● 1988–89 Platinum bullion issue – *see* T-3
KM-205 ● 1 noble ● 1988–89 Platinum bullion issue – *see* T-3
KM-206 ● 5 crowns ● 1988 *Queen Mary* – *see* T-9

Circulation Coins

KM-209.1 ● 5 pence ● 1988–90 copper-nickel, 23.6 mm
KM-209.2 ● 5 pence ● 1990–93 copper-nickel, 18 mm

The reverse features a windsurfer on a sailboard and the legend ELLAN VANNIN, the name of the Isle of Man in Manx, the Celtic language of the island that is now nearly extinct.

Fishing Trawler

KM-215 ● 5 pounds ● 1988–92 virenium

The reverse features a modern inshore-fishing trawler with Peel registration, the name of the Isle of Man in Manx and the triskeles of its coat-of-arms above, and a lobster and two herrings below.

200th Anniversary of Australia

KM-223 ● 1 crown ● 1988 – *see* T-10

200th Anniversary of Steam Navigation – *Number One*

KM-228 ● 1 crown ● 1988 copper-nickel

The reverse depicts the small experimental paddle boat driven by a steam engine that was tried out on Dalswinton Loch in Scotland on 14 October 1788. She was never officially named but is called *Number One*. She was built as a pleasure boat in 1785, had twin hulls and was fitted with two paddle wheels. Her length was 25 ft (7.6 m), her beam 7 ft (2.1 m) and her draft 2 ft (0.6 m). Her owner, the Edinburgh banker Patrick Miller, had commenced experimenting with pleasure boats that had double or triple hulls, providing them with cranked paddle wheels placed between the hulls to be able to extricate them from perilous situations. In 1787 James

Taylor suggested to Miller to use steam instead of the manual propulsion of the paddles. Miller commissioned the engineer William Symington to design a steam engine to turn the paddle wheels of the boat. The vessel with Symington's engine on the deck is shown on the reverse. It made 5 miles (8 km) an hour on the loch near Miller's home. The experiment was successfully repeated several times. The following year a larger engine was installed in a larger boat which made 7 miles (11 km) an hour; however, the project's expenses were much higher than expected and Miller abandoned the endeavor. The engine used in *Number One* is on exhibit in the Science Museum in London. It is the oldest surviving maritime steam engine. Symington was later engaged by Lord Dundas, a governor of the Forth and Clyde Canal, to build a steam tug, the *Charlotte Dundas*. In 1802 the tug, propelled by Symington's patented steam engine, pulled two 70-ton barges on the canal over a distance of 19 miles (31 km) in six hours. This vessel has been called the first practical steamboat but it was not used on the canal any more because it caused disintegration of its banks. Many years later the British government gave Taylor's widow an annuity in recognition of her husband's pioneering work, in which he was the first to "practically and successfully apply steam to the propulsion of vessels."

200th Anniversary of Steam Navigation – *Sirius*

KM-229 ● 1 crown ● 1988 copper-nickel

The reverse depicts the 703-ton two-masted paddle wheel steamer PS *Sirius*. She is credited with being the first vessel that made an Atlantic crossing from Europe to America under continuous steam. *Sirius* was built in 1837 at the yard of Robert Menzies & Son in Leith, Scotland for the St. George Steam Packet Company's service between Cork in Ireland, Liverpool in England and Glasgow in Scotland. She measured 178 ft (54 m) long and 25 ft (7.6 m) in the beam, and drew 15 ft (4.6 m) of water. Her crew numbered 35. She was named for the Dog Star, the brightest star in the sky. In 1838 *Sirius* was chartered by the British and American Steam Navigation Company because their own vessel, PS *British Queen*, would not have been ready in time to compete with the *Great Western* that was owned by a rival company. *Sirius*' voyage started the first Northern Atlantic steamship service. She left from Cork on 4 April 1838 with 40 passengers on board in three classes; those in first class paid 25 guineas for the passage. The passage to New York took 18 days at an average speed of 6.7 knots. She burned 24 tons of coal a day. In order to keep going she had to burn cabin furniture, spare yards and even a spare mast. The competing PS *Great Western*, designed by Isambard Kingdom Brunel (*see* Gibraltar KM-919), left on her maiden voyage from Bristol on 8 April 1838. After a voyage of 15 days at an average speed of 8.8 knots she arrived in

New York $3^1/_2$ hours after *Sirius*—with more than 40 tons of coal left. These passages showed that steam was practicable for Atlantic crossings. *Sirius* made two transatlantic voyages before commencing the Irish Sea trade for which she was built. She was wrecked in 1847 in Ballycotton Bay off the south coast of Ireland on a voyage from Glasgow to Cork with a loss of 19 of the 90 persons aboard.

200th Anniversary of Steam Navigation – *Chaperon*

KM-230 ● 1 crown ● 1988 copper-nickel

The reverse depicts the 800-ton wooden stern-wheel Mississippi river steamboat *J. C. Kerr*. Launched in 1884, she was one of over 5,000 paddle steamers built for service on the Mississippi and its tributaries in the 19th century. She was 121 ft (37 m) long, had a beam of 21 ft (6.4 m), and drew only 4 ft (1.2 m) of water. Her top speed was 8 knots. In 1904 she was sold and renamed *Chaperon*. In 1917 she was sold again and renamed *Choctaw*. She sank in 1922.

200th Anniversary of Steam Navigation – *Mauretania*

KM-231 ● 1 crown ● 1988 copper-nickel

The reverse depicts the British 31,938-ton ocean liner RMS *Mauretania*, named for the ancient Roman province on the north coast of Africa. Built by Swan, Hunter and Wigham Richardson Ltd. at Wallsend-on-Tyne in 1907, she was for four years the largest and most modern passenger vessel in the world. She measured 790 ft (241 m) in length and had a beam of 88 ft (27 m) and a draft of 60 ft (18 m). She could carry 2,165 passengers—563 in first class, 464 in second class and 1,138 in third class. Her crew numbered 812. First class fares on the luxury liner were up to £200. Fares in steerage—second and third class—were £10 and £6. In World War I she was requisitioned by the British Admiralty. She served from 1914 until 1919 as an armed troop transport and hospital ship, carrying a total of 66,264 troops and 8,605 wounded and medical staff. For 22 years, from 1907 to 1929, *Mauretania* held the Blue Riband. Her top speed was 27 knots. She lost the Riband to the German *Bremen* (*see* Sahara Republic 1000 pesetas 1998, not yet listed). *Mauretania* was scrapped in 1935. *Mauretania*, *Queen Mary* (*see* T-9) and *Queen Elizabeth 2* (*see* KM-233) were operated by the Cunard line. This shipping line was started in 1840 by Samuel Cunard after winning the mail franchise between Liverpool and Boston when the British Post Office decided to issue licenses to shipping lines instead of purchasing and operating the new steamships as it had done with the older sailing vessels. The prefix

RMS stands for Royal Mail Ship, a ship licensed to carry mail. The Blue Riband was an imaginary trophy for the fastest crossing of the Atlantic Ocean by a passenger liner. Its title originates from the blue insignia of the British Order of the Garter, the most exclusive decoration in the world. The Blue Riband was created in the 1860s by an agreement between transatlantic shipping lines to give publicity to the fastest ship. There were no official rules for the competition. Since distances of transatlantic routes vary, the record was claimed by the ship with the highest average speed for the crossing in either direction, eastbound and westbound. The eastbound crossings were usually slightly faster as westbound ships had to sail into the oncoming wind. It was common for one ship to hold both records at the same time. Over time, the best route for a record attempt was found to be between Ambrose lightship, New York and Bishop Rock lighthouse, Cornwall. In 1930 the British engineer Sir Harold Hales initiated a silver trophy. The last superliner to hold the trophy was SS *United States* (*see* Congo-Kinshasa KM-26).

200th Anniversary of Steam Navigation – *Queen Mary*

KM-232 ● 1 crown ● 1988 – see T-9

200th Anniversary of Steam Navigation – *Queen Elizabeth 2*

KM-233 ● 1 crown ● 1988 copper-nickel

KM-233
1 crown
1988 copper-nickel, 38.6 mm

The reverse depicts the 65,863-ton ocean liner RMS *Queen Elizabeth 2* (pronounced Queen Elizabeth Two), commonly known as *QE 2*. She is 963 ft (294 m) long, has a beam of 105 ft (32 m), and draws 32 ft (9.8 m) of water. She was built in Glasgow by John Brown & Co. at a cost of over £29 million. She was launched by Queen Elizabeth II in 1967; however, she is not named for the queen but her name denotes that she is the second Cunard liner named *Queen Elizabeth*. (The first *Queen Elizabeth* was launched in 1938 and was withdrawn from service by Cunard in 1968. This liner was named for Queen Elizabeth, the consort of King George VI.) *QE 2* has a capacity of 3,825 passengers—564 in first class, 1,441 in tourist class and 1,820 in second class. Her crew numbers 906. She is capable of making 29 knots. She made her maiden voyage in 1969. In 1982 she was requisitioned as a troopship for the Falklands war between Great Britain and Argentina. As of 2005 *QE 2* is still going strong, demonstrating a demand for sea voyages even in this jet age. The liner has made more than 1,300 voyages, carrying approximately three million passengers and sailing more than 5.3 million nautical miles (as of 2006)—more than any other ship in history.

200th Anniversary of the Mutiny on the *Bounty* – Tahiti

KM-241 • 1 crown • 1989 copper-nickel, issued also in .925 silver

The reverse depicts the arrival of HMAV *Bounty* at Tahiti in 1788 (*see* Pitcairn KM-4).

200th Anniversary of the Mutiny on the *Bounty* – William Bligh

KM-242 • 1 crown • 1989 copper-nickel, issued also in .925 silver

The reverse depicts the stern of HMAV *Bounty* and the mutineers putting Captain William Bligh and the 18 crew members loyal to him in the ship's launch in April 1789 (*see* Pitcairn KM-4), and features a medallion portrait of Bligh near the rim legend at 1 o'clock. Bligh was married to a Manx woman.

KM-242
1 crown
1989 copper-nickel, 38.6 mm

200th Anniversary of the Mutiny on the *Bounty* – Fletcher Christian

KM-243 • 1 crown • 1989 copper-nickel, issued also in .925 silver

The reverse depicts HMAV *Bounty* approaching Pitcairn Island in early 1790 (*see* Pitcairn KM-4) and features, near the rim legend at 11 o'clock, a medallion portrait of Manxman Fletcher Christian, the master's mate. He was the leader of the mutineers who set the ship's captain, William Bligh, and 18 loyal members of his crew adrift in the ship's longboat.

200th Anniversary of George Washington's Presidential Inauguration

KM-246 • 1 crown • 1989 copper-nickel, issued also in .925 silver

The reverse depicts General George Washington (1732–1799) in a troop-laden rowboat crossing the Delaware River on Christmas Day of 1776 (*see* United States KM-292). The design is a reproduction of part of the painting *Washington Crossing the Delaware* made in 1849/50 by Emanuel Leutze. Washington took the oath of office as first president of the United States on 30 April 1789 in New York City, the first capital of the United States, after he had been unanimously elected by the Electoral College. He served two terms until 1797. Earlier he had been commander-in-chief of the Continental Army, elected by the Continental Congress in 1775, leading the army to victory in the independence struggle of the United States.

200th Anniversary of Australia

KM-258 ● 10 crowns ● 1988 – see T-10

Crowned Shields

KM-260 ● 1/2 sovereign ● 1984 .917 gold, Queen's portrait by Arnold Machin
KM-261 ● 1 sovereign ● 1984 .917 gold, Queen's portrait by Arnold Machin
KM-262 ● 2 sovereigns ● 1984 .917 gold
KM-263 ● 5 sovereigns ● 1984 .917 gold
KM-264 ● 1/2 sovereign ● 1988 .917 gold, Queen's portrait by Raphael Makhlouf
KM-265 ● 1 sovereign ● 1988 .917 gold, Queen's portrait by Raphael Makhlouf

The reverse depicts four crowned shields; the one at 12 o'clock depicts a lumphad (*see* KM-90).

Platinum Bullion Issue

KM-266 ● 1/20 noble ● 1989–92 – see T-3

Christmas 1990

KM-282 ● 50 pence ● 1990 copper-nickel, seven-sided planchet, issued also in .925 silver, .917 gold and .950 platinum

The reverse depicts the TSS (twin screw steamer) *Lady of Mann* bringing visitors for Christmas to the pier at Douglas and in the foreground people watching the ship dock. The 3,104-ton ship was 371 ft (113 m) long, measured 50 ft (15 m) in beam, and drew 19 ft (5.7 m) of water. She was built in 1930 by Vickers Armstrong Ltd. at their Barrow-in-Furness yard in England for the Isle of Man Steam Packet Company at a cost of £249,073. She was the packet company's centennial ship, marking the 100th year of its existence. The steamer had two masts and a single funnel. She made 23 knots and carried up to 3,239 passengers on five decks in first and third class. Third-class passengers were confined to the after part of the ship. There was sleeping accommodation for only a few hundred passengers as the voyages generally took not more than a couple of hours. The "*Lady*" provided regular crossings between England, Scotland and Ireland and the Isle of Man during the summer season. She did not transport cargo or cars. On 3 September 1939, the day Britain declared war on Germany, she was called up for war service to serve as a personnel ship. In 1940 she took part in the evacuation of Allied troops from Dunkirk and other French ports. On her last voyage from Le Havre, under air and shell attack, she made passage with 5,000 troops on board. In preparation for D-Day she was converted into a Landing Ship, Infantry (Hand-hoisting), capable of carrying six landing assault craft, 55 officers and 435 men. On D-Day she was the headquarters ship of the 512th Assault Flotilla that was responsible for the landings on Juno Beach. *Lady of Mann* re-entered the service of the Isle of Man Steam Packet Company in 1946 and remained its flagship until it was decided that the vessel was no longer economic. She was sold for scrap in 1971.

200th Anniversary of Australia

KM-287 ● 1/2 crown ● 1988 – see T-10

America's Cup

KM-299 ● 5 crowns ● 1987 Cup and Statue of Liberty – see T-8
KM-300 ● 10 crowns ● 1987 Cup and sailboats – see T-7
KM-302 ● 1/5 crown ● 1991 Sailboats and *Star of India* – see T-11
KM-308 ● 5 crowns ● 1987 Sailboats and map – see T-6
KM-309 ● 10 crowns ● 1987 Sailboats and map – see T-6
KM-320 ● 1 crown ● 1991 Sailboats and *Star of India* – see T-11
KM-321 ● 5 crowns ● 1991 Sailboats and *Star of India* – see T-11
KM-322 ● 1/25 crown ● 1992 Sailboats and *Star of India* – see T-11
KM-323 ● 1/10 crown ● 1992 Sailboats and *Star of India* – see T-11
KM-324 ● 1/5 crown ● 1992 Sailboats and *Star of India* – see T-11
KM-325 ● 1/2 crown ● 1992 Sailboats and *Star of India* – see T-11
KM-326 ● 1 crown ● 1992 Sailboats and *Star of India* – see T-11
KM-327 ● 5 crowns ● 1992 Sailboats and *Star of India* – see T-11

America's Cup Challenge – San Diego

KM-523 ● 1/5 crown ● 1995 .999 gold
KM-524 ● 1 crown ● 1995 copper-nickel, issued also in .925 silver

KM-524
1 crown
1995 copper-nickel, 38.6 mm

The reverse depicts the three-masted sailing ship *Star of India*, in the background a modern sailing ship and, at the top within a medallion, the America's Cup (*see* Bahamas KM-100). The *Star of India* is the world's oldest seagoing merchant sailing ship. The 1,197-ton vessel is 205 ft (63 m) long and 35 ft (11 m) in the beam, and draws 23 ft (7.1 m) of water. She was built in 1863 by Gibson, McDonald & Arnold at Ramsey on the Isle of Man for Wakefield Nash & Co. of Liverpool to be used in the Indian jute trade. She was named *Euterpe* after the Greek goddess of music. In 1901 *Euterpe* was converted to a bark and her tonnage was increased to 1,318. In 1906 she was renamed *Star of India*. Her major owners were Shaw, Savill and Co. which used her in the years 1871–1897 on the New Zealand trade, mostly taking emigrants, and the Alaska Packers Association of San Francisco which owned the ship from 1901 until 1926 and used her to carry fish workers and tin plate to Alaska, and tinned salmon on returning to California. For many years she was sailed by a Manx crew. The *Star of India* made her last voyage to Alaska in 1923—the sailing ship had become uneconomical in the age of steam. In 1926 she was bought by James Wood Coffroth who gave her to the San Diego Zoological Society to be fitted out as a floating museum and aquarium. This project got stuck in the days of the American Depression and the Zoological Society gave the ship to the Maritime Museum Association of San Diego, California in 1957. The *Star of India* was named a National Historic Landmark in 1966, was restored, and was put to sea in 1976 for the first time in 50 years. She is now a floating museum in San Diego. The races for the America's Cup of 1995 were held in San Diego. The winner was the New Zealand team in *Black Magic*.

Olympic Games 1996 Atlanta

KM-563 ● 1/5 crown ● 1996 .999 gold
KM-569 ● 1 crown ● 1996 copper-nickel, issued also in .925 silver

The reverse features a modern sailship and an ancient Greek sailship. The ancient Greek ship alludes to the ancient Olympic Games and to the 100th anniversary of the first of the modern Games that were held in Athens, Greece in 1896.

200th Anniversary of the Death of Robert Burns – Ships

KM-574 ● 1/5 crown ● 1996 – see T-12

200th Anniversary of the Death of Robert Burns – Burns Seated

KM-577 ● 1 crown ● 1996 copper-nickel, issued also in .925 silver

The reverse depicts Scotland's national poet Robert Burns (*see* T-12) seated near a stream, likely composing a poem, and in the background on the stream a rowboat.

200th Anniversary of the Death of Robert Burns – Ships

KM-578 ● 1 crown ● 1996 – see T-12

Circulation Coin

KM-591 ● 10 pence ● 1996–97 – see T-13

Famous Discoverers – Ferdinand Magellan

KM-625 ● 1/5 crown ● 1996 .999 gold
KM-626 ● 1 crown ● 1996 copper-nickel, issued also in .925 silver

KM-626
1 crown
1996 copper-nickel, 38.6 mm

The reverse depicts Ferdinand Magellan (1480–1521) with the carrack *Vittoria* (Victoria) and a map of the Strait of Magellan which lies between the continent of South America and Tierra del Fuego. *Vittoria* was the only one of the five ships in Magellan's fleet that completed the first circumnavigation of the world in 1522. In the course of the voyage, in 1520, Magellan became the first European to navigate from the Atlantic Ocean to the Pacific Ocean through the strait that now bears his name (*see* Portugal KM-731).

Famous Discoverers – Francis Drake

KM-628 ● 1/5 crown ● 1996 .999 gold
KM-629 ● 1 crown ● 1996 copper-nickel, issued also in .925 silver

The reverse depicts Sir Francis Drake (1540–1596) and his flagship *Golden Hind* below a world map. Drake made his global circumnavigation in *Golden Hind* in 1577–1580 (*see* Great Britain KM-844). The map includes Australia, even though this continent was first visited by a European ship, *Duyfken* (*see* Australia KM-653), only after Drake's death.

Douglas Coat-of-Arms

KM-655 ● 1 pound ● 1996 – *see* T-5

50th Anniversary of D-Day

KM-695 ● 1 crown ● 1994 TSS *Ben-My-Chree IV* – *see* T-14
KM-696 ● 1 crown ● 1994 Omaha Beach – *see* T-15
KM-699 ● 1 crown ● 1994 British troops – *see* T-16
KM-700 ● 1 crown ● 1994 Dwight Eisenhower – *see* T-17
KM-701 ● 1 crown ● 1994 Omar Bradley – *see* T-18
KM-702 ● 1 crown ● 1994 Bernard Montgomery – *see* T-19
KM-703 ● 1 crown ● 1994 TSS *Ben-My-Chree IV* – *see* T-14
KM-704 ● 1 crown ● 1994 Omaha Beach – *see* T-15
KM-707 ● 1 crown ● 1994 British troops – *see* T-16
KM-708 ● 1 crown ● 1994 Dwight Eisenhower – *see* T-17
KM-709 ● 1 crown ● 1994 Omar Bradley – *see* T-18
KM-710 ● 1 crown ● 1994 Bernard Montgomery – *see* T-19

Platinum Bullion Issue

KM-717 ● 1/4 noble ● 1996 – *see* T-3

Leiv Eiríksson

KM-763 ● 1/5 crown ● 1997 .999 gold
KM-764 ● 1/2 crown ● 1997 .999 gold
KM-765 ● 1 crown ● 1997 copper-nickel, issued also in .925 silver

The reverse depicts the Norse explorer Leiv Eiríksson (late 970s – circa 1020) viewing a Viking knarr. A grid map of the region from Labrador to Europe is depicted on the sail of the ship. The deep-draft knarr was a merchantman approximately 54 ft (16 m) long and 15 ft (4.6 m) in the beam. It could carry 15 tons of cargo. It was the only Viking vessel to rely primarily on sails rather than oars. In the year 986 Eric the Red had set out to settle in south-west Greenland. A trader named Bjarni Herjólfsson who intended to join Eric's group was blown off course and sighted lands unknown to the Norse to the west and southwest of Greenland before he turned east to reach Greenland. In approximately 1000 CE (the reverse inscription states the years 999–1001), Eric's eldest son, Leiv Eiríksson (often written Leif Ericson or Eriksson), decided to explore the region which Bjarni had sighted. He bought Bjarni's ship and set sail in her from Greenland with a crew of 35. Upon reaching the eastern coast of North America, Leiv set up a short-lived settlement in a region that he named "Vinland" because of the vine growing there. The remains of this settlement, the oldest European settlement in North America, have been found at L'Anse-aux-Meadows on the northern tip of Newfoundland's Great Northern Peninsula. The site has been included on the UNESCO world heritage list of cultural and natural properties of universal value. It is not clear whether Leiv and his men ever returned to Europe.

Fridtjof Nansen

KM-766 • 1/5 crown • 1997 .999 gold
KM-767 • 1/2 crown • 1997 .999 gold
KM-768 • 1 crown • 1997 copper-nickel, issued also in .925 silver

The reverse features the Norwegian polar explorer Fridtjof Nansen (1861–1930), his ship *Fram* (*see* Norway KM-459) and, at the top, a map of the North Pole region. The coin marks Nansen's attempt in 1893–1895 to reach the North Pole.

KM-768
1 crown
1997 copper-nickel, 38.6 mm

500th Anniversary of the Discovery of the Sea Route to India

KM-826 • 1/5 crown • 1998 .999 gold
KM-827 • 1 crown • 1998 copper-nickel, issued also in .925 silver

The reverse shows the portrait of Vasco da Gama (1460–1524), a Portuguese nau and a map of Africa. On his journey of 1497–1499 da Gama became the first European to reach India by sailing along the African coast, around the Cape of Good Hope and crossing the Indian Ocean to Calicut (*see* Portugal KM-709).

Year of the Ocean

KM-899 ● 1 crown ● 1998 copper-nickel, issued also in .925 silver

The reverse depicts three sailboats on the ocean. The coin acknowledges the United Nations' declaration of 1998 as the "International Year of the Ocean" and serves as a reminder of the importance of the ocean to life on earth.

Circulation Coin

KM-903 ● 10 pence ● 1998–99 – see T-13

Russian Revolution 1917

KM-917 ● 1/5 crown ● 1999 .999 gold
KM-918 ● 1 crown ● 1999 copper-nickel, issued also in .925 silver

The reverse shows the armored cruiser *Aurora* (*see* Russia Y-138) and, at the top, a medallion portrait of Vladimir Ilich Lenin (1870–1924) against the background of the Winter Palace in St. Petersburg, in front of which revolutionaries have assembled. Lenin was the leader of the Great October Socialist Revolution of 25 October 1917 (the date according to the Julian calendar then still in use in Russia). The revolution toppled the temporary government of Prime Minister Alexander Kerensky and later resulted in the formation of the Russian Soviet Socialist Republic. *Aurora* is the symbol of the revolution as her shots gave the signal for the storming of the Winter Palace. Lenin is shown on the reverse with his typical gesture urging the people who have assembled to revolt. The reverse also features the Greenwich Meridian 2000 logo.

KM-926
1 crown
1999 copper-nickel, 38.6 mm

Olympic Games 2000 Sydney

KM-925 ● 1/5 crown ● 1999 .999 gold
KM-926 ● 1 crown ● 1999 copper-nickel, issued also in .925 silver

The reverse depicts a sailboat marked KA15a against the background of the Sydney Opera House and the Sydney Harbor Bridge. It also features the Greenwich Meridian 2000 logo.

KM-943
5 pounds
1999 .925 silver, 36.1 mm

175th Anniversary of the Royal National Lifeboat Institution

KM-943 ● 5 pounds ● 1999 virenium, issued also in .925 silver and .917 gold

The reverse depicts lifeboat 47-032, named *Sir William Hillary*, against the background of the Tower of Refuge. The 26-ton boat is 47 ft (14 m) long and has a beam of 15 ft (4.5 m) and a shallow draft. It is slipway launched. It has a crew of six and can make a speed of 18 knots. The buoyancy of the air contained in the watertight aluminum superstructure combined with the weight of the engines low in the boat enables the boat to self right in five seconds in the event of a capsize. The number of the boat, 47-032, signifies that it is 47 ft long, that it is made of steel (indicated by the zero) and that it is the 32nd Tyne class built. This class was introduced in 1982. Forty of them were built up to 1990. *Sir William Hillary*, built in 1986, is stationed at Douglas and is named for the initiator of the founding of the Royal National Lifeboat Institution (*see* KM-50), who resided at Douglas. The idea to build the Tower of Refuge was also conceived by Hillary (*see* KM-167).

Walter Raleigh

KM-954 • 1/5 crown • 1999 .999 gold
KM-955 • 1 crown • 1999 copper-nickel, issued also in .925 silver

The reverse depicts the English navigator Sir Walter Raleigh (1552–1618), a ship of the 16th century, and a map of the Americas. Raleigh made voyages to North and South America (*see* Cook Islands KM-188).

525th Anniversary of the Birth of Francisco Pizarro

KM-1020 • 1/5 crown • 2000 .999 gold
KM-1021 • 1 crown • 2000 copper-nickel, issued also in .925 silver

The reverse features an armored portrait of the Spanish conquistador Francisco Pizarro (1475–1541), a typical ship of the 16th century he would have sailed, and a map of the northwestern part of South America. The route that Pizarro took from Panama to Cuzco, the capital of the Inca empire, is indicated on the map. Superimposed on the map is a scene of Pizarro arresting Atahualpa, the ruler of that empire, and the inscription PIZARRO SEIZES INCA EMPEROR. The ship depicted may be *San Cristobal*, a vessel Pizarro had refitted, which he used as his flagship on his first trip to South America. Between the years 1531 and 1533, Pizarro, an illiterate Spanish soldier, conquered the 2,500-mile (4,000-km)-long Inca empire for its gold, subduing the Inca army of perhaps 80,000 with a force of 180 men and 27 horses through the use of European weaponry. He arrested Atahualpa, who gave Pizarro a vast amount of gold and silver in exchange for his release, but nevertheless the Inca was garroted. In 1535 Pizarro founded a capital for the new colony on the Rimac River, at a more convenient place than Cuzco. He named it Ciudad de Los Reyes (City of the Kings). Through corruption of the word Rimac the city became known as Lima. A war between Pizarro and his former partner, the mercenary Diego de Almagro, ended with Almagro's execution in 1538. Three years later Pizarro was murdered by partisans of Almagro's son. After the conquest of the Inca empire, the Spanish sent so much gold to Spain over a few decades that it caused severe inflation in Europe. Even after most of the Inca's gold and silver treasures had been found and melted down, rumors persisted that somewhere beyond the Andes lay a land so rich in gold that its king, whom the Spaniards came to call El Dorado (the Gilded Man), bathed in gold dust. It is believed that this story refers to a ceremony held annually by the Chibcha Indians at Lake Guatavita in what is now the republic of Colombia, during which the ruler was covered with gold dust and floated onto a sacred lake into which emeralds and gold objects were thrown.

450th Anniversary of the Birth of Willem Barents

KM-1022 • 1/5 crown • 2000 .999 gold
KM-1023 • 1 crown • 2000 copper-nickel, issued also in .925 silver

The reverse depicts a portrait of the Dutch navigator Willem Barents (1550–1597), his ship in the ice of the Barents Sea, and an outline map of northwestern Russia. The map shows the Kola Peninsula and the land to the east of it that borders the Barents Sea. Barents led three expeditions to discover a Northeast Passage from the Atlantic Ocean to Asia. In 1594 he set out with four ships—two from Amsterdam of which the names are unknown, *Zwaan* (Swan) from Zealand, and *Mercurius* (Mercury) from Enkhuizen. On this voyage Barents discovered Novaya Zemlya ("New Land" in Russian). Two of the ships found the sea on their route to be almost without ice. The men were convinced that Cape Tabin, the point where the north coast of Asia was supposed to end, was very close by and went back to Holland with the information that the sea route to China was open. Thus next year's fleet was a trading fleet stocked with merchandise. It consisted of seven ships with a cargo capacity of probably 50-100 burden—*Griffioen* (Griffon) and *Zwaan* from Zealand, *Hoop* (Hope) and *Mercurius* from Enkhuizen, *Winthont* (Greyhound) and a yacht from Amsterdam, and a yacht from Rotterdam. Barents was on the *Winthont*. Due to the ice they could not proceed and returned. After this failure it was decided to try the route around the Cape of Good Hope for trading purposes; however, Barents and a few merchants continued to believe in the northern route, and two ships were equipped for a third voyage in 1596. Both ships were from Amsterdam, but their names are not known for sure. Barents' ship may have been the *Seehont* (Seal). With a cargo capacity of 50 and 30 burden they were smaller than the ships on the previous voyage so as to facilitate navigation. On this expedition Barents discovered the archipelago of Spitsbergen (Steeple

Mountains in Dutch), now named Svalbard. One of the ships returned home but Barents proceeded southward across the wide northern sea to the north of Russia between Spitsbergen and Novaya Zemlya that is now named for him, and made land on Novaya Zemlya. Due to the floating ice and heavy winds, Barents and his men were obliged to stay at a bay on the coast of Novaya Zemlya which Barents called Ice Harbor. Here the 17 men built a wintering shelter from a find of large amounts of driftwood and parts of the ship. In this log cabin they remained for the long winter months, surviving on the flesh of walruses and foxes that they hunted. In June 1597 the ship was still trapped in the ice and the men set out in two of the ship's small boats. Barents died at sea but the others managed to reach the Russian mainland. The structure built by Barents and his men at Ice Harbor was found in 1871. A large number of tools and other relics found there can be seen in the Rijksmuseum at Amsterdam.

Global Challenge Sail Competition

KM-1034 ● 1/5 crown ● 2000 .999 gold
KM-1035 ● 1 crown ● 2000 copper-nickel, issued also in .925 silver

KM-1035
1 crown
2000 copper-nickel, 38.6 mm

The reverse gives a partial view of the sailing yacht *Isle of Man* and, in the background, a small part of a world map. The coin commemorates the BT Global Challenge Round the World Yacht Race 2000/01 that was organized by The Challenge Business International Ltd. The race has been billed as the world's toughest yacht race as it requires the yachts to circumnavigate the earth in westerly direction, the "wrong way"—against the prevailing winds and currents. The twelve participating yachts were identical and had identical equipment. They were steel-hulled, 72 ft (22 m) long and 18 ft (5.5 m) in beam, their draft was 10 ft (3 m) and their tonnage was 37. The total sail area was 6,254 sq ft (581 m^2). The yachts were built in 1999/2000, ten of them by Devonport Yachts at Plymouth, England, the other two by Kim's Yacht Company in China. The skipper of each yacht participating in the race was a professional yachtsman, the 17 crewmen were all volunteers. The competition started on 10 September 2000 in Southampton, England. The boats sailed to Boston, United States; Buenos Aires, Argentina; Wellington, New Zealand; Sydney, Australia; Cape Town, South Africa; and La Rochelle, France, returning to Southampton after ten months, on 30 June 2001. They made the voyage of over 32,000 nautical miles (nearly 60,000 km) at an average speed of 7.6 knots. Winner of the race was Conrad Humphreys of Plymouth and his crew in *LG Flatron*. The coin marks the participation of the *Isle of Man*, the only yacht representing a nation (the other boats were backed by multinational corporations).

Circulation Coin

KM-1037 ● 2 pence ● 2000–03 brass-plated steel

The reverse features a fishing sailboat. The reverse inscription CLASHT ROOIN, O HIARN translates as "Hear us, O Lord." The coin was first issued to mark the 2,000th anniversary of Christianity.

KM-1037
2 pence
2000 brass-plated steel, 26 mm

Platinum Bullion Issue

KM-1066 ● 1/4 noble ● 1995 – *see T-3*

Famous Explorers

KM-1078 ● 1/5 crown ● 2001 Martin Frobisher – *see T-20*
KM-1079 ● 1/5 crown ● 2001 Roald Amundsen – *see T-21*
KM-1080 ● 1 crown ● 2001 Martin Frobisher – *see T-20*
KM-1081 ● 1 crown ● 2001 Roald Amundsen – *see T-21*

Harry Potter

KM-1088 ● 1/25 crown ● 2001 .999 gold
KM-1089 ● 1 crown ● 2001 copper-nickel, issued also in .925 silver

The reverse depicts a boat with four children on a lake and, at the top, the coat-of-arms of the Hogwarts School of Witchcraft and Wizardy. The children are new students at this school who cross the lake on their way to the castle that houses the school. The lake is enchanted—the boat moves across without the use of oars. Harry Potter, who attends Hogwarts, is the hero of a series of books by British author J. (Joan) K. Rowling (rhymes with bowling, not howling). The coin was issued in 2001 upon the release of the movie adapted from the first book in the series, *Harry Potter and the Sorcerer's Stone*.

140th Anniversary of the Launching of the *Star of India*

KM-1174 ● 1 crown ● 2003 – *see T-22*

Olympic Games 2004 Athens

KM-1181 ● 1/5 crown ● 2003 .999 gold
KM-1182 ● 1 crown ● 2003 copper-nickel, issued also in .925 silver

The reverse depicts three sailing windsurfers, each maneuvering the sail while standing on the rudderless sailboard.

400th Anniversary of the Death of Queen Elizabeth I

KM-1184 • 130 crowns • 2003 – see T-23

Windsurfing

KM-1216 • 1 crown • 2004 copper-nickel, issued also in .925 silver
KM-1217 • $^{1}/_{25}$ crown • 2004 .999 gold

As reported, the reverse depicts three Olympic windsurfers. For lack of an image of the coin it cannot be determined whether this design is different from the windsurfing design of the issue of 2003 marking the Olympic Games held in 2004 in Atlanta (*see* KM-1181).

Queen Mary 2

KM-1219 • 64 crowns • 2004 .999 silver, 140 mm, 2000 gr

The reverse depicts the ocean liner *Queen Mary* 2 (pronounced Queen Mary Two) that was built by ALSTOM Chantiers de l'Atlantique in Saint Nazaire, France in 2003 for Carnival Corporation's Cunard Line. She cost an estimated 800 million dollars to build and outfit. With a length of 1,132 ft (345 m), a beam of 135 ft (41 m), a draft of 33 ft (10 m) and a height from the keel to the funnel of 236 ft (72 m), at the time she was completed, the 151,400-ton British liner was the largest, longest, tallest, widest and most expensive passenger ship ever built. Her crew of 1,253 serves up to 2,620 passengers. *Queen Mary* 2 has 14 decks and can make a speed of 30 knots. The electric power generated by her 157,000-horsepower gas turbine and diesel electric engines is enough to light a city of 200,000 residents. In 2004 Queen Elizabeth II formally named the ship in her home port of Southampton, England. She is named for the first *Queen Mary* which is now berthed at Long Beach, California (*see* T-9). *Queen Mary* 2 was built for the transatlantic run between Southampton and New York. She maintains a six-night/five-day schedule regardless of adverse weather conditions, averaging 24 knots.

175th Anniversary of the Death of John Quilliam

KM-1220 • 1 crown • 2004 copper-nickel, issued also in .925 silver

The reverse depicts a scene of the battle of Trafalgar on 21 October 1805 (*see* Gibraltar KM-12), a medallion portrait of Manxman Lieutenant John Quilliam (1771–1829) who steered Vice Admiral Lord Horatio Nelson's flagship *Victory* at the battle (*see* KM-98), and at the bottom Nelson's official signature *Nelson & Bronte*. The battle scene shows the British breaking the line of the French and Spanish fleets. In 1799 Ferdinand, King of the Two Sicilies, made Nelson Duke of Bronte and conferred on him the towns and lands of Bronte on Sicily.

The Battle of Trafalgar

KM-1221 ● 1 crown ● 2005 – see T-24

Norway's War Medal

KM-1232 ● 1 crown ● 2004 copper-nickel, issued also in .925 silver
KM-1233 ● 1/5 crown 2004 .999 gold

KM-1232
1 crown
2004 copper-nickel, 38.6 mm

The reverse depicts warships in Norwegian waters, three sailors clutching a lifeboat at the bottom, and Norway's War Medal in the center. The ship at the front of the reverse is the British destroyer HMS *Acasta*, marked by her pennant number H09. The other ships depicted are probably the British destroyer HMS *Ardent* at left, the German battle cruiser *Scharnhorst* at far right, and the silhouette of the sinking British aircraft carrier HMS *Glorious* in front of the *Scharnhorst*. The design relates to the naval engagement west of Narvik in June 1940 between the three British ships and the German battle cruisers *Scharnhorst* and *Gneisenau* which took place during the Allied evacuation of northern Norway. *Glorious*, carrying Hurricanes and Gladiators monoplane fighters of the Royal Air Force to Britain and escorted by the two destroyers, was surprised by the two German ships. All three British ships sank by gunfire in a little over two hours, with a loss of 1,500 and only 42 survivors. *Glorious* was built in 1916 by Harland & Wolff in Northern Ireland as a large light cruiser and converted to an aircraft carrier in 1930. She displaced 26,518 tons, had a length of 786 ft (240 m) and a beam of 90 ft (28 m), drew 24 ft (7.3 m) of water, and made 30 knots. She carried 48 aircraft and had a complement of 1,245. *Acasta* and *Ardent* were sister ships that were built in Scotland in 1929—*Acasta* by John Brown Shipbuilding & Engineering Company Ltd., *Ardent* by Scott's Shipbuilding & Engineering Company Ltd. Each of them displaced 1,350 tons, had a length of 323 ft (98 m), a beam of 32 ft (9.8 m) and a draft of 12 ft (3.7 m), made 35 knots, and had a complement of 138. *Scharnhorst* was 770 ft (235 m) long and 98 ft (30 m) in the beam, and had a draft of 33 ft (9.9 m). She was built at the naval shipyards in Wilhelmshaven and put into service in 1939. Her combat displacement was 38,092 tons. She attained 32 knots and had a complement of 1,968. She sank in battle with a British fleet in 1943, with only 36 survivors. The War Medal depicts King Haakon VII (1872–1957, born Prince Carl of Denmark, elected as the first king of newly-independent Norway in 1905). The medal was instituted by the king in 1941, who, at that time, headed the Norwegian government-in-exile in London. The medal was awarded to civilians and military personnel, both Norwegian and non-Norwegian, who served honorably in the war for Norway's liberation or the country's defense.

T-1 Odin's Raven

KM-51 • 50 pence • 1979 copper-nickel, seven-sided planchet, Royal visit, varieties exist, issued also in .925 silver and .950 platinum
KM-53 • 50 pence • 1979 copper-nickel, seven-sided planchet, circulation coin, issued also in .925 silver
KM-69 • 50 pence • 1980 copper-nickel, seven-sided planchet, Viking exhibition New York, issued also in .925 silver, .917 gold and .950 platinum

KM-53
50 pence
1979 copper-nickel, 30 mm

The reverse depicts *Odin's Raven* passing the Point of Ayre lighthouse. Her sail displays the logo of the Tynwald millennium. *Odin's Raven* is a reconstruction of a Viking longship (*see* KM-24), modeled after the ship found at Gokstad, Norway, but built to a two-thirds scale. *Odin's Raven* is 50 ft (15 m) long and 11 ft (3.4 m) in beam, draws some 3 ft (0.9 m) of water and has 16 oars. Her tonnage is about 15 and her square sail measures 484 sq ft (45 m^2). She was built in 1979 by Rod Batbyggeri at Frederikstad, Norway. Her name was the winning entry in a contest held among the school children on the Isle of Man. The reverse legend denotes 5 July, the ancient Midsummerday, as the Day of Tynwald. This day in 1979 marked the 1,000th anniversary of the founding of Tynwald, the parliament of the Isle of Man (*see* KM-46). To celebrate this millennium, *Odin's Raven* was rowed from Trondheim, Norway to Peel on the Isle of Man. The voyage was made according to the old Viking route, via the Shetlands, Orkneys, Hebrides and Ireland, a total of 1,500 miles (2,400 km). *Odin's Raven* arrived at Peel on 4 July 1979 and performed a mock invasion, demonstrating how the original Vikings invaded the island. In 1980 she was the main attraction at the Viking exhibition in New York. The vessel is now on display in the House of Manannan Museum in Peel Harbor. The edge inscription of KM-51 reads H.M / Q.E-II / ROYAL / VISIT / I.O.M / JULY / 1979. KM-53 has a plain edge. The edge inscription of KM-69 is ODIN'S / RAVEN / VIKING / EXHIBN / NEW / YORK / 1980. The Point of Ayre lighthouse (built 1818) at the northernmost tip of the Isle of Man was the first part of the island reached by *Odin's Raven* on her voyage to Peel.

T-2 150th Anniversary of the Founding of the Isle of Man Steam Packet Company

KM-57 • 50 pence • 1980 copper-nickel, seven-sided planchet, "mule"
KM-71 • 50 pence • 1980 copper-nickel, seven-sided planchet, issued also in .925 silver, .917 gold and .950 platinum

The reverse depicts the arrival in December 1830 in Douglas of the 200-ton paddle steamer *Mona's Isle* with the Christmas mail from Liverpool and in the foreground a Dickensian horse-drawn coach—a "coach and four." *Mona's Isle* was built in 1830 by John Wood & Co. in Glasgow for the passenger service of Mona's Isle Company at a cost of £7,052. She was 116 ft (35 m) long, 19 ft (5.8 m) in the beam and 10 ft (3 m) deep. The steamer was fast for her day, making 8.5 knots and doing the passage between Liverpool and Douglas in about eight hours on average—once weekly in winter, three times weekly in summer and twice weekly in the other months. At low water the steamers arriving in Douglas lay rocking about in the bay and the passengers were taken off in boats, often becoming wet to the skin by both sea and rain. In 1831 the company was given the contract for regular mail service between the Isle of Man and England, and the ship became HM Royal Mail Steam Packet *Mona's Isle*. The contract stipulated that the mails had to be conveyed twice weekly each way in summer and once weekly during the rest of the year. In 1832 the company—renamed the Isle of Man Steam Packet Company—ordered another ship, *Mona*, because *Mona's Isle* was too large and valuable to risk on the winter service. *Mona's Isle* was broken up in 1851. The obverse legend of KM-71 is ISLE OF MAN – ELIZABETH II. KM-57 is an error coin struck from two dies not meant to be used with one another. It combines the reverse of KM-71 with the obverse of KM-69 (*see* T-1) on which the legend is ELIZABETH THE SECOND. Because of the error, KM-57 does not have "Isle of Man" on it anywhere.

T-3 Platinum Bullion Issues

KM-110 ● 1 noble ● 1983–84 .999 platinum, Queen's portrait by Arnold Machin
KM-137 ● 1/10 noble ● 1984 .999 platinum, Queen's portrait by Arnold Machin
KM-153 ● 1/10 noble ● 1985–87 .999 platinum, Queen's portrait by Raphael Makhlouf, date at 6 o'clock on obv.
KM-154 ● 1 noble ● 1985–87 .999 platinum, Queen's portrait by Raphael Makhlouf, date at 6 o'clock on obv.
KM-168 ● 1/4 noble ● 1986–87 .999 platinum, date at 6 o'clock on obv.
KM-169 ● 1/2 noble ● 1986–87 .999 platinum, date at 6 o'clock on obv.
KM-170 ● 5 noble ● 1986–88 .999 platinum
KM-171 ● 10 noble ● 1986–88 .999 platinum, 63 mm
KM-202 ● 1/10 noble ● 1988–89 .999 platinum, date at 4 o'clock on obv.
KM-203 ● 1/4 noble ● 1988–90 .999 platinum, date at 4 o'clock on obv.
KM-204 ● 1/2 noble ● 1988–89 .999 platinum, date at 4 o'clock on obv.
KM-205 ● 1 noble ● 1988–89 .999 platinum, date at 4 o'clock on obv.
KM-266 ● 1/20 noble ● 1989–92 .999 platinum
KM-717 ● 1/4 noble ● 1996 .999 platinum
KM-1066 ● 1/4 noble ● 1995 .999 platinum in a .999 gold ring

KM-203
1/4 noble
1988 .999 platinum, 22 mm

The reverse depicts a Viking longship under full sail (*see* KM-24). Most of the issues display on the sail a hologram—a three-dimensional photograph made with the aid of a laser—

causing the sail to change hues based on the angle of the light. The noble denomination is reserved by the Isle of Man for its platinum bullion issues. Originally the noble was a denomination for English gold coins. Gold nobles were first issued by King Edward III in 1344 and depicted the king standing in a ship holding a sword in one hand and a shield with the royal arms in the other. This design referred to the king's victory over the allied fleets of France, Spain and Genoa of over 400 sail off Sluys on the coast of Flanders in present-day Belgium. The battle of Sluys was the first major engagement of the Hundred Years' War (1337–1453). King Edward's ship in the battle was the 200-ton cog *Thomas*.

T-4 Circulation Coins

KM-125 ● 50 pence ● 1984 copper-nickel, seven-sided planchet, Queen's portrait by Arnold Machin, issued also in .925 silver and .917 gold
KM-148 ● 50 pence ● 1985–87 copper-nickel, seven-sided planchet, Queen's portrait by Raphael Makhlouf, issued also in .925 silver, .917 gold and .950 platinum

KM-148
50 pence
1985 copper-nickel, 30 mm

The reverse features a lumphad (a one-masted galley, *see* KM-90) within a scrolled shield. The galley's prow is carved like the head of a dragon, the tail of the dragon is carved at the sternpost. The scrolled shield is a heraldic theme that alludes to the 500th anniversary of the incorporation by King Richard III in 1484 of the College of Arms, the college of royal heralds that grants coats-of-arms. The London headquarters of the College of Arms is in the Derby House that was once the town-house of the Earls of Derby who were the Lords of Mann. (Later the Dukes of Atholl were the Lords of Mann, until the lordship was bought by the United Kingdom government for the Crown in 1765.)

T-5 Douglas Coat-of-Arms

KM-136 ● 1 pound ● 1986 .925 silver, Queen's portrait by Arnold Machin, issued also in .917 gold and .950 platinum
KM-175 ● 1 pound ● 1986 virenium, Queen's portrait by Raphael Makhlouf
KM-655 ● 1 pound ● 1996, virenium, Douglas centennial, issued also in .925 silver and .917 gold

The reverse depicts the seal of the city of Douglas. The upper left of its four quarters displays a lumphad or galley of the Age of the Vikings (*see* KM-90), the upper right features an eagle and child (representing the arms of the Derby family), the lower left a lion (representing the Atholl family), and the lower right quarter the Manx triskeles. The scroll under the shield bears the motto in Manx KIANNOORTYS CHEUS THIE JEH KIANNOORTYS (Government within a Government). KM-655 marks the 100th anniversary of Douglas as the capital city of the Isle of Man.

T-6 America's Cup – Sailboats and Map

KM-179 ● 1 crown ● 1987 copper-nickel, issued also in silver clad copper-nickel, .925 silver and .999 palladium
KM-308 ● 5 crowns ● 1987 .999 silver, 65 mm
KM-309 ● 10 crowns ● 1987 .999 silver, 75 mm

The reverse features three sailboats and a map of Australia that denotes Fremantle in Western Australia. The coin marks the race that took place in February 1987 off Fremantle in which Dennis Conner and the crew of *Stars and Stripes* representing the San Diego Yacht Club won back the America's Cup from *Kookaburra III* which represented the Australian Yacht Club. *Stars and Stripes* had a winged keel and a special rounded nose, designed by the use of computer techniques. Her name is a nickname for the flag of the United States. Prior to the America's Cup races *Stars and Stripes* had won the Louis Vuitton Cup races in which 13 boats from six countries competed to determine which sloop would challenge the Australian boat that represented the holder of the America's Cup. The competing boats were of the 12-meter class, their design based on a formula that takes into account length, sail area, freeboard and a girth measurement, with the results of the calculation not to exceed 12 meters (39 ft). The design was also subject to other limitations. The boats were 60–70 ft (18–21 m) long and could reach a speed of 12 knots. Their main sail area was usually about 1,200 sq ft (111 m^2) and that of their jib ranged from 500 sq ft (46 m^2) to over 1,200 sq ft (111 m^2). Conner, sailing in *Liberty* for the New York Yacht Club, had lost the Cup in 1983 to John Bertrand in *Australia II* who sailed for the Royal Perth Yacht Club. The reverse inscription is THE AMERICA'S CUP CHALLENGE – FREMANTLE.

T-7 America's Cup and Sailboats

KM-180 ● 5 crowns ● 1987 .999 silver, 65 mm
KM-183 ● 1 crown ● 1987 copper-nickel, issued also in .925 silver and .999 palladium
KM-300 ● 10 crowns ● 1987 .999 silver, 75 mm

The reverse depicts the America's Cup trophy (*see* Bahamas KM-100) against the background of two competing sailboats. The reverse inscription is THE AMERICA'S CUP CHALLENGE – FREMANTLE.

KM-184
1 crown 1987 copper-nickel, 38.6 mm

T-8 America's Cup and Statue of Liberty

KM-181 ● 10 crowns ● 1987 .999 silver, 75 mm
KM-184 ● 1 crown ● 1987 copper-nickel, issued also in .925 silver and .999 palladium
KM-299 ● 5 crowns ● 1987 .999 silver, 65 mm

The reverse depicts two sailboats participating in the America's Cup race of 1887 in the harbor of New York against the background of the Statue of Liberty, which had been completed the year before (*see* United States KM-212). The race was won by Henry Haff in *Volunteer* for the United States. He competed with John Barr in *Thistle* who sailed for Scotland. The reverse inscription is THE AMERICA'S CUP CHALLENGE – FREMANTLE.

T-9 200th Anniversary of Steam Navigation – *Queen Mary*

KM-206 ● 5 crowns ● 1988 .999 silver, 65 mm
KM-232 ● 1 crown ● 1988 copper-nickel

KM-232
1 crown
1988 copper-nickel, 38.6 mm

The reverse features the 81,237-ton ocean liner RMS *Queen Mary*, built by John Brown & Co., Clydebank, Glasgow for Cunard White Star Ltd. The ship was launched in 1934 by Queen Mary, the consort of King George V. She is 1,020 ft (311 m) long, has a beam of 119 ft (36 m), and draws 39 ft (12 m) of water. She reached a speed of 32 knots. She could accommodate 2,139 passengers in cabin class, tourist class and third class, and had a crew of 1,101 men, including 750 "hotel" staff. *Queen Mary* made her maiden voyage in 1936 from Southampton to New York. At the time she was the ultimate in size, speed and luxury. She was built to take the Blue Riband (*see* KM-231), which she held from 1936 to 1937 when she lost it to the French liner *Normandie* (*see* France KM-1341), and from 1938 to 1952 when she lost it to the US liner *United States* (*see* Congo-Kinshasa KM-26). In World War II *Queen Mary* was conscripted and converted to carry troops—15,000 at a time in summer, 12,000–13,000 in winter. She and her sister ship RMS *Queen Elizabeth* together transported 320,000 of the 856,000 American troops sent to Britain. After the war *Queen Mary* reverted to her transatlantic passenger liner role until 1967 when, after having made 1,001 Atlantic crossings, she was sold to the City of Long Beach, California to become a shipping museum, hotel and convention center. Some 1,000 couples a year get married in her chapel.

T-10 200th Anniversary of Australia

KM-223 ● 1 crown ● 1988 copper-nickel, issued also in .999 silver
KM-258 ● 10 crowns ● 1988 .999 silver, 75 mm
KM-287 ● $^1/_2$ crown ● 1988 .948 gold
KM-360 ● $^1/_2$ crown ● 1988 .999 platinum

The reverse depicts a koala in a tree, in the background one of the ships of the First Fleet anchoring in Sydney Cove (*see* Australia KM-103) and at left the hoisting of the Union Jack, the flag of Great Britain, upon arrival of the fleet in Australia. "First Fleet" is the name given to the squadron of ships which arrived in Australia in 1788 to found a penal colony at Botany Bay in New South Wales.

T-11 America's Cup – Sailboats and *Star of India*

KM-326
1 crown
1992 copper-nickel, 38.6 mm

KM-302 ● 1/5 crown ● 1991 .999 gold (est. 250 pcs.)
KM-320 ● 1 crown ● 1991 copper-nickel, issued also in .925 silver (est. 115 pcs.)
KM-321 ● 5 crowns ● 1991 .999 silver, 65 mm (est. 15 pcs.)
KM-322 ● 1/25 crown ● 1992 .999 gold
KM-323 ● 1/10 crown ● 1992 .999 gold, issued also in .999 platinum
KM-324 ● 1/5 crown ● 1992 .999 gold
KM-325 ● 1/2 crown ● 1992 .999 gold
KM-326 ● 1 crown ● 1992 copper-nickel, issued also in .925 silver and .999 gold
KM-327 ● 5 crowns ● 1992 .999 silver, 65 mm

The reverse features two competing sailboats and the *Star of India* (*see* KM-523) in a medallion. The *Star of India* was built in 1863 and is the world's oldest seagoing merchant sailing ship. She is now a floating museum in San Diego, California—the venue at which the 28th America's Cup races were held in 1992. The reverse legend on the 1991 coins is AMERICA'S CUP CHALLENGE SAN DIEGO 1992. The reverse legend on the 1992 coins is XXVIII AMERICA'S CUP SAN DIEGO 1992. Neither the *Standard Catalog of World Coins* nor Schön's German-language catalog of world coins provide illustrations for all of the coins. Therefore part of the details mentioned is conjectural and may be incorrect.

T-12 200th Anniversary of the Death of Robert Burns – Ships

KM-578
1 crown
1996 copper-nickel, 38.6 mm

KM-574 ● 1/5 crown ● 1996 .999 gold
KM-578 ● 1 crown ● 1996 copper-nickel, issued also in .925 silver

The reverse depicts two sailing ships—one of them run aground—and armed persons standing in the water. One of the ships is the smuggling brig *Rosamond* of Plymouth, about 100 tons burden. Robert Burns, Scotland's national bard (1759–1796), was a customs officer in Dumfries, southwestern Scotland. In February 1792, *Rosamond* struck a shoal in the Solway Firth on the border with England. While waiting for the tide to lift her off the ship was assaulted by three teams of excisemen, one of which was commanded by Burns. During the assault the excise officers found themselves wading chest-deep into the cold waters of the Solway. This scene is depicted on the reverse. The smugglers escaped to England by leaving the ship on her opposite side. *Rosamond* with her cargo was confiscated and auctioned off. The sale realized £167. About this incident Burns wrote the poem *The de'il awa wi' th' Exciseman*. Burns is best known for *Auld Lang Syne*

(Times Gone By), an old Scottish song transcribed by Burns; the song is traditionally sung at midnight on New Year's Eve.

T-13 Circulation Coins

KM-591 ● 10 pence ● 1996–97 copper-nickel, Queen's portrait by Raphael Makhlouf, issued also in .925 silver
KM-903 ● 10 pence ● 1998–99 copper-nickel, Queen's portrait by Ian Rank-Broadley, varieties exist

The reverse features a sailboat.

KM-591
10 pence
1996 copper-nickel, 25 mm

T-14 50th Anniversary of D-Day – *Ben-My-Chree IV*

KM-695 ● 1 crown ● 1994 copper-nickel, issued also in .925 silver
KM-703 ● 1 crown ● 1994 .999 gold

The reverse depicts the troop ship HMS *Ben-My-Chree* and, in front of her, LCAs (Landing Craft, Assault). The 2,586-ton TSS (twin screw steamer) *Ben-My-Chree* was built in 1927 by Cammell Laird & Co. Ltd. at Birkenhead, England for the Isle of Man Steam Packet Company at a cost of £200,000—the fourth ship of this name that was owned by the company. She was 366 ft (112 m) long and 46 ft (14 m) in beam, and had a draft of some 18 ft (5.6 m). She could carry 2,495 passengers, of whom 1,642 in first class and 853 in third class. She made an average speed of 22 knots. Her name means "Woman of My Heart" in Manx. She was regularly used to ferry people, cars and goods between England and the Isle of Man until she was requisitioned for war service in 1940 and became a troop transport. In 1944 she was converted to carry landing craft. On D-Day, 6 June 1944, she saw action off the Normandy coast, taking US Rangers to Omaha Beach. After the war she returned to the passenger trade. She was broken up in 1965. The Rangers were US Army elite troops that had been trained in specialized assault tactics and equipped with ladders and ropes to scale cliffs. On Omaha Beach they were assigned the task to destroy German guns located at the top of a 125-ft (38-m)-high cliff prominence known as Pointe-du-Hoc.

T-15 50th Anniversary of D-Day – Omaha Beach

KM-696 ● 1 crown ● 1994 copper-nickel, issued also in .925 silver
KM-704 ● 1 crown ● 1994 .999 gold

The reverse depicts American troops disembarking from an LCVP at Omaha Beach on the Normandy coast on D-Day, 6 June 1944, and in the background at sea another LCVP. The LCVPs (Landing Craft, Vehicles and Personnel) were manufactured according to a design by Andrew Jackson Higgins of New Orleans, Louisiana. The Higgins

Industries LCVP was 36 ft (11 m) long and had a beam of 11 ft (3.3 m). Its draft was 3 ft (0.9 m) aft and 2 ft 2 inches (0.7 m) forward. It displaced 15,000 pounds (6.8 tons) and could make 12 knots. The boat had a crew of three or four—a coxswain, an engineer and one or two deck hands. It was basically constructed of wood, had a bow ramp and was used in transporting fully armed troops, light vehicles, and other equipment and supplies essential to amphibious operations. It could land a platoon of 36 men with their equipment, or a jeep and 12 men, or 8,100 pounds (3.7 tons) of cargo. The highly maneuverable boat was designed to beach, lower a ramp, discharge men and cargo, retract, and return to its transport to get more troops and/or supplies. The transports carried the boat on deck or in davits. The LCVPs made the D-Day landings possible by allowing Allied commanders to land troops on less-fortified beaches rather than be forced to capture enemy-held ports with facilities to offload men and matériel and sweep harbors of mines before landing an assault force. The boats served also as tugs, water ambulances, ferries and lifeboats. In the last years of the war they took a major part in the Allied amphibious operations. In the years 1942–1945, 23,358 LCVPs were built at the eight New Orleans plants of Higgins Industries which employed more than 20,000 workers, and by other plants licensed to use the designs. "Higgins boats" landed more Allied troops during World War II than all other types of landing craft combined. In addition to various types of landing craft, Higgins Industries also manufactured high-speed PT boats, antisubmarine boats, dispatch boats, freight supply vessels, and patrol craft. The company's total output during the war was 20,094 boats. A replica of an LCVP has been built for display at the National D-Day Museum in New Orleans.

T-16 50th Anniversary of D-Day – British Troops

KM-699 ● 1 crown ● 1994 copper-nickel, issued also in .925 silver
KM-707 ● 1 crown ● 1994 .999 gold

The reverse depicts British troops storming a beach, in the background at left the LCVP (*see* T-15) that has taken them to the beach, and at right an LSM with its ramp down. The LSM (Landing Ship Medium) was an ocean-going tank landing ship that could carry five medium tanks, or three heavy tanks, or six LVTs (Landing Vehicle, Tracked), or nine DUKWs (amphibious trucks), or any other cargo not exceeding 165 tons, to maintain landing draft. The LSM was 204 ft (62 m) long and 35 ft (11 m) in the beam. When fully loaded it displaced 1,095 tons and had a draft of 8 ft 3 inches (2.5 m) aft and 6 ft 4 inches (1.9 m) forward. Its speed was 13 knots. Its complement numbered 58. The first LSM was built in 1944. Its construction lasted 80 days but some shipyards later managed to reduce the construction period to 53 days. The coins mark the landings on the Normandy coast on D-Day, 6 June 1944. British troops landed on the Gold and Sword Beaches (*see* Great Britain KM-966).

T-17 50th Anniversary of D-Day – Dwight Eisenhower

KM-700 ● 1 crown ● 1994 copper-nickel, issued also in .925 silver
KM-708 ● 1 crown ● 1994 .999 gold

The reverse depicts US General Dwight D. Eisenhower (*see* Gibraltar T-17) observing a landing on the Normandy coast during the D-Day landings. The silhouette of a ship can be discerned on the horizon in the center of the reverse; a landing craft is depicted more to the left in the middle of the background scene; and the troops still more to the left in the foreground are standing in a landing craft, probably an LCVP (Landing Craft, Vehicles and Personnel), of which the coin shows only the bow and ramp area.

T-18 50th Anniversary of D-Day – Omar Bradley

KM-701 ● 1 crown ● 1994 copper-nickel, issued also in .925 silver
KM-709 ● 1 crown ● 1994 .999 gold

The reverse depicts US Lieutenant General Omar N. Bradley (1893–1981) observing a landing on the Fox Green Beach in Normandy. The landing scene includes two ships, in the foreground at right. At Normandy, Bradley was the commanding general of the US 1st Army that made landings at Omaha and Utah Beaches. Fox Green Beach was part of the Omaha Beach Head. Bradley was made army chief of staff in 1948 and became chairman of the joint chiefs of staff in 1949.

T-19 50th Anniversary of D-Day – Bernard Montgomery

KM-702 ● 1 crown ● 1994 copper-nickel, issued also in .925 silver
KM-710 ● 1 crown ● 1994 .999 gold
KM-? ● 1/2 crown ● 1994 gold

The reverse depicts British General Bernard L. Montgomery (1887–1976) observing the landings on the Normandy coast. At the very left of the landing scene troops are disembarking from HMCS *LCI(L)* 299—HMCS being short for His Majesty's Canadian Ship and LCI(L) for Landing Craft, Infantry (Large). The ship was built in 1943 by New Jersey Shipbuilding in Barber, New Jersey and displaced 389 tons (loaded). Her length was 158 ft (48 m), her beam 23 ft (7.1 m) and her draft (loaded) was almost 6 ft (1.8 m). She could make a speed of 16 knots, had a complement of 23, and could transport 188 troops. Her cargo capacity was 75 tons. Upon completion she was transferred to the United Kingdom. During most of 1944 she was commissioned in the Canadian Navy. During the D-Day landings, *LCI(L)* 299 landed troops of the Stormont Dundas Glengarrian

Highlanders of Canada on the Nan White sector of Juno Beach in Normandy. After the war, in 1946, she was returned to US Naval custody and in that same year she was transferred to France, designated *LC-1299*, to be used for spare parts. She was scrapped at an unknown date. During World War II, 923 LCI(L) were built in the United States by ten shipyards. They had a double bottom, and when approaching the beach the troops moved to the stern, so that bows of the landing craft would rise in the water and the craft could ram beach obstructions, ride over them and land the troops with the least possible human loss. Montgomery had commanded the British 8th Army at the battle of El Alamein in North Africa and during the landings in Italy, and in 1944 was commander of the 21st Army Group which consisted of all Allied ground forces that took part in the invasion of Normandy ("Operation Overlord"). Later he was promoted to Field Marshal.

T-20 Famous Explorers – Martin Frobisher

KM-1078 • 1/5 crown • 2001 .999 gold
KM-1080 • 1 crown • 2001 copper-nickel, issued also in .925 silver

KM-1080
1 crown
2001 copper-nickel, 38.6 mm

The reverse depicts the English navigator, explorer and naval officer Martin Frobisher (circa 1535–1594) and one of his ships on his voyages from England to northeastern Canada in 1576–1578 above a map. The map shows the route of Frobisher's three voyages to find the Northwest Passage from Europe to the East Indies. On his first voyage, in 1576, Frobisher's fleet consisted of *Gabriel* of 20 tons, *Michael* of 25 tons and a smaller pinnace the name of which is not known. The two ships together carried only 35 men. The pinnace was lost in a storm. *Michael* returned to England because of the heavy ice near Greenland. Frobisher in *Gabriel* discovered a large bay on southeastern Baffin Island, which was later named for him. He thought this to be the passage to Cathay, as China was then known. He took possession of the island in the name of Queen Elizabeth I and returned to England with some mineral samples. An "expert" found that they contained gold but actually it was iron pyrite ("fool's gold"). The next year Frobisher, who had been named Admiral of Cathay by the queen, made his second voyage, to bring more of that rich ore for the newly formed Cathay Company. His fleet consisted of *Ayde* (Aid), a vessel of some 200 tons provided by the queen, *Gabriel* and *Michael*. The 120 men in the fleet included 30 soldiers and eleven gentlemen. The three ships returned with some 200 tons of the worthless ore which they mined from Baffin Island. The investors, assuming that Frobisher had just mined in the wrong place, financed also his third expedition. It set off in 1578 and consisted of 15 ships, including the three ships of the second voyage. *Ayde* was the flagship. Frobisher set up a temporary mining settlement near what is now known as Frobisher Bay and returned with more than 1,300 tons of the ore, still believing it to contain precious metals and causing a 16th-century gold rush. Later, in 1585, Frobisher was a vice admiral for Sir Francis Drake's voyage to the West Indies. Frobisher participated in several battles against the Spanish. He was knighted for his part in the destruction of the armada in 1588. He died at sea in another battle with Spanish ships.

T-21 Famous Explorers – Roald Amundsen

KM-1079 ● 1/5 crown ● 2001 .999 gold
KM-1081 ● 1 crown ● 2001 copper-nickel, issued also in .925 silver

KM-1081
1 crown
2001 copper-nickel, 38.6 mm

The reverse depicts the Norwegian polar explorer Roald Amundsen (1872–1928) with his ship *Fram*, a map that denotes her route to the South Pole, three dogs at left below and the dirigible *Norge* at left above. The ship and the dirigible represent Amundsen's achievements with regard to respectively the South Pole and the North Pole—in 1911 Amundsen in *Fram* (*see* Norway KM-459) was the first man to reach the South Pole with the use of a dog sled (*see* Zambia KM-100) and in 1926 he directed the first ever flight over the North Pole by the dirigible *Norge* (*see* Russia Y-462).

T-22 140th Anniversary of the Launching of the *Star of India*

KM-1174 ● 1 crown ● 2003 copper-nickel, issued also in .925 silver
KM-? ● 1/5 crown ● 2003 .999 gold

KM-1174
1 crown
2003 copper-nickel, 38.6 mm

The reverse depicts the sailing ship *Star of India*, the world's oldest seagoing merchant sailing ship that was built on the Isle of Man in 1863 (*see* KM-523).

T-23 400th Anniversary of the Death of Queen Elizabeth I

KM-1184 ● 130 crowns ● 2003 .999 silver with gold-plated medallion portrait and an embedded ruby, 130 mm, 4000 gr
KM-? ● 32 crowns ● 2003 .999 gold, 100 mm, 1000 gr

The reverse features a medallion portrait of Queen Elizabeth I (1533–1603, queen of England from 1558) surrounded by two of the naval vessels in her fleet, at 4 o'clock and at 11 o'clock; a compass at 2 o'clock; a sextant at 8 o'clock; and four portraits. The portraits are those of William Shakespeare at 12 o'clock; Sir Francis Drake (*see* Great Britain KM-844) at 3 o'clock; Henry VIII, King of England, at 6 o'clock; and Sir Walter Raleigh (*see* Cook Islands KM-188) at

9 o'clock. The English dramatist William Shakespeare (1564–1616) is England's greatest writer. Thirty-six plays by him, in whole or part, survive. His works have been translated into nearly every language in the world. Henry VIII (1491–1547, king from 1509) was Queen Elizabeth's father. He initiated the English Reformation and became the head of the English Church that broke with Rome. The schism with Rome enabled the king to divorce his first wife, Catherine of Aragon. His five other wives were Anne Boleyn, the mother of Elizabeth I, who was beheaded; Jane Seymour, the mother of Edward VI, who died in childbirth; Anne of Cleves, who was divorced; Catherine Howard, who was beheaded; and Catherine Parr, who outlived the king. The gold-plated medallion portrait of Queen Elizabeth on KM-1184 has a .035 carat ruby embedded in the queen's forehead.

T-24 200th Anniversary of the Battle of Trafalgar – Battle Scene With Portraits

KM-1221 ● 1 crown ● 2005 copper-nickel, issued also in .925 silver
KM-? ● 64 crowns ● 2005 .999 silver with gold-plated inscriptions, 140 mm, 2000 gr

The reverse depicts a scene of the battle of Trafalgar of 1805 (*see* Gibraltar KM-12) and medallion portraits of Vice Admiral Lord Horatio Nelson at right and Emperor Napoleon Bonaparte at left. The scene displays ship-to-ship action as the British and the combined French–Spanish fleets sailed into the battle. Trafalgar was the most decisive battle in Britain's war against France. Nelson was the commander of the British fleet and was killed in the battle. Napoleon (1769–1821) was emperor of the French in the years 1804–1815. On the 64-crown coin the inscriptions NAPOLEON and NELSON below the medallions and Nelson's signature below the battle scene are gold-plated.

T-25 200th Anniversary of the Battle of Trafalgar – Battle Scene Without Portraits

KM-? ● 1/25 crown ● 2005 .999 gold
KM-? ● 1/10 crown ● 2005 .999 gold
KM-? ● 1/5 crown ● 2005 .999 gold, also issued in .999 platinum
KM-? ● 1 crown ● 2005 copper-nickel, issued also in .925 silver

The reverse features HMS *Victory* cutting the French line at the battle of Trafalgar (*see* Gibraltar KM-12) above Vice Admiral Lord Horatio Nelson's signature. The signature on one or more of the issues is struck into a piece of copper embedded in the coin which originates from *Victory*'s hull. The inscription around the rim on the reverse is THE BICENTENARY OF TRAFALGAR, the inscription below the battle scene reads THE BATTLE OF TRAFALGAR 1805.

T-26 175th Anniversary of the Isle of Man Steam Packet Company – *King Orry III*

KM-? • 1 crown • 2005 copper-nickel, issued also in .925 silver
KM-? • $^1/_5$ crown • 2005 gold

KM-?
1 crown
2005 copper-nickel, 38.6 mm

The reverse depicts the 1,877-ton HMS *King Orry* leading the German fleet into Scapa Flow in November 1918. *King Orry* was built in 1913 for the Isle of Man Steam Packet Company by Cammell Laird & Co. Ltd. Her length was 313 ft (95 m), her beam 43 ft (13 m) and her draft 17 ft (5.2 m). She made 21 knots and carried 1,600 passengers—884 in first class, 716 in third class. She was the third *King Orry* of the packet company, named for the Viking leader King Gorry whose name in old Manx was pronounced King Orry and who is also known as King Godred Crovan (ruled 1066–1087). In World War I, *King Orry* was one of the 11 ships out of the packet company's fleet of 15 that was requisitioned by the British government. She was fitted out as an armed boarding vessel and was attached to the British Grand Fleet. From the harbor at Scapa Flow in the Orkney Islands off the northeast coast of Scotland that was Britain's chief northern naval base during the war, *King Orry* was engaged on patrol duty. She intercepted and captured many ships carrying contraband to Germany, at least once disguised as a merchant vessel named *Viking Orry* by adding two letters in front of her name. She was also employed in towing targets for practicing gun fire by Royal Navy battleships. During the war she covered a total of more than fifty thousand miles (eighty thousand km). In recognition of the part played in the war by British merchant ships, *King Orry* was awarded the honor of leading the disarmed German fleet into internment at Scapa Flow at the end of the war, which is the scene depicted on the reverse. (Ten months later the German admiral in command—having waited for the bulk of the British fleet to leave on exercises—gave the order to scuttle the 74 ships to deny them to his enemy; 52 ships sank, the rest were beached.) At the outbreak of World War II *King Orry* was requisitioned once again to serve as an armed boarding vessel. At Dunkirk she saved many thousands of soldiers but on her second voyage to that harbor she sank after a German air attack, becoming one of the four vessels of the packet company lost at the evacuation.

T-27 175th Anniversary of the Isle of Man Steam Packet Company – The First and the Latest Ship

KM-? • 1 crown • 2005 copper-nickel, issued also in .925 silver
KM-? • $^1/_5$ crown • 2005 gold

The reverse features conjoined images of the 411-ft (125-m)-long MV *Ben-My-Chree* built in 1998 and the rather diminutive 116-ft (35-

m)-long paddle steamer *Mona's Isle* built in 1830 (*see* T-2) against the background of the Tower of Refuge in Douglas Bay (*see* KM-167). They are respectively the latest addition to the fleet of the Isle of Man Steam Packet Company and its first vessel. The company maintains the ferry service to and from the Isle of Man across the Irish Sea. *Ben-My-Chree* ("Woman of My Heart" in Manx) is the sixth ferry of this name owned by the company and the second ferry of this name to be depicted on a coin (*Ben-My-Chree IV* is featured on T-14). *Ben-My-Chree VI* was built in 1998 for the company by Van der Giessen de Noord B.V. in The Netherlands at a cost of 40 million US dollars. Her registered tonnage is 12,503. She is 411 ft (125 m) long and 77 ft (23 m) in the beam, and has a draft of 19 ft (5.8 m). She has a crew of 15 and makes a speed of 19 knots. *Ben-My-Chree* is operated as a combined car/passenger ferry with large freight decks and limited passenger accommodation for people wishing to travel with their cars. She has a total trailer lane capacity of 4,050 ft (1,235 m) for 275 cars and can carry up to 500 passengers—80 in cabins, the others in ordinary seating. The ferry is the flagship of the packet company and the largest ship ever to operate to the Isle of Man. On workdays she makes four daily crossings, two in each direction, between Douglas on the Isle of Man and Heysham in Lancashire in the north of England. The passage, which is 60 miles (111 km) long, takes approximately 3.5 hours. In the weekends the ferry is operated on the service from Douglas to Liverpool.

KM-?
1 crown
2005 copper-nickel, 38.6 mm

T-28 200th Anniversary of the Battle of Trafalgar – Horatio Nelson

KM-? ● 1 crown ● 2005 copper-nickel, issued also in .925 silver
KM-? ● 1/25 crown ● 2005 .999 gold

The reverse depicts Vice Admiral Lord Horatio Nelson (*see* Gibraltar KM-12) with a warship in the background and his official signature below his portrait.

T-29 200th Anniversary of the Death of Horatio Nelson – Battle of Cape St. Vincent

KM-? ● 1 crown ● 2005 copper-nickel, issued also in .925 silver

The reverse depicts the British 100-gun HMS *Victory* and the Spanish 112-gun *Salvadore del Mundo* at the battle of Cape St. Vincent of 1797 (*see* Gibraltar KM-605) and, at the bottom, the official signature of Vice Admiral Lord Horatio Nelson, *Nelson & Bronte*, above the year 1805. Nelson was killed at the battle of Trafalgar in 1805. *Victory* (*see* Gibraltar KM-12) was the flagship of Admiral Sir John Jervis at the battle of Cape St. Vincent. The 2,398-ton *Salvadore del Mundo* was built in 1787. She was 190 ft (58 m) long, had a beam of 54 ft (17 m) and drew 23 ft (7.1 m) of water. The reverse design is probably based on *The* Victory *Raking the Spanish at the Battle of Cape St Vincent, 14 February, 1797* painted in oil in 1798 by Robert Cleveley. The painting, which is in the collection of the National Maritime Museum, London, shows the commencement of the action at St. Vincent, at the point when the *Victory* raked the *Salvadore del Mundo*, causing her to strike her flag. The Spanish ship is shown in the right foreground, her stern swathed in the smoke of *Victory*'s broadside. In both the left and the right background other groups of ships are in action. Cleveley was a marine painter who specialized in naval battle scenes. *Salvadore del Mundo* served in the Royal Navy until she was broken up in 1815.

T-30 200th Anniversary of the Death of Horatio Nelson – Battle of the Nile

KM-? ● 1 crown ● 2005 copper-nickel, issued also in .925 silver

The reverse depicts a scene of the battle of the Nile and at the bottom the signature of Rear Admiral Lord Horatio Nelson above the inscription 1805. The design is probably based on the painting *The Destruction of* L'Orient *at the Battle of the Nile, 1 August 1798* by George Arnald in the National Maritime Museum, London. At center left is the French *Orient*, a 118-gun, 2,000-ton ship that had a length of 209 ft (64 m), a beam of 53 ft (16 m) and a draft of 27 ft (8.1 m). She was built by Jacques-Noël Sané at Toulon in 1791 as *Dauphin Royal*, named for the heir apparent to the French throne. In 1792 she was renamed *Sans Culotte* for the revolutionary extremists and in 1795 she became *Orient*. Her complement numbered 1,010. She was the flagship of the fleet in which General Napoleon Bonaparte sailed to Egypt in 1798. After seizing Alexandria, Vice Admiral François-Paul Brueys with 13 ships-of-the-line anchored in the sandy Aboukir Bay, east of Alexandria. Here he was found by Nelson, who ordered five of his ships to make their way inshore and subjected the French line to a simultaneous cannonade from both sides that caused *Orient* to explode. The reverse shows her engulfed in fire and smoke. The ship at center right is the 74-gun, 1,612-ton HMS *Swiftsure*. Her length was 167 ft (51 m) and her beam 46 ft (14 m). Her complement numbered 590. She was built in 1787, captured by France in 1801 and recaptured from the French at Trafalgar in 1805. Renamed HMS *Irresistible* she served as a prison until she was scrapped in 1816. In the foreground are boats with sailors rescuing men from the water. At far left is the French 80-gun *Franklin*, built in Toulon in 1798. She had a complement of 800 and was captured at the battle by the British. Renamed *Canopus* she served in the Royal Navy. In 1863 she became a receiving hulk at Devonport. She was broken up in 1887. The French ship at far right is probably *Tonnant*, a 80-gun, 2,190-ton ship that was 198 ft (60 m) long and had a beam of 51 ft (15 m), a draft of 24 ft (7.2 m), and a complement of 800. She was built in Toulon in 1791. At the battle of the Nile she was captured by the British who commissioned her into the Royal Navy without change of name. In the course of the night Nelson destroyed five ships-of-the-line and took six as prizes; only two French ships-of-the line and two frigates escaped. The French lost 1,400 men, the British 218. Nelson was made Baron Nelson of the Nile.

T-31 200th Anniversary of the Death of Horatio Nelson – Battle of Copenhagen

KM-? ● 1 crown ● 2005 copper-nickel, issued also in .925 silver

The reverse depicts ships of the squadron of Vice Admiral Lord Horatio Nelson bombarding shore defenses during the battle of Copenhagen on 2 April 1801, his signature, and the inscription 1805 which refers to the year of Nelson's death at the battle of Trafalgar. Nelson's flagship at Copenhagen was the 74-gun third-rate HMS *Elephant* that was built by George Parsons in Bursledon, Hampshire in 1786. She was 168 ft (51 m) long and 47 ft (14 m) across the beam. She was broken up in 1830. In 1801 Nelson was second-in-command to Admiral Sir Hyde Parker in an expedition to defeat a coalition of Russia, Sweden, Prussia and Denmark which threatened crucial British interests. Nelson convinced Parker that an attack on the Danish fleet at Copenhagen would be the most effective way to break up the northern league. Nelson made the attack with a squadron that included the 12 ships-of-the-line with the shallowest draft, 5 frigates, 7 bomb ketches and 6 other vessels. The Danish ships, forts and floating batteries returned heavy fire. After four hours of cannonade the battle was still undecided and Parker signaled to discontinue the action. Nelson considered it safer to continue firing rather than having his men raising sail to withdraw. It is told that he ignored Parker's signal by putting his telescope up to his right eye—the sight in which had been badly damaged in 1794 by stone splinters from a wall struck by an enemy shell—claiming that he did not see the signal and remarking that he had a blind eye and sometimes had a right to use it. An hour later most of the Danish ships had ceased fire or surrendered. Nelson sent a message ashore suggesting a ceasefire, which was agreed to by Crown Prince Frederick, regent for King Christian VII of Denmark, who had been watching the battle from the ramparts of the citadel. Danish casualties—killed and wounded—numbered 1,600, those of the British 950. Parker was recalled after the battle. Nelson was appointed commander-in-chief of the fleet in the Baltic in his place and made a viscount.

T-32 200th Anniversary of the Battle of Trafalgar – Horatio Nelson's Funeral

KM-? ● 1 crown ● 2005 copper-nickel, issued also in .925 silver

The reverse depicts Charles II's royal barge and other rowboats taking part in the funeral procession of Vice Admiral Lord Horatio Nelson against the background of Greenwich Hospital, his signature below, and the year of his death, 1805, in the exergue. The design is probably based on the engraving *Nelson's Funeral Procession on the Thames* by Augustus Charles Pugin in the collection of the National Maritime Museum, London. The royal barge of Charles II (1630–1685, king of England from 1660) was built during his reign as king. Its length is probably about 29 ft (8.8 m) and its beam about 6 ft (1.8 m). It had eight oars with one man per oar. The barge was lent for the funeral by King George III. At the funeral it was accompanied by over 60 rowboats, including 16 other principal barges and smaller craft and gunboats that followed the procession up river. Among the barges were those of the king, the admiralty and the lord mayor of London, and those of the fishmongers, goldsmiths, skinners, merchant tailors, ironmongers, stationers and apothecaries. Nelson died on HMS *Victory* during the battle of Trafalgar on 21 October 1805 (*see* Gibraltar KM-12). His body—preserved in brandy—was placed in a coffin made of timber cut from a chunk of *Orient*'s mainmast that had landed on HMS *Swiftsure* which he had received as a memento of the battle of the Nile. Nelson's remains were brought to Gibraltar where the brandy was replaced by spirits of wine for the journey to Britain. The body was laid in state for three days at the Painted Hall at Greenwich Hospital where about 100,000 people came to pay their respects. On 8 January 1806 seamen from the *Victory* carried the coffin to the funeral barge to begin the three-hour procession up the Thames River from the hospital to the admiralty buildings. Nelson was buried the next day in the crypt of St. Paul's Cathedral. It was the last full heraldic funeral staged in Britain and the largest ever. The barge was preserved as a Nelson relic and is now on display in the Royal Naval Museum in Portsmouth.

ITALY

The Italian Republic is situated in southern Europe. Its mainland is a peninsula that is bordered by the Tyrrhenian Sea in the west, the Adriatic Sea in the east and the Ionian Sea in the south. Italy was a kingdom in the years 1861–1946. In ancient times, Italy was the core of the Roman Republic and the Roman Empire between the 4th century BCE and the 5th century CE.

Circulation Coins

KM-40 • 1 centesimo • 1908–18 bronze
KM-41 • 2 centesimi • 1908–17 bronze
KM-42 • 5 centesimi • 1908–18 bronze
KM-43 • 10 centesimi • 1908 bronze

The reverse shows Italia standing on the prow of a galley and, in the background at left, two indiscernible sailing vessels under sail. Italia, the personification of the country, holds a laurel branch in her right hand. KM-40 and KM-41 are composed of 96 percent copper and 4 percent tin, the other two coins of 95 percent copper, 4 percent tin and one percent zinc. Thus all four coins are bronze, rather than copper as listed in some catalogs. KM-43 is rare as only a few pieces were struck to mark the placing of the foundation stone of the new building of the Mint in Rome.

50th Anniversary of the Kingdom of Italy

KM-51 • 10 centesimi • 1911 copper
KM-52 • 2 lire • 1911 .835 silver

The reverse depicts two allegorical figures, an unidentified sailing vessel at a quay in the background and a plow at right in the foreground. The female figure in front is standing, while behind her a personification of maritime Italy is sitting on a pedestal.

50th Anniversary of the Kingdom of Italy

KM-53 • 5 lire • 1911 .900 silver
KM-54 • 50 lire • 1911 .900 gold

The reverse depicts two allegorical figures, in the background at left a steamship with four smokestacks at a quay, and in the foreground at left a plow. One of the allegorical figures is a woman standing with her arms outstretched and behind her is Italia sitting on a pedestal.

Circulation Coin

KM-72 • 100 lire • 1931–33 = years IX–XI of the fascist era, .900 gold

The reverse depicts Italia standing on the prow of a galley, a laurel branch in her right hand and a torch in her left. A fasces (the bundle of rods containing an axe with the blade protruding that symbolized the authority of ancient Roman magistrates) decorates the prow. This symbol was adopted by the followers of Benito Mussolini (1883–1945). Following their march on Rome in October 1922, Mussolini became the head of a fascist government. The Roman numeral "IX" or "X" on the reverse under the year 1931 ("X" on the coins of 1932; "XI" on those of 1933) denotes the number of years since the establishment of the fascist government. The fascist era started in October 1922, year 1 corresponding to 1922/23. Thus, for any calendar year, there can be two different fascist era years. Italy struck coins with double dating—common calendar and fascist era—in the years 1927–1943.

Circulation Coin

KM-80 ● 10 lire ● 1936–41 = years XIV–XX of the fascist era, .835 silver

The reverse depicts Italia on the prow of a galley. In her right hand she holds a fasces and in her left a statue of a winged Nike standing on a globe. The obverse legend on the previous coins was VITTORIO EMANVELE III RE D'ITALIA (Victor Emmanuel III, King of Italy). Following the occupation of Ethiopia by Italian troops and the proclamation of Italy's king as emperor of Ethiopia in 1936 to replace Emperor Haile Selassie, the obverse legend is now VITTORIO EMANVELE III RE E IMPERATORE (Victor Emmanuel III, King and Emperor).

Circulation Coin

KM-98 ● 500 lire ● 1958–2001 .835 silver

The obverse depicts the ships of the Genovese discoverer Christopher Columbus on his voyage to America in 1492—*Santa Maria*, *Niña* and *Pinta* (*see* Andorra KM-78). The reverse features the portrait of a woman dressed and coiffured in Renaissance style surrounded by 19 shields. The portrait is taken from a bronze marriage anniversary medal designed by Pietro Giampaoli, chief engraver of the Rome Mint. The model was his wife Letizia Savonitto. The shields are those of cities and regions. From the bottom on the left they are those of Genoa (capital of the Liguria region), Turin (capital of Piedmont), Aosta (capital of Valle d'Aosta), Milan (capital of Lombardy), Trento (capital of Trentino-Alto Adige), Venice (capital of Veneto or Venetia), Trieste and Udine in the Friuli-Venezia Giulia region, Bologna (capital of Emilia-Romagna), Florence (capital of Tuscany), Ancona (capital of Marche or The Marches), Perugia (capital of Umbria), Rome (capital of Lazio or Latium), L'Aquila (capital of Abruzzi), Naples (capital of Campania), Bari (capital of Apulia), Potenza (capital of Basilicata), Catanzaro (capital of Calabria), Sicily, and Cagliari (capital of Sardinia). The shield representing the 20th of Italy's 20 regions, Molise, is hidden by the exergue under the woman's bust. The date appears on the edge of the coin in raised lettering.

100th Anniversary of the Taranto Naval Yard

KM-130 ● 200 lire ● 1989 aluminum-bronze

The reverse depicts a sailing ship passing a drawbridge. Taranto is a well-protected naval base in southern Italy at the end of a roadstead that is closed at the seaward end by two fortified islands. The city was founded by Greek settlers in the 7th century BCE.

500th Anniversary of the Discovery of America – 1989 Issue

KM-139 ● 500 lire ● 1989 .835 silver

The reverse depicts three ships in the harbor of Genoa. The design is based on a 15th-century painting. The obverse features a portrait of Christopher Columbus (1451–1506) (*see* Andorra KM-78) on an astrolabe background. Columbus was born in Genoa in 1451 and discovered America in 1492. The reverse legend is V CENTENARIO DELLA SCOPERTA DELL' AMERICA (5th Centennial of the Discovery of America).

500th Anniversary of the Discovery of America – 1990 Issue

KM-140 ● 500 lire ● 1990 .835 silver

The reverse features a medallion with a caravel. The design commemorates the voyage in 1492 by Christopher Columbus (1451–1506) during which he discovered America (*see* Andorra KM-78). The reverse depicts a bust of Columbus and a map of the New World in a medallion. The reverse legend is V CENTENARIO DELLA SCOPERTA DELL' AMERICA (5th Centennial of the Discovery of America).

250th Anniversary of the Death of Antonio Vivaldi

KM-141 ● 500 lire ● 1991 .835 silver

The reverse depicts the bow of a gondola against the background of the Rialto bridge in Venice and a music staff at the top. A typical gondola is a 32-ft (9.8-m)-long flat-bottomed boat that carries two to six passengers. Its design is peculiar to the canals and lagoon of Venice and is more than 700 years old. A prominent steel beak rises from the prow and a lesser one from the stern. A single rower, the gondolier, who stands near the stern, propels the boat by using a single sweep which also acts as rudder. Thanks to an efficient rowing technique, a good gondolier doesn't exert any more effort pushing a half-ton boat with three people than he would walking.

In the 17th century, the time of the mighty Venetian Republic, as many as 10,000 gondolas weaved their way through the city's canals. The present-day Rialto Bridge was built during the years 1588–1592 by Antonio da Ponte. It is hump-backed to allow an armed galley to pass under it. Its central street is lined with shops and gangways on either side that afford views of the Grand Canal, the central artery of Venice. The obverse shows a portrait of the composer and violinist Antonio Vivaldi (1678–1741) playing a violin against the background of the Doge's Palace, the most impressive secular building in Venice. In the period 1703–1738 Vivaldi held a post in Venice at the girls' orphanage Ospedale della Pietà, successively as *maestro di violino*, *maestro de' concerti* and *maestro di cappella*. The reverse legend reads MUSICO DI VIOLINO E MAESTRO DE CONCERTI. The Doge's Palace (Palazzo Ducale) served as the senate house, administrative center, hall of justice, public archive and prison until the fall of the Venetian Republic in 1797. Its façades date from 1309–1424.

500th Anniversary of the Discovery of America – 1992 Issue

KM-150 ● 500 lire ● 1992 .835 silver

The reverse depicts Christopher Columbus and his landing party disembarking from *Santa Maria* upon his arrival in America in 1492 (*see* Andorra KM-78). The obverse features the letter "C" (for Christopher Columbus) formed by a billowing sail of a caravel, a bust of Columbus, and a ship's wheel. The reverse legend reads SCOPERTA DELL' AMERICA 1492 (Discovery of America 1492).

Genova '92

KM-151 ● 200 lire ● 1992 aluminum-bronze

The reverse depicts three stylized sails above four waves—the logo of the Genova '92 stamp exposition held in Genoa in September 1992. The three sails allude to the three ships on the discovery voyage in 1492 of Christopher Columbus, who was born in Genoa in 1451. The reverse inscription reads ESPOSIZIONE MONDIALE DI FILATELIA TEMATICA (World Exposition of Thematic Philately).

900th Anniversary of St. Mark's Basilica in Venice

KM-165 ● 1000 lire ● 1994 .835 silver

The reverse depicts an oared galley of the early Middle Ages representing the ship that brought the remains of the apostle St. Mark to Venice. The obverse depicts the front façade of St. Mark's Basilica in which the saint's body is contained in a sarcophagus. In the year

828 two Venetian merchants stole St. Mark's remains from the church in Alexandria where they were interred to prevent Muslims from desecrating them. Allegedly the merchants packed the remains between slices of pork to deter inspection by Arab customs officers. Construction of the basilica began in order to house the body. This basilica was consecrated in 832 and St. Mark became the patron saint of Venice. His attribute of a winged lion is Venice's official symbol. The present church is a Byzantine building in the form of a Greek cross surmounted by five domes. It was consecrated in 1094 but its decoration was completed only centuries later.

Circulation Coin

KM-183 ● 50 lire ● 1996–2001 copper-nickel

The reverse features a large numeral 50 surrounded by a garland of grapes, vine, olive and oak leaves, a cog wheel, and a boat below.

100th Anniversary of the Italian Naval League

KM-186 ● 200 lire ● 1997 brass

The reverse features a lightship and the logo of the Italian Naval League. The league, an affiliate of the Italian Navy, works under the auspices of Italy's president to advance maritime subjects and to increase awareness of the sea through maritime research.

300th Anniversary of the Birth of Canaletto

KM-189 ● 5000 lire ● 1997 .835 silver

The reverse shows numerous sailboats in the harbor of Venice and in front at right the column in St. Mark's Square that depicts a winged lion, the symbol of St. Mark. The obverse features the portrait of the Venetian painter Giovanni Antonio Canal (1697–1768), known as Canaletto, and at right a view of his city. Canaletto is famous for his precise views of Venetian architecture.

KM-189
5000 lire
1997 .835 silver, 32 mm

Genoa, European Capital of Culture

KM-240 ● 10 euro ● 2004 .925 silver

The obverse shows a collage of sculpture, art works and other design elements connected with Genoa's history, including part of the rigging of a ship. The rigging may allude to Christopher Columbus who was born in the city in 1451. The reverse depicts *La Lanterna*, the city's lighthouse, and a map of the city's harbor. The lighthouse is situated on Capo di Faro (Beacon Promontory) at the western end of the Port of Genoa arc and is 384 ft (117 m) above sea level. Its light can be seen from a distance of 36 nautical miles (67 km).

Europe of the Arts

KM-242 • 20 euro • 2004 – see T-1
KM-244 • 50 euro • 2004 – see T-1

T-1 Europe of the Arts

KM-? • 20 euro • 2003 .900 gold, rev. Marini's *Horseman*
KM-? • 50 euro • 2003 .900 gold, rev. Klimt's *The Three Ages of Woman*
KM-242 • 20 euro • 2004 .900 gold, rev. Magritte's *The Man with the Bowler Hat*
KM-244 • 50 euro • 2004 .900 gold, rev. Thorvaldsen's *Night with Her Children*
KM-? • 20 euro • 2005 .900 gold, rev. Aalto's Technical University
KM-? • 50 euro • 2005 .900 gold, rev. Degas' *Little Dancer Aged Fourteen*

The obverse depicts an ancient sailing ship below the motif of the European flag—12 stars in a circle. The number 12 symbolizes perfection and completion; the stars represent the peoples of Europe; the circle is a sign of their unity. The flag was adopted at the time of the founding of the European Union; the number 12 does not denote the number of countries in the union. The European theme is continued on the reverses that depict works of artists from different European countries. The 20-euro coin of 2003 depicts the 1947 sculpture *Il Cavaliere* (*Horseman*) by the Italian sculptor Marino Marini (1901–1980). The 50-euro coin of 2003 features a detail from *Die drei Lebensalter der Frau* (*The Three Ages of Woman*) painted in 1905 by the Austrian expressionist painter Gustav Klimt (1862–1918). KM-242 shows *L'homme au chapeau melon* (*The Man with the Bowler Hat*) painted in 1964 by the Belgian surrealist painter René Magritte (1898–1967). KM-244 is the relief *Night with Her Children, Sleep and Death* executed in Rome in 1815 by the Danish sculptor Bertel Thorvaldsen (1770–1844). The 20-euro coin of 2005 depicts the Technical University in Otaniemi near Helsinki that was designed by the Finnish architect Alvar Aalto (1898–1976). The 50-euro coin of 2005 features the sculpture *Little Dancer Aged Fourteen* by the French impressionist Edgar Degas (1834–1917). The original figure, modeled in wax, to which Degas added a hair wig and fabric tutu, was shown at the Impressionist exhibition of 1881. On these coins with a European motif, the name of the Italian Republic (Repubblica Italiana) is denoted only by a small monogram "RI" on the obverse. The common reverse legend reads EUROPA DELLE ARTI (Europe of the Arts).

JERSEY

The island of Jersey in Western Europe in the Channel between England and northwestern France, 15 miles (24 km) west of Normandy, France is the largest and most southerly of the Channel Islands. The bailiwicks of Jersey and Guernsey represent the last remnants of the medieval Duchy of Normandy. Ever since William the Conqueror, Duke of Normandy, became King William I of England in 1066 (*see* Alderney KM-3), the Channel Islands are British crown dependencies. The king or queen of England, who is also duke of Normandy, is their head of state. Edge inscriptions on certain coins read CAESAREA INSULA (Island of Jersey), the Latin name given to Jersey by the Romans in 300 CE.

25th Wedding Anniversary of Queen Elizabeth II and Prince Philip

KM-37 ● 2 pounds ● 1972 .925 silver

KM-37
2 pounds
1972 .925 silver, 36 mm

The reverse features the 306-ton bark *Alexandra*. She was 126 ft (38 m) long, had a beam of 25 ft (7.6 m), and drew 15 ft (4.6 m) of water. She was built in 1865 in Jersey by Mallet for Le Quesne, Pallot & Mallet and had a crew of 12 men. She was in operation through 1877. During the 19th century shipbuilding was one of Jersey's major industries. In 1860 the island had 18 shipyards that built vessels ranging from small fishing smacks to full-rigged ocean-going ships. Later the shipbuilding industry declined because of the steamboat and the replacement of wooden vessels by iron.

Silver Jubilee of Queen Elizabeth II's Accession to the Throne

KM-44 ● 25 pence ● 1977 copper-nickel, issued also in .925 silver

The reverse depicts fishing smacks in the little harbor of Gorey against the background of the castle of Mont Orgueil. The castle dates back to the 13th century and was for centuries the residence of the Lords, Keepers and Governors of Jersey. It looks out to the French coast.

40th Anniversary of the Liberation

KM-64 ● 2 pounds ● 1985 copper-nickel, issued also in .925 silver and .917 gold

The reverse depicts the 1,360-ton British destroyer HMS *Beagle*. Her pennant number, H30, is incribed on the hull. *Beagle* was built by John Brown in 1931. Her length was 323 ft (98 m), her beam 32 ft

(9.8 m) and her draft 12 ft (3.7 m). She could make a speed of 35 knots and had a crew of 138. In World War II *Beagle* was modified for escort work. She served on the Northern Atlantic, Russian and Channel convoy routes. In April 1944, assisted by carrier aircraft, she sank the German submarine *U355* during the passage of Russian convoy JW58. She was sold for scrap in 1946. On 1 July 1940 the Island of Jersey was occupied by German troops and became, along with the other Channel Islands, the only part of the British isles to be occupied during World War II. The war in Europe ended by the unconditional surrender of all German armed forces, signed at Reims, France, on 7 May 1945 at 2:41 a.m. Hostilities were to cease at 00:01 a.m. on 9 May. On this day a British force comprising the *Beagle* and HMS *Bulldog* (*see* Guernsey KM-64) liberated the islands. Generalmajor Rudolf Wulf, commander of the German forces in Jersey, surrendered to Brigadier General Alfred E. Snow aboard *Beagle* in St. Helier harbor in the afternoon. The edge of the coin bears the incuse inscription OUR DEAR CHANNEL ISLANDS WILL ALSO BE FREED TODAY, a quote from the speech by Prime Minister Winston Churchill in which he announced the German surrender to the British nation.

Shipbuilding – *Tickler*

KM-84 ● 1 pound ● 1991 nickel-brass, issued also in .925 silver and .917 gold

The reverse features the 96-ton two-masted schooner *Tickler*. She measured 93 ft (28 m) long, had a beam of 19 ft (5.8 m), and drew 10 ft (3 m) of water. She was built in 1858 by Le Vesconte and Vautier at Havre des Pas, St. Helier for Le Boutillier and Company, and sailed between northern Europe, the Mediterranean Sea and Newfoundland. In 1868 *Tickler* was mortgaged with the Jersey Joint Stock Bank and was subsequently sold to Charles Robin. Three years later she was bought by Robin and Company, a ship-owning company on the island. In 1888 she was sold to France. The 1991–1994 shipbuilding series (this coin and the next five coins) commemorates shipbuilding in Jersey in the 19th century. The edge inscription is CAESAREA INSULA.

Shipbuilding – *Percy Douglas*

KM-85 ● 1 pound ● 1991 nickel-brass, issued also in .925 silver and .917 gold

KM-85
1 pound
1991 nickel-brass, 22.5 mm

The reverse depicts the three-master *Percy Douglas* in full sail. The 781-ton square-rigged ship was built at Beaumont by Edward Allen in 1861 and was named for Major General Sir Robert Percy Douglas, Lieutenant Governor of Jersey. She was 172 ft (52 m) long, had a beam of 33 ft (10 m), and drew 20 ft (6.1 m) of water. Her builder went bankrupt during the construction and the ship was registered to Thomas Hayley of Liverpool, the principal financier. *Percy Douglas* worked the China route. She was wrecked in 1871 after running aground off Rangoon, Burma. The edge inscription reads CAESAREA INSULA.

Shipbuilding – *Hebe*

KM-86 ● 1 pound ● 1992 nickel-brass, issued also in .925 silver and .917 gold

The reverse depicts the *Hebe* in full sail. The two-masted square-rigged brig was built in 1861 by Daniel Le Vesconte at First Tower for J. Le Boutillier and Company and registered at 236 tons. She measured 119 ft (36 m) long, with a beam of 24 ft (7.4 m) and a draft of 13 ft (4 m). In Greek mythology, Hebe, a daughter of Hera and Zeus, is the goddess of youthful beauty. She married Hercules after he won immortality. The Romans worshipped her under the name of Juventas. *Hebe* plied her trade on the North Sea and the Northern Atlantic, traveling regularly between Jersey and Canada. Primarily a cargo vessel, she was also used to ferry emigrant workers from Europe to Canada. Her captains were David Le Boutillier (until 1874) and Philip Le Brun. She was wrecked in 1887 off Bryon (Byron) Island, just north of the Magdalen (Madeleine) Islands in the Gulf of St Lawrence. The edge inscription reads CAESAREA INSULA.

Shipbuilding – *Gemini*

KM-88 ● 1 pound ● 1993 nickel-brass, issued also in .925 silver and .917 gold

The reverse depicts the three-masted bark *Gemini* in full sail. She measured 138 ft (42 m) in length and 28 ft (8.4 m) in the beam and had a draft of 17 ft (5.2 m). She was built in 1864 by Daniel Le Vesconte at First Tower for Messrs. Deslandes and Pallot, and registered at 430 tons. She made regular voyages to China, South America, the West Indies and New York. The crew numbered 14. The pay of the mate was £5 per month and that of the seamen half of this amount. In 1872 *Gemini* was sold to Geo. Shaddick and James Burgess of Swansea, Wales. She was declared unseaworthy in Singapore in 1880. It is unclear whether she was then broken up or continued to sail under a different name. The edge inscription reads CAESAREA INSULA.

Shipbuilding – *Century*

KM-90 ● 1 pound ● 1993 nickel-brass, issued also in .925 silver and .917 gold

The reverse depicts the two-masted brigantine *Century*, built by Daniel Le Vesconte at First Tower in 1866 for Charles Robin and Company. She was 107 ft (33 m) long, her beam was 21 ft (6.5 m) and she drew 13 ft (4 m) of water. She was registered at 186 tons.

The *Century* was so named to commemorate the centennial of the founding of the Robin firm. (This firm still exists, in Canada. It is now named Robin, Jones and Whitman.) The *Century* worked on the triangle run of South America, Jersey and Gaspé Bay. She was stranded at Val Bay, Gaspé in 1898 and declared a total loss. The edge inscription reads CAESAREA INSULA.

Shipbuilding - *Resolute*

KM-91 ● 1 pound ● 1994–97 – see T-1

50th Anniversary of the Liberation

KM-93 ● 10 pounds ● 1995 .999 gold

The reverse depicts the British destroyer HMS *Beagle* aboard which the commander of the German forces surrendered on 9 May 1945 (*see* KM-64).

Shipbuilding - *Resolute*

KM-101 ● 1 pound ● 1998–2003 – see T-1

T-1 Shipbuilding - *Resolute*

KM-91 ● 1 pound ● 1994–97 nickel-brass, Queen's portrait by Arnold Machin, issued also in .925 silver and .917 gold
KM-101 ● 1 pound ● 1998–2003 nickel-brass, Queen's portrait by Ian Rank-Broadley

KM-91
1 pound
1994 nickel-brass, 22.5 mm

The reverse depicts the two-masted topsail schooner *Resolute*. She was built in 1877 by Thomas Le Huquet in St. Catherine's Bay and registered at 63 tons. Her length was 80 ft (24 m), her beam 19 ft (5.8 m) and her draft 9 ft (2.7 m). She was owned throughout her life by the Noel family—until 1896 by George Noel Senior and then by his son George. They used the schooner for trade until she was wrecked by a hurricane at Friar's Cove, Newfoundland in 1905, with the loss of one of her five crew members. The edge inscription reads CAESAREA INSULA.

T-2 The History of the Royal Navy - 9th–20th Centuries

KM-? ● 5 pounds ● 2003 copper-nickel

The reverse depicts at right five vessels of the British Royal Navy of different periods and at left portraits of famous British naval commanders. The vessels are, from top to bottom, *Mary Rose* (*see*

Alderney T-1), HMS *Victory* (*see* Gibraltar KM-12), HMS *Warspite* (*see* Gibraltar T-7), HMS *Ark Royal* (*see* Gibraltar T-11) and the nuclear-powered submarine HMS *Conqueror* (*see* T-5). The naval commanders on the reverse are, from top to bottom, King Alfred the Great who was the first British ruler to organize a navy, at the end of the 9th century, to defeat Viking raiders (*see* Alderney KM-45), Sir Francis Drake who circumnavigated the globe in the 16th century (*see* Great Britain KM-844), Admiral Lord Horatio Nelson who foiled Napoleon's plans for European domination in the 18th century (*see* Gibraltar KM-12), Admiral Sir John Fisher who prepared the Royal Navy for World War I and won many victories until his resignation in 1915, and the former submariner Admiral Sir John "Sandy" Woodward who commanded the Falkland Island Task Groups in the Falkland Islands War of 1982 and assured Britain of victory.

T-3 The History of the Royal Navy – Francis Drake

KM-? • 5 pounds • 2003 copper-nickel

The coin depicts Sir Francis Drake and his flagship *Golden Hind* in which he made a voyage around the world in 1577–1580 (*see* Great Britain KM-844).

T-4 The History of the Royal Navy – HMS *Victory*

KM-? • 5 pounds • 2004 silver
KM-? • 25 pounds • 2004 gold

The reverse depicts HMS *Victory*, the flagship of Vice Admiral Lord Horatio Nelson at the battle of Trafalgar in 1805 during which he was killed (*see* Gibraltar KM-12).

T-5 The History of the Royal Navy – HMS *Conqueror*

KM-? • 5 pounds • 2005 copper-nickel

The reverse depicts the nuclear-powered submarine HMS *Conqueror* with some of her crew lined up in a row on her forward part, and in the background at right a tugboat that has its fire-fighting water nozzles spraying. *Conqueror* (S48) was built by Cammell Laird in Birkenhead in 1971. She displaced 3,500 tons on the surface, 4,800 tons submerged. She was 285 ft (87 m) long and 33 ft (10 m) in the beam, and had a draft of 27 ft (8.2 m). On the surface she could make 25 knots, submerged 30 knots. Her complement numbered 103. In the Falkland Islands War of 1982, torpedoes launched by the *Conqueror* sank the Argentine light cruiser ARA (Armada Republica Argentina) *General Belgrano* (ex USS *Phoenix* [1938–1946], later ARA *17 de Octubre* [1951–1956]) with the loss of 323 of the Argentine crew. *Conqueror* was decommissioned in 1990.

LATVIA

The republic of Latvia in Eastern Europe on the Baltic Sea is bordered by Estonia to the north and Lithuania to the south. Latvia attained independence from Russia in 1918 but in 1940 it came once again under Russian rule as a Soviet Socialist Republic. It regained sovereignty in 1991 after its parliament voted to restore the pre-war independence.

Circulation Coin

KM-6 ● 50 santimu ● 1922 nickel

The reverse depicts the stern of a boat on which Latvia, the personification of the Latvian republic, is standing at the helm. The design was taken from a stamp issued in 1920 to commemorate the first session of the assembly of deputies who had been elected in that year.

Olympic Games 1996 Atlanta

KM-24 ● 10 latu ● 1994 .925 silver

The reverse features a rower in a canoe with his oar raised for a stroke. Olympic canoe races for men (single) are held over a distance of 3,279 ft (1,000 m) and 1,640 ft (500 m). Latvian rowers first took part in the Olympic Games of 1968 in Mexico and over the years have brought home several Olympic medals. Ivans Klementjevs has been world champion seven times. In the 1996 Olympic Games he was awarded a silver medal. The obverse features Latvia's coat-of-arms. The three stars at the top represent the original duchies of Latgale, Kurzeme (Courland) and Vidzeme (Livonia).

100th Anniversary of Julia Maria

KM-25 ● 10 latu ● 1995 – *see T-1*

800th Anniversary of Riga – 14th Century

KM-27 ● 10 latu ● 1995 – *see T-2*

800th Anniversary of Riga – 12th Century

KM-28 ● 10 latu ● 1997 .925 silver

KM-28
10 latu
1997 .925 silver, 38.6 mm

The reverse depicts at the bottom the remains of a 12th-century ship and, at the top, a model of the vessel. The wreck was found in 1939 in excavations in Old Riga in the area of the old port that was once located on the bank of the Riga River, some 21 ft (6.5 m) below the present street level. The ship was clinker-built and had a high bow and one mast. She had a length of 56 ft (17 m), a beam of 16 ft (4.9 m) and a draft of 3.3 ft (1 m). Her carrying capacity was 30 tons. Both the wreck and the 1:10 model are on display at the Museum of the History of Riga and Navigation. The reverse legend RĪGAS KUGIS XII GS translates as "Riga Ship 12th Century." The coin is part of a series marking the 800th anniversary of Riga, Latvia's capital. The city on the banks of the Daugava River is first mentioned in chronicles of 1201. It developed into a trade center and joined the Hanseatic League in 1282 to further its trade with the leading European cities. The Hanseatic League was an association of northern European trading towns formed in the 13th century to protect their economic interests in foreign countries. The league fought against pirates and robbers, and built lighthouses to aid in safe navigation. In its heyday in the 14th century and in the first half of the 15th century the league included some hundred towns, eight of which were located in the present territory of Latvia—Riga, Cēsis, Valmiera, Koknese, Straupe, Limbazi, Kuldiga and Ventspils.

800th Anniversary of Riga – 14th Century

KM-29 ● 10 latu ● 1998 – see T-2

History of Seafaring – *Krišjānis Valdemārs*

KM-32 ● 10 latu ● 1998 .925 silver

KM-32
10 latu
1998 .925 silver, 38.6 mm

The reverse depicts the steam-icebreaker *Krišjānis Valdemārs* in the middle of an ice-pack. The 1,932-ton ship was built in 1925 in Glasgow by two British companies, William Beardmore and Vickers. She was 197 ft (60 m) long and 56 ft (17 m) in the beam and had a draft of 22 ft (6.7 m). She could make 14 knots in ice-free water and 3 knots in water covered with hard and smooth ice. She was owned by the government and was named for Krišjānis Valdemārs (1825-1891) who established the first naval college and promoted shipbuilding in Latvia. The ship was used to free the Riga port from ice in winter and to escort state visits. During World War II the icebreaker was evacuated to Tallinn, Estonia. In August 1941 she struck a mine and sank. The reverse legend is LEDLAUZIS KRIŠJĀNIS VALDEMĀRS (Ledlauzis meaning Icebreaker).

800th Anniversary of Riga – 16th Century

KM-34 ● 10 latu ● 1996 .925 silver

The reverse shows the city of Riga as depicted on a woodcut of 1547, in the foreground two sailing ships on the river and at left the inscription XVI GS. (16th century). The city's skyline is dominated by the church towers of St. Jakob's, the Dome and St. Peter's. The woodcut is the oldest known of the city. The obverse features Riga's 16th-century coat-of-arms supported by two lions. The country name is inscribed on the edge of the coin.

800th Anniversary of Riga – 17th Century

KM-35 ● 10 latu ● 1997 .925 silver

The reverse gives an aerial view of the fortified city of Riga in the first half of the 17th century with seven sailing ships of the period in the foreground. The reverse inscription is RIGAS NOCIETINAJUMI XVII GS. (Riga's Fortifications 17th century). Because of its strategic place on the Baltic and economic importance, Riga was encircled by high ramparts with mighty bastions and a wide and deep canal that made the city even stronger than Stockholm, the capital of Sweden. The obverse depicts Riga's coat-of-arms—an open gate with two towers, a lion's head in the gate, above the gate two crossed keys and above the keys a cross. The country name is inscribed on the edge of the coin.

History of Navigation – *Gekrönte Ehlendt*

KM-41 ● 20 latu ● 1997 .583 gold with 24-carat gilding

The reverse features the three-masted frigate *Gekrönte Ehlendt* (Crowned Elk in German) constructed in Ventspils (Windau) in 1642. Her length was 93 ft (28 m) and she could carry 320 tons. The frigate was in the fleet of Duke Jacob of Courland and Semigallia until she was seized by Spanish pirates in 1645.

100th Anniversary of *Julia Maria*

KM-42 ● 10 latu ● 1997 – see T-1

Hansa Cities – Ventspils

KM-46 ● 1 lats ● 2000 .925 silver

The reverse can be viewed either with the inscription HANZAS PILSETA (Hanseatic City) at the top or—rotating 180°—with VENTSPILS at the top. Below HANZAS PILSETA a Hanseatic cog (*see* Danzig KM-145) is depicted on a stretch of sea waves. Below VENTSPILS there is a view of Venta Castle. The coin honors the city of Ventspils (Windau), a major port on the Baltic Sea coast that was a member of the Hanseatic League from the 14th to the 16th centuries. Venta Castle, built by the Livonian Order on the banks of the Venta River, is first referred to in chronicles in 1290. The obverse depicts the coat-of-arms of Ventspils that was adopted in 1925. The country name is inscribed on the edge of the coin.

Hansa Cities - Cēsis

KM-49 ● I lats ● 2001 .925 silver

KM-49
I lats
2001 .925 silver, 38.6 mm

The reverse can be viewed either with the inscription HANZAS PILSETA (Hanseatic City) at the top or—rotating 180°—with CĒSIS at the top. Below HANZAS PILSETA a Hanseatic ship is depicted on a stretch of sea waves. Such ship may have been a cog or a transitional type between the Viking ship and the cog, wide and heavy, some 36 ft (11 m) long, weighing about 15 tons including ballast, with four oars, but not suited for rowing long distances. Below the inscription CĒSIS there is a view of Cēsis Castle. Cēsis (Wenden), one of Latvia's eight Hanseatic cities, is first mentioned in chronicles of 1206. Situated approximately 55 miles (90 km) northeast of Riga on both banks of the Gauja River, it was declared a town in 1323 and is Latvia's second oldest city after Riga. Wenden is named for the Vendi tribe. It was the name of the wooden castle that stood on the city's site in the 11th century. In the 13th century a stone castle was built. The city flourished in the late 14th and early 15th centuries due to the Gauja River trade and became a member of the Hanseatic League by the end of the 14th century. The city hosted the Livonian *Landtag* (assembly) on several occasions and gave Latvia its national colors—maroon-white-maroon. The obverse features the Hanseatic coat-of-arms of Cēsis. The country name is inscribed on the edge of the coin.

Hansa Cities - Kuldiga

KM-53 ● I lats ● 2002 .925 silver

KM-53
I lats
2002 .925 silver, 38.6 mm

The reverse can be viewed either with the inscription HANZAS PILSETA (Hanseatic City) at the top or—rotating 180°—with KULDIGA at the top. Below HANZAS PILSETA three Hanseatic cogs are depicted. Below KULDIGA there is a view of the city of Kuldiga (Goldingen) with its church towers, to its right the brick arch bridge across the Venta River, while the center of the reverse depicts the 6.5-ft (2-m)-high Ventas Rumba waterfall near Kuldiga, with a width of approximately 780 ft (240 m), probably the widest waterfall in Europe. Kuldiga is 93 miles (150 km) west of Riga. Its stone castle is first mentioned in chronicles in 1242. The town of Kuldiga, which joined the Hanseatic League in 1368, was built next to the castle in the 14th century. The obverse features the city's Hanseatic coat-of-arms. The country name is inscribed on the edge of the coin.

Kurzeme

KM-60 • 1 lats • 2003 .925 silver

The obverse depicts the hull of a 17th-century sailing ship under construction and, at the top, the coat-of-arms of the Duchy of Courland and Semigallia (Kurzeme and Zemgale in Latvian), a maritime region in western Latvia. The reverse depicts two men weighing packs of hemp against the background of a brick wall and an iron foundry. These design elements refer to the Duchy's prosperity in the 17th century when trade flourished and iron foundries and other industries developed, and ships were constructed at the region's shipyards for the sea trade. The country name is inscribed on the edge of the coin.

T-1 100th Anniversary of *Julia Maria*

KM-25 • 10 latu • 1995 .925 silver
KM-42 • 10 latu • 1997 .999 gold

KM-25
10 latu
1995 .925 silver, 38.6 mm

The reverse features the three-masted 274-ton gaff-sail schooner *Julia Maria*. She was built in 1895, measured 115 ft (35 m) long and 28 ft (8.5 m) in beam, and drew 14 ft (4.3 m) of water. Her tallest mast was 102 ft (31 m) high. Her crew consisted of a captain, a navigator, four sailors and a cook. *Julia Maria* was owned by the brothers Mucenieks. Although normally a transport in the Baltic Sea region, she also made many transatlantic voyages from Riga. She sank in the North Sea in 1920. Shipbuilding in Latvia at the end of the 19th century and the beginning of the 20th century was stimulated by the cheap timber and labor. The main types of sailing ships built were two-, three- and four-masted schooners and gaff-sail schooners. Their crews were mainly Latvians who got their training at the so-called Valdemärs naval colleges (*see* KM-32). By World War I, about 550 sailing ships suited for long voyages had been built in Latvia. The reverse inscription is GAFELŠONERIS JULIA MARIA 1895 (Gafelšoneris meaning gaff-sail schooner).

T-2 800th Anniversary of Riga – 14th Century

KM-27 • 10 latu • 1995 .925 silver
KM-29 • 10 latu • 1998 .999 gold

The reverse features a motif of the Great Guild's coat-of-arms of 1354—a ship with Riga's symbol, two crossed keys crowned with a cross at the top of the mast, representing overseas trading. The Great Guild was a guild of wealthy German traders. The reverse inscriptions on the silver coin, KM-27, are LIELAS GILDES GERBONIS (The Great Guild's Coat-of-Arms) and XIV GS. (14th century). The obverse depicts Riga's symbol as shown on the secret seal of Riga's

Town Council of 1368. In the 14th century Riga was decreed the central harbor for the Hanseatic League for discharging transit goods and the main intermediary for trade between Russia, Lithuania and Western Europe. The country name is inscribed on the edge of the coin.

T-3 Hansa Cities – Valmiera

KM-? ● 1 lats ● 2003 .925 silver

KM-?
1 lats
2003 .925 silver, 38.6 mm

The reverse can be viewed either with the inscription HANZAS PILSETA (Hanseatic City) at the top or—rotating 180°—with VALMIERA at the top. A Hanseatic cog on the Gauja River is featured below HANZAS PILSETA. The Romanesque St. Simanis church in the city of Valmiera (Wolmar) that was built in 1283 is depicted below VALMIERA. Valmiera on the Gauja, some 62 miles (100 km) northeast of Riga, came under the rule of the Order of the Swordbearers in 1224 and was a member of the Hanseatic League from the 14th century. It is now the largest city in the Vidzeme region (formerly Livonia). The obverse features Valmiera's Hanseatic city seal, which features a linden tree. The country name is inscribed on the edge of the coin.

LITHUANIA

The Republic of Lithuania is situated in Eastern Europe on the Baltic Sea, south of Latvia. Lithuania attained independence from Russia in 1918 but in 1940 it came once again under Russian rule as a Soviet Socialist Republic. It regained sovereignty in 1991 at the break-up of the Soviet Union.

750th Anniversary of Klaipėda

KM-131 ● 10 litų ● 2002 copper-nickel

The obverse gives an aerial view of the city of Klaipėda (Memel) and its harbor on the Curonian Lagoon in which a few indistinguishable watercraft are depicted. The reverse depicts the city's shield superimposed on a view of the city with harbor cranes in the background. This shield, based on a city seal dated to the second half of the 13th century or the 14th century, incorporates a gate tower and adjoining wharf walls, two wharf cranes behind the walls and a mastless ship hull below the gate, symbolizing the city's fortifications and a shipyard. The Baltic Sea city of Klaipėda, 200 miles (320 km) from the capital Vilnius, is the third largest city in Lithuania and its only sea port. The coin marks the signing of an agreement with the Livonian Order in 1252 following which the Teutonic Knights, also known as *Deutscher Orden* (German Order), built the brick castle of Memelburg on the estuary of the Dane River. In 1254 the area was formally established as a sea trading town. The region was German territory until the end of World War I. After the war Klaipéda and the surrounding territory were administered by France under a League of Nations mandate. In 1923 the Memel Territory became a part of the Lithuanian state but in March 1939 Lithuania bowed to Hitler's demands and returned the region to Germany without a fight. After the conquest of the region by the Soviet Army in 1945 it was incorporated into the Lithuanian Soviet Socialist Republic.

MALTA

The Republic of Malta, mainly including the islands of Malta and Gozo, is situated in the center of the Mediterranean Sea, 56 miles (90 km) south of the Italian island of Sicily. Malta attained independence from Great Britain in 1964.

The Order of Malta—officially named the Sovereign Military Hospitaller Order of St John of Jerusalem, of Rhodes and of Malta (*see* KM-69)—has issued symbolic coins since 1961. Some of them depict watercraft but are not included herein as the Order's territory is confined to just a few churches and palaces in Italy.

Barge of the Grand Master

KM-11 ● 10 cents ● 1972-81 – see T-1

Coat-of-Arms 1974–1986

KM-several – see T-2

Gold Coin

KM-27 ● 20 pounds ● 1974 .917 gold

The reverse features a navicello—a Gozo fishing boat with lateen sails. The obverse features the coat-of-arms with a dghajsa (*see* T-2). The dghajsa (pronounced die-sah) is a small, gaily painted local boat with stem and stern carved in the shape of a scimitar which is now mostly used for short sightseeing trips. When Malta served as a British naval base it was much in use ferrying sailors from the navy ships to various places around the Grand Harbour.

World Food Day

KM-52 • 2 pounds • 1981 .925 silver

The reverse depicts two fishermen hauling in their nets over the side of a traditional high-prowed Maltese fishing boat against the background of the island of Malta. The obverse features the coat-of-arms with a dghajsa (*see* T-2). The coin was issued under the auspices of the Food and Agriculture Organization of the United Nations (FAO) to mark World Food Day on 16 October 1981.

Barge of the Grand Master

KM-60 • 10 cents • 1982 Tenth anniversary of decimalization – *see* T-1

FAO World Fisheries Conference

KM-63 • 1 lira • 1984 copper-nickel
KM-64 • 5 liri • 1984 .925 silver

The reverse depicts a lobster fisherman in a rowboat loaded with two lobster traps. The obverse features the coat-of-arms with a dghajsa (*see* T-2). The coins commemorate the World Fisheries Conference held in Rome in June/July 1984 by the Food and Agriculture Organization of the United Nations. It adopted a strategy for fisheries management and development. In 1983 the Maltese pound (£M) was replaced by the Maltese lira (plural liri), written as Lm.

Maltese Maritime History – *Strangier*

KM-67 • 5 liri • 1984 .925 silver

The reverse depicts the three-masted merchantman *Strangier*. The obverse features the coat-of-arms with a dghajsa (*see* T-2). *Strangier* was a 263-ton full-rigged ship built in Malta in 1813 that was mainly employed on service between the United Kingdom and the Mediterranean Sea, and occasionally to the Black Sea. She was first owned by the Valletta merchant and shipowner John R. Stuart. In 1816 she was under the command of Biagio Tagliaferro (1777–1862)—the shipper, merchant and banker who has been called "the father of the Maltese merchant fleet." The vessel was later acquired by the Tagliaferro family. This is the first of the 12 coins issued in 1984–1986 to highlight the major changes in Maltese shipping from the second decade of the 19th century to the end of the 20th century. The series depicts representative types of ships owned by Maltese merchants from the age of sail down to steamships and the diesel powered vessel.

Maltese Maritime History - *Tigre*

KM-68 ● 5 liri ● 1984 .925 silver

KM-68
5 liri
1984 .925 silver, 35.2 mm

The reverse depicts the 274-ton barquentine *Tigre* completed in 1839. The obverse features the coat-of-arms with a dghajsa (*see* T-2). *Tigre* was one of the largest vessels of her type in the Maltese merchant fleet. She was owned by the Tagliaferro family and employed on their various trade routes until approximately 1861.

Maltese Maritime History - *Wignacourt*

KM-69 ● 5 liri ● 1984 .925 silver

The reverse depicts the 436-ton bark *Wignacourt* that was built in 1844. The obverse features the coat-of-arms with a dghajsa (*see* T-2). *Wignacourt* was owned by the Valletta merchants Giuseppe Garcin, Antonio Borg and Salvatore Isouard. She was mainly employed on the UK, Mediterranean Sea and Black Sea routes and was considered one of the fastest Maltese ships of her time. Two scions of the Wignacourt family were Grand Master of the Order of St. John of Jerusalem—Alof de Wignacourt in the years 1601–1622 and Adrienne de Wignacourt from 1690 to 1697. The Order, which originated from a hospital in Jerusalem, was founded in 1099 and was named for St. John the Baptist, the patron saint of the hospital. It soon became a militant order; the knights, recruited from Europe's nobility, vowed celibacy and obedience to the Order's Grand Master. With the fall of Jerusalem to Saladin in 1187 the Order fell back to Acre (now in Israel). Acre was captured in 1291 by the Egyptian Sultan al-Ashraf, bringing an end to the crusaders' Kingdom of Jerusalem, and the Order moved to Cyprus. In 1309 it conquered the island of Rhodes. In 1522 Sultan Suliman II (the Magnificent) of Turkey attacked Rhodes with a force of 200,000 Turkish soldiers against the knights' force of 10,000. After a siege of six months L'Isle Adam surrendered. The knights were allowed to leave and eventually found a refuge on Malta in 1530, L'Isle Adam becoming the first Grand Master of the Order in Malta. Malta remained the knights' permanent headquarters and home until Napoleon Bonaparte drove them out in 1798. After a period of wandering the Order established its headquarters in Rome in 1834, where it is still based. The churches and palaces in Rome and elsewhere in Italy that are owned by the Order have extraterritorial status. The official name of the Order is now the Sovereign Military Hospitaller Order of St John of Jerusalem, of Rhodes and of Malta. It has 11,000 members and 80,000 volunteers who carry out humanitarian work on every continent, such as running hospitals. The Order maintains diplomatic relations with many countries and issues its own symbolic coins.

Maltese Maritime History - *Providenza*

KM-70 • 5 liri • 1984 .925 silver

KM-70
5 liri
1984 .925 silver, 35.2 mm

The reverse depicts the 235-ton brig *Providenza*. The obverse features the coat-of-arms with a dghajsa (*see* T-2). The *Providenza* is representative of a large class of this type of vessel built by Maltese shipyards for local and foreign owners. She was built to the order of Biagio Tagliaferro and was employed on his Black Sea grain trade. The coins in the Maltese Maritime History series denote the year of building of the ship. On the reverse of this coin the year 1848 is inscribed; however, the Central Bank of Malta's publications give 1825 as the year of building. The author has been unable to ascertain the correct date.

Maltese Maritime History - *Malta*

KM-72 • 5 liri • 1985 .925 silver

The reverse depicts the wooden 1,336-ton bark *Malta* that was built in 1862 for Emmanuel Scicluna of Valetta. The obverse features the coat-of-arms with a dghajsa (*see* T-2). *Malta* was 157 ft (48 m) long and 32 ft (9.8 m) in beam and drew some 21 ft (6.4 m) of water. A full-rigged ship, she was one of the largest sailing vessels ever built in a Maltese shipyard. She carried cargo and passengers to various ports worldwide. *Malta* was last listed at Lloyd's in 1891.

Maltese Maritime History - *Tagliaferro*

KM-73 • 5 liri • 1985 .925 silver

KM-73
5 liri
1985 .925 silver, 35.2 mm

The reverse features the 1,588-ton iron paddle steamer *Tagliaferro*. The obverse features the coat-of-arms with a dghajsa (*see* T-2). *Tagliaferro* was built in 1880 in Newcastle for the Tagliaferro family. She measured 260 ft (79 m) long and 35 ft (11 m) in beam and drew 21 ft (6.4 m) of water. She was the first notable steamship to join the Maltese merchant fleet, and is described as a steam/schooner, meaning she carried sails to back up her engines. Her life in Malta was short—she was sold in 1882 to Australian buyers.

Maltese Maritime History – *L'Isle Adam*

KM-74 ● 5 liri ● 1985 .925 silver

The reverse depicts the 841-ton combination sail/steam passenger/cargo vessel *L'Isle Adam*. The obverse features the coat-of-arms with a dghajsa (*see* T-2). *L'Isle Adam* was built in 1883 in Birkenhead, England as the *Perferb*. She measured 201 ft (61 m) in length and had a beam of 28 ft (8.5 m) and a draft of 16 ft (4.9 m). In the fleet of the Gollcher family she plied the trade routes of the Mediterranean Sea until she was sunk in World War I in 1917. The ship was named for Philippe Villiers de L'Isle-Adam who was Grand Master of the Order of St. John of Jerusalem in 1521–1534 (*see* KM-69).

Maltese Maritime History – *Maria Dacoutros*

KM-75 ● 5 liri ● 1985 .925 silver

The reverse depicts the 210-ton barquentine *Maria Dacoutros*. The obverse features the coat-of-arms with a dghajsa (*see* T-2). *Maria Dacoutros* was built in 1902 as *Argo* by F. Bonifacio in Castellamare, Italy. Her length was 117 ft (36 m), her beam 26 ft (7.9 m) and her draft 12 ft (3.7 m). Her name was changed a couple of times and became *Maria Dacoutros* when she was bought by Pietro Dacoutros, a Maltese wine merchant. One of the few surviving vessels after World War II and Malta's last sailing vessel, she made trips from Malta to Gozo carrying grain and other commodities as well as mail and passengers. She sank off Cyprus in 1952.

Maltese Maritime History – *Valetta City*

KM-83 ● 5 liri ● 1986 .925 silver

The reverse depicts the 5,501-ton freighter *Valetta City*. The obverse features the coat-of-arms with a dghajsa (*see* T-2). *Valetta City* was built in 1917 as *Clan Ranald*. She had a length of 409 ft (125 m), a beam of 54 ft (16 m) and a draft of 29 ft (8.8 m). She was acquired by Pace Brothers in 1947 who named her either *Valetta City* (as denoted on the reverse) or *Valletta City* (as used by the Central Bank of Malta in its publications). At that time she was the largest ship on the Maltese Register. She was employed on world-wide tramp routes. Valletta, Malta's capital city, was named for its founder, Jean de La Vallette-Parisot, Grand Master of the Order of St. John of Jerusalem from 1557 to 1568.

Maltese Maritime History – *Knight of Malta*

KM-84 ● 5 liri ● 1986 .925 silver

The reverse depicts the 1,553-ton RMS *Knight of Malta*. The obverse features the coat-of-arms with a dghajsa (*see* T-2). *Knight of Malta* was built in 1929 by Swan Hunter & Wigham Richardson in Newcastle, England. The packet was 261 ft (80 m) long, had a beam of 37 ft (11 m), and drew 18 ft (5.5 m) of water. She was especially built as a Royal Mail Ship and was the first ship to operate a regular mail and passenger service between Malta and Sicily. Her owner was the Cassar Company. At the outbreak of World War II she was requisitioned by the British government. She was stranded on the Libyan coast in 1941.

Maltese Maritime History – *Saver*

KM-85 ● 5 liri ● 1986 .925 silver

The reverse shows the 2,074-ton steam freighter *Saver*. The obverse features the coat-of-arms with a dghajsa (*see* T-2). *Saver* was built in 1943 as *Empire Villager*. Her length was 282 ft (86 m), her beam 40 ft (12 m) and her draft 18 ft (5.5 m). She was renamed *Saver* in 1959 and was the last ship owned by the Virtù Steamship Company. She was employed in general trading activities until 1967.

Maltese Maritime History – *Dwejra II*

KM-86 ● 5 liri ● 1986 .925 silver

The reverse depicts the 1,000-ton *Dwejra II*. The obverse features the coat-of-arms with a dghajsa (*see* T-2). The freighter was built in 1969. As the other ships of the Sea Malta Company, a government-controlled company founded in 1973, *Dwejra II* is named for one of the towns and villages of Malta. The small sea-inlet of Dwejra and the village of that name are situated on the coast of western Gozo. The ship is employed on various trade routes.

KM-86
5 liri
1986 .925 silver, 35.2 mm

430 Years in Defense of Christian Europe

KM-103 ● 1 lira – 2 ecu ● 1993 copper-nickel
KM-104 ● 5 liri – 10 ecu ● 1993 .925 silver
KM-105 ● 25 liri – 55 ecu ● 1993 .900 gold

The reverse depicts galleys clashing in the battle of Lepanto that took place on 7 October 1571. Lepanto is located near the Ionian Sea on the north bank of the Gulf of Pátrai (Patras) between mainland Greece and the Peloponnese Peninsula. The battle took place between the Ottoman fleet under the command of Ali Pasha and a fleet of several European nations—among them Venice, Spain and the Papal States—that was commanded by Don John (Juan) of Austria. Don John was the 24-year-old half-brother of Philip II of Spain. Following the attack in 1570 on the Venetian-held island of

Cyprus by the Ottoman Turks of Selim II, Pope Pius V and King Philip II of Spain formed a Holy League to bring a halt to Muslim influence in Europe. The fleet of the Christian nations consisted of 316 ships, including 208 galleys, six galleasses (vessels somewhat larger in beam and draft than galleys) and 24 large sailing transports. The fleet carried some 80,000 men—about 350 in each galley. The Ottoman fleet consisted of 250 galleys, including some galiots (smaller and swifter galleys) and other smaller craft. It carried about 88,000 men. The typical Mediterranean galley of that time was about 150 ft (46 m) in length and 20 ft (6.1 m) in beam, mounted two or three fixed masts and carried 54 oars—27 to a side—that were pulled by four to six men per oar. The oarsmen of the Muslim galleys were mostly slaves chained to benches, many of them Christians. The Christian galleys were propelled by volunteers. The battle was dominated by ramming and boarding tactics, heavy arquebus fire, and by fire from the heavy guns carried on the galleasses. It lasted but four hours, but in that brief time some 130 Ottoman galleys were captured and another 80 burned or sunk. It is estimated that 25,000 Turks died in the battle (among whom Ali Pasha) and 5,000 were taken prisoner. It was the first major defeat the Ottomans had suffered in two centuries and a great victory for Christian Europe. The Christians lost 17 ships and 7,500 of their men, but twice this number of Christian galley slaves were freed. The battle of Lepanto was the last major battle in which the oar- and sail-driven galley dominated and one of the largest sea battles in history. The reverse inscription reads 430 YEARS IN DEFENCE OF CHRISTIAN EUROPE; the coins were issued 422 years after the battle. The ecu denomination relates to the European Currency Unit, a precursor of the euro. The ecu was a unit of account, not a real currency.

Schooner *Valletta*

KM-108 • 5 liri • 1994 .925 silver

KM-108
5 liri
1994 .925 silver, 38.6 mm

The reverse features the Maltese schooner *Valletta* of 129 tons against the background of the Sant'Angelo fortress at Vittoriosa. *Valletta* was built in 1829 and plied the Mediterranean Sea. She is not reported in listings in Lloyd's after 1842. Fort Sant'Angelo is the oldest fort in Malta. When the knights of the Order of St. John of Jerusalem arrived in Malta in 1530 they settled in the village of Birgu on the Grand Harbour around the fort and the fort became the residence of the Grand Master of the Order, until 1574. The fort played a vital role in the siege of Malta in 1565. After the siege Valletta was built on the peninsula opposite Birgu. Birgu got the title Città Vittoriosa (Victorious City in Italian). For two centuries the fort served as a base for the British navy. In recent years it has been handed over to the Sovereign Military Order of Malta to be used for international humanitarian and cultural activities.

Xprunara

KM-119 ● 10 liri ● 2002 .999 gold

The reverse depicts a xprunara (in Italian: speronara), a Maltese type of oar- and sail-driven boat. The brightly colored, one-masted xprunara with sprit rig, or two- or three-masted xprunara with lateen rig, was a double-ended open boat, without a deck or sometimes half-decked. The three-masted xprunara with a length of some 60 ft (18 m) was introduced in the second half of the 19th century. The xprunara was built without written plans by master shipbuilders following traditional methods. Once the owner and the builder agreed on the length, the other dimensions would be calculated following family traditions—the length between the perpendiculars determining the size and hold capacity. A 26-ft (7.9-m) xprunara registered 3 ton burden, while one of 50 ft (15 m) registered 45 tons. The crew normally consisted of a master and six rowers who also handled the sails. As a rule the boat traveled under sail but oars were used to increase speed. The oarsmen generally rowed standing to better push on the oar. The xprunara was primarily a passenger carrying vessel designed for speed that was used as a ferry between Sicily and Malta but also often for making voyages to Genoa or Marseilles, or other destinations in the Mediterranean Sea. It carried up to eight passengers; however, it was also used for carrying grain and other provisions from Sicily. It made speeds of up to 15 knots. The flat-bottomed and somewhat narrow xprunara was not adapted to rough seas and therefore sailed close to land. In bad weather the boat was pulled ashore. Seafaring at night was normal, in order to evade marauding corsairs who constituted a constant danger until driven out of their last stronghold in Algiers in 1830. The xprunara was first described in a written document of 1576. The first dated painting on which it is featured was made in 1740. The last such painting dates from 1907. During the time Malta was ruled by the Order of St. John of Jerusalem, the names of all xprunari contained the prefix *Il Santissimo Crocifisso* (The Holy Crucifix). They had names such as *Il Santissimo Crocifisso e l'Anime del Purgatorio* (The Holy Crucifix and the Souls of Purgatory) and *Il Santissimo Crocifisso e la Madonna del Rosario* (The Holy Crucifix and the Madonna of the Rosary).

T-1 Barge of the Grand Master

KM-11 ● 10 cents ● 1972–81 copper-nickel, circulation coin
KM-60 ● 10 cents ● 1982 copper-nickel, Tenth anniversary of decimalization

The obverse features a three-masted galley of the 18th century—the ceremonial barge of Grand Master Emmanuel de Rohan de Polduc (1775–1797). It was the last barge of a Grand Master of the Order of St. John of Jerusalem on Malta prior to the expulsion of the knights by Napoleon Bonaparte in 1798. KM-11 is part of the first series of circulation coins issued after Malta attained independence. It symbolizes the renewal of indigenous coinage. Under British rule (1800–1964) Malta used the regular homeland coins of Great Britain. The British coins were demonetized in 1972 after issue of this series.

T-2 Coat-of-Arms 1974–1986

KM-29 ● 25 cents ● 1975 brass, eight-sided planchet
KM-76 ● 10 cents ● 1986 copper-nickel
KM-82 ● 1 lira ● 1986 nickel

The coins listed are just a sample of the coins issued during the years 1974–1986 that depict the country's coat-of-arms of that period.

KM-29
25 cents
1975 brass, 30 mm

The obverse of most coins issued during the years 1974–1986 features the coat-of-arms that depicts a traditional Maltese boat by a shore; a Barbary fig, a shovel and a three-pronged fork on shore; and a radiant sun above. The boat is a dghajsa (*see* KM-27). The long objects on shore below the boat are agricultural implements—not oars, as stated in some sources. This coat-of-arms was adopted following the parliament's resolution of December 1974 to become a republic. It was replaced in 1986 by a coat-of-arms that does not depict a boat.

MOLDOVA

The Republic of Moldova in Eastern Europe northeast of Romania attained independence in 1991 upon the break-up of the USSR.

Olympic Games 1996 Atlanta

KM-9 ● 100 lei ● 1996 .925 silver

The reverse depicts two men paddling in a canoe. The coin commemorates Moldova's participation in the Olympic Games of 1996—the first time Moldovan sportsmen competed in an Olympic tournament. In these Games, the country's canoe team won a silver medal in the 500-m (1,640-ft) Canadian canoe race for two men.

MONACO

The Principality of Monaco is a constitutional monarchy that borders France on the Mediterranean coast. Since 1419 it is ruled by the House of Grimaldi.

1,700th Anniversary of St. Dévoté

KM-180 ● 5 euro ● 2004 .900 silver

The reverse depicts Sainte Dévoté and a sailing vessel that purports to be a vessel of the 4th century. Dévoté was a young Corsican woman killed by order of the Roman emperor Gaius Aurelius Valerius Diocletianus (284–305). It was declared that the body should not be buried, so that the woman's place of burial would not become a place of worship, but some religious men managed to bring the body to a ship, to be transported to Africa; however, for reasons now unknown, the ship returned to the country that is now Monaco, Dévoté's body became venerated, and eventually she was proclaimed a saint.

NETHERLANDS

The Kingdom of the Netherlands is situated in Western Europe on the North Sea.

Circulation Coin

KM-174 ● 25 cents ● 1941–43 zinc

The obverse depicts a vessel similar to a Viking longship (*see* Isle of Man KM-24), shown to symbolize the Dutch people as seafarers who continously endure a hard life on the sea coast. This zinc coin was issued during the German occupation of the Netherlands during World War II to replace the silver coin of the same denomination of the pre-war type. It is the only zinc coin presented in this book. Zinc is used only rarely on its own in coinage. Its widest use was probably by the Germans in both world wars in occupied countries. The obverse of the pre-war 25-cent coin featured Queen Wilhelmina who reigned from 1898 until 1948 and was in London with the government-in-exile during the war (1940–1945).

T-1 Mintmastermark "Sails"

KM-235 ● 2 cents ● 2003–04 copper-plated steel
KM-238 ● 20 cents ● 2003–04 brass
KM-245 ● 5 euro ● 2003 .925 silver, Vincent van Gogh
The coins listed are just a sample of the coins struck from 2003 that depict the mintmastermark "Sails."

The mintmastermark "Sails" symbolizes the sails of the clipper *Nederland* (Netherlands). The 2,031-ton three-master was built in 1894 at the Concordia yard in Amsterdam for the W. A. Huijgens shipping company. One of the country's last sailing ships, she had a steel hull, was 264 ft (80 m) long, had a beam of 42 ft (13 m), and drew 24 ft (7.2 m) of water. Her total sail area was 21,926 sq ft (2,037 m^2). In 1910 she was sold to Thomas Berg's Fides shipping company of Stavanger, Norway for £3,750 and was renamed *Fides*. In 1917 she was resold to Risør, also in Norway, and renamed *Vigør*. She was scrapped in 1923. The captain of *Nederland* in 1897–1900 was Sipko Renger Brouwer (1875–1922), a great-grandfather of Maarten T. Brouwer, general manager and mintmaster of the Royal Dutch Mint in Utrecht from 1 May 2002, who chose this mintmastermark to honor his ancestor. Coins struck by the mint in Utrecht have both a mintmark—a caduceus—and a mintmastermark. The mintmastermark "Sails" appears on coins struck by the Dutch mint from 2003, including coins struck for other countries.

NORWAY

The Kingdom of Norway occupies the western part of the Scandinavian peninsula in northwestern Europe.

150th Anniversary of Organized Norwegian Emigration to America

KM-422 ● 5 kroner ● 1975 copper-nickel

KM-422
5 kroner
1975 copper-nickel, 29.5 mm

The reverse depicts the small 39-ton sloop *Restaurasjonen* (Restoration), built in Hardanger in 1801 as the yacht *Emanuel* and renamed *Haabet* (Hope) probably in 1815. She was 54 ft (16 m) in length and 16 ft (4.9 m) in beam, and used for transportation of herring and grain between Sweden and Denmark. In 1820 she was rebuilt and renamed *Restaurasjonen*. She was bought by Lars Larsen, a Quaker, for 1,800 speciedalers and fitted for a voyage to America. On 5 July 1825 she sailed from Bergen carrying a load of iron and 52 people including the crew. *Restaurasjonen* arrived in New York on 9 October and was placed under arrest because under the 1819 Passenger Act the small ship was allowed to enter the United States with only 16 passengers on board. A fine of $150 was imposed for each of the 21 excess passengers but later that year the owners of the vessel were pardoned by President John Quincy Adams. The ship was sold for $400—less than half of what the owners had paid for her in Norway. The newcomers settled in Kendall, Orleans County, New York under the leadership of Cleng Peerson, a member of the Quaker community in the Stavanger area in southern Norway. He had first come to the United States in 1821 to look into opportunities for the Quakers to settle in America. The Quakers' wish to emigrate stemmed from the fact that the Norwegian government did not approve of any Christian religious practice other than Lutheran. The voyage of *Restaurasjonen* was the beginning of Norwegian mass emigration to North America. Today there are more Americans of Norwegian ancestry than the whole population of Norway. The reverse inscription is VEIEN MOT VEST (The Way Westward). The obverse features the crowned lion rampant holding a straight-handled ax from Norway's coat-of-arms.

Circulation Coin

KM-453 ● 20 kroner ● 1994–2005 nickel-bronze

KM-453
20 kroner
2003 nickel-bronze, 27.4 mm

The reverse depicts the swan-necked prow of a Viking ship built around the year 820 that was used as a sailing vessel for many years before it was used as a burial ship. The oak-built ship was found in a mound at the Oseberg farm at Slagen on the Oslo Fjord and excavated in 1904. She is 71 ft (22 m) long, has a beam of 17 ft (5.1 m), drew 5.2 ft (1.6 m) of water, and had a tonnage of approximately 11. The prow rises 16 ft (4.9 m) above the deck. Under the shield rack there are on each side 15 oar-holes. All 15 pairs of oars were present, each oar is 12–13 ft (3.7–4.0 m) long. With a lookout and a steersman and either one or two oarsmen to each oar, the ship had a crew of either 32 or 62 men. She was fully rigged for sailing as well. It is estimated that she carried a sail of 969 sq ft (90 m^2) on a mast 43 ft (13 m) tall that could be unstepped and that she could make a speed of perhaps 12 knots. The ship is classified as a karfi—a kind of Viking-age yacht—and presumably served for cruising in the coastal waters of a fjord. Her stem and stern posts are elaborately carved. The Vikings buried their dead with the personal belongings they would need on their final journey or that would make afterlife more convenient—jewels, food, domestic items and sometimes even servants. The Oseberg ship was used as the tomb of a lady of high standing, presumably a queen, who died in the year 834. The ship was found fully laden, with the remains of an older female, most likely a slave that was sacrified to follow her mistress in death. The burial chamber of the Oseberg ship held the largest collection of Viking-age artifacts ever uncovered in Scandinavia. The ship has been fully restored and is on exhibit in the Viking Ship Museum on the Bygdøy Peninsula in Oslo which also houses a Viking warship found at Gokstad that was built around 890 and excavated in 1880. Both ships were well preserved in a bed of blue clay in which they were buried.

100th Anniversary of Fridtjof Nansen's Return from the Arctic

KM-459 ● 5 kroner ● 1996 copper-nickel

The reverse depicts the 402-ton three-master *Fram* (Forward). Built in 1892 at Larvik for the Norwegian polar explorer Fridtjof Nansen (1861–1930), the schooner is 128 ft (39 m) long, 34 ft (11 m) in beam and 15 ft (4.8 m) deep. She could make 6 knots. On a voyage to the Arctic Ocean in 1882 Nansen was intrigued by a piece of driftwood on the ice and concluded that it had drifted westward with an ocean current from Siberia toward the North Pole and on to Greenland. He developed a plan to build a ship strong enough to withstand the ice pressure, to sail her north until she froze in the ice pack and to drift in her west toward the Pole. *Fram* was fitted to this task. Her three-layered hull of oak and greenheart wood was both tough and slippery. Her rounded shape gave the ice nothing to grip. When the ice started to exert its pressure the ship was pushed upwards. In June 1893 Nansen sailed from Kristiania (now Oslo) with a crew of 12, including Otto Sverdrup as *Fram*'s captain. From Siberia they struck north and upon reaching the pack ice the vessel was frozen in the ice for her drift northwards. In March 1895 Nansen and Hjalmar Johansen left the ship with three sleds, two kayaks and 27 dogs to make for the North Pole. *Fram* was left in the hands of Sverdrup. Ice conditions at 86° 14' N. latitude, 240 miles (386 km) from the Pole, forced the two men to turn back. After five months they reached Franz Josef Land where they built a hut of stone and moss with a roof of walrus skins, and wintered for nine months living on polar bears and walruses that they hunted. They returned to Norway in August 1896. *Fram* drifted to Spitsbergen where Sverdrup managed to free her from the pack ice after three years during which she drifted some 2,200 miles (3,500 km) westward, as Nansen had predicted. In 1898–1902 *Fram* was used by Sverdrup to explore the islands to the northwest of Greenland. The Sverdrup Islands west of Ellesmere Island were named for him. Roald Amundsen used her in 1910–1912 for his successful expedition to the South Pole (*see* Zambia KM-100). She is now preserved in the Fram Museum at Bygdøy, Oslo. The reverse inscription is FRAM OVER POLHAVET (*Fram* in the Polar Ocean). The coin marks the centennial of Nansen's return from the Arctic and the 60th anniversary of the opening of the Fram Museum. After his return Nansen became a professor of zoology. He played a prominent part in the release of Norway from Swedish rule in 1905 and was Norway's first ambassador to Great Britain. In 1920 he became high commissioner for refugees of the League of Nations and directed the repatriation of millions of displaced persons and war prisoners in the aftermath of World War I and the Russian revolution. He also helped millions in the famine-stricken USSR and in exchanging populations of Greeks and Turks. In 1922 Nansen was awarded the Nobel Prize for Peace.

Arrival of the First Europeans in North America

KM-465 • 20 kronor • 1999 nickel-bronze

The reverse depicts the bow of the Viking ship of the Norse explorer Leiv Eiríksson (often written Leif Ericson or Eriksson) approaching L'Anse-aux-Meadows, Newfoundland in approximately 1000 CE (*see* Isle of Man KM-763). The reverse inscription is MOT UKJENT LAND (To Unknown Land). The coin commemorates the arrival of the first Europeans in North America. It was sold as a pair with Canada KM-398.

KM-465
20 kronor
1999 nickel-bronze, 27.4 mm

POLAND

The Republic of Poland in Central Europe to the east of Germany borders to the north on the Baltic Sea. The country was dissolved after the partition effected by Austria, Prussia and Russia at the end of the 18th century, and became independent only after World War I.

15th Anniversary of Gdynia Seaport

Y-30 • 2 złote • 1936 – see T-1
Y-31 • 5 złotych • 1936 – see T-1

1,000th Anniversary of Poland as a Separate State

Y-57 • 100 złotych • 1966 .900 silver

The obverse depicts the shields of the capital cities of Poland's 17 voivodships (provinces) surrounding the country's coat-of-arms, an eagle; the shield of the city of Łódź features an oar in front of a boat. At 12 o'clock is the shield of Warszawa (Warsaw), the country's capital, followed, going to right, by the shields of Poznań, Łódź, Opole, Kielce, Lublin, Rzeszów, Bialystok, Olsztyn, Katowice,

Zielona Góra, Szczecin, Bydgoszcz, Gdańsk (Danzig), Wrocław, Koszalin, and Kraków. The coin commemorates the first appearance of Poland as a separate state in 966. In that year Mieszko I (circa 930–992), the first duke of Poland, converted to Christianity. The reverse depicts Mieszko holding a sword in his right hand and a shield with the Polish eagle in his left, and his Bohemian wife Dabróvka.

50th Anniversary of *Dar Pomorza* under the Polish Flag

Y-112 ● 20 złotych ● 1980 copper-nickel

Y-112
20 złotych
1980 copper-nickel, 28 mm

The reverse depicts the three-masted steel bark *Dar Pomorza*. The 1,561-ton vessel is 299 ft (91 m) long and 41 ft (12 m) in the beam, draws 19 ft (5.8 m) of water, and has over 20,000 sq ft (1,850 m^2) of sails on her 134-ft (41-m)-high masts. She was built in 1910 by Blohm & Voss in Hamburg for the Deutscher Schulschiff-Verein (German Training Ship Association) as the German training ship *Prinzess Eitel Friedrich*. For four years she prepared cadets for the German merchant marine. When World War I broke out, she was laid up. After the war she was given to France as war reparations, plying the seas from 1921 for the Société Anonyme de Navigation "Les Navires Ecoles Français" (French Training Ships) that renamed her *Colbert*. In 1926 she was sold to the Baron de Forrest to be converted to a yacht. Donations by citizens of the Pomerania region in Poland enabled the City of Poznań to purchase the ship in 1929 for the Merchant Maritime Academy at Gdynia. In 1930 she was put into service under the Polish flag as a training ship for 150 cadets named *Pomorze* (Pomerania, literally "along the sea"), later *Dar Pomorza* (Pomerania's Gift). She had a regular crew of about 30 paid hands. Her best known voyage was that in 1934/35 during which she circumnavigated the world in 352 days. During the World War II years, 1939–1945, she sheltered in Swedish waters. She was the flagship of the Gdynia Merchant Maritime Academy until she was retired in 1982. In her fifty years as a Polish training ship she trained more than 13,000 cadets and sailed half a million miles (eight hundred thousand km), winning many regattas and the "Cutty Sark Trophy." She is now a museum ship moored in Gdynia.

500th Anniversary of the Discovery of America

Y-230 ● 200,000 złotych ● 1992 .999 silver

The left half of the reverse depicts Christopher Columbus above a compass and the right half *Santa Maria*, his flagship on his discovery voyage to America in 1492 (*see* Andorra KM-78).

Polish Soldiers at World War II Fronts – Protection of Convoys

Y-232 ● 200,000 złotych ● 1992 .750 silver

The reverse features the destroyer ORP (Ship of the Republic of Poland) *Garland* escorting a convoy of freighters to Murmansk, Russia in World War II. She displaced 1,335 tons, was 323 ft (98 m) long, had a beam of 32 ft (9.8 m), drew 8 ft (2.6 m) of water, and could make 32 knots. Her crew numbered 145. Built in 1936 by Fairfield Shipbuilding & Engineering Co. Ltd. at Govan, Scotland for the Royal Navy, HMS *Garland* was leased in 1940 by Britain to the Polish government-in-exile, which retained her original name. She survived the war and was returned to the Royal Navy in 1946. A year later she was sold to the Royal Netherlands Navy to serve as the school ship Hr.Ms. (Her Majesty's) *Marnix*. The ship was broken up in 1964. The Polish vessels in England were sovereign Polish territory. They were commanded by Polish officers, manned by Polish crews and subject to Polish regulation, but they were subordinated to the operational control of the British Admiralty. The Polish navy participated in the war in numerous sea battles, convoy escorting and invasions.

Polish Soldiers at World War II Fronts – Narvik

Y-236 ● 100,000 złotych ● 1991 .750 silver

The reverse depicts gunners manning a battery on a mountain overlooking a fjord, and in the fjord the Polish destroyer ORP *Grom* (Thunder). *Grom* was built in 1937 by John Samuel White in Cowes on the Isle of Wight in the UK. She displaced 2,144 tons fully loaded, was 374 ft (114 m) long, had a beam of 37 ft (11 m), and drew some 14 ft (4.3 m) of water. She could make 39 knots. In 1940 she sank in three minutes in the Rombaken Fjord near Narvik, Norway with a loss of 55 men of the 213 on board after being hit by a German *He111* aircraft. *Grom* was one of three Polish destroyers sent to England on 30 August 1939, just prior to the invasion of Poland by the Germans on 1 September which started World War II. The others were ORP *Blyskawica* (Lightning) and ORP *Burza* (Storm). These formed the nucleus of the Polish navy-in-exile.

Olympic Games 1992 Barcelona

Y-241 ● 200,000 złotych ● 1991 .925 silver

The reverse features two racing sailboats, *PZ 56* and *PZ 88*.

Bronisław Malinowski

Y-431 ● 2 złote ● 2002 brass

Y-431
2 złote
2002 brass, 27 mm

The reverse depicts the Polish anthropologist Bronisław Malinowski (1884–1942) and, at left, two outrigger native sailing vessels and inhabitants of the Trobiand Islands in New Guinea. On these islands Malinowski found four types of canoes: the *kewo'u*, a single dugout for coastal transportation in the lagoon of Boyowa, the largest island of the Trobiand group; the *kalipoulo*, a larger dugout that serves as a fishing canoe; the *masawa*, a trading canoe with a lateen sail made of strips of dried pandanus leaf, which is constructed and owned by a group; and the *nagega*, a larger, more seaworthy trading canoe than the *masawa* and of greater carrying capacity. In the years 1914–1918 Malinowski did extensive ethnographic research on New Guinea and on the nearby Trobiand Islands. He lived in a tent among the tribesmen, mastered their language, and thanks to this pioneering fieldwork obtained much material for his book *Argonauts of the Western Pacific – An Account of Native Enterprise and Adventure in the Archipelagoes of Melanesian New Guinea* (1921) and for other publications. The watercraft on the reverse probably allude to the *Argonauts of the Western Pacific*. In his works Malinowski also described ceremonial practices connected with the various stages in the building of a canoe. In 1927 Malinowski became a professor, heading the faculty of social anthropology at the University of London—a position that was created especially for him. He believed that all components of a society—beliefs, ceremonies, customs, institutions, religion, and ritual and sexual taboos—should be considered as an integrated system, and thus founded functionalism as a field of social anthropology.

History of the Złoty

Y-521 ● 2 złote ● 2005 – see T-1

T-1 *Dar Pomorza*

Y-30 ● 2 złote ● 1936 .750 silver, Fifteenth anniversary of Gdynia seaport
Y-31 ● 5 złotych ● 1936 .750 silver, Fifteenth anniversary of Gdynia seaport
Y-521 ● 2 złote ● 2005 brass, History of the złoty
Y-? ● 10 złotych ● 2005 .925 silver, History of the złoty – listed separately below (see T-2)

Y-31
5 złotych
1936 .750 silver, 28 mm

The reverse of the coins of 1936 depicts the sail training ship *Dar Pomorza* (*see* Y-112). The reverses of the two coins of 1936 are featured on the reverses of the coins of 2005. The coins of 1936 commemorate the founding of the port of Gdynia in 1921, Poland's first seaport. Gdynia is located 15 miles (24 km) north of the Polish city of Gdańsk (which was the Free City of Danzig in the years between the two world wars). The port gave Poland direct access to the Baltic and obviated the need for using the port of Danzig. The reverse inscription of the 2-złote coin of 2005 is DZIEJE ZŁOTEGO (History of the Złoty).

T-2 History of the Złoty

Y-?
10 złotych
2005 .925 silver, 32 mm

Y-? ● 10 złotych ● 2005 .925 silver

The obverse depicts at right the training ship *Dar Pomorza* (*see* Y-112) and at left the obverse of the 5-złotych coin of 1936 (Y-31, *see* T-1). The reverse features the reverse of that 1936 coin, which depicts the same vessel. The obverse gives a starboard bow view of the ship; the reverse of the 1936 coin shows her from a full port broadside view. The reverse inscription is DZIEJE ZŁOTEGO (History of the Złoty). The edge inscription is 75-LECIE CHRZTU "DARU POMORZA" (75th Anniversary of the Christening of *Dar Pomorza*).

T-3 25th Anniversary of the Founding of the Solidarity Trade Union

Y-? ● 10 złotych ● 2005 .925 silver

The reverse depicts a ship in the Gulf of Gdańsk north of an outline of the northern coast of Poland with silhouettes of people waving flags and holding their hands upwards in the "V" gesture for Victory. The ship resembles a ship of the era of the Hanseatic League. She flies the flag of the Solidarity trade union. Solidarity was formed in 1980 in the Lenin shipyard at Gdańsk under the leadership of Lech Walesa. The union was banned by the Communist government in 1982 and many of its leaders were imprisoned, but it continued to operate as an underground movement to promote freedom and destabilize the Communist regime. Following nationwide strikes, the union was legalized in 1989. Walesa's election as the country's president in 1990 confirmed the fall of Communism in Poland. The obverse features the Solidarity logo. The reverse inscription is NSZZ SOLIDARNOSC (The Independent, Self-Governing Trade Union Solidarity).

PORTUGAL

The Portuguese Republic on the Iberian peninsula in southwestern Europe, west of Spain, borders the northern Atlantic Ocean. Its name derives from Portus Cale, a pre-Roman or Roman settlement near the mouth of the Douro River.

Circulation Coins

KM-580 ● $2^1/_2$ escudos ● 1932–51 .650 silver
KM-581 ● 5 escudos ● 1932–51 .650 silver
KM-582 ● 10 escudos ● 1932–48 .835 silver
KM-586 ● 10 escudos ● 1954–55 .835 silver, modified design

KM-586
10 escudos
1955 .835 silver, 30 mm

The obverse depicts a type of vessel used in numerous Portuguese explorations in the 16th century, shown at sea under full sail. It was probably a carrack or a caravel. Such vessels varied in tonnage, averaging several hundred tons and having a length of about 100 ft (30 m). They were characterized by a broad bow and three lateen sails, and were developed by the Portuguese. These vessels were sturdier and far more seaworthy than any previous ships had been, which allowed for ever longer voyages. The obverse design may have been inspired by *Santa Catarina do Monte Sinai*, the flagship of Antonio de Abreu on his exploration of the Moluccas Islands in 1511/12 (*see* KM-682) or by *São Gabriel*, the flagship of Vasco da Gama on his journey of 1497–1499 during which he was the first European to reach India by sailing around the Cape of Good Hope (*see* KM-709).

Circulation Coins

KM-590 ● $2^1/_2$ escudos ● 1963–85 – see T-1
KM-591 ● 5 escudos ● 1963–86 – see T-1

Opening of the Salazar Bridge

KM-592 ● 20 escudos ● 1966 .650 silver

The obverse depicts the Salazar bridge that connects the two banks of the Tagus River, and a freighter on the river. The 1.4-mile (2.3-km)-long highway bridge connects Lisbon–Alcantara on the north bank of the river with Almada on its south bank. It was opened in 1966 and is similar in appearance to the Golden Gate Bridge in San Francisco. The bridge was named for António de Oliveira Salazar (1889–1970), who was Portugal's prime minister in the years 1932–1968. Later it was renamed the 25th of April Bridge to mark the "revolution of the carnations" on 25 April 1974, in which

Salazar's dictatorship regime was overthrown in a military coup; during that week, soldiers were seen in the streets with seasonal red carnations in the barrels of their guns—images which became a symbol of the absence of violence in the revolution.

Circulation Coin

KM-600 ● 10 escudos ● 1971–74 – see T-1

50th Anniversary of the Death of Fernando Pessoa

KM-628 ● 100 escudos ● 1985 copper-nickel, issued also in .925 silver

The reverse features four overlapping profiles of Fernando Antonio Nogueira Pessoa (1888–1935) facing the sea on which a ship sails in the background. The repetition of the portrait alludes to the fact that Pessoa published his works under four different names: his own name, and the pseudonyms Alberto Caelro, Álvaro de Campos and Ricardo Reis. Pessoa is considered by many as Portugal's greatest modern poet.

Circulation Coin

KM-636 ● 50 escudos ● 1986–2000 copper-nickel

The reverse features a three-masted ship as depicted on a 15th-century Spanish–Moorish ceramic bowl exhibited in the Victoria and Albert Museum in London. The design is the earliest known picture of a three-masted ship, a type that had its origins in Portugal's nautical technology. The bowl was made in circa 1425–1430 in Málaga of tin-glazen earthenware painted in blue and lustre. It is rather large, about 24 inches (60 cm) in diameter and about 12 inches (30 cm) deep. A shield of arms on the mainsail identifies the ship as Portuguese. All design details on the bowl, even the four decorative fishes under the hull of the ship, are included on the reverse.

Exploration of the Atlantic Coast of Africa – Gil Eanes

KM-639 ● 100 escudos ● 1987 copper-nickel, issued also in .925 silver and .917 gold

KM-639
100 escudos
1987 copper-nickel, 34 mm

The reverse depicts the 50-ft (15-m)-long barca (bark) of the Portuguese explorer Gil Eanes sailing south with a map of the Cape Bojador area on the northwest coast of Africa (now Sahara Republic) and the Canary Islands. Barks were the ships in which the Portuguese began their ocean voyages of discovery. They were sturdy square-rigged vessels that had an average length of 52 ft (16 m) and were 10–13 ft (3–4 m) across the beam. They had a maximum tonnage of 38 and generally had a main mast with a lookout. The larger ships also had a foremast. Oars were used when necessary. The crew varied in number from eight to twenty men, according to the size of the ship. Late in 1434 or 1435, on an expedition commissioned by Prince Henry the Navigator, Eanes reached a bay 50 leagues beyond Cape Bojador which he named Angra dos Rivos (Rivos Bay). The coin marks the rounding of Cape Bojador by Eanes. This "Cape of No Return" was considered the farthest limit of navigation along the African coast, as it was believed that beyond it the sea became boiling hot and white men were turned black by the extreme temperatures; that the prevailing winds and currents would make a return from south of the cape impossible; and/or that sea-serpents were lurking to devour the seafarers. Eanes' accomplishment marks the beginning of the discoveries along the western coast of Africa, beyond the traditional limits of Christendom. Eanes was made a knight at arms for having rounded Cape Bojador. He also participated in expeditions in 1444 and 1445. This coin and the next three constitute the first series in the 15-year "Coins of Discovery" program that commemorates Portugal's landmark sea voyages of exploration and discovery in the 15th and 16th centuries. This first series is titled "The Dawn of the Age of Discovery" and focuses on the explorations along the African coast until Bartolomeu Dias proved in 1488 the existence of a sea route to the Orient.

Exploration of the Atlantic Coast of Africa – Nuno Tristão

KM-640 • 100 escudos • 1987 copper-nickel, issued also in .925 silver, .917 gold and .999 palladium

The reverse depicts the caravel of the Portuguese navigator Nuno Tristão sailing up the Gambia River, and a map of the area of the river delta. The caravel had two masts rigged with lateen sails. Its average length was 49–66 ft (15–20 m) and its tonnage 50–60. Its crew rarely exceeded 20 men. The caravel could sail in shallow waters with variable currents and winds. Thus it was more suited for the exploration of the many inlets, bays and rivers that the Portuguese met along the African coast to the south of Cape Bojador than the bark that preceded it. Tristão undertook three voyages along the Atlantic coast of Africa which were sponsored by Prince Henry the Navigator. In 1441 Tristão was the first European to reach Cape Blanco (now Cabo das Barbas in the south of the area claimed by the present-day Sahara Republic, the point at which the African mainland begins to extend southward). He made a landing near the mouth of the Rio de Oro, at the Tropic of Cancer, where he captured a number of natives who were taken back to Portugal as slaves. On his exploration voyage in 1443 Tristão reached the Senegal River delta, becoming the first

European to visit West Africa south of the Sahara. During this voyage he discovered the Arguin and Garças Islands, just beyond Cape Blanco. (Five years later the Portuguese erected a fort on Arguin Island that served as Europe's first slave station. The slave trade became a strong incentive for later Portuguese explorations along the African coast.) In 1446 Tristão discovered the Gambia River, the discovery marked by this coin. While exploring the delta of this river, Tristão and 19 of his men met their death at the hands of armed natives with poisoned arrows. Only five of the crew survived and managed to return to Lisbon. Tristão's voyages brought about the first contacts between Europeans and non-Muslim black Africans.

Exploration of the Atlantic Coast of Africa – Diogo Cão

KM-641 ● 100 escudos ● 1987 copper-nickel, issued also in .925 silver and .917 gold

The reverse depicts the caravel of the Portuguese navigator Diogo Cão (Diego Cam) (circa 1450–1486), a compass and a map of western Europe and the part of the western African coast which Cão explored. Cão was chosen by King João II to continue the exploration of the Atlantic coast of Africa. He made two voyages of discovery into the Southern Atlantic Ocean to ascertain the southern limit of the African continent. He was the first to carry *padrões* (limestone pillars) surmounted by a cross and bearing inscriptions proclaiming Portuguese suzerainty which were to be erected as signposts of discovery. On the first of his voyages (1481–1484) Cão was the first European to explore the western African coast beyond the equator. After passing Cape Santa Catarina in present-day Gabon, the farthest point previously reached, he continued and discovered the mouth of the Congo River. He set up a *padrão* on the northern bank of this river (6° 6' S. latitude) in 1483. He continued southward until he reached Cape Santa Maria in present-day Angola (13° 26' S.), where a second *padrão* was erected which is now preserved in the museum of the Geographic Society in Lisbon. On his return to Portugal, Cão was richly rewarded by the king, who granted him an annuity of 10,000 reais brancos as well as the privileges of a lord and a coat-of-arms. The second voyage (1485/86) took Cão to a point at 22° 10' S. On this voyage two more *padrões* were erected— the first at Cabo Negro in present-day Angola (15° 40' S.), the second at Cape Cross in what is now Namibia (21° 51' S.). The latter *padrão* stood at Cape Cross until the end of the 19th century and is now in the Humboldt University in Berlin. Cão probably died on the Namibian coast south of Cape Cross. The rim of the reverse denotes the latitudes of three *padrões* which Cão placed on the coast of Africa—6° S., 13° S. and 22° S.—and lines connecting these latitudes to Portuguese badges superimposed on the map of Africa to indicate where Cão placed the *padrões*.

Exploration of the Atlantic Coast of Africa – Bartolomeu Dias

KM-642
100 escudos
1988 copper-nickel, 34 mm

KM-642 ● 100 escudos ● 1988 copper-nickel, issued also in .925 silver, .917 gold and .999 platinum

The reverse depicts the caravel *São Cristóvão* superimposed on a map of Africa. This caravel was the flagship of Bartolomeu Dias (also spelled Diaz) (circa 1450–1500) on his discovery voyage of 1487/88 during which he and his men became the first Europeans to round the Cape of Good Hope, in 1488. The other two ships in Dias' fleet were the caravel *São Pantaleão* under João Infante and a supply ship under Bartolomeu's brother Pêro (or Diogo) Dias. Both caravels were newly built and 59 ft (18 m) long. The ship on the reverse is shown twice, to illustrate the rounding of the continent. Dias was sent by João II (King of Portugal in 1481–1495) to ascertain the southern limit of the African continent. He had with him *padrões* (stone pillars) to stake the claims of the Portuguese crown on the territories he discovered. Beyond 32° S. latitude the caravels stood out to sea and were blown around the southern tip of Africa. Dias continued the voyage several hundred miles east of the Cape of Good Hope until his unwilling crew forced him to return. It was only on the return voyage that Dias sighted the cape and gave it the name by which it is known today. (While the Cape of Good Hope is the renowned cape, it is not the southernmost point of Africa, which is Cape Agulhas, 100 miles (161 km) east–southeast.) The two caravels returned to Portugal after a voyage of 16 months and 16,000 miles (26,000 km). Dias' voyage opened for Portugal a sea route to the East Indies, propelling the country into a period of prosperity. In 1500 Dias commanded a squadron in the fleet led by Pedro Álvares Cabral which discovered Brazil. After leaving Brazil, four ships were lost in a storm, including that commanded by Dias. A replica of Dias' ship, a two-masted lateen-rigged caravel, has been built in the shipyards of Vila do Conde in the north of Portugal. The ship is 77 ft (23 m) long and has a beam of 22 ft (6.6 m) and a draft of 9.2 ft (2.8 m). She has a tonnage of 120 and a crew of 17. Christened *Bartolomeu Dias* and launched in 1987, the vessel set sail from Lisbon to arrive in Mossel Bay in South Africa on 3 February 1988, exactly 500 years after Dias' disembarkation at the bay.

Conquest of the Atlantic Ocean – The Discovery of the Canary Islands

KM-646 ● 100 escudos ● 1989 copper-nickel, issued also in .925 silver and .917 gold

The reverse depicts a three-masted Portuguese ship against the background of the Pico de Teide on Tenerife. The coin marks the rediscovery of the Canary Islands by the Portuguese in 1336. These islands were known in ancient times as the Fortunate Isles but were since forgotten. Their Roman name was Canaria, for the large numbers of wild dogs (*canes* in Latin) that roamed the islands. The importance of the Canary Islands as a strategic port of call for future discoveries made their ownership a constant cause of dispute for over a century. The Spanish conquered the archipelago island by island in the 15th century. The sovereignty of Castile over the islands was recognized by Portugal in the Treaty of Alcáçovas of 1479. The reverse inscription ILHAS CANÁRIAS 1336–1479 refers to the period in which the Canary Islands were held by the Portuguese. The shield of Portugal on the obverse is supported by two *Guanches*, the residents of the Canary Islands of Berber origin with whom the Portuguese made contact. They entered history with the name given them by the chroniclers of the time, and which is incribed on a scroll below the shield: HOMINES SYLVESTRES DE INSULA CANARIA (The Savage Men of the Canary Islands in Latin). The 12,198-ft (3,718-m)-high Pico de Teide is the highest point on the Canary Islands. This coin and the next three constitute the second series in the 15-year "Coins of Discovery" program that commemorates Portugal's landmark sea voyages of exploration and discovery in the 15th and 16th centuries. This series is titled "Conquest of the Atlantic Ocean." It presents the discovery of the island groups in the Atlantic Ocean after the Portuguese learned to navigate far from the relative security of the coastline they were accustomed to, using celestial navigation which made it possible to sail from one place to another across uncharted open sea. The gold coins in this series contain a "J" mark to denote that they were made of gold from the Jales mine in Portugal.

Conquest of the Atlantic Ocean – The Discovery of Madeira

KM-647 • 100 escudos • 1989 copper-nickel, issued also in .925 silver, .917 gold and .999 palladium

The reverse depicts the square-rigged vessel *São Lourenço* of the Portuguese navigator João Gonçalvez Zarco in 1419/20, and relief maps of Madeira (below the ship) and of Porto Santo (at top right). The time of this voyage strongly suggests that Zarco's vessel was a barinel. The barinel resembled the cog, the major vessel of trade in northern Europe, and is generally described as being a little larger than the barca (bark), which was commonly used in southern Europe. A barinel was perhaps 50–60 ft (15–18 m) long and 15–18 ft (4.6–5.5 m) in beam. The bonnet of the sail with the words AVE MARIA inscribed on it was a common nautical motif of the time. The reverse legend 1420 MADEIRA – PORTO SANTO 1419 marks the rediscovery of these two islands by Zarco and his companion Tristão

Vaz Teixeira. They first discovered Porto Santo. From there they sailed out to the island nearby that could be seen in clear weather. They named it Ilha da Madeira (Island of Timber) as the island was densely covered with trees. The long tongue of land on Madeira they named São Lourenço, for Zarco's ship. At the time of discovery, Madeira was uninhabited. Settlers soon followed after the discovery. Their sugar plantations created a demand for slave labor, which served as an incentive to explore the western coast of Africa.

Conquest of the Atlantic Ocean – The Discovery of the Azores

KM-648 ● 100 escudos ● 1989 copper-nickel, issued also in .925 silver and .917 gold

The reverse depicts a Portuguese bark used by the discoverers of the Azores in the 15th century, and nine stars that represent the nine largest islands of the Azores group. In 1427 Diogo de Silves discovered seven of the islands (São Miguel, Santa Maria, Faial, Pico, São Jorge, Terceira and Graciosa). The last two islands, Flores and Corvo, were discovered by Diogo de Teive in 1452. In 1439, Prince Henry the Navigator was given the right to settle the Azores, which were uninhabited. The islands gained considerable importance as a strategic and logistic base for Atlantic voyages, especially those heading to America. In both world wars in the 20th century they served as a base for naval and air operations. The reverse inscription ARQUIPELAGO DOS AÇORES translates as Archipelago of the Azores, the years 1439–1989 on the reverse mark the 550th anniversary of the granting of the right to settle the islands, and 1427 and 1452 are the years in which the islands were discovered.

Conquest of the Atlantic Ocean – Celestial Navigation

KM-649 ● 100 escudos ● 1989 copper-nickel, issued also in .925 silver, .917 gold and .999 platinum

The reverse depicts a stylized caravel of the era of the Portuguese discoveries, and a compass and a portion of an astrolabe that symbolize the nautical instruments of the 15th century. The seven stars on the obverse represent the celestial bodies which navigators observed to chart their course—the sun, the polar star and the five stars of the Southern Cross constellation. When the Portuguese set out on their discovery voyages along the African coast, the only tools available to guide them on their way were the compass and some very simple charts. Knowing that the only measurable point of reference when sailing north to south was the height of the stars, they developed astrolabes and quadrants, and so became the first to measure latitude. With the new techniques of celestial navigation they could construct more accurate charts and sail farther across the seas. (Only with the sextant and chronometer that were developed in the 18th century did it become possible to calculate longitude.) The reverse inscription NAVEGAÇÃO ASTRONÓMICA translates as Celestial Navigation. The second reverse inscription, ATLANTICO – 1455–1485, refers to the conquest of the Atlantic Ocean by the Portuguese in those years.

500th Anniversary of the Discovery of America

KM-657 • 1000 escudos • 1992 .500 silver, issued also in .925 silver

The reverse depicts a 16th-century Portuguese caravel on the Atlantic Ocean as shown on an old map that depicts parts of North and South America and of Europe and Africa. Superimposed on the map of the Brazil area are the Portuguese coat-of-arms and the inscription MONDO NOVO (New World). Badges on the map mark areas that were under Portuguese sovereignty. The inscription along the rim of the reverse is ENCONTRO DE DOIS MUNDOS (Meeting of Two Worlds). The coin was issued in the Ibero-American series—a joint program of Portugal, Spain and various Central and South American countries to issue similar coins. Usually all coins in this series are of identical size and weight and are in .925 silver. The .500 silver version of the coin is the exception to this rule. The coat-of-arms of Portugal on the obverse is surrounded by the coats-of-arms of all countries participating in the series.

Discovery of America – Pre-Columbian Voyages to the West

KM-659 • 200 escudos • 1991 copper-nickel, issued also in .925 silver, .917 gold, .999 platinum and .999 palladium

The reverse depicts a stylized ship with three sailors holding the tiller, an astrolabe, a chart and a sword with a cross, sailing west over Toscanelli's six-sided map of 1474 that shows a direct sea route between Europe and Asia. The ship design with the sailors and the cross is based on the oil painting *The Navigators* (1991) by Paulo Guilherme d'Eça Leal. The obverse features the same hexagonal map by Toscanelli. The coin marks the Portuguese pre-Columbian voyages westward between 1452 and 1486 which were part of a long, continous undertaking and could have provided clues regarding the existence of islands in the Western Atlantic Ocean, even though their whereabouts were uncertain. This information may have reached the ears of Columbus when he lived in Portugal and may have been used by him to set out his plan to reach India by sailing west. He first presented his plan to the king of Portugal in 1484 but was turned down and left for Spain. This coin and the next two are part of the third series in the 15-year "Coins of Discovery" program that commemorates Portugal's landmark sea voyages of exploration and discovery in the 15th and 16th centuries. This series is titled "Discovery of America."

Discovery of America – 500th Anniversary of the Voyage of Christopher Columbus

KM-660 ● 200 escudos ● 1992 copper-nickel, issued also in .925 silver, .917 gold, .999 platinum and .999 palladium

The reverse features a portrait of Christopher Columbus (1451–1506) with a reproduction of his signature below, and the three ships in his fleet of 1492 above an outline map of the north-eastern coast of the island of Hispaniola to which he sailed toward the end of that year. Columbus' vessels on the voyage during which he discovered America were the carrack *Santa Maria* and the caravels *Niña* and *Pinta* (*see* Andorra KM-78).

Discovery of America – 450th Anniversary of the Voyage of João Cabrilho

KM-661
200 escudos
1992 copper-nickel, 36 mm

KM-661 ● 200 escudos ● 1992 copper-nickel, issued also in .925 silver, .917 gold, .999 platinum and .999 palladium

The obverse depicts the caravel *San Salvador*, the flagship of the Portuguese navigator João Rodrigues Cabrilho (circa 1500–1543) on his expedition for Spain in 1542/43 during which he discovered California. His second ship was an open-decked vessel named *Victoria*. The aim of the expedition was to reconnoiter the western coast of North America to as far north as possible, to see if there was a passage to the Atlantic Ocean. Cabrilho set sail from the port of Navidad, New Galicia in western Mexico. He followed the Pacific coast, put into the bays at San Diego and Monterey, and continued until he reached about 40° N. latitude, close to the California-Oregon state line. He died from the complications of a broken leg after an Indian attack. The reverse features a statue of Cabrilho wearing armor and sword, with a map of southwestern North America and Central America.

Europe Meets Japan – 450th Anniversary of Relations between Portugal and Japan

KM-665
200 escudos
1993 copper-nickel, 36 mm

KM-665 ● 200 escudos ● 1993 copper-nickel, issued also in .925 silver and .917 gold

The reverse features a 16th-century Portuguese sailing vessel and a map of part of the island of Tanega Shima in the extreme south of the Japanese archipelago, as depicted on a screen of the Namban period. The vessel represents the commercial and other relations between Portugal and Japan. These began in 1543, when the Portuguese traveler Fernão Mendes Pinto (1509–1583) and two other Portuguese merchants sailing on a junk bound for China were blown by a typhoon to the island of Tanega Shima, thus becoming the first Europeans to visit Japan. Pinto, a soldier and sailor, merchant and missionary, traveled, fought and traded in India, China and neighboring countries for 21 years. During these years he was captured 13 times, and 17 times he was sold into slavery. The musket that the Portuguese brought with them was copied by the Japanese. The name of the island of Tanega Shima came to mean "firearms" to the Japanese. In later years Pinto was a travel companion of Francisco Xavier (*see* KM-697). He joined the Jesuit order and worked as a missionary in Japan. After a number of years he was dispensed of his vows but he really may have been expelled from the order because he was found to be a marrano, i.e. to possess Jewish blood. After his return to Portugal, Pinto wrote a book on his travels, *The Peregrination*, which was published posthumously. The arrival of the Portuguese, whom the inhabitants of Tanega Shima called *Namban-jin* (barbarians from the Southern Seas), is the beginning of the Namban century (1543–1639) during which Japan maintained commercial relations with Europe and introduced Western technology, Christianity, medicine, cuisine, music, art and culture, until it was decided to close the country to foreigners. The obverse depicts a compass rose and two outline maps of parts of the island of Tanega Shima. This coin and the next one are part of the fourth series in Portugal's "Coins of Discovery" program, which is titled "Europe Meets Japan." The coins of this series are the first European coins with a legend in Japanese.

Europe Meets Japan – Envoys of the Daimios of Kyushu

KM-667 ● 200 escudos ● 1993 copper-nickel, issued also in .925 silver and .917 gold

KM-667
200 escudos
1993 copper-nickel, 36 mm

The obverse features a 16th-century Portuguese nau (merchant ship). Naus were broad-beamed, multidecked, square-rigged carracks or galleons used as cargo carriers on the long route between Portugal and its trading posts in India and beyond. The reverse depicts four 12 to 13-year-old samurais of the daimios (feudal lords) of Omura, Arima and Otomo on the island of Kyushu who are dressed in western clothing, and a Doric column in Rome. The young noblemen were Christian converts who studied at a Jesuit seminary. They became the first Japanese ambassadors to Europe when, in 1582, the Jesuits organized for them a mission to Lisbon and Rome. In Rome, the envoys were received in an audience with Pope Gregory XIII. They returned to Japan in 1590. The reverse inscriptions are in Portuguese, ENVIADOS DOS DAIMIOS KIUSHU (Envoys of the Daimios of Kyushu), and in Japanese.

600th Anniversary of the Birth of Henry the Navigator

KM-670 • 200 escudos • 1994 copper-nickel, issued also in .925 silver and .917 gold

Two Portuguese caravels are depicted on the obverse. The reverse features the portrait of Infante (Prince) Henry the Navigator (1394–1460). Prince Henry—a son of King João I who had established the Aviz dynasty in Portugal—did not actually participate in any sea voyages but sponsored scientific explorations across uncharted water routes to find a way to the rich spice trade of the Indies and spread the Christian faith. In 1420 Henry became master of the Order of Christ. The resources of the Order were used to draw together at Sagres, a town on the Atlantic coast in southwestern Portugal, skilled mathematicians, astronomers, naval architects, geographers and navigators, and to equip a series of expeditions. Prince Henry also erected a shipyard where caravels were built. It was through his inspiration that the shape of the African coast was determined. Every ship sent out to Africa between 1418 and 1460 went under his personal supervision. The reverse inscription is HENRIQUE O NAVIGADOR (Henry the Navigator). This coin and the next three constitute the fifth series in the 15-year "Coins of Discovery" program that commemorates Portugal's landmark sea voyages of exploration and discovery in the 15th and 16th centuries. This series is titled "Dividing Up the World."

500th Anniversary of the Treaty of Tordesilhas – Issue I

KM-671 • 200 escudos • 1994 copper-nickel, issued also in .925 silver, .917 gold and .999 palladium

The obverse depicts the line of demarcation between the areas of influence of Spain and Portugal established by the Treaty of Tordesilhas (Tordesillas), and a Portuguese caravel sailing east of the line between Africa and Brazil. The division of the world outside Europe between the two countries was decreed by the pope, who was regarded by these Christian nations as the ultimate global sovereign power. In a papal bull of 1481, Africa south of the Canary Islands was granted to Portugal. This decree was followed by a bull of 1493, issued less than a year after the discovery of America by Christopher Columbus, in which Pope Alexander VI decreed a line along a circle through the two poles passing 100 leagues west of the Cape Verde Islands. Lands discovered to the west of this line would be Spanish, while Portugal would be entitled to all lands discovered east of the line. Negotiations between the two countries resulted in the Treaty of Tordesilhas which moved the line of demarcation farther west, to 370 leagues (1,453 miles; 2,338 km) west of the Cape Verde Islands (approximately 46° 37' W. longitude). The treaty was signed in the town of Tordesilhas in northwestern Spain in 1494, and was sanctioned by Pope Julius II in 1506. Due to the treaty, Brazil became Portuguese upon its discovery, while Spain's zone of influence included all the Americas with the exception of Brazil. The reverse depicts the signatories to the treaty and a dividing line between them—a portrait of King João II at right to the east of the line with the flag of Portugal and the conjoined portraits of the Spanish monarchs Queen Isabella and King Ferdinand at left to the west of the line with the flag of Castile-Leon.

500th Anniversary of the Treaty of Tordesilhas – Issue II

KM-672 ● 200 escudos ● 1994 copper-nickel, issued also in .925 silver and .917 gold

The reverse features at right a Portuguese caravel, at left a map of South America divided by the north–south line of demarcation established by the Treaty of Tordesilhas (*see* KM-671) and the flags of the countries—that of Portugal to the east of the line and that of Aragon and Castile to its west. The obverse shows a map of Africa and southwestern Europe. The reverse inscription reads PARTILHO DO MUNDO (Dividing the World).

King João II

KM-673 ● 200 escudos ● 1994 copper-nickel, issued also in .925 silver, .917 gold and .999 platinum

The reverse depicts King João (John) II holding a caravel in his hands. King John, "The Perfect Prince" (1455–1495), was king of Portugal over the period 1481–1495. He continued as a leader in the enterprise of the Portuguese discoveries that was launched by his great-uncle Prince Henry the Navigator (*see* KM-670), sending out explorers to find a seaway to India. During his reign, in 1488, Bartolomeu Dias found the passage from the Atlantic Ocean into the Indian Ocean but the king did not live to see India's discovery by Vasco da Gama in 1498. The reference to King John as the "Perfect Prince" alludes to his strategy for the Treaty of Tordesilhas, in which he guaranteed Portuguese rights and influence in large parts of the world. The obverse features Portugal's shield and the king's personal device and motto.

The Sea Route to the Spice Islands - Afonso de Albuquerque

KM-681 ● 200 escudos ● 1995 copper-nickel, issued also in .925 silver and .917 gold

KM-681
200 escudos
1995 copper-nickel, 36 mm

The obverse features the galleon *Flor de la Mar*, the flagship in the fleet of Afonso de Albuquerque (1453–1515) in 1511. No details are available on the size of the vessel. In *Flor de la Mar*, accompanied by two other vessels, Albuquerque first set out to India in 1503 with orders to safeguard Portuguese interests on the Malabar coast of western India. On his way he discovered the island of Zanzibar. In 1509 he became viceroy of India. In 1511 he took the rich trading center Malacca with only 1,100 men, even though its sultan had an army of 20,000 men. Here he built the A Formosa fortress (also known as A Fomosa or A Famosa) that overlooked the Strait of Malacca—the strategic channel between Sumatra and peninsular Malaysia that links the Indian Ocean with the Pacific Ocean and controls the sea route to the Spice Islands. On the return voyage from Malacca to Goa, India *Flor de la Mar* ran on to reefs and was wrecked with the treasures looted in Malacca. Most of her men managed to construct a raft and survive. The reverse depicts Albuquerque and the entrance gate to the A Formosa fortress, the Porta de Santiago. Albuquerque was a man of many talents—soldier, sailor, administrator, statesman, diplomat and strategist. His conquests gave Portugal control of all the main maritime trade routes across the Indian Ocean, ousting the Muslim traders who had monopolized the spice trade and laying the foundations of Portuguese hegemony in the East. Malacca remained Portuguese until it fell into Dutch hands in 1641. This coin and the next three constitute the sixth series in the 15-year "Coins of Discovery" program that commemorates Portugal's landmark sea voyages of exploration and discovery in the 15th and 16th centuries. This series is titled "The Sea Route to the Spice Islands."

The Sea Route to the Spice Islands - Moluccas

KM-682 ● 200 escudos ● 1995 copper-nickel, issued also in .925 silver, .917 gold and .999 palladium

The reverse depicts the carrack *Santa Catarina do Monte Sinai* and maps of several spice islands, including Ternate and Tidore. The four-masted *Santa Catarina do Monte Sinai* was the flagship of Antonio de Abreu who in 1512 commanded the first Portuguese expedition to the Molucca Islands in present-day Indonesia. The ship was built around 1500. According to one source, her tonnage was about 400, her length approximately 90 ft (27 m), her beam about 30 ft (9.1 m), and her depth some 17 ft (5.2 m). Other sources state vastly different measurements. *Santa Catarina do Monte Sinai* had six decks and a complement of some 400. She is the largest vessel on a painting dated to circa 1520 in the collection of the National Maritime Museum at Greenwich, England and must have been one of the largest men-of-war of her times. The obverse depicts clove and nutmeg plants and fruits. These are two of the coveted spices that made the Moluccas famous. From 1513, the Portuguese sent an annual trading fleet to the spice islands.

The Sea Route to the Spice Islands – Solor and Timor Islands

KM-683 ● 200 escudos ● 1995 copper-nickel, issued also in .925 silver and .917 gold

The obverse depicts a 16th-century ship and a sandalwood tree (*pterocarpus santalinus*). The reverse features a cartographic representation of Timor and the smaller islands of Solor and Atauro, the Portuguese cross of the Order of Christ, an island native, and various design elements representing myths, traditions and customs of the islanders. These elements include a snake as a symbol of life, a buffalo and a horse as symbols of wealth, and a crocodile reminiscent of the legend of the creation of Timor. The coin marks the establishment of the Portuguese on the Lesser Sunda Islands of Solor and Timor east of Java in 1515 which was aimed at purchasing sandalwood, a fragrant wood highly prized in Europe.

The Sea Route to the Spice Islands – Australia

KM-684 ● 200 escudos ● 1995 copper-nickel, issued also in .925 silver, .917 gold and .999 platinum

The reverse depicts three caravels, an outline map of Australia and coastal cliffs. The obverse features an armillary sphere. Following the division of the world between Spain and Portugal under the Treaty of Tordesilhas (*see* KM-671), Portugal concentrated its discovery voyages on the East Indies and South Asia. While exploring that part of the world, a Portuguese expedition reached even the west coast of Australia. The coin commemorates the Portuguese exploration of the waters surrounding Australia in the years 1522–1525.

500th Anniversary of the Death of João II

KM-685 ● 1000 escudos ● 1995 .500 silver, issued also in .925 silver

The reverse features a portrait of King João (John) II (1455–1495) (*see* KM-673) and a ship of Portugal's era of discoveries. The obverse features the king's personal device and his motto.

150th Anniversary of the Maiden Voyage of *Dom Fernando II e Glória*

KM-688
1000 escudos
1995 .925 silver, 40.1 mm

KM-688 ● 1000 escudos ● 1995 .500 silver, issued also in .925 silver

The lower half of the reverse depicts the 1,849-ton frigate *Dom Fernando II e Glória*, while the upper half shows the portraits of Queen Maria II da Glória (1819–1853) at right and her consort King Fernando (Ferdinand) II (1816–1885) at left. The ship was named for the king and for Our Lady of Glory, a figure of special devotion among the inhabitants of Goa, to whom she was dedicated. The obverse features the ship's hull and her original figurehead—the bust of King Ferdinand. *Dom Fernando II e Glória* was built of teak at the Naval Dockyard at Damão in India and was launched in 1843. She was then towed to Goa where she was fitted out as a full-rigged ship. She measures 284 ft (87 m) long and has a beam of 42 ft (13 m) and a draft of 21 ft (6.4 m). The total area of her sails is 22,190 sq ft (2,062 m^2). She could carry 650 persons, bringing army and navy units and colonists with their families to the Portuguese colonies in India, Mozambique and Angola. She made her maiden voyage from Goa to Lisbon in 1845 with a crew of 145. *Dom Fernando II e Glória* was the last sail-powered frigate of the Portuguese Navy and the last warship to serve on the India run that linked Portugal to her colonies in India. She made her last sea voyage in 1878. From 1865 until 1938 she served as the naval artillery school. During the years 1938–1963 she was used as a school that provided training in seamanship. In 1963 the ship was partially destoyed by fire and until 1992 lay heeled over to port on the mud-flats of the Tagus River. Subsequently the hull was refloated, placed in a floating dock and towed to the Ria-Marine shipyard at Aveiro for rebuilding and restoration. In 1997 the frigate returned to Lisbon for the completion of the restoration work and to be transformed into a floating museum. She was delivered to the Maritime Museum in Lisbon in 1998 and was a major attraction at the world exhibition Expo '98 that marked the 500th anniversary of the discovery of India by Vasco da Gama. Proceeds from the sale of the coin raised 15 percent of the nearly $8.5 million rebuilding costs.

Opening of the China Sea in the 16th Century – Siam

KM-689 ● 200 escudos ● 1996 copper-nickel, issued also in .925 silver and .917 gold

The obverse shows the ship of Duarte Fernandes at left and Siamese stupas at right. In 1511 Fernandes was sent by Afonso de Albuquerque, Viceroy of the Indies (*see* KM-681), to the king of Siam (now Thailand) with a message of friendship. This was followed by a mission led by António de Miranda de Azevedo that resulted in a military and commercial alliance laid down in a treaty of 1512 between the kingdoms of Portugal and Siam. This alliance caused a strong Portuguese influence in this region. The reverse, which carries inscriptions both in Thai and in Portuguese, depicts the joined arms of Manuel I of Portugal (1495–1521) and Ramathibodi II of Siam (1491–1529). This coin and the next three constitute the seventh series in the 15-year "Coins of Discovery" program that commemorates Portugal's sea voyages of exploration and discovery in the 15th and 16th centuries. This series is titled "Opening of the China Sea."

Opening of the China Sea in the 16th Century – China

KM-690
200 escudos
1996 copper-nickel, 36 mm

KM-690 ● 200 escudos ● 1996 copper-nickel, issued also in .925 silver, .917 gold and .999 palladium

The reverse features the ship of Jorge Álvares, a Chinese junk, an outline map of the Chinese coastline, and the emperor's palace in Beijing. The reverse inscription CHINA is written both in Western and in Mandarin characters. In 1513 Álvares, a factor (commission merchant and sales agent) of the Portuguese king sailed into Chinese waters. He landed on an island near Guangzhou (Canton), set up a traditional Portuguese pillar marking his landing and began trade negotiations with the Chinese. This was the first time Portuguese navigators set foot in China. The Portuguese arms on the obverse are surrounded by fields with bamboo plants.

Opening of the China Sea in the 16th Century – Macao

KM-691
200 escudos
1996 copper-nickel, 36 mm

KM-691 ● 200 escudos ● 1996 copper-nickel, issued also in .925 silver and .917 gold

The reverse depicts a Chinese junk and the Macao lighthouse Farol da Guia, the first in Southeast Asia. The reverse inscription MACAU is written both in Western and in Mandarin characters. The coin marks the granting in 1557 of authorization by the local Mandarin authority to Portuguese merchants to establish a presence at Macao in return for clearing the local waters of pirates. This was the first European settlement in the Far East. Macao, with an area of 6.2 square miles (16 km^2), is situated on a peninsula of the estuary of the Xun (Pearl) River on the South China Sea, 90 miles (145 km) south of Guangzhou (Canton). It became the base of operations for Portuguese commerce in Japan and China, although Portugal's sovereignty to the territory was not officially recognized by China prior to the Treaty of Tianjin of 1862. The coat-of-arms on the obverse is joined by a Chinese dragon rising behind the ornate façade of the ruins of Macao's Church of St. Paul that was built between 1602 and 1608. This is the only part of the Jesuit college of Madro de Deus that remained after the fire of 1835 and is the most celebrated early monument of Macao. Macao remained a Portuguese colony until 1999, when it reverted to China shortly after Great Britain returned Hong Kong to China.

Opening of the China Sea in the 16th Century – Taiwan

KM-692 • 200 escudos • 1996 copper-nickel, issued also in .925 silver, .917 gold and .999 platinum

The reverse features the caravel of the Portuguese navigator Andre Feio, a relief map of the island of Taiwan (Formosa) and the inscription TAIWAN in both Western and Mandarin characters. In 1582 Feio ran his ship aground on the island of Taiwan that had not yet been visited by Portuguese ships. Discovery of the island resulted in its first relations with Europe. The branch of flower blossoms on the obverse signifies Taiwan as "beautiful national flower."

100th Anniversary of Oceanographic Expedition of 1896/97

KM-695 • 1000 escudos • 1997 .500 silver, issued also in .925 silver

The reverse features the busts of King Carlos I of Portugal at top right and of Prince Albert I of Monaco at top left, the yacht *Amélia* and the logo of "Expo '98." The 1,370-ton yacht, named *Banshee*, was built in Scotland in 1900 along the lines of a British cruiser. She was 230 ft (70 m) long and 30 ft (9.1 m) in beam, and drew some 11 ft (3.4 m) of water. She could steam at 15 knots. King Carlos purchased the vessel in 1901 and fitted her to provide for oceanographic scientific expeditions, particularly in the field of ichthyology (study of fishes). He renamed the yacht *Amélia* for his wife, the name of all vessels that were owned by the royal family between 1887 and 1910. After the declaration of the Republic in 1910, King Manuel II, Queen Amélia and other members of the royal family escaped to Gibraltar in *Amélia*. In 1911 the yacht was incorporated into the navy as a dispatch vessel and in 1930 she became a hydrographic ship. In 1938 she was decommissioned and dismantled; however, the quarters of King Carlos and Queen Amélia were preserved and are now on exhibit in the Maritime Museum at Lisbon. Prince Albert (ruler of Monaco 1889–1922) and King Carlos (ruler of Portugal from 1889 until his assassination in 1908) were both interested in oceanography and did much to advance knowledge in this field. The coin marks an oceanographic expedition in 1896/97 under the command of Prince Albert, in King Carlos' *Amélia*. The fish on the obverse represent the field of study to which the king was dedicated.

Golden Age of Discovery – Francisco Xavier

KM-697 ● 200 escudos ● 1997 copper-nickel, issued also in .925 silver and .917 gold

KM-697
200 escudos
1997 copper-nickel, 36 mm

The obverse depicts a nau (merchant ship) like that in which the Spanish priest Francisco Xavier (1506–1552) traveled in eastern Asia to spread the Christian religion. The reverse features Xavier's portrait and the seal of the Society of Jesus (the Jesuit Order) of which he was one of the founding members. In 1540 Xavier was named papal nuncio to the Indies. He did missionary work and established missions in the Malay Peninsula, the Molucca Islands, India, Ceylon, Japan and China. In 1549 he led a group of missionaries to Japan, where he met up with the Portuguese traveler Fernão Mendes Pinto (*see* KM-665). Xavier died in China and later his remains were transferred to Goa, India. He was canonized in 1622. The coin commemorates the Portuguese missionaries that brought the Christian religion to Portuguese territories overseas.

Opening of the Vasco da Gama Bridge

KM-705 ● 500 escudos ● 1998 .500 silver, issued also in .925 silver with .917 gold lamination on reverse

KM-705
500 escudos
1998 .500 silver, 30 mm

The reverse features the Vasco da Gama bridge and in the exergue the sails of a ship. Large crosses are depicted on the sails, similar to the crosses on the sails of the caravels of Portugal's Age of Exploration. The 11-mile (17-km)-long Vasco da Gama bridge was opened in 1998 to relieve the traffic-congested 25th of April Bridge (*see* KM-592) and accommodate visitors to the Expo '98 world fair in Lisbon. The Vasco da Gama bridge spans the Tagus River estuary and is named for the discoverer who was the first European to reach India by sailing around the Cape of Good Hope exactly 500 years before (*see* KM-709). The bridge is the longest in Europe and one of the longest in the world. Its cable-stayed main span is 534 ft (163 m) long. The bridge was designed to withstand earthquakes four times the strength of the one that flattened Lisbon in the 18th century. Its construction took only 18 months, at a cost of one billion US dollars.

Expo '98 and International Year of the Ocean

KM-707 ● 1000 escudos ● 1998 .500 silver, issued also in .925 silver

KM-707
1000 escudos
1998 .500 silver, 27.2 mm

The reverse features a sail, a seahorse, an astrolabe, stars and other celestial bodies, the map of Portugal, and a stylized representation of the Atlantic Ocean. The design elements symbolize Portugal's ties to the sea. The obverse design includes a partial compass and the Expo '98 logo. The coin commemorates both the Expo '98 world fair in Lisbon and the Year of the Ocean that was proclaimed for 1998 by the United Nations to emphasize the need to preserve this world resource. The fair's central theme was "The Oceans, A Heritage for the Future." The coin was chosen as best crown for 1998 in the annual Coin of the Year contest.

500th Anniversary of Vasco da Gama's Voyage to India – From Lisbon to Calicut

KM-709 ● 200 escudos ● 1998 copper-nickel, issued also in .925 silver, .917 gold and .999 platinum

The obverse features three ships of the fleet of Vasco da Gama on his voyage of 1497–1499 during which he was the first European to reach India by sailing around the southern tip of Africa. The reverse shows da Gama's portrait. In July 1497 da Gama left Lisbon with approximately 150 men in a squadron of four specially built ships. They were *São Gabriel* and *São Rafael*, three-masted sailing ships of about 175 tons each, the 50-ton caravel *Berrio*, and a 200-ton storeship. It is assumed that *São Gabriel* was a nau about 106 ft (32 m) long, about 28 ft (8.5 m) in beam and about 11 ft (3.4 m) deep, and that *São Rafael* had similar measurements—100 ft (30 m) length, 27 ft (8.2 m) beam and 10 ft (3 m) draft. *São Gabriel* and *São Rafael* were especially built for this voyage under the supervision of Bartolomeu Dias. Captain of *São Rafael* was Vasco's brother Paolo; captain of *Berrio* was Nicolau Coelho. Da Gama was under orders to go around Africa to India. To avoid the unfavorable winds off West Africa, he swung out into the Atlantic Ocean on a great looping course to escape the doldrums, without sight of land for an unnerving 95 days. After rounding the Cape of Good Hope he anchored in Mossel Bay, where the storeship was broken up. Da Gama then followed the African coast, reaching Natal on Christmas Day. In Malindi in what is now Kenya he met a pilot, Ahmad ibn-Majid, who agreed to show the Portuguese the route to India. After a 23-day voyage across the Indian Ocean, da Gama reached Calicut on 20 May 1498, becoming the first European to discover the sea route to India. Calicut is situated on the Malabar coast of India which is the subcontinent's southwest coast. At Mossel Bay and at Calicut da Gama erected *padrões* (stone pillars) to claim possession of the area for Portugal. His arrival in India secured for Portugal the hegemony over the Indian Ocean. On the return voyage *São Rafael* was burned because the crew that remained was not enough to handle her, after many had died of scurvy. *São Gabriel* and *Berrio* returned home in September 1499 with a full cargo of spices, the voyage showing a profit of 600 percent. Da Gama was made Almirante do Mar das Indias. He made additional voyages to India, and died there after he had become viceroy of India. The route and dates of the journey are inscribed on the reverse—from Lisbon to Calicut, 8 July 1497 until 20 May 1498. This coin and the next three constitute the eighth series in the 15-year "Coins of Discovery" program that commemorates Portugal's landmark sea voyages of exploration and discovery in the 15th and 16th centuries. This series is titled "India, at last!" and documents the stages of da Gama's discovery voyage.

500th Anniversary of Vasco da Gama's Voyage to India – The Discovery of Natal

KM-710 • 200 escudos • 1998 copper-nickel, issued also in .925 silver and .917 gold

The obverse depicts *São Gabriel*, the flagship in the fleet of Vasco da Gama on his voyage of 1497–1499 (*see* KM-709), sailing on the Atlantic side of southern Africa and a palm tree on the continent's west coast. The reverse shows the same ship on the Indian Ocean after rounding the southern tip of Africa, to the right of an outline map of Natal on the east coast of South Africa on which a cross with the arms of Portugal has been planted, and at top right an African native with bow and arrows. The reverse inscription commemorates the discovery by da Gama on 25 December 1497 of the territory on the east coast of Africa which he named Terra do Natal, referring to Christ's Nativity on that day.

500th Anniversary of Vasco da Gama's Voyage to India – The Discovery of Mozambique

KM-711 • 200 escudos • 1998 copper-nickel, issued also in .925 silver and .917 gold, and palladium (unlisted)

The reverse depicts *São Gabriel* sailing on the Indian ocean close to a dhow in front of the coastline of Mozambique. *São Gabriel* was the flagship in the fleet of Vasco da Gama on his voyage of 1497–1499 (*see* KM-709). The date of 1 March 1498 denoted on the reverse is the date of da Gama's landing on the coast of Mozambique.

500th Anniversary of Vasco da Gama's Voyage to India – The Arrival at India

KM-712 • 200 escudos • 1998 copper-nickel, issued also in .925 silver, .917 gold and .999 palladium

The reverse depicts *São Gabriel* and a portolan map of part of the Malabar coast in southwest India. The coin marks Vasco da Gama's arrival in India in 1498 in his flagship *São Gabriel* (*see* KM-709). The map shows the locations of Goa and Calcutta (Calicut). The obverse shows a dhow and a sprig of the pepper plant, symbolizing the importance of spices to the journey. The coin was selected as the most historically significant coin for 1998 in the annual Coin of the Year contest.

King Manuel I

KM-713 ● 1000 escudos ● 1998 .500 silver, issued also in .925 silver

The obverse depicts two caravels of the era of Portuguese discovery voyages, an armillary sphere and the crowned arms of Portugal. The reverse features King Manuel I (1469–1521, reigned from 1495) seated on the throne. The king succeeded João II (*see* KM-673) and continued the royal support to the Portuguese exploration voyages. During his reign the Portuguese discovered the sea route to India and in the wake of this discovery obtained a monopoly to the maritime routes across the Indian Ocean, opening the way to the rich trade in spices and other commodities from the East.

Landfall in Brazil – Death on the Sea

KM-716 ● 200 escudos ● 1999 copper-nickel, issued also in .925 silver and .917 gold, and platinum (unlisted)

The reverse depicts a stylized sinking ship with rolling waves below and raining storm clouds above, illustrating the perils early explorers encountered on their voyages. The reverse inscription is MORTE NO MAR (Death on the Sea). The obverse features an armillary sphere, the coat-of-arms of Brazil, the Portuguese shield and ship rigging ropes. This coin and the next three constitute the ninth series in the 15-year "Coins of Discovery" program that commemorates Portugal's landmark sea voyages of exploration and discovery in the 15th and 16th centuries. This series is titled "Landfall in Brazil."

Landfall in Brazil – Pedro Álvares Cabral

KM-717 ● 200 escudos ● 1999 copper-nickel, issued also in .925 silver and .917 gold, and palladium (unlisted)

The ships on the obverse represent the 13 ships in the fleet of Pedro Álvares Cabral (circa 1467–1526) who discovered Brazil in 1500. Only *El Rei*, *São Pedro* and *Anunciada* can be named. No data exists about their construction. The flagship was *El Rei*. The fleet had more than 1,200 men on board—merchants, soldiers, Franciscan missionaries and a number of convicts. Cabral's voyage was the second major Portuguese expedition to India by way of the Cape of Good Hope. His mission was to capitalize on the discovery of this route by Vasco da Gama, who had returned in 1499, to trade and to claim what lands he could for Portugal. Cabral left Lisbon on 9 March 1500. Da Gama had been becalmed in the waters of the Gulf of Guinea, so Cabral was instructed to sail a circular path to the southwest and then to the southeast to avoid this area. This route brought him to the coast of Brazil, that had already been sighted before by other navigators who explored the extension of known coastlines. (Vicente Yáñez Pinzón visited Brazil a few months before Cabral.) Cabral, however, sailed into an area where no land had been anticipated. On 22 April 1500 the fleet sighted the South American mainland at about 17° S. latitude. They sailed northward to present-day Porto Seguro (Secure Harbor) and a few days later Cabral went ashore, took possession of the land for Portugal and named it Terra da Vera Cruz (Land of the Holy Cross). Only later was the area named Brazil, because of the brazilwood tree from which a red dye is extracted. Cabral then turned east to the Cape of Good Hope and from there to the Malabar coast of southwest India, where he reached Calicut on 13 September. He arrived back in Lisbon in July of 1501. *Anunciada* was the first ship to return to Portugal. Six other ships also eventually found their way home again, with on board nearly 900 of his original complement of 1,200 men. The other ships were lost at sea. Cabral's portrait is featured on the reverse against the background of an outline map of the coast of Brazil with an anchor below that denotes the location of Porto Seguro.

Landfall in Brazil – Brazil

KM-718
200 escudos
1999 copper-nickel, 36 mm

KM-718 ● 200 escudos ● 1999 copper-nickel, issued also in .925 silver and .917 gold

The reverse depicts an outline map of Brazil, superimposed on which are a native Indian and a Portuguese ship. The obverse design features an outline map of the northern coast of Brazil with a native Indian and palm trees thereon. The designs with scenes of Brazil's trees and native people in feather clothes are inspired by a map made by Lopo Homem-Reineis in 1519 that features native people as well as local flora and fauna.

Landfall in Brazil – Duarte Pacheco Pereira

KM-719 ● 200 escudos ● 1999 copper-nickel, issued also in .925 silver and .917 gold

The obverse depicts two Portuguese caravels. The reverse features an armored portrait of the navigator and cosmographer Duarte Pacheco Pereira (1460–1533) holding a sword. He was the first person to write about supposedly "secret" voyages to northern Brazil.

Expo '98 and Millennium of Atlantic Sailing

KM-721 ● 1000 escudos ● 1999 .500 silver; issued also in .925 silver

The reverse features a sailing ship on stormy waves that take the form of a sea monster. The design marks the Millennium of Atlantic Sailing. The obverse features the logo of Expo '98, the world fair held in Lisbon in 1998.

Opening Up New Frontiers - Labrador

KM-728 ● 200 escudos ● 2000 copper-nickel, issued also in .925 silver and .917 gold

The reverse depicts at right a caravel on the Atlantic Ocean and at left a map of Labrador—that part of the Canadian province of Newfoundland on the eastern coast of the North American continent that is located between Hudson Strait and the island of Newfoundland. The reverse inscription 1491–1500 denotes the period of Portuguese discovery voyages to northern America. The Portuguese Crown thought this area to be in the part of the world assigned to Portugal in 1494 under the Treaty of Tordesilhas (*see* KM-671). In 1499, the year after John Cabot reported on his discovery of Newfoundland, King Henry VII of England granted a patent to an Anglo-Portuguese syndicate that included João Fernandes (?–1505), a *lavrador* (landowner) from the Azores. In the same year, Fernandes also obtained a charter from the Portuguese King Manuel that promised him governorship of any islands which he might discover. A map of 1503 shows Greenland as Terra de Labrador, probably because the labrador Fernandes was the first to give information on it to the English. The name was later given to the area now known as Labrador. This coin and the next three constitute the tenth and last series in the 15-year "Coins of Discovery" program that commemorates Portugal's landmark sea voyages of exploration and discovery in the 15th and 16th centuries. This series is titled "Opening Up New Frontiers."

Opening Up New Frontiers - Newfoundland

KM-729 ● 200 escudos ● 2000 copper-nickel, issued also in .925 silver, .917 gold and .999 palladium

The reverse depicts a caravel and an outline map of Newfoundland that was prepared in 1506. The reverse inscriptions are TERRA DOS CORTE REAIS (Land of the Corte Reals) and 1501–1502. The coin commemorates the Portuguese navigators and explorers Gaspar Corte Real and his elder brother Miguel. Gaspar made voyages of exploration to North America in 1500 and 1501 by charter of King Manuel I. On his first voyage Gaspar explored the east coast of the island of Newfoundland. He was lost with his ship on his second voyage but the two other vessels of this expedition returned safely to Portugal, bringing the king a present of more than 50 kidnapped Indians. Miguel made a voyage with two ships in 1502 to look for his brother. The vessel that carried him was also lost at sea. These voyages did not result in land claims by the Portuguese government in northern America but Portuguese fishermen continued to fish cod in Newfoundland waters to such extent that King Manuel imposed payment of a tithe on the products of fishing activity in Newfoundland in 1506. A statue of Gaspar Corte Real in St. John's, Newfoundland donated by the Portuguese Fisheries Organization recognizes the hospitality of Newfoundlanders toward Portuguese Grand Banks fishermen.

Opening Up New Frontiers – Florida

KM-730 • 200 escudos • 2000 copper-nickel, issued also in .925 silver and .917 gold

KM-730
200 escudos
2000 copper-nickel, 36 mm

The reverse depicts a caravel to the right of a map of the east coast of the United States. The reverse inscription TERRA FLORIDA is superimposed on the lower part of the map; the year 1501 is denoted in the exergue. The discovery of Florida is generally attributed to the Spaniard Juan Ponce de León, who was likely the first European to set foot in the area in 1513; however, the shoreline of Florida is shown already on a map published in 1502. The most likely candidate for the early discovery of Florida is a Portuguese explorer, whose discovery may have been kept secret; but all known (including secret) geographical knowledge was taken into account in drawing the world map maintained by the Portuguese crown, of which the 1502 map seems to be a copy.

Opening Up New Frontiers – Circling the World

KM-731 • 200 escudos • 2000 copper-nickel, issued also in .925 silver, .917 gold and .999 platinum

The obverse features *Trinidad*, the flagship in the fleet of five ships of the Portugese sailor Fernão de Magalhães (Ferdinand Magellan) (1480–1521) on the first circumnavigation voyage ever made. Magellan's bust appears on the reverse. The 110-ton *Trinidad* was a carrack of 79 ft (24 m) long, had a beam of 23 ft (7.1 m), and drew 10 ft (3 m) of water. She was built in 1511 and sank in 1522. Her crew numbered 55. *Vittoria*, built in 1514, was an 85-ton carrack with 42 men. She was 55 ft (17 m) long, had a beam of 20 ft (6.1 m), and drew 9 ft (2.7 m) of water. She went on to make two transatlantic voyages to Hispaniola. On the return leg of the second voyage she sank in mid-Atlantic in 1525. The other ships in the fleet were the 120-ton *San Antonio* with a crew of 60, the 90-ton *Concepción* with

45 men and the 75-ton *Santiago* with 42 men. Magellan, after having renounced his Portuguese citizenship, got the backing of King Charles I of Spain for a voyage to find a westward route to the Spice Islands (the Moluccas) around South America, that would prove them to be situated within the Spanish hemisphere demarcated by the Treaty of Tordesilhas. The voyage would be completed by sailing westward back to Spain without intruding into Portuguese territories. The fleet left Sanlúcar de Barrameda in September 1519 and sailed to the coast of South America. After having lost *San Antonio* and *Santiago*, Magellan entered into the strait that now bears his name. In November 1520 he reached the great ocean that he later named "Pacific" because for a long time the ships were not surprised by any storms. After crossing the Pacific Ocean, Magellan was fatally wounded by poison-tipped arrows on the Philippine island of Cebu in April 1521, while fighting in a local war. Command of *Vittoria* was taken over by the master of *Concepción*, the Basque navigator Juan Sebastián del Cano (or de Elcano). Only *Vittoria* completed the voyage, the first ship to circumnavigate the earth. She arrived home at Sanlúcar on 6 September 1522. Only 18 men survived the voyage. Although most of the ships had been lost, the spices taken on in the Moluccas more than paid for the initial investment in the expedition.

Ibero–American Series - Navigation

KM-748 • 10 euro • 2003 .500 silver, issued also in .925 silver

KM-748
10 euro
2003 .500 silver, 40 mm

The reverse depicts a caravel of the era of the discoveries, a quadrant used to determine latitude, and three stars, one of which is aligned with the quadrant as the reference point to determine the position of the ship. The obverse features the coat-of-arms of Portugal surrounded by those of all countries participating in the issue of the Ibero–American series—a joint scheme of Portugal, Spain and various Central and South American countries to issue similar coins. The theme of the 2002–2003 series was "Navigation."

T-1 Circulation Coins

KM-590 • $2\frac{1}{2}$ escudos • 1963–85 copper-nickel
KM-591 • 5 escudos • 1963–86 copper-nickel
KM-600 • 10 escudos • 1971–74 copper-nickel clad nickel

KM-590
$2\frac{1}{2}$ escudos
1984 copper-nickel, 18.2 mm

The obverse depicts a caravel, probably *São Rafael*, one of the ships in the fleet of Vasco da Gama on his journey of 1497–1499 during which he was the first European to reach India by sailing around the Cape of Good Hope (*see* KM-709). The caravel used several types of rigs. Commonplace was the three-masted lateen sails format, such as depicted on the obverse.

ROMANIA

Romania is a republic in southeastern Europe between Bulgaria and the Ukraine.

Olympic Games 1996 Atlanta

KM-122 ● 10 lei ● 1996 Windsurfing – see T-1
KM-123 ● 10 lei ● 1996 Sailing – see T-2
KM-124 ● 10 lei ● 1996 Canoeing/Kayaking – see T-3
KM-125 ● 10 lei ● 1996 Sweep boat racing – see T-4
KM-129 ● 100 lei ● 1996 Windsurfing – see T-1
KM-130 ● 100 lei ● 1996 Sailing – see T-2
KM-131 ● 100 lei ● 1996 Canoeing/Kayaking – see T-3
KM-132 ● 100 lei ● 1996 Sweep boat racing – see T-4

Antarctic Expedition

KM-148 ● 100 lei ● 1999 .925 silver

KM-148
100 lei
1999 .925 silver, 37 mm

The reverse depicts the wooden steamer *Belgica* that made the Antarctic expedition of 1897–1899 and the expedition's Romanian biologist, Emil Racovita (1868–1947). *Belgica* was originally a Norwegian whaler named *Patria* that was built in 1884 by Christian Jacobsen at Svelvig, Norway. The three-masted bark of 336 gross tons was 118 ft (36 m) long and 25 ft (7.6 m) in beam, and drew 13 ft (4.1 m) of water. Her engine enabled her to make seven knots. In 1886 she was bought by Adrien Victor Joseph de Gerlache de Gomery (1866–1934), a lieutenant in the Royal Belgian Navy, for 70,000 francs and renamed *Belgica*. De Gerlache used her for the expedition of 1897–1899 that is marked by the coin. After the expedition de Gerlache sold the ship to the Belgian government but he bought her back to be used once again as a whaler. In 1905 the vessel was sold to Prince Philippe, Duke of Orleans. In 1905–1907 *Belgica* was used for research voyages to the Kara and Greenland Seas, and to Franz Josef Land in the Arctic Ocean. *Belgica* was sold in 1916 to a mining company that sold her in 1917 to Kristian Holst of Harstad, Norway. She was renamed *Isfjord* after a fjord in Svalbard (Spitsbergen) and engaged in carrying coal. In later years she served as a barge. In 1940 she was used for the storage of explosive shells and was scuttled to prevent her from falling into the hands of the German invaders. The expedition of 1897–1899 was the first to carry out a scientific research program in Antarctica. The men were also the first to winter in the Antarctic and the first to bring back actual photographs of the continent. For 13 months *Belgica* was trapped in the ice. Over those long months the crew of 19, from six different nationalities, had difficulty in communicating because of language barriers. Two of them died, others came down with scurvy and muscular spasms, and many lost their sanity. The biologist was Emil Racovita, who brought back 400 botanical and 1,200 zoological specimens. Later he became the founder of biospeleology (cave biology) as an independent science. He became president of the Romanian Academy of Sciences and was a senator.

T-1 Olympic Games 1996 Atlanta – Windsurfing

KM-122 ● 10 lei ● 1996 nickel plated steel
KM-129 ● 100 lei ● 1996 .925 silver

The reverse features a Mistral windsurfer. Windsurfing—introduced at the 1984 Olympic Games in Los Angeles—is the latest form of watercraft racing in the Olympic Games. Sailing and rowing entered in 1900, motorboating in 1908 and canoeing in 1936.

T-2 Olympic Games 1996 Atlanta – Sailing

KM-123 ● 10 lei ● 1996 nickel plated steel
KM-130 ● 100 lei ● 1996 .925 silver

The reverse depicts a catamaran with three crewmen.

KM-130
100 lei
1996 .925 silver, 36.9 mm

T-3 Olympic Games 1996 Atlanta – Canoeing/Kayaking

KM-124 ● 10 lei ● 1996 nickel plated steel
KM-131 ● 100 lei ● 1996 .925 silver

The reverse depicts a kayak with two paddlers.

T-4 Olympic Games 1996 Atlanta – Sweep Boat Racing

KM-125 ● 10 lei ● 1996 nickel plated steel
KM-132 ● 100 lei ● 1996 .925 silver

The reverse features a 62-ft (19-m)-long sweep-oared rowboat with eight oarsmen and a coxswain. It is steered by the non-rowing coxswain (pronounced cox-n) who manipulates tiller ropes attached to a rudder. A sweep oar has an average length of 12 ft (3.8 m).

RUSSIA

Coins of the years 1967–1991 were issued by the **Union of Soviet Socialist Republics** (USSR). Those of later years were issued by the Bank of Russia, the central bank of **Russia** (the Russian Federation).

HISTORICAL OVERVIEW

To better appreciate Russia's ship coins in their historical context, the major events reflected by them are shown below chronologically, followed by their Y-numbers:

1240	Victory over Sweden in the battle on the Neva River (503)
1581	Occupation of the Tatar city of Sibir (683)
1643	Exploration of eastern Siberia (684)
1648	Discovery of the northeast passage to the Orient (685)
1696	Founding of the Russian fleet by Czar Peter I (504–512, 542–548)
1700	Great Northern War (801, 865)
1703	Founding of St. Petersburg (249–250, 836, 873, 877) and surrounding fortifications (878–879)
1714	Victory over Swedish fleet at the battle of Gangut (542)
1725	First Kamchatka Expedition (809, 866, 875)
1732	Discovery of Alaska (245)
1733	First rounding of Cape Chelyuskin (461)
1740	Second Kamchatka Expedition (243, 244)
1762	Accession of Empress Catherine II (353)
1770	Victory over the Turkish fleet at Chesme (358, 543)
1784	Founding of the first Russian settlement in Alaska (265)
1803	First Russian circumnavigation of the world (464, 517–519)
1819	First Russian expedition to Antarctica (466, 521–523)
1853	Crimean War (545, 755, 785)
1904	Russo-Japanese war (546)
1917	October Revolution – *Aurora* (138, 143, 206)
1941	Great Patriotic War (World War II) (304, 403, 548, 666, 668)
1980	Olympic Games in Moscow (148, 159)

50th Anniversary of the October Revolution

Y-138 ● 20 kopeks ● 1967 copper-nickel-zinc

The reverse depicts the 6,630-ton armored cruiser *Aurora*, 416 ft (127 m) long, with a beam of 55 ft (17 m) and a draft of 22 ft (6.6 m). *Aurora* was completed in 1900 at the Galerni Island Shipyard in St. Petersburg for the Imperial Russian Navy. Her steam engines gave her a speed of 20 knots. She had a complement of 571. She was named for the frigate of the same name that defended

Petropavlovsk on Kamchatka against French and British naval units during the Crimean War of 1853–1856. In the battle of Tsushima Strait of 1905 in the Russo-Japanese War she was badly damaged, with ten dead, including Captain Egorev, and 86 wounded. *Aurora* played an important role in the October Revolution in 1917. While at St. Petersburg for repairs, she was ordered to sea for trials as a way of removing her revolutionary crew from the capital. These orders were countermanded by the Central Committee of the Baltic Fleet and she took up station on the Neva River. On 25 October 1917 according to the Julian calendar then still in use in Russia (corresponding to 7 November 1917 according to the Gregorian calendar), *Aurora* fired blanks to signal the Bolsheviks' determination to force the ouster of the government. This signal triggered the attack on the Winter Palace in St. Petersburg which resulted in the resignation of the provisional government that same day. The reverse alludes to this event by showing a gun on *Aurora*'s bow with a puff of smoke from the powder explosion in front of the gun. The straight line on the reverse may represent the ray from a searchlight. The old ship occupied a special place in the Communist pantheon. She was used for training and after 1930 was permanently moored in the Neva. In World War II she was badly damaged by bombing but after the war she was salvaged and moved to a permanent berth in the Bolshaya Nevka River, a small tributary which joins the Neva very close to the scene of her exploit in 1917. She is now a floating museum and a cadets' training ship of the Nakhimov Navy school. The obverse legend translates to "50 Years of Soviet power."

60th Anniversary of the October Revolution

Y-143 ● 1 rouble ● 1977 copper-nickel-zinc, varieties exist

The reverse features the bust of Vladimir Ilich Lenin (1870–1924), the cruiser *Aurora* and the monument to space explorers in Moscow. The coin marks the 60th anniversary of the October Revolution of 1917 (*see* Y-138 about *Aurora* and her place in that revolution). Lenin—whose original surname was Ulyanov and who named his alias after the Lena River—was a Marxist theoretician. He believed that the revolution must be guided by a single centralized party of professional revolutionaries. In 1903 he formed the Bolsheviks (literally, those in the majority). Lenin was the originator of the guiding doctrine of the Soviet Union, Marxism–Leninism. In 1917 he called for the transfer of power from the provisional government to the soviets (workers' councils) and led the Bolsheviks in the revolution which overthrew the provisional government and established the ruling Soviet of People's Commissars under Lenin's chairmanship. He was the first premier of the Soviet Union. The characters CCCP on the obverse are the Cyrillic alphabet letters corresponding to the Roman alphabet letters SSSR (the initial letters of "Union of Soviet Socialist Republics" in Russian). The translation of the edge inscription is "One Rouble."

Olympic Games 1980 Moscow – Sailing

Y-148 ● 5 roubles ● 1977 .900 silver

The reverse shows two sailboats against the background of the city of Tallinn, the capital of Estonia, where the sailing races of the 1980 Olympic Games were held. Estonia is now independent. Upon issue of the coin it was the Estonian Soviet Socialistic Republic, part of the USSR.

70th Anniversary of the October Revolution

Y-206 ● 1 rouble ● 1987 copper-nickel

The reverse pictures the cruiser *Aurora* and the crossed-hammer-and-sickle Soviet symbol on a globe which is superimposed on a ribbon tied in a bow (*see* Y-138 about *Aurora* and her place in the revolution of 1917).

250th Anniversary of the Discovery of Russian America – James Cook on Unalaska Island

Y-242 ● 3 roubles ● 1990 .900 silver

Y-242
3 roubles
1990 .900 silver, 39 mm

The reverse depicts the encounter in 1778 on the Aleutian island of Unalaska between the party of Captain James Cook and a Russian expedition led by Gerasim Grigorevich Izmailov, and in the background HMS *Resolution* (*see* Gibraltar KM-622) and HMS *Discovery*. *Resolution* and *Discovery* were Cook's ships on his third circumnavigation voyage (1776–1780). *Discovery* was built by G. & N. Langborn in 1774 as *Diligence* for Mr. William Herbert, from whom she was bought in 1775 by the admiralty for Cook's expedition and renamed *Discovery*. The 299-ton bark measured 91 ft (28 m) long and had a beam of 27 ft (8.4 m) and a draft of 11 ft (3.5 m). She cost the admiralty £2,415 including alterations. Her complement numbered 70 and she was put under the command of Lieutenant Charles Clerke. She was broken up at Chatham in 1797. The aim of Cook's third voyage was to explore the west coast of North America looking for the Northwest Passage. En route in December 1777 Cook sighted a barren atoll on which he landed on Christmas Day, naming it Christmas Island. In January 1778 Cook discovered the Hawaiian Islands, which he named Sandwich Islands after the Earl of Sandwich, First Lord of the Admiralty. Cook was killed at Kealakakua Bay in a fight with natives of Hawaii when he tried to capture Chief Teraiobu in order to hold him as a hostage until the return of *Discovery*'s largest cutter that had been stolen by the natives. Clerke took command of the expedition and Lieutenant Gore was appointed to take charge of *Discovery*. Later Clerke died, Gore took over command of the expedition and Lieutenant King succeeded Gore in *Discovery*. The translation of the reverse inscriptions is "250th Anniversary of the Discovery of Russian America" and "Cook's Expedition to Russian America."

250th Anniversary of the Discovery of Russian America – *Sviatoi Pyotr*

Y-243 ● 25 roubles ● 1990 .999 palladium

The reverse depicts the two-masted brig *Sviatoi Pyotr* (St. Peter), the ship of Vitus Jonassen Bering (1681–1741) on his second Kamchatka expedition (1740–1742), and a small portrait of Bering. The second ship on the expedition was *Sviatoi Pavel* (St. Paul) (*see* Y-244). Both vessels were of about 90 tons and were very much alike, measuring 80 ft (24 m) in length and 22 ft (6.9 m) in beam, and drawing 12 ft (3.7 m) of water. They were built in Okhotsk in 1736–1740 by master shipwright Andrei Kuzmin with materials brought overland from the European part of Russia. Bering, a Danish explorer who was a captain in the Russian navy, had been the leader of the first Kamchatka expedition (*see* Y-809). On his second expedition Bering sailed to Avacha Bay on the east coast of the Kamchatka Peninsula, where he founded Petropavlovsk, which was named for his two ships. In 1741 he saw the American coast at 58° 14' N. latitude and sailed along it for four days. On his return voyage Bering sighted several of the Aleutian Islands. His ship was wrecked on an island he discovered, which was later named for him. During the winter spent there 19 men died of scurvy, including Bering. In the spring of 1742 the 45 survivors built a 12-ft (3.7-m)-long boat from timber salvaged from *Sviatoi Pyotr*, which they also named *Sviatoi Pyotr*. In this boat they reached Petropavlovsk in August with 600 fur pelts. This voyage resulted in the Russian colonization of Alaska. The region was under the trade control of the Russian American Company from the founding of this company in 1799 until 1867 when the territory was purchased by the United States for $7 million. The translation of the reverse inscriptions is "250th Anniversary of the Discovery of Russian America" and "Packet-ship *Sv. Pyotr* – Captain Commander V. Bering." Palladium, an element of the platinum group, was discovered in 1803. It was named for the asteroid Pallas, which had recently been discovered. Russia's first palladium coin was issued in 1988.

250th Anniversary of the Discovery of Russian America – *Sviatoi Pavel*

Y-244 ● 25 roubles ● 1990 .999 palladium

The reverse depicts *Sviatoi Pavel* (St. Paul), the second vessel in the fleet of Vitus Bering (1681–1741) on his second Kamchatka expedition (1740–1742). *Sviatoi Pavel* and Bering's ship *Sviatoi Pyotr* were very much alike (*see* Y-243). *Sviatoi Pavel* was commanded by the Russian seafarer Aleksey Ilyich Chirikov (1703–1748) who had been second-in-command of Bering's first Kamchatka expedition (1728–1730) and had assisted Bering from 1733 in organizing the Great Northern Expedition. The second Kamchatka expedition was part of the Great Northern Expedition and had the task of reaching the coast of North America. Chirikov in *Sviatoi Pavel* left Okhotsk in 1740. He sighted the American coast in 1741 at 55° 36' N. latitude, mistaking the Alexander Archipelago for the mainland, and landed at what is now Prince of Wales Island, Alaska—becoming the first European to set foot in Alaska. On his return voyage Chirikov sighted several of the Aleutian Islands. At 57° 58' N. latitude he attempted to send a party ashore but both of the ship's boats and the 15 men in them were lost and Chirikov returned to Kamchatka in 1742. Chirikov proceeded to Europe. *Sviatoi Pavel* was laid up at Okhotsk. Chirikov's report is the first description of the northwest coast of North America and of the Aleutian Islands. The translation of the reverse inscriptions is "250th Anniversary of the Discovery of Russian America" and "Packet-ship *Sv. Pavel* – Captain A. Chirikov – 1741."

Y-244
25 roubles
1990 .999 palladium, 37 mm

250th Anniversary of the Discovery of Russian America – *Sviatoi Gavriil*

Y-245 ● 150 roubles ● 1990 .999 platinum

The reverse depicts the sailing ship *Sviatoi Gavriil* (St. Gabriel) and names the Russian surveyor Mikhail Spiridonovich Gvozdev and the year 1732 in which Gvozdev together with the navigator Ivan Fedorov discovered Alaska. *Sviatoi Gavriil* was built in 1728 at Nizhne Kamchatsk on the east coast of the Kamchatka Peninsula. She measured about 60 ft (18 m) in length and had a beam of about 20 ft (6 m) and a draft of some 8 ft (2.4 m). Her complement numbered 44. In 1728 and 1729 Vitus Bering made exploration voyages along the east coast of Asia in *Sviatoi Gavriil* (*see* Y-809) and confirmed that Asia and North America are not connected. In August 1732 Fedorov and Gvozdev crossed the Bering Sea and reached Alaska in the region of Cape Prince of Wales. They were the first Europeans to see both the Asian and the American coasts bordering upon the Bering Sea. For a long time the name of Fedorov was lost and Gvozdev was considered to be the discoverer of Alaska. In 1738 *Sviatoi Gavriil* was one of three ships that made an expedition during which nearly 30 new islands in the Kurile chain between Kamchatka and Japan were discovered. Her fate is unknown. The translation of the reverse inscriptions is "250th Anniversary of the Discovery of Russian America" and "Ship *Sv. Gavriil* – M. Gvozdev – 1732."

Y-245
150 roubles
1990 .999 platinum, 29 mm

500th Anniversary of the Unified Russian State – Peter the Great's Fleet

Y-248 ● 3 roubles ● 1990 .900 silver

The reverse depicts the battleship *Poltava* (*see* Y-547) at front, another battleship at left and, at the top left, a contemporary medal that features Peter I (the Great). *Poltava* was the first Russian battleship, built for its Baltic navy in 1712. Peter I (1672–1725) became czar in 1682 and emperor in 1721. The reverse inscriptions translate to "500th Anniversary of the Unified Russian State" and "Peter the Great's Fleet."

500th Anniversary of the Unified Russian State – Peter and Paul Fortress

Y-249 ● 3 roubles ● 1990 .900 silver

The reverse depicts a sailing ship and a rowboat in front of the Peter and Paul fortress in Leningrad (now St. Petersburg). The fortress, which is the oldest structure in the city, was built in 1703 at the orders of Czar Peter I (the Great) who cut two strips of turf with a bayonet on Zayachy Island (Hare Island) and laid them in the form of a cross to dedicate the founding of St. Petersburg. At a massive cost in human lives, tens of thousands of workers raised the level of the swampy island above the reach of the Neva River, constructed the ramparts of the fortress of earth and timber, and later made the walls thicker and higher with stone. The fortress covers the entire island and was built as a strategic stronghold at the mouth of the Neva River to protect the Russian interior from the Swedes. Its designer was Lambert, a pupil of the French military engineer Sébastian de Vauban. Within the fortress is the Saints Peter and Paul Cathedral for which the fortress is named. The cathedral was founded on the feast day of the Apostles Peter and Paul. The golden needle-thin spire on its bell tower, the overall height of which is 402 ft (122 m), is a landmark of St. Petersburg. Also within the fortress is the mint that struck Russia's first rouble-denominated coins. The translation of the reverse inscriptions is "500th Anniversary of the Unified Russian State" and "Peter and Paul Fortress – 1703."

Y-250
25 roubles
1990 .999 palladium, 37 mm

500th Anniversary of the Unified Russian State – Peter the Great

Y-250 ● 25 roubles ● 1990 .999 palladium

The reverse depicts a half-length portrait of Czar Peter I (the Great, 1672–1725) holding a scroll, at right in the background a two-masted sailing ship, and at left in the background the Peter and Paul fortress with the spire on the bell tower of the Saints

Peter and Paul Cathedral and ship masts behind the fortress. (The usual description, according to which the spire is that on the top of the central tower of the Admiralty, appears to be incorrect.) The czar is shown as the founder of his capital St. Petersburg. He built the city on the delta of the Neva River at the eastern end of the Gulf of Finland, an arm of the Baltic Sea, on land conquered from Sweden. St. Petersburg was the capital of the Russian Empire from 1712 to 1918. From 1914 to 1924 the city's name was Petrograd. When the Bolshevik revolutionary leader Vladimir Lenin died in 1924 the city's name was changed to Leningrad and in 1991 it reverted to its original name. The reverse inscriptions translate to "500th Anniversary of the Unified Russian State" and "Peter I – Reformer."

250th Anniversary of the Discovery of Russian America – Fort Ross

Y-264 ● 3 roubles ● 1991 .900 silver

Y-264
3 roubles
1991 .900 silver, 39 mm

The reverse depicts the two-masted brig *Maria* and at left in the background the Russian trading colony Fort Ross in northern California. *Maria* was built in 1804 for Governor Aleksandr Baranov (*see* Y-266) as a company vessel for the Russian American Company to transport passengers and cargo between Russia and the Russian outposts in Alaska and California. She met her end in 1815. Fort Ross was founded in 1812 on Baranov's orders 50 miles (80 km) north of present-day San Francisco. The need for this fur trading colony arose after the Russians had depleted populations of sea otters off the coast of Alaska and were forced to move south. The founder of the fort was Ivan A. Kuskov, an assistant of Baranov. Fort Ross remained a Russian outpost until 1841. It is now an historical site. The translation of the reverse inscriptions is "250th Anniversary of Discoveries in Russian America" and "Fort Ross – 1812."

250th Anniversary of the Discovery of Russian America – Three Saints Harbor

Y-265 ● 25 roubles ● 1991 .999 palladium

According to an advertisement of the Russian Central Bank the reverse depicts the sailing ship *Elizaveta* anchoring at Three Saints Harbor on Kodiak Island in the Gulf of Alaska. No information has been found on this vessel or her place in the history of Russian America. The ship depicted may be a fur trader of the hooker type. Such Russian ships were 54–98 ft (16–30 m) long and 15–24 ft (4.7–7.2 m) wide, and had a draft of 5.9–13.4 ft (1.8–4.1 m) and a cargo capacity of 60–200 tons. The fortified settlement of Three Saints (now

Kodiak) was founded in 1784 by the fur trader Grigori Ivanovich Shelekhov (1747–1795). It was the first Russian settlement in Russian America and was named for Shelekhov's flagship, the galiot *Tri Sviatitelia* (Three Saints or, in a more exact translation, Three Hierarchies) that had been built in 1783 and sank in 1790. A galiot is a Russian vessel somewhat similar in appearance to a topsail schooner measuring up to 72 ft (22 m) in length and up to 20 ft (6 m) in beam. Shelekhov's other two ships on this voyage were another galiot, *Sviatoi Archistratig Mikhail* (St. Archangel Michael), which was wrecked on the voyage, and the sloop *Sviatoi Simeon Bogopriimets i Anna Prorochitsa* (St. Simeon Who Took God and Anna the Prophetess, referring to the episode in the Temple described in Luke 2:25–38 in which the old man Simeon took the child Jesus in his arms and the old prophetess Anna gave thanks to God and spoke about the child). The three ships set out from Okhotsk to Alaskan waters and carried over 200 men, cattle, seeds and other supplies. Three Saints Harbor served for the trade in the heavy furs of the region which were in great demand in Russia. Later other settlements were founded, extending south to Fort Ross in northern California (*see* Y-264). Initially the fur trade was conducted by various Russian trading companies. In 1799 the Russian American Company was granted a monopoly by Czar Paul I. It prospered under the direction of Aleksandr Baranov (*see* Y-266). Russia's presence in America lasted until 1867. The reverse inscriptions translate to "250th Anniversary of Discoveries in Russian America" and "Three Saints Harbor 1784."

250th Anniversary of the Discovery of Russian America – Novo Archangelsk

Y-266 ● 25 roubles ● 1991 .999 palladium

According to an advertisement of the Russian Central Bank the reverse depicts the sailing ship *St. Nikolay* anchored off the outpost Novo Archangelsk on rocky Sitka Island, and the portrait of Aleksandr Andreyevich Baranov (1746–1819). No information has been found on this vessel or her place in the history of Russian America. Baranov was the general manager of the Russian American Company and the first governor of Russian America (1802–1818). In 1795 Baranov, in charge of the fur trade operations of Grigori Shelekhov (*see* Y-265), had discovered Sitka Island, later renamed Baranof Island in his honor. In 1799 he established on the island the settlement of Fort St. Archangel Mikhail. In 1802 the fort was overrun and burned by members of the Tlingit-Haida tribe, with a loss of more than 400 persons and half of Baranov's fleet of baidarkas (leathern canoes). In 1804 Baranov led an attempt by 120 Russians in four small ships and 800 Aleutians in 300 baidarkas to retake the fort but their attack failed. After *Neva*'s arrival on her voyage around the world (*see* Y-518), Baranov requested her captain,

Yuri Lisyansky, to assume command of the combat against the Sitkans. Lisyansky, convinced of the importance to the Russian trade of recovering the settlement, had *Neva* positioned under the fort and opened fire. A few days later, after negotiations with the Tlingit, they deserted the fort and Baranov ordered the fort to be completely destroyed. A new fort was built nearby and named Novo Archangelsk (New Archangelsk) after the port of Archangelsk in European Russia on the White Sea. The settlement that grew out of the fort (now Sitka) became the center of Russian America. The reverse inscriptions translate to "250th Anniversary of Discoveries in Russian America" and "Novo Archangelsk 1799."

250th Anniversary of the Discovery of Russian America – Ioann Veniaminov

Y-267 ● 150 roubles ● 1991 .999 platinum

The reverse depicts Ioann Veniaminov (1797–1879) in front of a 19th-century sailing ship. Veniaminov served as a Russian Orthodox missionary to Kamchatka, Alaska and the Aleutian Islands for 37 years. He learned the native Alaskan language, created a written alphabet for it, and translated liturgical texts into that language. In 1840 he was consecrated as Bishop Innokenty, the first bishop of Russian America. Later he became the metropolitan of Moscow. He was canonized and is now known as St. Innocent Veniaminov. The reverse inscriptions translate to "250th Anniversary of Discoveries in Russian America" and "Ioann Veniaminov Missionary and Enlightener."

50th Anniversary of the Northern Supply Convoys

Y-304 ● 3 roubles ● 1992 copper-nickel

Y-304
3 roubles 1992 copper-nickel, 33 mm

The reverse depicts a German bomber attacking the first of three ships sailing in a convoy to Murmansk, a bomb exploding near the lead ship, and the flags of the United States, Great Britain and the Soviet Union. The years 1941–1945 denoted on the reverse are the years in which the Soviet Union participated in World War II as one of the Allied Powers. During the war Allied convoys delivered cargo from the Northern Atlantic Ocean to Murmansk and Archangelsk in northwestern Russia. Murmansk is an ice-free port on an inlet of the Barents Sea. Archangelsk is situated near the White Sea. The Allied convoys were special groups of transportation and patrol ships organized by the United States and Great Britain that brought to the Soviet Union tanks, guns, planes, vehicles, food and other vital cargo such as tin and aluminum, and took back strategic raw materials.

The first British convoy arrived at Arkhangelsk on 31 August 1941. In all, 42 convoys that comprised 722 transportation ships reached Soviet ports during the war, and 36 convoys were sent back from the Soviet Union. A total of 682 transportation ships reached their ports of destination. The convoys ran the constant risk of attack from German submarines and aircraft, and also had to cope with the forbidding weather conditions north of the Arctic Circle. The reverse inscription translates to "North Convoy." The US flag on the reverse is the flag with 50 stars that was in use upon issue of the coin. At the time of World War II the US flag had only 48 stars (Alaska and Hawaii were admitted into the Union in 1959). The obverse depicts the cupolas of the Cathedral of Intercession on the Moat and the Savior's Tower near the main Kremlin tower in Red Square, Moscow. The denomination in Russian, "three roubles," is inscribed twice on the edge.

190th Anniversary of the Birth of Pavel Nakhimov

Y-306 ● 1 rouble ● 1992 copper-nickel

The reverse features a portrait of naval commander Pavel Stepanovich Nakhimov (1802–1855), and at right the ship-of-the-line *Imperatrista Maria*, Nakhimov's flagship at the naval battle of Sinop (*see* Y-545). Nakhimov commanded the Russian navy in the Black Sea in the Crimean War. At Sinop he achieved one of Russia's greatest victories over the Turks. Admiral Nakhimov was killed during the siege of Sevastopol (*see* Y-755). The Order of Nakhimov was instituted in 1944 in his honor and several naval cadet schools are named after him.

The 18th Century – Academy of Sciences

Y-350 ● 3 roubles ● 1992 .900 silver

Y-350
3 roubles
1992 .900 silver, 39 mm

The reverse shows two 18th-century sailing ships and a boat on the Neva River in front of the building of the Academy of Sciences on St. Petersburg's University Embankment. The Academy, founded in 1724 by Emperor Peter I, is the chief coordinating body for scientific research in Russia. Its building is an example of late classicism that was built in 1783–1789 according to a design by architect Giacomo Quarenghi. The reverse inscriptions translate to "The Age of the Enlightenment, the 18th Century" and "Academy of Sciences."

The 18th Century – Catherine the Great

Y-353 ● 25 roubles ● 1992 .999 palladium

The reverse features Empress Catherine II (1729–1796, empress from

1762), and in the background an 18th-century sailing ship at left and an altar with a burning fire and books at right. The ship on the reverse apparently represents Russia's naval power in the period of Catherine's reign. Catherine, a German princess named Sophie Augusta Frederika of Anhalt-Zerbst, married the future Peter III in 1745. The year before she had entered the Russian Orthodox Church and had taken the name Ekaterina (Catherine) Alexeyevna. Peter became czar in 1762 but was murdered the same year. Czarina Catherine, who is called Catherine the Great, introduced educational, legal and administrative reforms in line with the liberal philosophy of the Enlightenment. During her reign the Russian empire expanded its territories near the Black Sea following wars with Turkey in 1768–1772 and 1787–1792, and annexed the Crimea. The portrait of the empress holding a scepter is based on a painting by Dimitri Grigoryevich Levitzky (1735–1822). The reverse inscriptions translate to "The Age of the Enlightenment, the 18th Century" and "Catherine II, the Legislator."

The 18th Century – Battle of Chesme

Y-358 • 150 roubles • 1992 .999 platinum

The reverse depicts three Russian sailing ships at right and a sinking Turkish ship at left, representing a scene from the battle of Chesme against the Turks which took place in 1770 (*see* Y-543). The reverse inscriptions translate to "The Age of the Enlightenment, the 18th Century" and "The Chesme Naval Battle."

Y-358
150 roubles
1992 .999 platinum, 28.5 mm

250th Anniversary of the Birth of Feodor Ushakov

Y-363 • 2 roubles • 1994 .500 silver

The reverse depicts the naval commander Feodor Feodorovich Ushakov (1745–1817) in uniform holding a spyglass, and to his right two sailing ships. Ushakov was one of the founders of the Black Sea Fleet and its commander from 1790. He used original maneuvering tactics and won several major battles against the Turkish fleet, not losing a single battle. During a Russian naval expedition in the war against France in the Mediterranean Sea of 1798–1800 Ushakov seized the Ionian Islands in 1798.

50th Anniversary of the End of the Great Patriotic War

Y-403 • 50 roubles • 1995 aluminum-bronze

The reverse depicts two Soviet marines during fighting, against the background of a warship and a warplane. The coin commemorates the end of World War II fought by the USSR against Germany in the years 1941–1945. The war started in 1939 when Great Britain and France declared war against Germany following its invasion of Poland. Russia remained neutral and secured eastern Poland and the Baltic states; however, on 22 June 1941 the Germans invaded Russia. World War II is known in Russia as the Great Patriotic War. It resulted in 20 million dead, of whom 7.5 million were in the armed forces. US losses were 292,000 and those of British and Commonwealth forces 398,000. The reverse inscription translates to "50th Anniversary of the Great Victory."

Exploration of the Russian Arctic – Semyon Chelyuskin

Y-461 ● 3 roubles ● 1995 .900 silver

The reverse features at the top the portraits of five Russian Arctic explorers, in the center their wooden coast-dweller sailing/rowing vessel and a dog sled with travelers, and at the bottom a map of the Siberian coast. In 1742/43 Semyon Chelyuskin explored the Arctic coast of Russia and Siberia, sailing eastward from the White Sea off northwestern Russia to the Laptev Sea. When his ship was stopped by ice he resorted to sleds to travel over the frozen sea. He and his party made the first recorded journey around what is now Cape Chelyuskin, the tip of Taymyr Peninsula which is continental Asia's northernmost point. The explorers depicted on the reverse are Stepan Malygin, Dmitri Ovtsyn, Semyon Chelyuskin (whose name was given to Cape Chelyuskin) and Khariton and Dmitri Laptev (for whom the Laptev Sea is named—the part of the Arctic Ocean bordering northern Siberia between the Severnaya Zemlya and the New Siberian Islands). Chelyuskin's expedition was aimed at exploring the unknown Arctic coast of Siberia. It was part of Vitus Bering's Great Northern Expedition of 1733–1743 (*see* Y-243). The reverse inscriptions translate to "Exploration of the Russian Arctic" and "The Great Northern Expedition."

Exploration of the Russian Arctic – Roald Amundsen

Y-462 ● 3 roubles ● 1995 .900 silver

Y-462
3 roubles
1995 .900 silver, 39 mm

The reverse features the 392-ton wooden schooner *Maud* and a bust of the Norwegian polar explorer Roald Engelbregt Gravning Amundsen (1872–1928) below an airplane and a dirigible. *Maud* was built by Amundsen in 1917, had a length of 107 ft (33 m), was 51 ft (16 m) in beam, and had a draft of 22 ft (6.7 m). She was designed to withstand severe ice pressure. In 1918–1920 she was used by Amundsen in an attempt to reach the North Pole, crossing from Norway to Alaska through the Northeast Passage. In 1925 *Maud* was sold for $40,000 to the

Hudson's Bay Company which renamed her *BayMaud*. She was moored at Cambridge Bay from 1927 until she sank in 1930. In 1990 *BayMaud* was bought for $1 with the intention of raising her and returning her to Asker, Norway where she was built. Amundsen achieved many firsts in his career: he served on the *Belgica* (*see* Romania KM-148), the first vessel to winter in the Antarctic (1897); he was the first to navigate from east to west the Northwest Passage—the route from the Atlantic Ocean to the Pacific Ocean through the Arctic archipelago of Canada and Alaska that had eluded European sailors for so many centuries—and on this voyage in the 46-ton sloop *Gjøa*, 73 ft (22 m) long, he became the first to determine the precise position of the magnetic North Pole (1903–1906); he was the first man to reach the South Pole, in *Fram* (*see* Norway KM-459) (1911); he became the first person to circumnavigate the globe in Arctic waters, in *Maud* (1920); and he was one of the three men in the dirigible *Norge* (ex N-1) that made the first Europe-to-America flight by way of the North Pole (1926). (Commander of the 71-hour flight from Spitsbergen to Teller, Alaska was the Italian aeronautical engineer Umberto Nobile.) In 1928 Amundsen died in the Arctic during efforts to rescue Nobile, whose dirigible *Italia* had crashed on the polar ice (*see* Y-497). The coin marks Amundsen's voyage of 1918–1920 in *Maud* and his flight in 1926 over the North Pole. The reverse inscriptions translate to "Exploration of the Russian Arctic" and "Expedition of R. Amundsen."

First Russian Voyage Around the World – Map of Voyage

Y-464 ● 3 roubles ● 1993 .900 silver

Y-464
3 roubles
1993 .900 silver, 39 mm

The reverse depicts the three-masted sloops *Nadezhda* (*see* Y-517) and *Neva* (*see* Y-518) below a world map marked with the route of their voyage in 1803–1806. This was the first Russian circumnavigation of the world. The expedition was commanded by naval officer Ivan Fyodorovich Krusenstern (1770–1846). As a young Russian officer assigned to the British navy for experience during the 1790s, Krusenstern visited China where he witnessed the fortunes being made by English and American fur traders. He saw the need for ships to be built on the coast of Russian America to carry the pelts direct to Canton, instead of landing them at Okhotsk for transportation overland to China. The supply of the fur-trading posts of Alaska by sea would also be far more efficient than the tedious overland route across Siberia. In 1799 Krusenstern presented a proposal for an expedition to the Pacific Ocean. In 1802 he was appointed its commander. The voyage was made as a joint trading venture with the Russian American Company: the company embarked freight for barter in the East, the navy was responsible for the command and manning of the vessels and for the scientific and survey work to be undertaken. Also on board was a Russian ambassador to Japan. In 1803 *Nadezhda* under Krusenstern with 85 people on board and *Neva* under Captain Yuri Lisyansky with 54 people put out from Kronstadt and reached the Pacific Ocean. From the Hawaiian islands, *Neva* proceeded to Russian America (*see* Y-266) and *Nadezhda* to Petropavlovsk and then Nagasaki, the intended base of the embassy; however, after months of waiting for a decision from the Shogunate, the Russians were ordered to depart. *Nadezhda* returned to Petropavlovsk, charting en route the eastern shores of Japan, Sakhalin and the Kuril Islands north of Japan. Loaded with furs she proceeded to Macao. Here the two sloops met and then returned home after three years. Both captains, Krusenstern and Lisyansky, are immortalized in geographical names, such as Cape Krusenstern in northwestern Alaska and Lisianski Island near Midway Island in the Pacific Ocean. Krusenstern later became an admiral. Both ships completed the three-year voyage without losing a single man. The reverse inscriptions translate to "First Russian Voyage Around the World 1803–1806" and "Map of Voyage."

First Russian Expedition to Antartica – The Route of the Expedition

Y-466 ● 3 roubles ● 1994 .900 silver

Y-466
3 roubles
1994 .900 silver, 39 mm

The reverse depicts in the foreground the sloop *Vostok* (*see* Y-522) and in the background at left the sloop *Mirny* (*see* Y-521) below a sea chart of Antarctica that denotes the route of their discovery voyage in 1819–1821. This expedition was sent by Czar Alexander I to make discoveries in the higher southern latitudes, circumnavigating the ice-belt of the Antarctic Circle. Commander of the expedition and of *Vostok* was the Russian navigator Captain Faddey Faddeyevich Bellingshausen (1778–1852). The expedition numbered 189 men—117 in *Vostok* and 72 in *Mirny*. They discovered Antarctica in 1820 and made the European discovery of a total of 29 islands, one coral reef and one lagoon. Among the islands discovered were two Antarctic islands, which Bellingshausen named for Peter I, the czar who had founded the Russian navy, and for his monarch Alexander I. (Peter I Island is now Norwegian territory.) The vessels crossed and recrossed the Antarctic Circle several times, reaching as far south as 69° latitude. In the process they were the first ever to circumnavigate Antarctica. Upon return to Kronstadt after 751 days they had sailed more than 57,000 miles (91,000 km). Earlier, in 1803–1806, Bellingshausen had participated as a midshipman in the first Russian voyage around the world (*see* Y-464). He fought in the Russo–Turkish War of 1828/29 as a rear admiral and was promoted to admiral in 1831. The Bellingshausen Sea on the Pacific side of Antarctica is named for him. The reverse inscriptions translate to "First Russian Antarctic Expedition 1819–1821" and "Route of Expedition."

Exploration of the Russian Arctic – Events in 1937

Y-472 ● 25 roubles ● 1995 .900 silver, 65 mm

Y-472
25 roubles
1995 .900 silver, 65 mm

The reverse depicts in the center an icebreaker and four polar explorers on an ice floe, and, at the top, an airplane, a map of the Arctic coast, and the portraits of three Russian pilots. The coin marks two events that took place in 1937. That year the first drift station at the North Pole, SP-1 (*Severnyy Polyus*, North Pole), was set up. The explorers on the ice floe are four men who served on SP-1—Ivan Dmitriyevich Papanin (born 1894), the group's leader, Yevgeny K. Fedorov, Pyotr P. Shirshov and Ernst T. Krenkel. Four-engined aircraft based on Franz Josef Land were used to land the party at the station. The men became national heroes when they were rescued from their melting ice floe in the Greenland Sea after nine months, during which they had drifted 19° of latitude and 58° of longitude. The drift stations conducted hydrological, meteorological, magnetic and military research. Ultimately there were more than a hundred polar stations but most activity ceased with the collapse of the USSR in 1991. The second event marked by the coin is the first transarctic non-stop flight from Moscow to Vancouver. It was made—also in 1937—by the Russian pilots Valery Chkalov, Georgy Baidukov and Alexander Belyakov who are depicted at the top of the reverse. The reverse inscriptions translate to "Exploration of the Russian Arctic" and "North Pole Station – 1937 – Chkalov's Transarctic Flight."

Exploration of the Russian Arctic – Fridtjof Nansen's Expedition

Y-496 ● 50 roubles ● 1995 .900 gold

Y-496
50 roubles
1995 .900 gold, 22.6 mm

The reverse depicts the icebound sailing ship *Fram* and the Norwegian Arctic explorer Fridtjof Nansen (*see* Norway KM-459). The reverse inscriptions are "Exploration of the Russian Arctic" and "The Expedition of F. Nansen – 1893–1896."

Exploration of the Russian Arctic – Umberto Nobile

Y-497 ● 100 roubles ● 1995 .900 gold

The reverse depicts at left the Russian steam icebreaker *Krassin* and at right members of the expedition of Umberto Nobile waiting for their rescue on an ice floe in 1928. The 10,620-ton icebreaker was built in England in 1917 by Sir W. G. Armstrong, Whitworth & Co.

Ltd. at Newcastle-on-Tyne for the Russian government, based on a design by Vice Admiral Stepan Ossipovich Makarov (1848–1904), and was named *Suyatogor* for a hero of Russian folklore with supernatural powers. She is 327 ft (100 m) long, has a beam of 71 ft (22 m), and draws 30 ft (9.1 m) of water. She could make a speed of 14 knots. For 35 years she was the strongest icebreaker in the world. In the civil war (1918–1922) she was sunk at Arkhangelsk. In 1920 she was raised from the seabed and taken to England. In 1921, after efforts by the diplomat Leonid Krassin who was a trade representative in Britain, she was returned to the USSR. After Krassin's death in 1926 the icebreaker was renamed for him—first *Leonid Krassin*, later *Krassin*. The Italian aeronautical engineer Umberto Nobile (1885–1978) was the designer and pilot of the dirigible that made the first ever Europe-to-America flight over the North Pole (*see* Y-462). In 1928 Nobile led an Italian expedition to the North Pole in the dirigible *Italia*. The dirigible crashed onto the frozen sea, 180 miles (290 km) northwest of Spitsbergen. *Italia*'s control gondola, carrying Nobile and eight others, broke free, while the lighter-than-air portion of the airship, carrying seven other crewmen, became airborne once again and drifted out of control. No trace of it or the men aboard was ever found. A Russian radio fan picked up Nobile's SOS signal and a search was launched, in which 17 ships and 22 planes took part. *Krassin* under captain K. P. Eggy, with a plane on board, reached the men at 82° N. latitude and brought them to safety. In World War II *Krassin* cleared ice for the Allied ship convoys to the northern cities of Murmansk and Arkhangelsk. In 1976 the vessel was taken out of service and became a floating museum at the Neva embankment in St. Petersburg. *Krassin* was declared a historical monument in 1992. The reverse inscriptions are "Exploration of the Russian Arctic," "The Rescue of Nobile's Expedition" and "1928."

The Millennium of Russia – Alexander the Nevsky

Y-503 ● 150 roubles ● 1995 .999 platinum

The reverse depicts four Russian warriors fighting against a Swedish knight, and three 13th-century ships with square sails in the background. In 1240 Prince Alexander of Novgorod (1220–1263) and his troops defeated the Swedish army that had invaded the northwest of Russia in the battle on the Neva River, earning the prince his name of Nevsky (of the Neva). In 1242 he defeated the Teutonic Knights, also known as *Deutscher Orden* (German Order), on the frozen Lake Peipus (Lake Chudskoye) on the Estonian border. Alexander the Nevsky was an outstanding Russian military commander, statesman, political leader and diplomat in a period of Russian history in which the northeastern and southern part of the country languished under the Tatar–Mongol yoke, while its northwest was attacked by the German and Swedish knights. In 1252

Alexander the Nevsky became the grand prince of Vladimir. In 1547 he was canonized by the Russian Orthodox Church. The reverse inscriptions translate to "1,000 Years Russia – Alexander the Nevsky" and "Battle on the Neva River – 1240."

300th Anniversary of the Russian Fleet – Fishing Trawler

Y-504 ● 1 rouble ● 1996 brass

The reverse depicts a fishing trawler. The coin—like the other coins issued by Russia in 1996 narrated herein—marks the 300th anniversary of the creation of the Russian fleet. On 20 October 1696 a meeting of the Boyar's Parliament (Duma) took place in the village of Preobrazhenskoye near Moscow to discuss the future use of the fortress at Azov in the delta of the Don River. Czar Peter I had first attempted to seize this fortress in 1695 but the attack was repulsed by the Turkish defenders. Recognizing that the fortress could be taken only from the sea, the czar started building ships. The new flotilla captured the fortress in 1696, gaining a stronghold for Russia on the Black Sea. At the meeting of the Duma three months after the capture, the czar stated the need for sea-going ships and proposed to create a navy. The date of this proposal is considered the date of the creation of the Russian fleet. The reverse inscriptions translate to "300th Anniversary of the Russian Fleet" and "Fishing Trawler."

300th Anniversary of the Russian Fleet – *Tovarishtsh I*

Y-505 ● 5 roubles ● 1996 brass

The reverse features the 2,301-ton cadet ship *Tovarishtsh* (Comrade). The four-masted bark had a length of 285 ft (87 m), her beam was 42 ft (13 m) and she drew 22 ft (6.6 m) of water. The area of her sails was 32,346 sq ft (3,005 m^2). The ship, named *Lauriston*, was built in 1892 in Belfast by Workman, Clark & Co. for the London shipowners Galbraith & Moorhead to be operated in the jute trade. She was sold by her original owners in 1905 to Duncan & Co. of London, passed into the hands of Cook & Dundass in 1910 for £4,000, and from 1913 she was operated by the Taltal Shipping Company. In 1917 the Hudson Bay Company of London became her owner and in 1919 she was sold to the State Baltic Steamship Company of Petrograd. In 1922/23 she was converted into a training vessel for the Soviet trading fleet, in 1924 she was renamed *Tovarishtsh* and in 1928 she was incorporated into the Soviet State Shipping Line Sovtorgflot. The Germans took the vessel in 1941 in the port of Zhdanov (now Mariupol) on the Sea of Azov off the Black Sea, and used her to lodge the Croatian navy legion. *Tovarishtsh* sank in the Sea of Azov in 1943. One of her anchors is now a memorial in Mariupol. The ship is often referred to as *Tovarishtsh I* in order to avoid confusion with the sail training ship that was built in 1933 as *Gorch Fock*, served in the German navy until 1939, was scuttled at the end of World War II by the Germans, raised under Soviet supervision and repaired, and taken into the Soviet Navy in 1951 as the training ship *Tovarishtsh* (*see* Korea-North 7 won 2003). The reverse inscriptions, translated, are "300th Anniversary of Russian Fleet" and "Sailing Ship *Tovarishtsh*."

300th Anniversary of the Russian Fleet – Cargo Vessel

Y-506 • 10 roubles • 1996 copper-nickel

The reverse features a cargo ship below the ancient Greek god Hermes, the patron of trade. The reverse inscriptions translate to "300th Anniversary of the Russian Fleet" and "Cargo Vessel."

300th Anniversary of the Russian Fleet – Research Ship

Y-507 • 20 roubles • 1996 copper-nickel

The reverse features a scientific research ship. The reverse inscriptions translate to "300th Anniversary of the Russian Fleet" and "Research Ship."

300th Anniversary of the Russian Fleet – Submarine Cruiser

Y-508 • 50 roubles • 1996 aluminum-bronze

The reverse depicts a submarine below the St. Andrew's flag, the flag of the Russian navy. The reverse inscriptions translate to "300th Anniversary of the Russian Fleet" and "Submarine Cruiser."

300th Anniversary of the Russian Fleet – *Arktika*

Y-509 • 100 roubles • 1996 copper-nickel

The reverse features the 18,172-ton icebreaker *Arktika* which entered service in 1975, leading convoys between Murmansk and Vladivostok through the Northeast Passage across the top of Russia. Built by the Baltic Shipbuilding and Engineering Works of Leningrad (now St. Petersburg) for the Murmansk Shipping Company, the steel vessel is 435 ft (148 m) long, has a beam of 92 ft (28 m), and draws 36 ft (11 m) of water. Her three screws are propelled by steam turbines powered by nuclear energy. This technology is particularly suited for vessels operating in remote and inaccessible places because it obviates the need for regular supplies of fuel. *Arktika* makes a speed of 18 knots. Originally she was named *Leonid Brezhnev* after the secretary of the Soviet Communist Party and president of the Soviet Union (1906–1982). In 1977 *Arktika* was the first surface ship ever to break through the Arctic ice pack and reach the North Pole. In 1983 she led a flotilla of 12 icebreakers which released a convoy of 51 ships trapped north of Chukotka. The translation of the reverse inscriptions is "300th Anniversary of the Russian Fleet" and "Nuclear-Powered Icebreaker *Arktika*."

300th Anniversary of the Russian Fleet – *Yermak*

Y-511 ● 3 roubles ● 1996 .900 silver

Y-511
3 roubles
1996 .900 silver, 39 mm

The reverse depicts the 8,730-ton icebreaker *Yermak* and a portrait of Vice Admiral Stepan Ossipovich Makarov (1848–1904). Built under Makarov's direction by Sir W. G. Armstrong, Whitworth & Co. at Elswick on the Tyne, England for the Imperial Russian Navy, *Yermak* was launched in 1898. She measured 320 ft (98 m) long, had a beam of 71 ft (22 m), and drew some 25 ft (7.6 m) of water. She was one of the earliest purpose-built icebreakers and was specially reinforced to withstand the heavy pressures on her hull from the ice. One of her unusual features was her screws set-up. She was the first ship to have three screws in the stern and one in the bow. One of her three engines could be disconnected from an aft screw and connected to a forward screw. She was capable of moving at a speed of 14 knots. Her crew numbered 112. She was named for Cossack chief Yermak Timofeyevich (?–1584) (*see* Y-683). *Yermak* made her first voyage to the Arctic in 1899 and for many years she kept the route from Murmansk to Vladivostok open for as long as possible. In 1938 she participated in the evacuation of the polar station *SP-1* (*see* Y-472). *Yermak* was scrapped in 1965 after more than 60 years' service of allowing Russian shipping to continue during the winter months. Admiral Makarov was a navy officer, oceanographer and polar researcher. In charge of defense in the Russo–Japanese War of 1904/05, he went down with his flagship, *Petropavlovsk*, outside Port Arthur. The translation of the reverse inscriptions is "300th Anniversary of the Russian Fleet" and "Icebreaker *Yermak*."

300th Anniversary of the Russian Fleet – *Admiral Kuznetsov*

Y-512 ● 3 roubles ● 1996 .900 silver

The reverse depicts the aircraft carrier *Admiral Kuznetsov* and a portrait of the naval commander for whom she was named. *Admiral Kuznetsov* was built at the Nikolayev South Shipyard on the Black

Sea and completed in 1991. Laid down as *Riga*, she was renamed in 1982 *Leonid Brezhnev*. In 1988, after Mikhail Gorbachev had denounced Brezhnev, she was renamed *Tbilisi*. After the outbreak of anti-Soviet violence in Georgia she became *Admiral Flota Svetskogo Soyuza Kuznetsov* (Admiral of the Fleet of the Soviet Union Kuznetsov). The carrier is 984 ft (300 m) long and has a beam of 125 ft (38 m) and a draft of 36 ft (11 m). Including the flight deck she has an extreme width of 239 ft (73 m). Her displacement is 60,000 tons standard (67,000 tons fully loaded); she reaches a speed of 29 knots. The crew, including the air group, numbers 2,626. The flight deck area is 158,000 sq ft (14,700 m^2). The carrier was built as a heavy aviation cruiser to support and defend strategic missile-carrying submarines, surface ships and maritime missile-carrying aircraft. *Kuznetsov* has the capacity to support 18 fixed-wing aircraft and 12 helicopters. Admiral Nikolai Gerassimovich Kuznetsov (1904–1974) served as People's Commissar of the Navy and Admiral of the Fleet of the USSR throughout World War II. He initiated the building of aircraft carriers. At the end of the war he was made a Hero of the Soviet Union. The reverse inscriptions translate to "300th Anniversary of the Russian Fleet" and "Aircraft Carrier *Admiral Kuznetsov*."

First Russian Voyage Around the World – *Nadezhda*

Y-517 • 25 roubles • 1993 .999 palladium

Y-517
25 roubles
1993 .999 palladium, 37 mm

The reverse depicts the three-masted naval sloop *Nadezhda* (Hope) anchoring at Petropavlovsk, Kamchatka and the portrait of the Russian navigator and admiral Ivan Fyodorovich Krusenstern (1770–1846). *Nadezhda* was Krusenstern's flagship on the first Russian circumnavigation of the world in 1803–1806 (*see* Y-464). The 450-ton wooden vessel was built in 1800 in England as the merchant ship *Leander*. Two years later the Russians purchased her for Krusenstern's expedition and renamed the vessel. The fate of the ship after traveling around the world is unknown. The reverse inscriptions translate to "First Russian Voyage Around the World 1803–1806" and "Sloop *Nadezhda* – I. F. Krusenstern."

First Russian Voyage Around the World – *Neva*

Y-518 • 25 roubles • 1993 .999 palladium

The reverse depicts the three-masted square-rigged naval sloop *Neva* and at left a patch of land with buildings and a portrait of Yuri Fyodorovich Lisyansky (1773–1837). Lisyansky was *Neva*'s captain on the first Russian circumnavigation of the world in 1803–1806 (*see* Y-464). In the 1790s Lisyansky was assigned to the

British navy as a young Russian officer for experience. In 1803 he was sent to England to purchase two ships for the Russian navy to make the voyage to the Pacific Ocean that would become the first Russian circumnavigation of the world. On the Thames he found two merchant ships—the 375-ton *Thames* that had been built in London in 1801, which he renamed *Neva* for the Neva River that flows through St. Petersburg, and *Leander* which he renamed *Nadezhda* (*see* Y-517). *Neva*'s crew numbered 43. In 1804 *Neva* took part in the recapture of Fort St. Archangel Mikhail on Sitka Island from the Tlingit natives (*see* Y-266). She sailed home in 1805/06 with a cargo of 150,000 fur seal pelts which were sold in China and replaced by a cargo of teas, chinaware and nankeens for Russia. *Neva* made another voyage to the Pacific Ocean in 1806/07 under Lieutenant Leontiy Andrianovich Gagemeister who later became manager of the Russian-American Company. She was the first Russian ship to call in at the newly founded British colony at Sydney Cove. The reverse inscriptions translate to "First Russian Voyage Around the World 1803–1806" and "Sloop *Neva* – Y. F. Lisyansky."

First Russian Voyage Around the World – The English Embankment

Y-519 • 150 roubles • 1993 .999 platinum

Y-519
150 roubles
1993 .999 platinum, 28.6 mm

The reverse depicts the sloops *Nadezhda* and *Neva* and a rowboat against the background of the house of Count Nikolai P. Rumyantsev (1754–1826) on the English Embankment of the Neva River in St. Petersburg, and, at the top, Rumyantsev's portrait. As Russia's State Chancellor, Rumyantsev enthusiastically supported the voyage of the two sloops to the Pacific Ocean in 1803 that would become the first Russian circumnavigation of the world (*see* Y-464). The translation of the reverse inscriptions is "First Russian Voyage Around the World 1803–1806" and "English Embankment."

First Russian Expedition to Antartica – *Mirny*

Y-521 • 25 roubles • 1994 .999 palladium

Y-521
25 roubles
1994 .999 palladium, 37 mm

The reverse depicts the sloop *Mirny* (Peaceful), the portrait of the Russian naval commander and navigator Mikhail Petrovich Lazarev (1788–1851) at right, and a map of Antarctica at the bottom. The 530-ton *Mirny* was 120 ft (37 m) long and 30 ft (9.1 m) in beam and drew 15 ft (4.6 m) of water. Built as the merchantman *Ladoga*, she was converted in 1818 for the first Russian Antarctic expedition (*see* Y-466). On this expedition she was commanded by Lazarev who had served four years in the British navy. Lazarev participated in two more voyages around the globe—in 1813–1816 in *Suvorov* for the Russian-American Company from Kronstadt to the company's settlement at Sitka off the coast of Alaska and in 1822–1825 as commander of the Russian frigate *Kreiser*. Lazarev took part in the battle of Navarino in 1827 and in other naval operations against the Ottoman Empire in the Greek War of Independence. Later he organized and commanded Russia's Black Sea Fleet and became an admiral in 1843. The reverse inscriptions translate to "First Russian Antarctic Expedition 1819–1821" and "Sloop *Mirny* – M. P. Lazarev."

First Russian Expedition to Antartica – *Vostok*

Y-522 ● 25 roubles ● 1994 .999 palladium

Y-522
25 roubles
1994 .999 palladium, 37 mm

The reverse depicts the sloop *Vostok* (East), at top left the portrait of the Russian navigator Faddey Faddeyevich Bellingshausen (1778–1852) and at the bottom a map of Antarctica. The 900-ton *Vostok* was built in 1818 at the Okhta Shipyard of Stoke and Kolodnin in St. Petersburg. She was 130 ft (40 m) long and 33 ft (10 m) in beam, drew 10 ft (2.9 m) of water and had a complement of 127. She was built of softwood that had been reinforced and copper-sheathed for the first Russian Antarctic expedition (*see* Y-466). Bellingshausen was the leader of the expedition and *Vostok*'s captain. *Vostok* was also the name chosen by the USSR for the world's first manned spaceship which took Yuri Gagarin into space in 1961. The reverse inscriptions translate to "First Russian Antarctic Expedition 1819–1821" and "Sloop *Vostok* – F. F. Bellingshausen."

First Russian Expedition to Antartica – *Mirny* and *Vostok*

Y-523 ● 150 roubles ● 1994 .999 platinum

The reverse depicts two sloops and a rowboat with oarsmen, at the top a map of Antarctica and in the foreground penguins on an ice floe. The sloops are *Mirny* (*see* Y-521) and *Vostok* (*see* Y-522) that made the first Russian Antarctic expedition in 1819–1821 (*see* Y-466). The reverse inscriptions translate to "First Russian Antarctic Expedition 1819–1821" and "In the Antarctic Seas."

300th Anniversary of the Russian Fleet – Battle of Gangut

Y-542 ● 25 roubles ● 1996 .900 silver, 60 mm

Y-542
25 roubles
1996 .900 silver, 60 mm

The reverse depicts sailing ships at the battle of Gangut in 1714 and, at the top, a portrait of General Admiral Count Fedor Matveyevich Apraksin (1671–1728). In 1700 Czar Peter I (the

Great) put Apraksin in charge of shipbuilding and the construction of naval installations, creating the Russian navy. That year also marks the beginning of the Great Northern War between Sweden and Russia. In 1708 Apraksin repulsed a Swedish attack on St. Petersburg. The next year he was made a count for his services. In 1714 a fleet of scampavias (small galleys) under Apraksin defeated a Swedish squadron under the command of Rear Admiral Nils Erenskjold and captured all the enemy ships—the 18-gun frigate *Elephant*, six galleys and two skerry boats. The battle took place off the Gangut (Hanko in Finnish, Hangø in Swedish) Peninsula south-west of Helsinki. The Great Northern War came to an end in 1721 by the Treaty of Nystad, Finland under which Apraksin gained for Russia considerable territory, including Estonia and Swedish Livonia, which gave it access to the Baltic Sea. Following ratification of the treaty, the Senate conferred upon Czar Peter I the title of emperor. The translation of the reverse inscriptions is "300th Anniversary of the Russian Fleet" and "Gangut Naval Battle 1714."

300th Anniversary of the Russian Fleet – Battle of Chesme

Y-543 ● 25 roubles ● 1996 .900 silver, 60 mm

The reverse shows a scene of the battle of Chesme of 1770 and, at the top, the portrait of Admiral Grigory Andreevich Spiridov (1713–1790). The scene depicts the Russian ships *Tri Sviatitelia* (Three Hierarchies) and *Sviatoi Yevstafy*, both of 66 guns, and the Turkish ship *Burcu Zafer* of 84 guns. Spiridov's flagship in the battle was *Sviatoi Yevstafy*, a ship-of-the line of 156 ft (48 m) long with a beam of 48 ft (15 m) and a draft of 16 ft (4.9 m) that had been built in 1762. The battle took place in the Russian–Turkish war of 1768–1774 in the Bay of Chesme (Çeşme) off the west coast of Asia Minor near Izmir. Empress Catherine II had sent a Russian fleet from Kronstadt on the Baltic Sea to the Aegean Sea, to divert some of the Turkish naval might from the Danube and the Black Sea. The Russian fleet included nine battleships, three frigates, one bombardier ship and 17 support ships fitted with 820 guns. The Turkish fleet in the Aegean under Admiral Hassan-bey Djezairly included 16 battle-ships, six frigates and at least 50 support ships fitted with more than 1,400 guns. Spiridov in *Yevstafy* attacked near Chesme and engaged the Turkish admiral, who had changed shortly before the battle from his flagship, the 84-gun *Real Mustapha*, to *Burcu Zafer*. During the attack the Turkish ship caught fire, her burning mast crumbled on the Russian ship, and Spiridov and his men had to abandon ship. Spiridov transferred his flag to *Tri Sviatitelia*. Both *Yevstafy* and *Burcu Zafer* exploded. The Turks withdrew to Chesme and were blocked in its harbor by the Russian fleet. Four Russian fire-ships penetrated into the harbor. One of them managed to come near a 84-gun Turkish battleship, and when set on fire it caused a blaze which set off a chain reaction of ships that were ignited by burning parts of other ships. All of the Turkish ships exploded. The Turks lost 15 battleships, 6 frigates and 46 other ships. Their death toll was at least 11,000. Only the Turkish battleship *Rhodos* and five galleys were salvaged from the fire. The Russians lost 620 men upon the explosion of *Sviatoi Yevstafy* and 45 men on other ships. The victory gave Russia control of the Aegean Sea and the Dardanelles. The translation of the reverse inscriptions is "300th Anniversary of the Russian Fleet" and "Chesme Naval Battle 1770."

300th Anniversary of the Russian Fleet - Corfu Fortress

Y-544 ● 25 roubles ● 1996 .900 silver, 60 mm

Y-544
25 roubles
1996 .900 silver, 60 mm

The reverse depicts sailing ships during the assault on the Corfu fortress in 1799 and, at the top, the portrait of Admiral Feodor Feodorovich Ushakov (*see* Y-363). In November 1798 a Russian–Turkish squadron commanded by Ushakov in *Sviatoi Pavel*, a second-rate ship-of-the-line, laid siege to the fortress of Corfu. (Corfu is the Italian name of the Venetian fortress built from the 14th century on the Ionian island of Kerkira that was seized by France in 1797.) The French defenders surrendered after 102 days. The tactics used by Ushakov during the assault is a textbook example of co-ordination between a landing force and shipborne artillery. *Sviatoi Pavel* was built in 1794 and survived until 1804. The reverse inscriptions translate to "300th Anniversary of the Russian Fleet" and "Storming of the Corfu Fortress."

300th Anniversary of the Russian Fleet - Battle of Sinop

Y-545 ● 25 roubles ● 1996 .900 silver, 60 mm

The reverse depicts a fortress and sailing ships during the battle of Sinop and, at the top, a portrait of Vice Admiral Pavel Stepanovich Nakhimov (1802–1855). Nakhimov's flagship at the battle was the 84-gun ship-of-the line *Imperatrista Maria*. She was built around 1830 and served until 1855. The 3,575-ton ship had a length of 196 ft (60 m), her beam was 51 ft (16 m) and she drew about 21 ft (6.4 m) of water. In 1853 she headed a Russian squadron under Nakhimov's command that was sent by Czar Nicholas I across the Black Sea after the outbreak of the Crimean War with Turkey. The squadron trapped nine Turkish ships in the harbor of Sinop on Turkey's northern coast, totally destroyed the Turkish squadron with a loss of more than 4,000 Turks, captured the Ottoman commander and burned part of the city and its harbor installations. Admiral Nakhimov was killed during the siege of Sevastopol (*see* Y-755). After the battle of Sinop, Great Britain, France and later Sardinia joined the war on the side of Turkey. Notwithstanding the victory at Sinop, Russia lost the Crimean War—the 19th-century war with the largest number of casualties except for the Napoleonic wars. At the Treaty of Paris of 1856 Russia had to agree to the neutralization of the Black Sea area, being allowed to keep in the Black Sea only six screw corvettes, nine screw transportation ships and four wheel steam ships. The translation of the reverse inscriptions is "300th Anniversary of the Russian Fleet" and "Sinop Naval Battle 1853."

300th Anniversary of the Russian Fleet – *Varyag*

Y-546 ● 50 roubles ● 1996 .900 gold

Y-546
50 roubles
1996 .900 gold, 22.6 mm

The reverse features the 6,500-ton protected cruiser *Varyag*. Built by Cramp in 1900, *Varyag* had a length of 425 ft (130 m), a beam of 52 ft (16 m) and a draft of 21 ft (6 m). Her crew numbered 580. At the beginning of the Russo-Japanese war in January 1904, *Varyag* and the gunboat *Koreyets* were attacked by a Japanese squadron of 14 warships off Chemulpo, Korea. After suffering heavy damage the crews of the Russian ships scuttled them rather than let them fall into the hands of the enemy. *Varyag* was refloated in August 1905 and served in the Japanese navy as *Soya*. Sold to Russia in 1916, she was sent to Britain for repairs that were never carried out. She was scrapped in 1921. The reverse inscriptions translate to "300th Anniversary of the Russian Fleet" and "Cruiser *Varyag* 1904."

300th Anniversary of the Russian Fleet – *Poltava*

Y-547 ● 100 roubles ● 1996 .900 silver, 100 mm, 1111 gr

Y-547
100 roubles
1996 .900 silver, 100 mm

The reverse depicts the 54-gun ship *Poltava*, at left the main building of the Admiralty, and at right a portrait of Czar Peter I (the Great, 1672–1725), a drawing of the keel of the ship and a four-line inscription. *Poltava* was the first Russian battleship. The czar was closely involved in her design, which was adapted to the high waves on the Baltic Sea. *Poltava* was launched at the admiralty shipyard in St. Petersburg in 1712 and was named for the Russian victory at the city of Poltava a few years before. She displaced almost 1,000 tons, was 131 ft (40 m) long, and had a beam of 38 ft (12 m) and a draft of 15 ft (4.6 m). Her complement numbered around 260. *Poltava* saw action in the Great Northern War, served until 1725, and was scrapped in 1732. The Ukrainian city of Poltava is situated on the Vorskla River, a tributary of the Dnieper, 190 miles (304 km) east-south-east of Kiev. In 1709 the Swedes under their King Charles XII had laid siege to this city. The siege ended in the death or capture of virtually the entire invading army. Only Charles and a few hundred of his troops escaped to exile in Turkish Moldavia. He was not able to return to Sweden until 1715. The Russian victory at Poltava ended forever Swedish military power and marks the beginning of Russian ascendancy in Europe. The four-line inscription on the reverse translates to "There Must Be Sea-Going Ships. Peter I." The czar said these words at the meeting of the Duma at which the Russian navy was created (*see* Y-504). The translations of the reverse inscriptions are "300th Anniversary of the Russian Fleet" and "First Battleship *Poltava* 1712."

300th Anniversary of the Russian Fleet – *Gremyashiy* and *Soobrazitelny*

Y-548 ● 100 roubles ● 1996 .900 gold

The reverse features the destroyers *Gremyashiy* and *Soobrazitelny*. The 1,860-ton destroyer–minelayer *Gremyashiy* (Thunder) was built in 1939. She was 380 ft (116 m) long and had a beam of 36 ft (11 m) and a draft of 13 ft (4 m). Her crew numbered 240 and her speed was 37 knots. She served until 1958. The 1,686-ton *Soobrazitelniy* (Quick-witted) (ex *Prozorliviy*) was adapted for operating in the Arctic. She was built in 1941 by 61 Kommunar Yard, Nikolaiev. Her length was 370 ft (113 m), her beam 33 ft (10 m) and her draft 13 ft (4 m). She could make 36 knots and her crew numbered 207. In World War II *Soobrazitelny* made a number of runs into beleaguered Sevastopol with the flotilla leader *Tashkent*. When *Tashkent* was sunk by air attack, *Soobrazitelniy* rescued her survivors. *Soobrazitelniy* was decommissioned in 1966 and served as a museum ship in Sevastopol to commemorate the deeds of the Black Sea Fleet in World War II. Apparently she was later broken up. The reverse inscriptions translate to "300th Anniversary of the Russian Fleet" and "Destroyer *Gremyashiy* – Destroyer *Soobrazitelny*." The reverse also denotes the years 1941–1945 in which the USSR participated in World War II.

525th Anniversary of the Death of Afanasy Nikitin – Nikitin in Russia

Y-558 ● 2 roubles ● 1997 .500 silver

The reverse depicts the Russian merchant Afanasy Nikitin (?–1472) against the background of a Viking-type ship on the Volga River and Russian city buildings on the river front. In 1466 Nikitin sailed from Tver near Moscow down the Volga, reached Baku on the Caspian Sea and then sailed over to Persia, where he spent about a year. In

1469 Nikitin crossed the Arabian Sea to India, where he traveled for three years. On his way back he visited Somalia, Persia, Muscat and Turkey, crossed the Black Sea and arrived in Cafa (Feodossia) in the Crimea. He died in 1472 near Smolensk on his way back to Tver. While traveling in India, Nikitin made a close study of its population, state system, economy, religion, people's everyday life, and nature. His travel notes *The 1466–1472 Voyage Beyond The Three Seas* contain one of the earliest descriptions of India and its people in European literature and is a major work of ancient Russian literature. The book was translated into many foreign languages. Nikitin accomplished his voyage 25 years before Vasco da Gama discovered another way to reach India. The reverse inscription translates to "525th Anniversary of Afanasy Nikitin's Voyage to India."

525th Anniversary of the Death of Afanasy Nikitin – Nikitin in India

Y-559 ● 2 roubles ● 1997 .500 silver

The reverse shows a portrait of the Russian merchant Afanasy Nikitin (*see* Y-558) surrounded by scenes of India—at right a sailing dhow, an elephant and a palace, and at left a peacock. This design alludes to Nikitin's travel throughout India in 1469–1472. The reverse inscription translates to "525th Anniversary of Afanasy Nikitin's Voyage to India."

Krusenstern Seen From the Bow

Y-588 ● 100 roubles ● 1997 .900 silver, 100 mm, 1111 gr

The reverse depicts the 3,064-ton Russian sailing ship *Krusenstern* seen from her bow and at right the portrait of Admiral Ivan Fyodorovich Krusenstern for whom she was named. This four-masted steel bark is one of the largest modern sailing ships. Her length is 376 ft (115 m), her beam 46 ft (14 m) and her draft 22 ft (6.8 m). The surface of her sailing rig is 38,750 sq ft (3,600 m^2). The highest mast is 164 ft (50 m), the height of a 15-story building. *Krusenstern* can develop a speed of 15 knots when under sail, 10 knots by use of her two diesel engines. She serves as a training ship for naval cadets. Her crew numbers 272, of whom 208 are cadets. Built in 1926 for Ferdinand Laeisz's Flying "P" Line by Joh. C. Tecklenborg at Bremerhaven–Geestemünde in Germany, the vessel was first named *Padua*. (All Laeisz's ships had names beginning with "P".) She was used for carrying nitrates from Chile and then wool from Australia; later she became a survey vessel. In 1933 she set a speed record by sailing from Hamburg to Port Lincoln, South Australia in 67 days. She was the last four-masted bark that was built as a cargo ship. At the end of World War II she was found in Flensburg, Germany and in 1946 she was taken over by the Soviet

Union. She came into operation in the Soviet fleet under the name *Krusenstern*. In 1952 her name was changed into *Floating Base No. 14*. In 1961 she got back her former name, *Krusenstern*. In 1957–1964 she was twice modernized and in 1996 she made a ten-month circumnavigation of the world to mark the 300th anniversary of the Russian fleet. Her home port is Kaliningrad on the Baltic Sea. Admiral Ivan Fyodorovich Krusenstern (1770–1846) led the first Russian voyage around the world in 1803–1806 (*see* Y-464). The reverse inscription is "Bark *Krusenstern*."

Krusenstern Seen From the Stern

Y-589 ● 1000 roubles ● 1997 .999 gold, 50 mm

The reverse depicts the Russian four-masted bark *Krusenstern* seen from her stern and at right the portrait of Admiral Ivan Fyodorovich Krusenstern for whom she was named (*see* Y-588). The reverse inscription is "Bark *Krusenstern*."

Y-589
1000 roubles
1997 .999 gold, 50 mm

Protect Our World – Polar Bears

Y-597 ● 100 roubles ● 1997 .900 silver, 100 mm, 1111 gr

The reverse features two polar bears in ice hummocks and at left a fisherman in a boat. The polar bear (*Ursus maritimus*) is a carnivorous animal found on the coast of the Arctic Ocean and in the ice of Arctic regions. It reaches 9.8 ft (3 m) in length and over 1,500 pounds (700 kg) in weight. In Russia it inhabits Franz Josef Land, and Vrangel Island on which a nursery was set up in 1976. The polar bear swims and dives well, and feeds chiefly on seals. The polar bear is an endangered animal and its hunting is forbidden in Russia. The reverse inscription translates to the motto "Protect Our World."

Protect Our World – Polar Bear

Y-598 ● 200 roubles ● 1997 .999 gold

The reverse depicts a seated polar bear (*see* Y-597) and at left a Viking-type one-masted sailing ship. The reverse inscription translates to the motto "Protect Our World."

100th Anniversary of the Birth of Sergei Eisenstein

Y-608 ● 2 roubles ● 1998 .925 silver

Y-608
2 roubles 1998 .925 silver, 33 mm

The reverse depicts the Russian film producer Sergei Mikhailovich Eisenstein (1898–1948) surveying a film strip, at the bottom his signature and in the background the battleship *Potemkin* (pronounced Potyomkin). At the Brussels Film Festival in 1958, Eisenstein's silent film *Battleship Potemkin* (1925) headed the list of the twelve best films ever made in the world. The film tells of the 1905 uprising on *Kniaz Potemkin Tavritcheski* (Prince Potemkin Tavritcheski). This vessel had a displacement of 12,582 tons, was 378 ft (115 m) long, had a beam of 73 ft (22 m), and drew 27 ft (8.2 m) of water. Built by the Nikolaev State Shipbuilding Works in 1903 and put into service on the Black Sea, she had a complement of 741 and could make 16 knots. The ship was named for Prince Grigory Aleksandrovich Potemkin (1739–1791), who under Catherine II (the Great) annexed the Crimea and built Russia's first Black Sea fleet. The uprising on *Potemkin* in 1905 began when the men refused to eat maggot-infested meat that had been brought aboard the ship by torpedo boat No. 267. Twelve sailors were ordered to be executed. In the ensuing struggle, Able Seaman Grigory Vakulinchuk was shot by Commander Ippolit Giliarovsky, whereupon seven officers were killed. Upon return to Odessa under the red flag the mutineers landed Vakulinchuk's corpse on the quay. Civilian demonstrators were attacked by mounted Cossacks and in the riots an estimated 6,000 people were killed. *Potemkin* and the torpedo boat sailed for Constanţa, Romania. The ships were allowed only a day's provisions and sailed again. Faced with a lack of food, fuel and fresh water, the mutineers returned to Constanţa, where their leader ordered to scuttle the battleship. The crew surrendered to the Romanian authorities. A few days later *Potemkin* was raised and towed back to Russia. She was recommissioned in Sevastopol on St. Panteleimon's day and renamed *Panteleimon*. In 1917 she became *Potemkin* and later *Boretz za Svobodu* (Fighter for Liberty). She served as the stage for Eisenstein's film in 1921/22 and was scrapped in 1922.

Nilo Stolobenskaya Hermitage

Y-631 ● 3 roubles ● 1998 .900 silver

The reverse depicts the Nilo Stolobenskaya hermitage on the water front, in front on the lake a sailing ship and a rowboat, and above the monastery the figure of St. Nil Stolobensky. The hermitage is a monastery for men on Stolobny Island in the Seliger Lake, midway between St. Petersburg and Moscow. It was founded in 1594. Its architectural monuments include the 18th-century hospital church, two gate churches and the refectory, and the 19th-century cathedral with a four-staged bell tower. The reverse inscription translates to "Nilo Stolobenskaya Hermitage – 16th Century."

55th Anniversary of the Victory in the Great Patriotic War – Murmansk

Y-666 ● 2 roubles ● 2000 copper-nickel-zinc

The reverse features two transportation vessels of a Murmansk ship convoy (*see* Y-304), at right a warship, at the top an airplane, and at left the Gold Star Medal. In 1985 the highest distinction class "Hero City" was conferred on the city of Murmansk, accompanied by the awarding of the Lenin Order and the Gold Star Medal, in recognition of the heroism and courage of its defenders displayed in the struggle for freedom of the Motherland in the Great Patriotic War of 1941–1945 (World War II).

55th Anniversary of the Victory in the Great Patriotic War – Novorossiysk

Y-668 ● 2 roubles ● 2000 copper-nickel-zinc

The reverse depicts two marines landing in Novorossiysk—one holding a rifle, the other a flag—and at left a warship, outlines of the city and the Gold Star Medal. Novorossiysk is situated on the northeastern shore of the Black Sea. In 1973 the highest distinction class "Hero City" was conferred on the city, accompanied by the awarding of the Lenin Order and the Gold Star Medal, in recognition of the heroism and courage of its defenders displayed in the Great Patriotic War of 1941–1945 (World War II).

Exploration of Siberia in the 16th and 17th Centuries – Yermak Timofeyevich

Y-683 ● 25 roubles ● 2001 .900 silver, 60 mm

The reverse depicts in the center a rowboat under sail with oarsmen and warriors firing guns, followed in the background by another rowboat under sail; at the left a half-length portrait of Cossack chief Yermak Timofeyevich holding a pole-axe; at the right four archers in boats at the foot of a fortification on a steep bank; and at the top the coat-of-arms of Siberia and a map of western Siberia that denotes the city of Tobolsk. The design marks the attack by Yermak and his men on the city of Sibir on the Irtysh River (near present-day Tobolsk) in 1581. Yermak, a hetman (leading commander) among the Cossacks of the Volga and Don rivers, spent his early career plundering the czar's ships on the Volga. Later he entered the service of the Stroganov merchant family. In 1581 they sent Yermak on an expedition to protect their lands in western Siberia from attack by local tribes. Advancing in riverboats, Yermak and his army of 840 Cossacks and soldiers crossed the Ural mountains and with the superior force of firearms overthrew the khanate of Sibir ruled by Kuchum Khan.

This khanate was the western part of the Mongol Empire of the Golden Horde that was founded in the 13th century after the Mongol (Tatar) conquest of Russia. Yermak occupied Kuchum Khan's capital, then known as the Tatar city of Sibir, which gave its name to the entire region that stretches eastward to the Pacific Ocean. Yermak was killed in an encounter with the Tatars in 1584. His campaign through western Siberia led to the annexation of this region by Muscovy. Tobolsk was the capital of Siberia in the 18th century. The reverse inscriptions translate to "The Development of Siberia 16-17[th centuries]" and "Yermak's Campaign 1582–1585."

Exploration of Siberia in the 16th and 17th Centuries – Vasili Poyarkov

Y-684 ● 50 roubles ● 2001 .900 gold

The reverse depicts at right a kotch under sail, at left the portrait of the explorer Vasili Danilovich Poyarkov, and at the top an outline map of eastern Siberia with the inscriptions Amur and Yakutsk, and the coat-of-arms of Siberia. A kotch is a Siberian single-masted sailing/rowing vessel suited to sailing in ice-strewn waters. In 1638 Poyarkov together with the governor of Siberia founded a fort on the Lena River that developed into the city of Yakutsk. The Lena is one of the longest rivers in the world; some 2,700 miles (4,300 km) are navigable. In 1643 Poyarkov started out on an expedition to eastern Siberia as the leader of a Russian military detachment of 133 men. They traveled up several of the tributaries of the Lena and reached the mouth of the Amur River where they spent the winter of 1644/45. They were the first Europeans to travel on the Amur. In the summer of 1645, after the mouth of the Amur became ice-free, Poyarkov set out into the Sea of Okhotsk. The next winter they spent in a camp on the Ulya River. In the spring of 1646 they headed up the Ulya on skis, crossed over the height of land, and then descended tributaries of the Lena, arriving back in Yakutsk in June 1646. Poyarkov's report on his expedition led to Russian expeditions to the Amur in the following years. Poyarkov died in 1668. The reverse inscriptions translate to "The Development of Siberia 16–17[th centuries]" and "Expedition of V. Poyarkov 1643–1646."

Exploration of Siberia in the 16th and 17th Centuries – Semyon Dezhnev

Y-685 ● 100 roubles ● 2001 .900 gold

Y-685
100 roubles
2001 .900 gold, 30 mm

The reverse depicts in the center a kotch under sail, at right the conjoined portraits of the navigator Fyodor Alekseyev Popov (died 1648) and the Cossack explorer and adventurer Semyon Ivanovich Dezhnev (1605–1673) who discovered the

Northeast Passage from Europe to the Orient, and at the top the coat-of-arms of Siberia and an outline map of the northeastern part of Asia and Alaska. In 1648 Popov and Dezhnev set sail from the Kolyma River in eastern Siberia with seven kotches that carried over 100 men. Four boats disappeared in the Arctic Ocean, the other three rounded the easternmost cape of Chukotka Peninsula in the northeastern corner of Asia (now Cape Dezhnev) in August 1648. These are the first known men to have navigated the Bering Strait, proving that there is no land connection between Asia and America. Later on their voyage one of the boats was lost, Popov's boat disappeared at sea, and after enduring shipwreck only Dezhnev with the 25 men of his kotch survived and reached the mouth of the Anadyr River on the Bering Sea after a long overland trek. Dezhnev's report on his expedition and the strait he discovered went unnoticed for almost a century, until 1736. A few years before the report received attention, in 1728, eighty years after Dezhnev's discovery, Vitus Bering (*see* Y-243) had sailed through the strait, and it now bears Bering's name. The reverse inscriptions translate to "The Development of Siberia 16–17[th centuries]" and "Expedition of F. Popov (Alexeyev) and S. Dezhnev."

Aleksandr Suvorov

Y-717 ● 25 roubles ● 2000 .900 silver, 60 mm

The reverse depicts at left the military commander Aleksandr Vasilyevich Suvorov (1729–1800) standing along with ordnance maps, in the background outlines of sailing ships, at the top soldiers assaulting a Turkish fortress, at right a group of soldiers with a standard bearer during a battle, and at the bottom cannons, sables and standards. The design probably alludes to Suvorov's capture by storm of the strongly fortified and defended Turkish fort at Izmail in Bessarabia (now the southern Ukraine) in 1790. Izmail is situated on the Danube some 50 miles (80 km) from the Black Sea. Suvorov was an outstanding military theorist, tactician and strategist. He fought in the Seven Years' War (1756–1763), the Polish Civil War (1768–1776), two Russo-Turkish Wars (1768–1774 and 1787–1791) and the French Revolutionary War (from 1799). In the course of his military career he was seriously wounded six times. His armies won 63 battles without suffering a single major defeat. After his victory over the Turkish forces at the great Turkish fort on the Rymnik River in Moldavia (1788) he was made Count Rymniksky by Empress Catherine II (the Great). Suvorov was appointed field marshal in 1794.

Ancient Russian Towns – Kostroma

Y-740 ● 10 roubles ● 2002 copper-nickel core in brass ring

The reverse depicts at the top the shield of the city of Kostroma that features an 18th-century river vessel, at left the Ostrovsky bower, and in the background the Ipatievsky Monastery that was built in the 17th and 18th centuries. The city of Kostroma and the monastery are situated at the confluence of the Volga and Kostroma Rivers, 211 miles (340 km) northeast of Moscow. The city was founded in 1152. Its shield features a galera, a sailing/rowing vessel with oars and a sail, which hoists the imperial flag. This shield was granted by Empress Catherine II (the Great) in 1767 following her visit to the city during a voyage on the Volga River with a large retinue in a flotilla of rowing and sailing vessels. The empress' vessel was named *Tver*. The "0" of the "10" denomination on the obverse contains a security element in the form of the figure "10" and the legend "**РУБ**" (the abbreviation for roubles) which are seen differently depending on the angle from which the coin is viewed.

200th Anniversary of the Birth of Pavel Nakhimov

Y-755 ● 3 roubles ● 2002 .900 silver

Y-755
3 roubles
2002 .900 silver, 39 mm

The reverse depicts in the background sailing ships during a battle, in front naval commander Pavel Nakhimov, and at left the Crimean War monument in Sevastopol (*see* Ukraine KM-342). Vice Admiral Pavel Stepanovich Nakhimov (*see* Y-545) is shown as the defender of Russian-held Sevastopol in 1854/55 in the Crimean War—standing alongside smoking artillery and looking to the sea, holding a spyglass in his hand. The city, which is situated on the Crimea Peninsula (now in the Ukraine), held out against a siege by British and French troops for 349 days until it surrendered. Nakhimov was killed during the siege.

Sei Whale

Y-759 ● 1 rouble ● 2002 .900 silver

The reverse shows a sei whale (*Balaenoptera borealis*) in the sea, its tail projecting unto the surface, and a ship in the background. This type of whale lives off the Kamchatka Peninsula and the Kuril Islands to its south, and in the White Sea and Barents Sea off north-western European Russia. The sei whale is an endangered species and is protected by the state.

Architectural Monuments - Kideksha

Y-778 ● 3 roubles ● 2002 .900 silver

The reverse depicts two river vessels in front of buildings in Kideksha—at right the Saints Boris and Gleb Church that dates back to 1152, and more to the left St. Stephen's Church with its 18th-century bell tower and the Holy Gate, also built in the 18th century.

The village of Kideksha on the Nerl River, some 120 miles (190 km) to the northeast of Moscow, was the country residence of the Suzdal princes. The reverse inscription translates to "Kideksha – 12th–18th centuries."

200th Anniversary of the Birth of Pavel Nakhimov

Y-785 ● 25 roubles ● 2002 .900 silver, 60 mm

The reverse depicts at right sailing ships during a sea battle, at left Vice Admiral Pavel Stepanovich Nakhimov in his flagship *Imperatrista Maria* (*see* Y-545) holding a spyglass in his hand, and at the top the St. Andrew's flag of the Russian navy which was instituted by Czar Peter I.

Y-785
25 roubles
2002 .900 silver, 60 mm

Sail Training Ship *Sedov*

Y-795 ● 100 roubles ● 2001 .900 silver, 100 mm, 1111 gr

The reverse of this large silver coin depicts the four-masted sail training bark *Sedov* and a medallion portrait of the Russian Arctic explorer Georgi Yakovlevich Sedov (1877–1914) for whom she was named. The vessel is shown from her port bow, her sails all set. The bark is 400 ft (122 m) long and has a beam of 47 ft (14 m) and a draft of 21 ft (6.5 m). Her sail area is 42,744 sq ft (3,971 m^2). The 3,709-ton vessel was built in 1921 at the Germania Shipyard of Friedrich Krupp in Kiel, Germany for the Bremen firm of F. A. Vinnen & Co. as a large cargo-carrying sail-training ship named *Magdalene Vinnen*. She was used to carry nitrate from Chile and then grain from Australia. In 1936 she was sold to the Norddeutsche Lloyd shipping company and renamed *Kommodore Johnsen*. She continued to be used for cargo service but was primarily used as a training vessel for navy school cadets, with accommodation for 70 cadets. At the end of World War II the Russians found her in a German port and towed her away to the Soviet Union, where she was given her present name. She was used as an oceanographic research ship until she was taken out of service in the mid-1970s. After a re-fit she returned to the sea as one of only two ex-working Cape Horners still sailing (the other is *Krusenstern*, *see* Y-588). She is a regular competitor in the Cutty Sark Races. *Sedov* now has a crew of 234 men, some two-thirds of which are trainees.

Sail Training Ship *Sedov*

Y-796 ● 1000 roubles ● 2001 .999 gold, 50 mm, 156 gr

The reverse features the four-masted sail training bark *Sedov* (*see* Y-795).

Y-796
1000 roubles
2001 .999 gold, 50 mm

The Window into Europe

Y-801 ● 3 roubles ● 2003 .900 silver

Y-801
3 roubles
2003 .900 silver, 38.7 mm

The reverse depicts two sailing ships in front of the Vyborg fortress, seen through a stylized window-arch. Vyborg ("Holy Fortress" in Swedish) is located 70 miles (112 km) northwest of St. Petersburg on an island in the Vyborg Bay on the Gulf of Finland. The island was captured by Czar Peter I in 1710 in the Great Northern War (1700–1721). The castle on the island was originally built by the Swedes in 1293. Its 157-ft (48-m)-high tower affords a view far out into the Gulf of Finland. The window-arch alludes to the expression coined by the poet Alexander Pushkin who said that by founding St. Petersburg, Peter I opened a window into Europe. The denomination of 3 roubles (ТРИ РУБЛЯ) is spelled out on the obverse.

First Kamchatka Expedition

Y-809 ● 3 roubles ● 2003 .900 silver

The upper half of the reverse depicts a sailing ship against the background of mountains, a fisherman in a boat is depicted near the rim at 3 o'clock, and the lower half shows three indigenous Kamchatkans who are scaling fish against the background of poles with dried fish. The coin commemorates the First Kamchatka Expedition of 1725–1730, which was sent overland by Czar Peter I to learn whether Asia was connected with North America. The expedition was commanded by the Danish explorer Vitus Bering (*see* Y-243). Second-in-command was Martin Petrovich Spanberg, who was accompanied by the senior Russian—the naval instructor Aleksey Ivanovich Chirikov. In January 1725 a team headed by Spanberg and Chirikov set out with 25 large waggons of provisions and equipment, followed shortly thereafter by Bering with a similar caravan. The journey by land and river was hindered by swamps and streams. Bering reached Okhotsk on the eastern Siberian coast in October 1726 but the second team failed to arrive there before the onset of winter. The party had their boats frozen in the ice of the Gorbeia River and were forced to march throughout the winter, hauling makeshift sleds. Provisions ran out and the starving men ate the horses and finally the leather harnesses. Many men died and the equipment and material dragged with such effort and hardship across the entire breadth of Russia were lost. In April 1727 the survivors reached Okhotsk, 28 months after their departure. For the sea portion of the exploration voyage a vessel was built at Okhotsk, *Fortuna*, which was launched in June 1727. She made two voyages from Okhotsk to the west coast of Kamchatka. Kamchatkans were employed to haul everything across the peninsula to Nizhne Kamchatsk on the east coast. Here *Sviatoi Gavriil* (St. Gabriel) was built in 1728 (*see* Y-245). In 1728 and 1729 Bering made exploration voyages along the east coast of Asia in *Sviatoi Gavriil* and *Fortuna*, sailing as far north as 67° 18' N. His voyages confirmed that Asia is divided from America by what was named the Bering Sea, in his honor. Bering sailed back to Okhotsk and then returned to St. Petersburg, where he arrived in 1730. The reverse inscription translates to "1st Kamchatka Expedition."

Ancient Russian Towns - Murom

Y-817 ● 10 roubles ● 2003 copper-nickel core in brass ring

The reverse depicts churches in the city of Murom among trees, in the foreground a fisherman in a boat on the Oka River, and at the top two shields of Murom. The city is situated 150 miles (241 km) east of Moscow. First mentioned in chronicles of 862, it is one of the oldest Russian towns. Surviving historic buildings include the Trinity and Annunciation monasteries and the churches of the Resurrection and Transfiguration, all from the 17th century. The "0" of the "10" denomination on the obverse contains a security element (*see* Y-740).

Ancient Russian Towns - Kasimov

Y-818 ● 10 roubles ● 2003 copper-nickel core in brass ring

The reverse features a steamship on the Oka River, a view of the city of Kasimov, and at the top the shield of the city which shows a medieval ship-like device with a crowned prow. Kasimov on the Oka River, about 160 miles (260 km) east–southeast of Moscow, is more than 800 years old. Several churches are prominent in the city skyline. The church at the right of the reverse contains the tomb of Alexander Nevskii (*see* Y-504). The "0" of the "10" denomination on the obverse contains a security element (*see* Y-740).

Ancient Russian Towns - Kemy

Y-826 ● 10 roubles ● 2004 copper-nickel core in brass ring

The reverse depicts boats on a river in front of a view of the city of Kemy with the Assumption Chapel and, at the top, the city's coat-of-arms. The city is a fishing and wood industry center on the west coast of the White Sea. It is first mentioned in chronicles in the 15th century. The "0" of the "10" denomination on the obverse contains a security element (*see* Y-740).

Second Kamchatka Expedition

Y-832 ● 100 roubles ● 2004 .900 gold

The reverse depicts a shaman performing a ritual dance in front of two sitting persons and in the background at right a sailing ship and at left two tents. The reverse inscription, translated, is "2nd Kamchatka Expedition" (*see* T-1). The denomination is spelled out on the obverse: СТО РУБЛЕЙ (100 roubles).

300th Anniversary of the Founding of St. Petersburg

Y-836 ● 1 rouble ● 2003 .925 silver

Y-836
1 rouble
2003 .925 silver, 25 mm

The reverse depicts an 18th-century frigate. The vessel is the gilded weather vane on the spire on the top of the 236-ft (72-m)-high central tower of the Admiralty in St. Petersburg, and has become the city's emblem. The wooden spire, like that of the Saints Peter and Paul Cathedral (*see* Y-249), asserted St. Petersburg's identity as a European city, rather than a traditional Russian city with onion domes. The site was first a shipyard and was later expanded to become a well-protected fortress that served as the headquarters of the Russian navy. The present building with the spire was constructed in 1806–1823 according to a design by the Russian architect A. D. Zakharov who received his training in France.

The Window into Europe

Y-865 ● 25 roubles ● 2003 .900 silver, 60 mm

Y-865
25 roubles
2003 .900 silver, 60 mm

The center of the reverse gives a view through a stylized window-arch of two sailing ships and a rowboat in front of the Shlisselburg fortress, and in the foreground a rider and two fighting men on the shore. Shlisselburg (Key Fortress in German) is situated on the island of Oreshek (Little Nut) in Ladoga Lake, some 25 miles (40 km) east of St. Petersburg. The island, which was first fortified in 1323, changed hands many times until it was captured in 1702 from Sweden by Czar Peter I in the Great Northern War. In World War II the town of Shlisselburg fell to the Germans in 1941 but the fortress held out for 500 days until the raise of the blockade of Leningrad. The denomination of 25 roubles (ДВАДЦАТЬ ПЯТЬ РУБЛЕЙ) is spelled out on the obverse.

First Kamchatka Expedition

Y-866 ● 25 roubles ● 2003 .900 silver, 60 mm

The reverse depicts the sailing ship *Sviatoi Gavriil* (*see* Y-245), and at top left a map of eastern Siberia from Kamchatka to the Chukchi

Peninsula in the extreme north. The map denotes the route followed by *Sviatoi Gavriil* on Vitus Bering's exploration voyages in 1728/29, which were part of the First Kamchatka Expedition of 1725–1730 (*see* Y-809). The reverse inscriptions translate to "1st Kamchatka Expedition" and "Vessel *Sv. Gavriil*."

The Window into Europe

Y-873 ● 100 roubles ● 2003 .900 silver, 100 mm, 1111 gr

Y-873
100 roubles
2003 .900 silver, 100 mm

The center of the reverse gives a view through a stylized window-arch of a sailing ship of the Russian navy and sail-boats against the background of St. Petersburg's Neva River Embankment and the Peter and Paul Fortress (*see* Y-249), while builders of the city are depicted in the foreground. The window-arch alludes to the words of the poet Alexander Pushkin that the founding of St. Petersburg by Czar Peter I opened a window into Europe. The denomination of 100 roubles (СТО РУБЛЕЙ) is spelled out on the obverse.

First Kamchatka Expedition

Y-875 ● 100 roubles ● 2003 .900 gold

The reverse depicts at right a sailing ship against the background of mountains and in the foreground an indigenous Kamchatkan with a bow and quiver with arrows and a pronged fishing spear. The reverse inscription translates to "1st Kamchatka Expedition," referring to the First Kamchatka Expedition of 1725–1730 (*see* Y-809).

The Window into Europe

Y-877 ● 200 roubles ● 2003 .900 silver, 130 mm, 3333 gr (7.3 pounds!)

The reverse is divided into five parts. The upper left part depicts sailing ships and a boat against the background of the Admiralty in St. Petersburg; the upper right shows the coat-of-arms of Russia against the background of a building; the lower right part features artillery guns with cannon-balls, banners, bayonets and a drum against the background of a fortress; the lower left part depicts books, a paper scroll, mathematical instruments and an astronomic instrument against the background of buildings; and the center part features the equestrian statue of Czar Peter I, *Bronze Horseman*, on the Decembrists' Square in St. Petersburg. This statue was commissioned by Empress Catherine II from the Frenchman Etienne Maurice Falconet who sculpted it in 1767–1782. The coin marks the founding in 1703 of St. Petersburg by Czar Peter I. The denomination of 200 roubles (ДВЕСТИ РУБЛЕЙ) is spelled out on the obverse.

The Window into Europe

Y-878 ● 1000 roubles ● 2003 .999 gold, 50 mm

The reverse depicts sailing ships and a boat between defense works of the Kronstadt Fortress within a stylized window-arch. Kronstadt is situated on Kotlin Island in the Gulf of Finland, 14 miles (22 km) west of St. Petersburg and commands the approach to St. Petersburg. It is a naval base with an arsenal, docks and shipyards that was founded by Czar Peter I in 1703. The denomination of 1000 roubles (ОДНА ТЫСЯЧА РУБЛЕЙ) is spelled out on the obverse.

The Window into Europe

Y-879 ● 10,000 roubles ● 2003 .999 gold, 100 mm, 1001 gr

The reverse depicts, clockwise from left, at 9 o'clock – defense works of the Kronstadt Fortress and a sailboat; at 10 o'clock – the Vyborg Fortress and a sailing ship; at 1 o'clock – armaments factory buildings in Petrozavodsk on the western shore of Onega Lake along an outline map of the lake; at 3 o'clock – the Shlisselburg fortress superimposed on an outline map of the Ladoga Lake; and at 6 o'clock – the Peter and Paul Fortress in St. Petersburg. All these military buildings in St. Petersburg and surroundings date back to Czar Peter I. The denomination of 10,000 roubles (ДЕСЯТЬ ТЫСЯЧ РУБЛЕЙ) is spelled out on the obverse.

Armed Forces – 18th-Century Marine

Y-917 ● 1 rouble ● 2005 .925 silver

The reverse depicts a marine of the time of Czar Peter I (1672–1725) against the background of a naval vessel with a landing party on board. The vessel flies the St. Andrew's flag, the flag of the Russian navy. The reverse inscription translates as "Marines."

Y-917
1 rouble
2005 .925 silver, 25 mm

Armed Forces – Marines

Y-918 ● 1 rouble ● 2005 .925 silver

The reverse depicts two marines against the background of a landing ship. The reverse inscription translates as "Marines."

Y-918
1 rouble
2005 .925 silver, 25 mm

T-1 Second Kamchatka Expedition

Y-? ● 3 roubles ● 2004 .900 silver

The reverse depicts a Kamchatka aborigin paddling a canoe and in the background at right a sailing ship and at left two boats and outlines of mountains on the horizon. The coin marks the Second Kamchatka Expedition of 1733–1743 (*see* Y-243) which was headed by Vitus Jonassen Bering (1681–1741) in *Sviatoi Pyotr* (St. Peter) and Aleksey Ilyich Chirikov (1703–1748) in *Sviatoi Pavel* (St. Paul). The men reached the shores of North America and discovered several islands of the Aleutian chain and the Commander Islands.

Y-?
3 roubles
2004 .900 silver, 39 mm

T-2 Second Kamchatka Expedition

Y-? ● 25 roubles ● 2004 .900 silver, 60 mm

The reverse depicts two sailing ships—one in the center, the other following in the background—and, at the top, a map of the Bering Sea. The inscriptions at the bottom of the reverse name the ships: Packet-boat *Sv. Pyotr* and Packet-boat *Sv. Pavel* (*see* T-1). The map shows at left the Kamchatka and Chukchee Peninsulas and at right the northwestern coast of North America. The inscription at the top of the reverse, translated, is "2nd Kamchatka Expedition." The denomination is spelled out on the obverse: ДВАДЦАТЬ ПЯТЬ РУБЛЕЙ (25 roubles).

Y-?
25 roubles
2004 .900 silver, 60 mm

T-3 Ancient Russian Towns – Kaliningrad

Y-? ● 10 roubles ● 2005 copper-nickel core in brass ring

The reverse features a view of the city of Kaliningrad on the Pregel River and, at the top, the city's shield that depicts a kotch of the time of Czar Peter I on a wave of amber beads. Kaliningrad is the capital of the region of that name. The annexation of the region to the USSR was agreed upon at the Potsdam conference of the Allied leaders in 1945 shortly after the end of World War II. The city (formerly Königsberg) was renamed for Mikhail Kalinin (1875–1946) who was the titular head of the Soviet state between 1919 and 1946. The region is part of the Russian Federation but is detached from it and can be reached overland only by passing through Lithuania or Poland. Prior to its annexation to the USSR it was the northern part of the German province of East Prussia. The city of Königsberg was founded by the Teutonic Knights, also known as *Deutscher Orden* (German Order), in 1254 and became the residence of their Great Master in 1456. It was a member of the Hanseatic League. In the 16th century the Great Master took the title of Duke of Prussia. From 1618 the dukedom was ruled by the electors of Brandenburg. In 1701 Brandenburg's elector was crowned in Königsberg as the first King of Prussia.

SAN MARINO

San Marino, with 23 square miles (61 km^2) one of the smallest states in the world, stands on the slopes of the ridge of Monte Titano, a triple-peaked mountain in the Appenine chain near the city of Rimini, Italy. It is the oldest republic in the world. The heads of state are two co-regents from opposing political parties who are chosen for six-month terms from among the members of the popularly elected Great and General Council.

Annual Series 1972

KM-20 • 100 lire • 1972 steel

The reverse depicts St. Marinus in a boat on the Adriatic Sea. According to tradition, Marinus (Marino) was a Christian stonemason who lived in the 2nd century CE and came to the town of Rimini in Italy with his companion Leo to find work. Here he met Christians who had been persecuted by the Roman emperor Diocletian and sentenced to hard labor on account of their refusal to sacrifice to the Roman gods. In his old age, in 301 CE, Marinus withdrew from the world to a hermitage on Monte Titano, not far from Rimini, where he founded a community for Christians seeking refuge from persecution. On the site of the hermitage a town was built which was called after Marinus and developed into San Marino. The first historical record mentioning San Marino is dated 951 CE. The obverse features three stylized towers, each surmounted by an ostrich plume, which is the design of San Marino's coat-of-arms that appears on most of the country's coins. The towers represent the tower fortifications of la Guaita (Rocca), la Cesta and Montale that are linked together by walls surrounding the mountain peak of Monte Titano and have made the Sammarinese independence possible. Giuseppe Garibaldi, the father of modern Italy, found safety in the republic with his troops after the fall of the Roman Republic in 1849. In gratitude, he excluded San Marino from his plans for the unification of Italy.

Annual Series 1973

KM-24 • 5 lire • 1973 aluminum

The reverse depicts five young men in a symbolic boat surrounded by stars. They represent the population of the earth and are placed together in the boat to illustrate the unity that should exist among mankind.

Annual Series 1973

KM-28 ● 100 lire ● 1973 steel

The reverse depicts Odysseus and his men passing the Pillars of Hercules (*see* Spain KM-839) in their oar- and sail-driven ship. In Greek mythology, Odysseus, King of Ithaca, was one of the Greek heroes in the Trojan War. His adventures on his voyage home from the war were written down in the 8th century BCE by the Greek poet Homer in the poem *Odyssey*. The reverse design represents the diffusion of culture in human progress.

Annual Series 1989

KM-240 ● 1000 lire ● 1989 .835 silver

The reverse depicts St. Marinus and St. Leo standing in a boat on the Adriatic Sea (*see* KM-20).

Olympic Games 1992 Barcelona

KM-272 ● 1000 lire ● 1991 .835 silver

The reverse depicts three stylized caravels below a runner with a Catalonian cap who holds the Olympic flame. The caravels symbolize the 500th anniversary of the discovery of America by Christopher Columbus, and the runner's cap alludes to the Olympic Games that were held in Barcelona, the capital of Catalonia. The Latin language edge legend reads RELINQUO VOS LIBEROS (I Leave You Free).

500th Anniversary of Discovery of America

KM-281 ● 10 lire ● 1992 aluminum

The reverse depicts a stylized caravel superimposed on a stylized map and at the bottom a dolphin.

500th Anniversary of Discovery of America

KM-282 ● 20 lire ● 1992 aluminum-bronze

The reverse depicts Christopher Columbus planting the flag of Spain on Hispaniola in the New World in 1492 and a small ship on the horizon at right. This image is a detail from *The Discovery of the New World*, a painting made in 1837 by John Vanderlyn that was placed in 1847 in the Rotunda of the US Capitol in Washington, DC.

500th Anniversary of Discovery of America

KM-284 ● 100 lire ● 1992 steel

The reverse depicts the three ships of Christopher Columbus—*Santa Maria, Niña* and *Pinta*—in the Sargasso Sea in 1492. The Sargasso Sea, named for the seaweed of the genus *Sargassum* that is found on it in abundance, is the calm section of the northern Atlantic Ocean between the Azores and the West Indies.

500th Anniversary of Discovery of America

KM-286 ● 500 lire ● 1992 aluminum-bronze core in steel ring

The reverse shows a caravel being blown by trade winds in the tropics. The inscription along the outer periphery of the reverse is SCOPERTA DELL'AMERICA ("Discovery of America" in Italian), that along the inner periphery is the mission statement which, according to legend, Christopher Columbus formulated when he set out across the Atlantic Ocean to find Cathai (China): BUSCAR EL LEVANTE POR EL PONIENTE ("Searching for the East by Way of the West" in Spanish).

Amerigo Vespucci – The Ship

KM-333 ● 5000 lire ● 1995 .835 silver

KM-333
5000 lire
1995 .835 silver, 32 mm

The reverse features the three-masted full-rigged training ship *Amerigo Vespucci* of the Italian navy. The 3,543-ton steel bark is 332 ft (101 m) long, has a beam of 51 ft (16 m), and draws 22 ft (6.6 m) of water. She was built in 1931 at the royal yard Castellamare di Stabia for the Academia Navale in Livorno and imitates a fourth- or fifth-rate ship-of-the-line of about 1800, with scuttles replacing gunports. This design of a frigate with a wide beam makes it possible to accommodate the crew of 450, of whom 150 are cadets, without making the vessel too large. *Amerigo Vespucci* carries 22,600 sq ft (2,100 m^2) of canvas in her 23 sails. The top of the main mast is 150 ft (46 m) above the main deck. Under auxiliary power she can make a speed of 10 knots. She makes frequent voyages to ports all over the globe, both to promote Italy and to instruct new seamen in the rigors of sail. She is named for the Florentine navigator Amerigo Vespucci (1451–1512), for whom America is named (*see* KM-334). The figurehead of the ship is a larger-than-life effigy of Vespucci. The edge legend reads RELINQUO VOS LIBEROS (I Leave You Free).

Amerigo Vespucci – The Explorer

KM-334 ● 10,000 lire ● 1995 .835 silver

The reverse depicts *Dauphine*, the 468-ton carrack of the Florentine navigator Amerigo Vespucci (1451–1512) on one or more of his exploration voyages, and a medallion portrait of Vespucci holding nautical instruments. *Dauphine* was built about 1480 and had a length of 115 ft (35 m), a beam of 19 ft (5.8 m) and a draft of 15 ft (4.6 m). Vespucci made voyages to America for the Spanish monarchs in 1499/1500 and for the king of Portugal in 1501/02. On the latter voyage he began to doubt that the coastline he explored was in Asia; he began to believe that they were exploring a totally unknown continent, a New World, although he continued to call it, as Columbus had, *Las Indias*. He put his thoughts on paper in a letter to a relative, describing the land as not an island but a previously unknown continent. This letter, published as the tract *Mundus Novus*, an account of his second voyage, was read around Europe thanks to the recent invention of printing by means of movable type. In 1507 a professor of geography in Lorraine, Martin Waldseemüller (circa 1470–circa 1520), used Amerigo Vespucci's (misspelled) first name, Americi, rather than that of Columbus, to denote the portion of the New World he had charted. This "Land of Americi" became America.

500th Anniversary of Vasco da Gama's Voyage to India

KM-370 ● 5000 lire ● 1997 .835 silver

KM-370
5000 lire
1997 .835 silver, 32 mm

The reverse depicts at right *São Gabriel*, the flagship of the Portuguese navigator Vasco da Gama (circa 1460–1524) on his journey of 1497–1499 during which he was the first European to reach India by sailing around the Cape of Good Hope (*see* Portugal KM-709), and at left a map of Africa on which the route of that journey from Portugal to India is denoted. The edge legend reads RELINQUO VOS LIBEROS (I Leave You Free).

500th Anniversary of Voyage of John Cabot

KM-371 ● 10,000 lire ● 1997 .835 silver

KM-371
10,000 lire
1997 .835 silver, 34 mm

The reverse features two 15th-century sailing ships and in the upper left a map of the Atlantic Ocean. One of the ships is *Matthew*, the three-masted ship of some 50 tons in which John Cabot made the first voyage from Europe to North

America since the time of the Norsemen, in 1497. *Matthew*, launched around 1490, was 112 ft (34 m) long, had a beam of 15 ft (4.6 m), drew some 13 ft (4 m) of water, and was manned by a crew of 18. John Cabot (circa 1455–1498) was an Italian who lived in London when the news was received that Columbus had sailed to the west and reached Asia. (Cabot is the Anglicized form of his name. In Italian it is Giovanni Caboto.) England decided to follow up on Columbus' discovery. In March 1496 King Henry VII granted letters patent to his "well-beloved John Gabote, citizen of Venice ... to seeke out, discover and finde whatsoever isles, countries, regions or provinces of the heathen and infidels which before this time have been unknown to all Christians." Cabot set sail from Bristol on 2 May 1497 aboard *Matthew* to find the Northwest Passage to Asia. He landed on 24 June 1497 on either Cape Briton Island in Nova Scotia or Cape Bonavista in Newfoundland. (The exact place cannot be determined, as one of Cabot's three sons destroyed all of his father's letters and papers after his death.) Cabot planted a wooden cross where he landed, claiming the region for England and naming it Newfoundland. On his return voyage Cabot explored the western and southern coasts of Newfoundland. Upon his return to England Cabot received from the king a reward of £10 for having discovered the "new island." In May 1498 Cabot sailed from Bristol on a follow-up expedition with five ships and 300 men, to proceed westward from his last discovery to the coast of Cipangu. He was never heard of again. The Cabot Strait between Newfoundland and Cape Breton Island is named for the explorer. The map on the reverse shows the Northern Atlantic route taken by Cabot from Britain to Canada. It is unclear why the reverse depicts two ships, as it is well documented that Cabot made his discovery voyage with only one ship.

Mankind and the Exploration of the World – The Old Sea

KM-391 ● 50 lire ● 1999 copper-nickel

The reverse depicts the stylized sail of a ship, the sun and waves, marking man's discoveries of our planet, by sea.

Mankind and the Exploration of the World – The Modern Sea

KM-392 ● 100 lire ● 1999 copper-nickel

The reverse depicts a stylized submarine below the Arctic icecap, symbolizing man's discoveries of our planet, undersea.

750th Anniversary of the Birth of Marco Polo

KM-466 ● 50 euro ● 2004 .900 gold

The reverse portrays the Venetian traveler Marco Polo (1254–1324) as part of a drawing that also depicts a boat in front of the gate of a wall and, below the boat, part of a ship with furled sails. Polo set sail for China in 1271 (*see* China / People's Republic Y-56).

SLOVAKIA

From 1993 Slovakia is an independent republic in central Europe. Prior thereto it was part of Czechoslovakia.

250th Anniversary of Birth of Moric Beňovský

KM-34 ● 200 korun ● 1996 .750 silver

KM-34
200 korun
1996 .750 silver, 34 mm

The obverse features a sailing ship on a stormy sea. The reverse depicts Slovak-born Count Moric Beňovský (Benovsky, Benyowsky) (1746–1786)—soldier, navigator, adventurer, author, and ruler of Madagascar. In 1769, while fighting against the Russians for the independence of Poland, he was captured and after an unsuccessful escape attempt he was deported to Kamchatka, where he organized a rebellion and managed to escape. In 1771 the conspirators sailed by way of the Kuril Islands, Japan and Taiwan to Macao. This is the first voyage from the northeast to the southeast of Asia reported by a European. From Macao Beňovský traveled to France where he managed to gain the favor of King Louis XV, who granted him the rank of colonel and "commander of the island of Madagascar" and entrusted him with the leadership of a corps of volunteers to colonize the island. In Madagascar Beňovský built up a network of trade centers and roads, and unified the clans and petty chiefdoms. In 1776 the local tribes granted him the title of "King of Kings" and the French made him a general; however, when his efforts met with opposition from France he left the island and sought support at the court of Vienna. In 1778 Empress Maria Theresa, at the request of her daughter Marie Antoinette of France, made Beňovský a count. He attempted to build an Austrian navy but failed in his mission. In 1779 Beňovský fought with American troops in the War of Independence. He joined a Polish contingent led by General Casimir Pulaski and fought in the siege of Savannah, Georgia. In 1784 Beňovský organized an

American expedition to Madagascar. He sailed in *Intrepid* from Baltimore to Madagascar, where he proclaimed himself emperor of Madagascar. The French regarded this as a threat to their interests and sent a military expedition against him. Beňovský fell in battle while defending Mauritania, the chief town of his Kingdom of Madagascar. His travel memoirs were published posthumously and have been translated into many languages. The edge legend IN ADVERSIS ET PROSPERIS (In Adversity and In Success), the Latin motto from Beňovský's coat-of-arms, is divided by two anchors.

SPAIN

The Kingdom of Spain occupies most of the Iberian peninsula in southwestern Europe.

Circulation Coin

KM-740 ● 25 centimos ● 1925 – *see* T-1

Circulation Coin

KM-833 ● 5 pesetas ● 1989–2001 aluminum-bronze

The reverse depicts a stylized three-masted sail ship.

500th Anniversary of Discovery of America

KM-839 ● 5000 pesetas ● 1989 .925 silver

KM-839
5000 pesetas
1989 .925 silver, 40 mm

The reverse features *Santa Maria*, the flagship of Christopher Columbus on his discovery voyage in 1492 (*see* Andorra KM-78). The obverse shows the coat-of-arms of Spain flanked by two crowned pillars. These represent the Pillars of Hercules—the two promontories at the entrance to the Mediterranean Sea on opposite sides of the Strait of Gibraltar that were known in ancient times as Calpe (modern Gibraltar) and Abyla (modern Jabel Musa at Ceuta on the African coast). According to legend, the promontories were joined until Heracles tore them apart. The liston draped around the pillars bears the Latin motto PLUS ULTRA (More Beyond) referring to the Spanish possessions in the Americas. The Pillars of Hercules design is adapted from the "piece of eight"—the 8 reales silver coin that was struck in

Spanish-American mints from 1537. The "pieces of eight" were struck in vast quantities. For hundreds of years they were one of the most famous and widely accepted of all silver coins. The size and weight of KM-839 correspond to those of the 8 reales silver coin of the past.

Regional Autonomy

KM-841 ● 10,000 pesetas ● 1989 .925 silver, 73 mm

The coat-of-arms of Spain on the reverse is surrounded by the arms of the 17 provinces (autonomous communities or regions). At 4 o'clock is the shield of Cantabria, the upper part of which features at left a galleon and at right a tower. Clockwise from top center the 17 provinces are: Andalucia (Andalusia), Aragón, Asturias, Baleares (the Balearic Islands), Islas Canarias (the Canary Islands), Cantabria, Castilla-La Mancha, Castilla-Leon, Cataluña (Catalonia), Extremadura, Galicia, La Rioja, Madrid, Murcia, Navarra (Navarre), Pais Vasco (the Basque Country) and Valencia. The obverse depicts the Spanish royal family.

500th Anniversary of Discovery of America

KM-844 ● 40,000 pesetas ● 1989 .999 gold

The reverse depicts a sea monster attacking a ship. The design alludes to the horrors envisaged by medieval sailors who made the discovery voyages and who believed that somewhere beyond the known shipping lanes lies the end of the earth where ships are swallowed by sea monsters. The size and weight of the coin correspond to those of the 4 escudos gold coins of Spain's colonial past.

Olympic Games 1992 Barcelona

KM-865 ● 2000 pesetas ● 1990 .925 silver

The reverse depicts an ancient riverboat with five oars, a helmsman at left who holds the steering oar, and three rowers opposite him. The design is adapted from a copper coin struck in southern Spain in the period between circa 100 BCE and the reign of Roman emperor Augustus (27 BCE–14 CE). It is assumed that the coin was minted in a town named Tamusia, the exact location of which is not known. The motif symbolizes (Olympic) rowing. The obverse depicts King Juan Carlos I and his son Don Felipe de Borbón, Prince of Asturias.

KM-865
2000 pesetas
1990 .925 silver, 40 mm

Expo Lisbon 1998

KM-1000 ● 1000 pesetas ● 1998 .925 silver

KM-1000
1000 pesetas
1998 .925 silver, 33 mm

The reverse features the four-masted sail training vessel *Juan Sebastián de Elcano*. The 3,750-ton topsail schooner was built in 1928 for the Royal Spanish Navy at the Echevarrieta y Larrinaga shipyard in Cadiz. She is 309 ft (94 m) long and has a beam of 43 ft (13 m) and a draft of 22 ft (6.9 m). Her sail area is 26,555 sq ft (2,467 m^2) and her highest sail is 164 ft (50 m) in height. Her crew numbers 332, including cadets. Her home port is Cadiz in Andalusia. *Juan Sebastián de Elcano* is Spain's most representative ship, visiting other countries on goodwill missions during six months of the year. The ship bears the name of the Basque captain of *Concepción*, one of the five ships in the fleet of the Portugese sailor Fernão de Magalhães (Ferdinand Magellan) that set out in 1519 on a westward voyage to the Far East to find the Spice Islands (the Moluccas) for Spain (*see* Portugal KM-731). After passing through the strait that now bears his name and crossing the Pacific Ocean, Magellan was fatally wounded on the Philippine island of Cebu in April 1521, while fighting in a local war. De Elcano then took over command of Magellan's flagship *Vittoria*, which became the first ship to circumnavigate the earth, completing the voyage in September 1522—the only ship remaining of the original fleet. Only 18 men survived the voyage. Near the rim of the reverse at 1 o'clock is the logo of EXPO '98, the world fair held in 1998 at Lisbon, Portugal. The theme of the exposition was "The Oceans: A Heritage for the Future."

End of Millennium

KM-1010 ● 1500 pesetas ● 1999 .925 silver, eight-sided planchet

The reverse depicts an astronaut floating over an image of the earth that shows a map of the Atlantic Ocean between Europe and northern America on which the three ships of Christopher Columbus are sailing. The design marks two major events of the millennium—the discovery of America and the conquest of space.

300th Anniversary of the House of Bourbon

KM-1026 ● 2000 pesetas ● 1997 .925 silver

The reverse depicts the 1,925-ton galleon *Real Phelipe*. She had 114 guns and was constructed in 1732 in Guarnizo, Cantabria. The obverse features the effigy of King Fernando (Ferdinand) VI (1713–1759), based on a portion of the painting of the Spanish royal family, *The Family of Felipe V*, by the French painter Louis Michel van Loo that is on exhibit in the Prado Museum in Madrid. Fernando VI reigned from 1746 as the second Bourbon king of Spain. The lilies on the obverse are the emblem of the Bourbon dynasty. Its present king is Juan Carlos I in whose name the coin is struck.

200th Anniversary of the Incorporation of Menorca into Spain

KM-1050 ● 10 euro ● 2002 .925 silver

The reverse depicts three men on horses on shore and in the background two sailing ships. The design, taken from a painting by Giuseppe Chiesa, depicts the transfer of Menorca by its British governor General Henry Cleophane to the Spanish General Don Miguel Vives following the signing of the Treaty of Amiens in 1802. Pursuant to this treaty, Menorca (or Minorca), one of the Balearic Islands to the east of the Spanish mainland, became Spanish territory in exchange for the island of Trinidad that became British. Menorca had been British since the Treaty of Utrecht of 1713. The size and weight of the coin are the same as those of the 8 reales silver coin of the past.

75th Anniversary of *Juan Sebastián de Elcano*

KM-1052 ● 10 euro ● 2003 .925 silver

The reverse features the sail training ship *Juan Sebastián de Elcano* that was built in 1928 (*see* KM-1000). The latent image in the sea below the ship is either seen as a crowned "M," the mintmark of the Madrid Mint, or the number "75," the age of the ship, depending on the angle at which the coin is viewed. In the annual Coin of the Year contest for 2003 the coin was selected as the best silver coin.

KM-1052
10 euro
2003 .925 silver, 40 mm

500th Anniversary of the Birth of Miguel López de Legazpi

KM-1053 ● 10 euro ● 2003 .925 silver

The coin depicts the Spanish conquistador Miguel López de Legazpi (1505–1572) in front of a 16th-century sailing ship. Legazpi's portrait is based on a painting by the Philippine artist Juan Luna. In 1564 Legazpi sailed from Mexico as commander of a colonization expedition to the Philippines. He took possession of the islands for the Spanish crown and became the first governor general of the archipelago, which was named for Philip II (1527–1598, king of Spain from 1556). In 1565 Legazpi founded Cebu, the oldest Spanish city in the Philippines, on the ashes of the town of Sugbu. In 1570 a company of 120 Spanish–Mexican conquistadors took Maynilad (now Manila) and a year later proclaimed it the archipelago's capital.

Salvador Dalí

KM-1058 ● 400 euro ● 2004 .999 gold

The girl on the reverse looks out from the window over the Bay of Cadaqués, in which good eyes can discern a sailing yacht far in the background. This design is a reproduction of the painting *Girl Standing by the Window* by the Spanish Catalonian painter Salvador Dalí (1904–1989) which is exhibited at the Museo Nacional Centro de Arte Reina Sofia in Madrid. The painting depicts Dalí's sister Ana-María looking out from the family's summer home. Dalí, who is featured on the obverse, is famous for his surrealistic paintings but *Girl Standing by the Window*, painted in 1925, is in the realistic style. The metal composition, size and weight of the coin correspond to the Spanish 8 escudos coin struck from the 17th century.

T-1 Galleon

KM-740 ● 25 centimos ● 1925 copper-nickel, circulation coin
KM-? ● 10 euro ● 2002 .925 silver, Ibero-American Series

A galleon is featured on the obverse of KM-740 and on the reverse of the 2002 coin. Galleons were well-built, steady ships that could stand up to the heavy ocean swell. They were large stern-squared four-masters and usually had three or four decks, all capable of supporting guns. They came in many sizes, ranging from a hundred to a thousand tons. Their exterior dimensions varied widely—100 ft (30 m) in length, 30 ft (9.1 m) in beam and 18 ft (5.5 m) in draft being about average. The galleon was the predominant type of ship that maintained the connection between Spain and its colonies in South America from the 16th century, transporting provisions and bringing treasure to the mother country. The reverse inscription of the 2002 coin reads ENCUENTRO DE DOS MUNDOS (Meeting of Two Worlds). Its obverse shows the coat-of-arms of Spain surrounded by those of the ten countries that participated in the issue of the 2002–2003 dated Ibero-American series, the theme of which is Navigation. These countries are Argentina, Cuba, Ecuador, Guatemala, Mexico, Nicaragua, Paraguay, Peru, Portugal and Spain. Almost all of the coins in the series are of identical size, weight and silver content.

SWEDEN

The Kingdom of Sweden occupies the eastern part of the Scandinavian peninsula in northwestern Europe.

300th Anniversary of the Founding of a Swedish Colony in Delaware

KM-807 ● 2 kronor ● 1938 .800 silver

The reverse depicts the three-masted pinnace *Calmare Nyckel* (Key of Kalmar, named for the Swedish city of Kalmar). She was one of the two ships that brought the first Swedish settlers to America in 1638. The second ship was *Fågel Grip* (Griffin Bird). *Calmare Nyckel* (sometimes spelled *Kalmar Nyckel*) was built in 1629. In 1638 she was sent out by the Dutch–Swedish–owned New Sweden Company, that had been founded in 1633 to exploit the fur trade then developing and in 1637 had obtained a charter by Queen Christina (1632–1654) for a settlement in America. The settlers on the two ships were lead by Peter Minuit. They built Fort Christina, named for the Swedish queen. The settlement became the Swedish colony Nya Sverige (New Sweden, *see* KM-867). Both *Calmare Nyckel* and *Fågel Grip* returned to Sweden with furs. In 1997 a replica of *Calmare Nyckel* was built by Allen C. Rawl, Inc. of Wilmington, Delaware to a design based on historical research but mostly from inference, as no accurate records of the original vessel exist. The replica measures 168 gross tons. It has a length of 93 ft (28 m) overall, 141 ft (43 m) sparred, a beam of 25 ft (7.6 m) and a draft of 12 ft (3.8 m). Its sail area is 7,600 sq ft (706 m^2). The Latin reverse inscription NOVAE SUECIAE SUECIA MEMOR translates to "Sweden commemorates New Sweden."

350th Anniversary of the Founding of a Swedish Colony in Delaware

KM-867 ● 100 kronor ● 1988 .925 silver, varieties exist

KM-867
100 kronor
1988 .925 silver, 32 mm

The reverse depicts the pinnace *Calmare Nyckel* and a map of New Sweden. *Calmare Nyckel* was one of the two ships that brought the first Swedish settlers to America (*see* KM-807). These settlers, among which were also Finns and Dutchmen, landed in 1638 at the mouth of the Delaware River and purchased from the Indians a strip of land about 60 miles (97 km) wide between the present-day cities of Trenton, New Jersey and Wilmington, Delaware, on which they founded the colony New Sweden. Leader of the expedition was a Walloon, Peter Minuit, the founder of the city of New York who had acquired the island of Manhattan in 1626. In 1632 Minuit offered his services to Sweden to establish a Swedish colony in North America. The settlers built Fort Christina, which they named for the Swedish queen and which developed into the present city of Wilmington. Its location is denoted on the map on the reverse of the coin. In 1642 the Swedish partners in the trading company acquired the share of their Dutch partners and the Delaware Valley became the Swedish colony Nya

Sverige (New Sweden). The Dutch West India Company, claiming rights to the same area, built a fort at the mouth of the Delaware River and in 1655 the colony was seized by Peter Stuyvesant, governor of the Dutch company. He sailed into Delaware Bay with more than 300 men and the colony became part of New Netherlands. The inscription on the reverse is NYA SVERIGE DELAWARE (New Sweden Delaware).

350th Anniversary of the Founding of a Swedish Colony in Delaware

KM-868
1000 kronor
1988 .900 gold, 21 mm

KM-868 ● 1000 kronor ● 1988 .900 gold

The reverse depicts the pinnace *Calmare Nyckel*, one of the two ships that brought the first Swedish settlers to America (*see* KM-807 about the ship and KM-867 about the colony of New Sweden). The inscription on the reverse is NYA SVERIGE DELAWARE (New Sweden Delaware).

Opening of the Vasa Museum in Stockholm

KM-875
200 kronor
1990 .925 silver, 36 mm

KM-875 ● 200 kronor ● 1990 .925 silver

The reverse depicts the 64-gun galleon *Vasa*, which was built at the royal dockyard in Stockholm for Gustavus II Adolphus (King of Sweden 1611–1632) and named for the king's family, the House of Vasa. She was meant to be the flagship of the Swedish navy. *Vasa*'s length was 180 ft (55 m) and her beam 38 ft (12 m). She drew 15 ft (4.6 m) of water and displaced approximately 1,300 tons. She had three masts and ten sails. The ship set out on her maiden voyage on 10 August 1628. Before she left Stockholm harbor there was a sudden squall. Her gun ports were still open having just fired farewell, and when she listed heavily to port, the gun ports sank below water level and water gushed in. The too-narrow-bottomed, top-heavy ship with too little ballast sank in a few moments. (The king himself had dictated her measurements. No one had dared argue against him.) It is believed that some 50 individuals were drowned with her. In 1664/65, 53 cannons were salvaged by divers in a diving bell that enabled them to remain underwater for about 15 minutes. In the course of time the location of the wreck was forgotten. In the 1950s Anders Franzén, a naval architect, started to research old archives to determine the place where *Vasa* had foundered. In 1955 he found a letter sent to the king in 1628 which indicated the area. Franzén combed the area in his motorboat and in August 1956 brought up a piece of black oak from the ship's wreck. After King Gustaf VI Adolf had expressed his interest, Franzén secured cooperation from the navy and a salvage company. Six tunnels were dug through the mud and clay under the keel using a water jet and cables were pulled through the tunnels to form a cradle. In August 1959 *Vasa* was ready for her lift from a depth of 115 ft (35 m). She was lifted up from her claybed and moved in several steps to shallower levels until she surfaced in April 1961 and could be treated in dry dock. Her wood was in good condition due to the fact that ship worm (*teredo navalis*) cannot exist in waters with a low salt content, such as the Baltic Sea. The ship is now in the Vasa Museum in Stockholm, the opening of which is marked by this coin. The reverse inscription is REGALSKEPPET VASA (Royal Ship *Vasa*).

SWITZERLAND

The Swiss Confederation is situated in central Europe. Its coins state the country's name in Latin—Confoederatio Helvetica, or just Helvetia—rather than in the four official languages German, French, Italian and Romansch. The Celtic Helvetians lived in the country 2,000 years ago.

Shooting talers are not listed herein as they are medallic issues with limited use during the shooting festival for which they are produced.

100th Anniversary of the Birth of Auguste Piccard

KM-63 • 5 francs • 1984 copper-nickel

KM-63
5 francs
1984 copper-nickel, 31 mm

The bathyscaph in the lower half of the reverse and the balloon in its upper half were designed by the Swiss physicist and inventor Auguste Piccard (1884–1962) to achieve the highest and lowest altitudes reached by man. In 1931, in *FRNS*, Piccard made the first manned balloon flight into the stratosphere to gather data on the upper atmosphere and to measure cosmic rays, reaching the record altitude of 51,775 ft (15,781 m). The balloon was named for the Fonds National de la Recherche Scientifique—the Belgian foundation that financed the experiment. After making 27 flights until 1937, having set an ultimate record of 72,177 ft (22,000 m), Piccard's interest shifted toward exploration of the ocean bottom when he realized that a modification of some of his balloon concepts would allow descent into the deep ocean. The bathyscaph was a free-moving submersible. Piccard coined its name from the Greek words *bathus* (deep) and *skaphe* (boat). It consisted of a tank with an observation chamber suspended below it. The tank had two compartments—one containing lighter-than-water fuel that was emptied when descending, the other filled with iron ballast that was released for ascent. The observation chamber could hold two men and had two portholes. Piccard's bathyscaphe *FRNS* 2 was built in 1948 at Emile Henricot Works in Court-St-Étienne, Belgium. In 1950 it was gifted to the French navy and renamed *FRNS* 3. In 1954 it took a man safely down off Dakar, Senegal to a record depth of 13,693 ft (4,176 m). Piccard's second bathyscaph was *Trieste*, built in 1953 by Navalmeccanica at Naples, Italy. It was 60 ft (18 m) long, had a diameter of 12 ft (3.5 m) and a height of 18 ft (5.5 m), and weighed 13 tons in air, 8 tons in water. It was named for the city of Trieste on the Adriatic Sea. Piccard made over 100 dives in *Trieste*, among which a descent in 1956 to a depth of 10,355 ft (3,156 m). In 1958 it was purchased by the US Office of Naval Research for $250,000. In 1960 Piccard's son Jacques and US Navy lieutenant Don Walsh took it to the bottom of Challenger Deep in the Marianas Trench in the western Pacific, the deepest point known in the ocean, reaching a depth of 35,802 ft (10,912 m). *Trieste* is now on exhibit at the Navy Museum in Washington, DC.

Landscapes and Legends – Gargantua

KM-76 • 20 francs • 1996 .835 silver

The reverse shows the giant Gargantua emptying the Doubs River, on which a boat is depicted. The design is inspired by a legend from the Jura in French-speaking western Switzerland. Gargantua's head looked like a mountain and his hair like a gigantic forest. When he got up, he left a valley behind him. His tears caused catastrophic floods. Once the giant was so thirsty that he emptied the Doubs River, leaving the stream without water for three days. The Latin edge inscription DOMINUS PROVIDEBIT (God Will Provide) is borrowed from Genesis 22:8.

Landscapes and Legends – Dragon of Breno

KM-77 • 20 francs • 1996 .835 silver

The reverse depicts a landscape typical of the Italian-speaking canton of Ticino—a lake on which a boat is depicted, a village in front and a mountain in the background, and above the lake "the dragon of Breno." Legend tells about the frightened mountain herdsman of Breno who at midnight saw a dragon milking the full-uddered cows. The dragon did this for many nights, until the herdsmen called in the help of the Madonna. After promising to make a pilgrimage every year to the church on Monte Sacro in Varese, they managed to kill the dragon. Many years later, when the pilgrimage made its way to that holy mountain, a black rider passed the procession and kidnapped a girl. The people feared that this was the revenge of the dragon and ever since have made the pilgrimage not farther than the nearby chapel of San Mattia. The Latin edge inscription is DOMINUS PROVIDEBIT (God Will Provide).

TURKEY

The Republic of Turkey consists of a small part in southeastern Europe, Thrace, that borders the Black Sea and the Aegean Sea, and a large part in southwestern Asia, Anatolia, between the Black Sea and the Mediterranean Sea. The name "Turkey" derives from Tu-Kui, the Chinese name for nomad peoples who lived in a 6th-century empire that stretched from Mongolia and the northern border of China to the Black Sea.

FAO Issue

KM-934 ● 5 kurus ● 1980 bronze
KM-938 ● 2 1/2 lira ● 1980 stainless steel
KM-939 ● 5 lira ● 1980 stainless steel

The obverse features a large flounder, within which a fishing boat is depicted in which two men are standing hauling in their net. The obverse inscription is "kalkınma için balıkcılık" (Fishing for Development).

Olympic Games 1984 Los Angeles

KM-970 ● 5000 lira ● ND (1984) .925 silver

The reverse depicts in the center the cauldron with the Olympic flame, surrounded along the rim by images representing twelve different sports, among which is canoeing at 4 o'clock.

500th Anniversary of the Birth of Turgut Reis

KM-976 ● 5000 lira ● 1985 – see T-1

75th Anniversary of the Battle of Gallipoli

KM-993 ● 20,000 lira ● 1990 .925 silver
KM-994 ● 200,000 lira ● 1990 .917 gold

The reverse depicts the Dardanelles monument at Gallipoli and to both its left and its right a sinking ship. Gallipoli is the peninsula at the southern end of the European part of Turkey stretching along the Dardanelles. The Dardanelles is the narrow strait that separates European and Asian Turkey and connects the Aegean Sea with the Black Sea through the Sea of Marmara and the Bosporus. In 1915, during World War I, the British and French allies tried to open this important waterway, first by forcing passage of the Dardanelles, and later by landing forces on Gallipoli. The battle of the Dardanelles began on 19 February 1915 with 18 British and French battleships and battle cruisers, supported by destroyers and minesweepers. Their gunfire continued for four weeks and on 18 March they made an all-out assault. Five British and two French battleships were lost and other vessels were struck by mines or damaged by shellfire and either sank or had to be withdrawn, before the command was given to withdraw the Allied fleet. This attack was followed by landings on Gallipoli during the period April–August. The Turkish forces, some of which were led by Colonel Mustafa Kemal (later Kemal Atatürk), held firm everywhere. A stalemate developed and finally the Allies called off the operation by evacuating the remaining troops in December 1915–January 1916. The battle cost the British and French some 250,000 casualties out of the 480,000 landed at Gallipoli. Turkish losses numbered some 100,000 but their defense had held the Dardanelles and effectively blocked all aid to Russia by this route. The reverse inscriptions read 1915 – ÇANNAKALE and ZAFERI 75. YIL – 1990 (Victory – 75 Years). Çannakale Boğazi is the Turkish name for the Dardanelles, named for the city of Çannakale on the Asian side of the Dardanelles.

Turkish Jews – 500 Years of Peace and Harmony

KM-1018
5,000 lira
1992 copper-nickel, 30 mm

KM-1016 • 50,000 lira • 1992 .925 silver
KM-1017 • 500,000 lira • 1992 .900 gold
KM-1018 • 5,000 lira • 1992 copper-nickel

The reverse shows in front a crowded three-master at a quay in the harbor of Constantinople against the background of the Sea of Marmara on which three vessels can be discerned, and a group of Turks standing on the quay in front of the ship. The scene depicts the arrival in Constantinople (now Istanbul) in 1492 of Jews that had been expelled from Spain. The expulsion was instigated by the Dominican friar Tomás de Torquemada. As the head of the Spanish Inquisition—the institution of the Catholic Church designated to combat heresy—he concluded that the persecution and mass burnings of Jewish converts to Christianity who secretly continued practicing Judaism was not enough to ensure that the converts would become faithful Christians obeying the rules of the Church, and that in order to establish the Catholic faith it was necessary to get rid of the Jews and their influence on the new Christians. After the Spanish army had defeated the forces of the Moorish Kingdom of Granada in January 1492, thereby restoring the whole of Spain to Christian rule, Queen Isabella and King Ferdinand felt that the Jews were expendable, and on 31 March 1492 they signed an edict whereby the entire Jewish community in Spain, estimated at some 200,000 people, was ordered to depart from the Kingdom of Aragon and Castile by the end of July of the same year, unless they agreed to receive baptism. In this short time span of four months the Jews had to sell their property, finding only buyers who were willing to pay a tiny fraction of its value. The majority of the Jews crossed the border to Portugal, others sailed to North Africa and Turkey. Tens of thousands of refugees died while trying to reach safety. By order of Sultan Bayezit II, the Spanish Jews were granted refuge in the Turkish empire, in which they were received favorably and their religion was respected on a par with Christianity. The reverse inscription is in English: 500 YEARS OF PEACE AND HARMONY – TURKISH JEWS – 1492–1992.

Piri Reis (2)

KM-1038 • 50,000 lira • 1995 – *see* T-2
KM-1039 • 500,000 lira • 1995 – *see* T-2

Endangered Wildlife – Mediterranean Seal

KM-1047 • 1,000,000 lira • 1996 .925 silver

The reverse depicts a vessel of indiscernible type on the horizon, in front a Mediterranean monk seal lying on a beach, and in the sea behind it the heads of two more seals. The Mediterranean monk seal (*Monachus monachus*) is Europe's most endangered mammal. Its name derives from the folds of skin around the neck that resemble monastic dress. The obverse shows an underwater scene with several fish and a crab.

Barbaros Hayreddin

KM-1082 • 1,500,000 lira • 1997 .925 silver

KM-1082
1,500,000 lira
1997 .925 silver, 38.7 mm

The reverse depicts a galleon, the flagship of Admiral Barbaros Hayreddin (Khair ed-Din) (1466–1546), followed by another ship. Barbaros' three-masted flagship was a frightening fortress equipped with 60–100 cannons on three decks that could serve as a battleship on the open sea and to fire at fortified harbors. In the early 16th century Barbaros (Barbarossa, Redbeard) and his elder brother Oruç (Aruj) had been leaders of corsairs—pirates who operated from the ports of

Tripoli, Tunis and Algiers along the Barbary coast of north Africa, targeting Christian shipping in the Mediterranean Sea. They controlled large fleets of galleys and operated under the protection of the Ottoman sultan and the dey of Tunis. In 1533 Barbaros, who was the governor of the independent state he had created in Algiers, with his 18 admirals and a powerful navy, offered his services to Sultan Süleyman the Magnificent. The sultan appointed him to the position of commander-in-chief of the Ottoman navy. Barbaros was the greatest and most successful of all the Ottoman naval commanders. In the battle of Preveza in 1538 he defeated Andrea Doria, the Genoese admiral in Spanish service, and he conquered Tunisia for the Ottomans. Ships under the Ottoman four half-moon flags could be distinguished from those of other countries because their figureheads were dragons, tigers, horses or lions, while the figureheads of ships of non-Muslim countries were human figures. The reverse inscription is BARBAROS HAYREDDIN PAŞA KAPTAN-I DERYA 1533, the year 1533 denoting the year of Barbaros' appointment as Kaptan-ı Derya (Naval Commander-in-Chief).

Fethiye

KM-1087 • 4,000,000 lira • 1999 .925 silver

The reverse depicts two sailing ships, one of them the three-masted *Fethiye*, a 96-gun ship-of-the-line, the result of the rebuilding and modernization of the Ottoman fleet in the years 1829–1831. Fethiya is the name of a town on the Gulf of Fethiya in southwestern Turkey opposite the Greek island of Rhodes.

KM-1087
4,000,000 lira
1999 .925 silver, 38.7 mm

80th Anniversary of Atatürk's Voyage to Samsun

KM-1088 • 4,000,000 lira • 1999 .925 silver

KM-1088
4,000,000 lira
1999 .925 silver, 38 mm

The reverse features the portrait of Mustafa Kemal Atatürk (1881–1938) above the 279-ton cargo/passenger ship SS *Bandirma*. Built by Macintyre in Glasgow in 1878 and registered as *Trocadero*, she was 156 ft (48 m) long and 22 ft (6.8 m) in beam. She was sold and renamed *Kymi* in 1885, sold and renamed *Panderma* in 1894, and sold and renamed *Bandirma* in 1910. On 16 May 1919 Atatürk left Istanbul in *Bandirma* for the port of Samsun on the Black Sea, disembarking at Samsun on 19 May. Here he formed a liberation army and started a national movement for independence. He overthrew the Turkish sultan and founded the Republic of Turkey in 1923, of which he was the first president (1923–1938). He worked to make Turkey a modern secular state, abolishing the caliphate, closing down monasteries and religious orders, setting up secular schools instead of the traditional, mainly religious, system of education, totally revising the legal system, replacing the Islamic calendar by the Gregorian calendar, replacing the Arabic script by a modified Latin alphabet, banning the fez and encouraging Western-style dress, and requiring all Turks to adopt surnames. The surname "Atatürk" (Father of Turks) was given to him in 1934 by the National Assembly. *Bandirma* was sold for scrap in 1925. Atatürk's cabin on his voyage in 1919 is preserved in the Naval Museum in Istanbul.

Piri Reis

KM-1098 ● 1,000,000 lira ● 1997 – see T-2

Bogaziçı'nde Yalilar

KM-1159 ● 10,000,000 lira ● 2001 .925 silver

The reverse depicts a rowboat on the Bosporus in front of waterfront mansions (*yalı*) in Istanbul. The Bosporus is the strait connecting the Black Sea with the Sea of Marmara. The mansions were built as summer residences for highly placed officials of the court.

T-1 500th Anniversary of the Birth of Turgut Reis

KM-976
5,000 lira
1985 .925 silver, 38.6 mm

KM-976 ● 5,000 lira ● 1985 .925 silver
KM-? ● 50,000 lira ● 1985 .917 gold

The reverse features a portrait of Turgut Ali Pasha (1485–1565)— known in Turkey as Turgut Reis and to Europeans as Dragut—and to the left of the portrait sailing ships of his fleet. Turgut started life at sea as a pirate. He served under the command of Barbarossa (*see* KM-1082) and was among the corsairs who joined the Ottoman navy at the invitation of the sultan. Turgut took a leading part in battles all over the Mediterranean Sea between the Ottoman empire and the Christian powers, more than once against the Genoese admiral in Spanish service, Andrea Doria. In 1540 Turgut's fleet was trapped in an inlet on Corsica, Turgut was taken captive and at the age of 56 became a galley slave. Four years later Barbarossa forced the Genoese to release him. In 1546 Barbarossa died and Turgut became the commander of the Barbary corsairs. He captured all of Tunisia but in 1550 lost the northern part of this region to Andrea Doria who commanded a large Christian allied fleet. Turgut managed to escape to the island of Djerba with 20 galleasses, galleys and brigantines. When surrounded by Doria's forces, Turgut hauled his ships overland to the other side of the island and escaped from there. In 1551 he captured Gozo, Malta's second island and took its entire population into slavery. In 1553 he conquered the island of Corsica. From 1554 Turgut served Sultan Süleyman I (the Magnificent, called Kanuni, the Lawgiver, by the Turks) as an admiral in the Ottoman navy. That same year Turgut conquered Tripoli (now Libya) and was appointed its governor. In 1558 the Turks together with the Barbary corsairs established control over most of the North African coast. In 1565 Turgut's squadron was a part of the fleet of 181 Ottoman ships that laid siege to Malta. He was killed at the age of 80 by a stone splinter from a rock that was struck by a cannon ball fired from a Maltese fortification. Turgut Reis was born on the Bodrum Peninsula opposite the Greek island of Kos. His home village is now named Turgutreis. The reverse inscriptions are TURGUT REIS and 1485–1985 BESYÜZÜNCÜ DOĞOM YILI (500th Birth Year).

T-2 Piri Reis

KM-1038 • 50,000 lira • 1995 .925 silver
KM-1039 • 500,000 lira • 1995 .917 gold
KM-1098 • 1,000,000 lira • 1997 .999 gold

KM-1039
500,000 lira
1995 .917 gold, 22 mm

The reverse features the flagship of the admiral and cartographer Muhji al-din Piri (1470–1554), known as Piri Reis. (Reis is Turkish for captain or admiral.) The ship depicted resembles a caramusal, the common Turkish vessel in the 16th to 19th centuries. The caramusal was similar to a galleon, carried four sails, and as a merchant ship had a cargo capacity of up to 900 tons. Piri spent his first 14 years at sea as a corsair with his uncle, Kemal Reis, fighting against other pirates and trying to seize ships. In 1494 Kemal accepted the invitation by the Ottoman government to join the imperial navy, along with his experienced crew. Piri was given command over a number of vessels in Kemal's fleet. He took part in the Ottomans' campaigns against the Venetians in 1502, against Egypt in 1516 and against Rhodes in 1523. Between campaigns in the fleet Piri worked at home, first on a map of the world, later on a book. He presented his first map of the world to Sultan Selim I in 1517. It already incorporated Columbus' discoveries. Piri's prime sources were probably captured Spanish and Portuguese ships but Piri's map is far more accurate than other maps of his time. The title of Piri's book is *Kitab-I Bahriye* (Book of Navigation). It contains more than 500 pages of text and 220 maps. The text describes the navigation routes along the coasts of the Aegean and the Mediterranean Seas, including details about ports and their facilities, ship repair possibilities and how to obtain drinking water and food. The book and Piri's second world map were presented to Sultan Süleyman I in 1526. After that year Piri served in the Red Sea, Arabian Sea, Persian Gulf and Indian Ocean, and was appointed Admiral of the Indian Ocean Fleet in 1547. He led successful campaigns against the Portuguese around the Persian Gulf and was instrumental in bringing southern Arabia under direct Ottoman control; however, after a failed attack on Ormuz he was condemned to death and executed at the age of 84.

UKRAINE

The Ukraine is a republic in southeastern Europe. It attained independence in 1991 upon the dissolution of the USSR. The original meaning of the name Ukraine is "border country"— the region that segregated the settled Slavs from the nomadic Tatars. The obverse of almost all of the Ukrainian coins features the country's coat-of-arms, the trident, which is already found on gold and silver coins of Volodymyr (Vladimir) the Great (979–1015), the grand prince of Kiev.

50th Anniversary of the End of World War II – Kerch

KM-11 • 200,000 karbovantsiv • 1995 copper-nickel

The reverse shows the "Obelisk of Glory" World War II monument in Kerch and a tanker in the background. Kerch is a port on the Crimea at the eastern end of the Kerch Peninsula between the Sea of Azov in the north and the Black Sea in the south. The obelisk stands at the top of the Mitridat Hill. It honors the soldiers of the Special Prymorsk Army, the seamen of the Black Sea Navy and the Azov battle fleet, and the citizens of the city who perished when defending the Crimea against the German invaders. Kerch was the fourth city in the Ukraine to be declared a "hero city" via a proclamation by the Supreme Soviet of the USSR for its contribution to the victory by the Soviets and their allies over the Axis powers in the Great Patriotic War of 1941–1945 (the years in which the Soviets participated in World War II). The proclamation was issued in 1973. The city was awarded both the Order of Lenin and the Gold Star Medal.

50th Anniversary of the End of World War II – Odessa

KM-12 • 200,000 karbovantsiv • 1995 copper-nickel

KM-12
200,000 karbovantsiv
1995 copper-nickel, 32.9 mm

The reverse shows in the center the World War II Monument for an Unknown Seaman in the Black Sea port of Odessa, at left a generic merchant vessel moored in a seaport with port cranes, and at right the Odessa lighthouse. The monument in Shevchenko Central Recreation Park honors the soldiers of the

Special Prymorsk Army, seamen of the Black Sea Navy and volunteers of the Odessa division of the emergency volunteer corps who died during the defense of Odessa against troops of Germany and its allies in August–October 1941. Kiev, the Ukraine's capital, Odessa and Sevastopol (*see* KM-14) were declared "hero cities" in 1965 and were awarded the Order of Lenin and the Gold Star Medal for their contribution to the victory by the Soviets and their allies over the Axis powers in World War II (1941–1945).

50th Anniversary of the End of World War II – Sevastopol

KM-14 • 200,000 karbovantsiv • 1995 copper-nickel

The reverse features in the center the Obelisk to the Hero City of Sevastopol, which is the city's World War II monument, at right the silhouette of a modern generic navy vessel and at left the Crimean War monument (*see* KM-342). The port city of Sevastopol on the southwestern point of the Crimean peninsula was founded in 1783 by Russia after the annexation of the Crimea. The obelisk stands on the bank of the North Bay. It honors the soldiers of the Special Prymorsk Army, seamen of the Black Sea Navy, emergency volunteers and fighter battalion warriors who died for the defense of Sevastopol against German and Romanian forces for 250 days in 1941/42. In 1965 the Supreme Soviet of the USSR issued a proclamation in which it honored Sevastopol, together with Kiev and Odessa (*see* KM-12), with the Order of Lenin and the Gold Star Medal and declared them "hero cities" for their contribution to the victory by the Soviets and their allies over the Axis powers in the Great Patriotic War of 1941–1945 (the years in which the Soviets participated in World War II). The Crimean war was the war with the largest number of troops fought in the present-day Ukraine in the 19th century. Participants included regiments raised in the Ukraine and units of the Black Sea Cossack's forces who opposed British, French, Turkish and Sardinian forces.

Annual Meeting of the Board of Governors of the European Bank for Regional Development

KM-48 • 2 hryvni • 1998 copper-nickel

The reverse features a Viking-like ship above the logo of the European Bank for Reconstruction and Development (EBRD). The ship is a monument to the legendary founders of Kiev erected in Primakov Park in that city. The persons standing in the ship are the three brothers Kyi, Schek and Khoriv and their sister Lybid, members of a Slavic tribe who founded the city of Kiev toward the end of the 5th century on the steep hills of the west bank of the

Dnieper River, 470 miles (756 km) southwest of Moscow. The city, Kyyiv in Ukrainian, was named for the eldest brother, Kyi. The reverse design—the monument above the EBRD logo—was the logo of the Annual Meeting of the Board of Governors of the EBRD that was held in Kiev in May 1998. Kiev was the capital of Kievan Rus, the Eastern Slavic state that was founded by the Varangians, warrior-merchants known in the west as Vikings. This state is considered the birthplace of Russian civilization. The hryvnia currency was introduced in 1996. The exchange rate was 100,000 karbovantsiv to 1 hryvnia (plural: hryvni, hryven).

200th Anniversary of the Opening of the Contract Fair in Kiev

KM-57 ● 20 hryven ● 1997 .925 silver

KM-57
20 hryven
1997 .925 silver, 38.6 mm

The reverse features the Kiev City Council building and in front a two-masted ship at the Podil embankment on the Dnieper River. The image of the building is based on the drawing *The Façade of the Old Kiev Fortress* by M. Razhen. The first contract fair took place in this building in 1797. This fair was an important annual event for commerce and a center of social–political life from the end of the 18th century until the beginning of the 20th.

Prince Askold

KM-86 ● 10 hryven ● 1999 .925 silver

KM-86
10 hryven
1999 .925 silver, 38.6 mm

The reverse features Prince Askold (?–882), a ruler of the state of Kiev, leading his armed men on a campaign in their Viking ships. In the middle of the 9th century Askold and Dir, two Varangians, took over power from leaders of local tribes who were unable to protect the land from the Khazars. The reverse legends are "Askold – 9th Century" and "Prince of the Ukraine."

Olympic Games 2000 Sydney

KM-93 ● 2 hryvni ● 2000 copper-nickel-zinc, sportswoman performing triple jump
KM-94 ● 2 hryvni ● 2000 copper-nickel-zinc, gymnast on parallel bars
KM-97 ● 2 hryvni ● 2000 copper-nickel-zinc, yachtsman
KM-101 ● 2 hryvni ● 2000 copper-nickel-zinc, female gymnast doing floor exercises

The stylized sportspersons depicted on the obverse are, from right to left, a yachtsman sailing in his yacht, a sportswoman performing a triple jump, a gymnast on parallel bars and a female gymnast doing floor exercises. Each of them is shown on the reverse of one of the coins in the series.

Peter Sahaidachny

KM-120 ● 10 hryven ● 2000 .925 silver

KM-120
10 hryven
2000 .925 silver, 38 mm

The reverse depicts a 17th-century sailing ship and two rowboats, and a medallion portrait of Peter Konoshevich Sahaidachny (1578?–1622). Each of the rowboats is propelled by nine rowers. Sahaidachny was a military leader, diplomat and Ukrainian nationalist. In 1614–1616 and in 1620–1622 he was the hetman of the Ukrainian Registered Cossacks. The supporters of the country's shield on the obverse are the archangel Michael, symbol of Kiev, and a crowned lion symbolizing the city of Lvov.

2,500 Years Yevpatoria

KM-186 ● 5 hryven ● 2003 copper-nickel-zinc

The reverse depicts a sailing ship at sea in front of the health resort of Yevpatoria in Crimea and in the foreground a seagull sitting on an amphora. In the 5th century BCE there was an ancient Greek settlement at the place of present-day Yevpatoria.

2,500 Years Balaklava

KM-205 ● 5 hryven ● 2004 copper-nickel-zinc

The obverse depicts two ancient Greek trading ships, each on one side of the national coat-of-arms. The upper part of the reverse gives a view of Balaklava Bay with two sailing ships at right and the shield of the city of Balaklava at left, while the lower part of the reverse features a column and two anchors that were found during archeological excavations. The origins of Balaklava (Fish Town) in the municipal area of Sevastopol in Crimea go back to an ancient settlement that was captured by the Greeks in the 4th century BCE.

110th Anniversary of the Birth of Oleksander Dovzhenko

KM-211 ● 2 hryvni ● 2004 copper-nickel-zinc

The obverse depicts a boy standing in a boat holding a candle in his hand, floating on the river of time to meet his destiny. The coin honors the writer and artist Oleksander P. Dovzhenko (1894–1956) who founded the Ukrainian national school of cinematography. His feature film *Earth* (1930) is listed among the best feature films ever produced.

Captain Bilousov's 50th Anniversary

KM-221 ● 5 hryven ● 2004 copper-nickel-zinc
KM-224 ● 10 hryven ● 2004 .925 silver

KM-221
5 hryven
2004 copper-nickel-zinc, 35 mm

The reverse depicts the icebreaker *Captain Bilousov* amid blocks of ice and a boat in open water in the background. The 5,350-ton ship was built in Finland in 1954 for the Soviet Union and was still in operation in 2004. She has a cruising radius of 8,760 miles (14,100 km) and has sufficient reserves of fuel, water and food to be self-sufficient for 28 days. The icebreaker is named for the Arctic explorer Captain Mykhailo P. Belousov (1904–1946), a Hero of the Soviet Union. Since 1994 the ship belongs to the Mariupil state merchant marine. The inscription at the top of the reverse is CAPTAIN BILOUSOV; that in the part of the water which is free from ice translates to "Icebreaker." The obverse depicts an anchor and a steering wheel.

150th Anniversary of the Defense of Sevastopol in the Crimean War

KM-342 ● 10 hryven ● 2004 .925 silver

The background of the reverse depicts sailing and steam ships and a fort protecting the entrance to the bay on which Sevastopol is situated, while in front ship cannons are shown along with various types of ammunition—case-shot, cannon balls, bombs and ramrods. The obverse features the Crimean War monument in Sevastopol against the background of bastions and batteries. This monument commemorates the ships of the Russian Black Sea Fleet scuttled across the entrance to the harbor when defending Russian-held Sevastopol for 349 days in 1854/55, to prevent access to the city's harbor by enemy steam ships. The monument is 55 ft (17 m) high.

T-1 Olympic Games 2006 Athens

KM-? ● 10 hryven ● 2004 .925 silver

The reverse depicts sportsmen representing various disciplines, among which is canoeing at 7 o'clock.

UNION OF SOVIET SOCIALIST REPUBLICS

Coins issued by the Union of Soviet Socialist Republics (USSR) are listed under **Russia**, the dominant republic of the USSR.

VATICAN CITY

The Vatican City occupies only 109 acres (44 hectares) and has less than a thousand inhabitants. It became an independent sovereign state by the Lateran Treaty of 1929 between Italy and the Holy See. Its coins conform to Italian standards and are legal tender in Italy.

Annual Issues

Y-7 ● 5 lire ● 1929–37 .835 silver, rev. Pius XI with years VIII–XVI of his pontificate
Y-17 ● 5 lire ● dual date 1933–1934 .835 silver
Y-28 ● 5 lire ● 1939–41 .835 silver, rev. Pius XII with years I–III of his pontificate

The reverse depicts St. Peter sitting in a small fishing rowboat, holding the tiller with his left hand and lifting his right arm toward heaven. The boat represents the Church. Peter was one of Jesus' twelve apostles and a fisherman by trade. He was the first bishop of Rome; the popes are his successors. Peter is often depicted as a fisherman, symbolic of his "fishing" of men to bring them into the Christian faith. The pope's title stated on the obverse, *Pontifex Maximus* (Supreme Pontiff), originally meant chief bridge builder, an important office in ancient Rome that was built on both sides of the Tiber. In the course of time, the chief bridge builder became the head of the Roman religion and in this meaning it became one of the imperial titles. Generally it is the first title on coins of Roman emperors, before the titles of holder of the tribunician power, consul and father of his country. With the introduction of Christianity as the state religion, the position of head of the religion was taken over by the bishop of Rome, i.e. the pope. Y-17 marks the extraordinary Holy Year 1933/34 declared by Pope Pius XI to mark the 1,900th anniversary of the death and resurrection of Jesus in 33 CE and to commemorate the fifth anniversary of the founding of the State of Vatican City by the Lateran Treaty. While the obverse of the coins of the other years denotes the year of the pontificate, on Y-17 the year denoted is A IVB (Anno Ivbilaei, Jubilee Year in Latin). In the Roman

Catholic tradition a Holy Year is a year of forgiveness of sins, in which pilgrims coming to Rome visit the four main basilicas in the city and pass through the Holy Doors. These doors are bricked over between Holy Years and are opened by the pope at the beginning of the Holy Year. In 1933, the Holy Doors were opened on Palm Sunday. They were closed in 1934 on the Monday immediately preceding Easter.

Annual Issue

Y-127 ● 10 lire ● 1975 (MCMLXXV) aluminum

The reverse features Noah in the Ark looking at the dove returning to the Ark with a fresh olive leaf in its beak (*see* Armenia T-1). The scene is symbolic of the reconciliation between God and the human race, as told in the Bible: God flooded the earth because it was corrupt and filled with violence. After the flood God vowed that there would never be another flood again to destroy the earth. The obverse features the coat-of-arms of the pope. On top of the shield is the tiara, the emblem of the papacy, below which are two crossed keys. The key pointing to the upper left signifies the power of the pope which extends even to heaven. The key pointing to the upper right symbolizes the pope's power over all the faithful on earth. The obverse legend is AN IVB MCMLXXV (Anno Ivbilaei MCMLXXV, Jubilee Year 1975).

Annual Issue

Y-139 ● 500 lire ● 1978 .835 silver, Year 16 of Paulus VI's pontificate

The reverse depicts Jesus walking on the water toward a boat in which there are two men. Jesus and the man in the front of the boat stretch out a hand toward the other. The Gospels tell about Jesus who sent his disciples to cross the Sea of Galilee by boat. In the night Jesus came to them, walking on the sea. Peter said that he wanted to go to Jesus, also walking on the water, to which Jesus agreed. Peter came out of the boat and walked on the water, but there was a wind, Peter became afraid, and with the boat beginning to sink, he prayed Jesus to save him. Jesus stretched out his hand and caught him, and asked Peter why he was of so little faith. The disciples took Jesus on board, the wind ceased, and in no time they reached their destination.

Annual Issue

Y-181 ● 200 lire ● 1984 aluminum-bronze, Year 6 of John Paul II's pontificate

The reverse depicts a ship sailing toward the word PAX (Peace) inscribed amid cruciform rays. The ship represents the Church.

Annual Issue

Y-190 ● 500 lire ● 1985 aluminum-bronze core in stainless steel ring, Year 7 of John Paul II's pontificate

The reverse depicts St. Paul in a sailing ship. He is holding his attributes—a sword in his right hand and a book in his left. Paul was the disciple who led the way in spreading the gospel of Jesus to non-Christians in the Church's earliest days. The theme of the coin was inspired by Pope John Paul II's travels throughout the world.

500th Anniversary of the Discovery of America

Y-235 ● 500 lire ● 1992 .835 silver, Year 14 of John Paul II's pontificate

The reverse features the three ships of Christopher Columbus—*Santa Maria*, *Niña* and *Pinta* (*see* Andorra KM-78)—sailing west on a map of the Atlantic Ocean from Spain to the Caribbean islands, guided by a cross. The obverse depicts the pope who, from the Old World, blesses the newly discovered Americas against the background of light beams focused on the New World. The edge inscription is V SAEC. EXPLETO AB INITA EVANGELIZATIONE AMERICAE (Completion of Five Centuries Since the Beginning of the Evangelization of America).

Annual Issue

Y-244 ● 10 lire ● 1993 aluminum, Year 15 of John Paul II's pontificate

The reverse depicts the sailboat of the apostle Peter. The theme of the coins issued in 1993 in the annual series was "The Catechism of the Catholic Church." The boat symbolizes the Church.

Toward the Holy Year 2000

Y-319 ● 10,000 lire ● 1997 (MCMXCVII) .835 silver

The reverse depicts Jesus and his disciples in a sailboat on a stormy sea. The theme of the coin is "The Calming of the Sea." As told in the Bible, Jesus and his disciples were in a boat on the sea when suddenly a great tempest arose. Jesus rebuked the winds and the sea, they obeyed, and the sea calmed. The reverse inscription is VERSO L'ANNO SANTO DEL 2000 (Toward the Holy Year 2000).

Y-319
10,000 lire
1997 .835 silver, 34 mm

The Roots of the Faith – Noah's Ark

Y-361 ● 20 euro ● 2002 (MMII) .917 gold, Year 24 of John Paul II's pontificate

The reverse depicts violent men and animals against the background of Noah's Ark, prior to the flood (*see* Armenia T-1). These men expired in the flood. Representatives of the animal species were saved in the ark. The theme of the coin is "The Roots of the Faith."

YUGOSLAVIA

Yugoslavia (Land of the South Slavs) in southeastern Europe on the Adriatic Sea was formed after World War I. In 1963 it was renamed the Socialist Federal Republic (SFR) of Yugoslavia. The federation fell apart in the 1990s; the break-up was completed in 2006. Yugoslavia's constituent parts are now six sovereign states—Croatia, Macedonia, Montenegro, Serbia, Slovenia, and Bosnia and Herzegovina.

Mediterranean Games 1979 Split

KM-66 • 150 dinara • 1978 .925 silver

The reverse features the 6,239-ton SS *Bakar*. The steamer was built in 1969 and had a length of 498 ft (152 m), a beam of 66 ft (20 m) and a draft of 37 ft (11 m). She was named for the port of Bakar east of Rijeka, Croatia. She served as a Yugoslavian freighter until being transferred to Jamaica in 1992 and ended her service in 1994. The 8th Mediterranean Games were held in 1979 in the Adriatic port city of Split, Croatia. The obverse depicts President Josip Broz (1892–1980), better known by his pseudonym Tito.

KM-66
150 dinara
1978 .925 silver, 30 mm

International Canoeing Championships 1982

KM-94 • 1500 dinara • 1982 .925 silver

The obverse depicts a paddler in a canoe against the background of two hemispheres. The 17th International Canoeing Championships were held in 1982 in Belgrade. The late President Josip Broz (Tito), who died in 1980, is shown on the reverse.

SELECT BIBLIOGRAPHY

Books

Albion, R. G. *Five Centuries of Famous Ships*. New York: McGraw-Hill, 1978.
Antoine, L. W. *Nautical Numismatics*. Palm Bay, FL: private issue, 2003.
Baker, D. B. (ed.). *Explorers and Discoverers of the World*. Detroit: Gale Research, 1993.
Bathe, B. W. *Seven Centuries of Sea Travel*. London: Barrie & Jenkins, 1972.
Beylen, J. v. *Maritieme Encyclopedie*. Bussum: de Boer, 1972.
Brouwer, N. J. *The International Register of Historic Ships*. Peekskill, NY: Sea History Press, 1999.
Bruce II, C. R. (ed.). *Standard Catalog of World Coins, 1801–1900*, 3rd edition. Iola, WI: Krause Publications, 2001.
Bruce II, C. R. (ed.). *Standard Catalog of World Coins, 1901–2000*, 34th edition. Iola, WI: Krause Publications, 2006.
Bruce II, C. R. (ed.). *Standard Catalog of World Coins, 2001–Date*. Iola, WI: Krause Publications, 2006.
Delpar, H. *The Discoverers – An Encyclopedia of Explorers and Exploration*. New York: McGraw-Hill, 1980.
Dodge, E. S. *Beyond the Capes – Pacific Exploration from Captain Cook to the* Challenger *1776–1877*. Boston: Little, Brown and Co., 1971.
Doty, R. G. *The Macmillan Encyclopedic Dictionary of Numismatics*. New York: Macmillan, 1982.
Dunan, M. (ed.). *Larousse Encyclopedia of Modern History*. New York: Crown Publishers, 1972.
Eggenberger, D. *An Encyclopedia of Battles*. Mineola, NY: Dover, 1985.
Fitzsimons, B. *The Illustrated Encyclopedia of 20th Century Weapons and Warfare*. New York: Phoebus, 1977.
Galuppini, G. *Weltenzyklopädie der Schiffe – Band I: Kriegsschiffe von den Anfängen bis heute*. München: Südwest, 1985. (original edition: *Enciclopedia delle Navi da Guerra*)
Gardiner, R. (ed.). *The Golden Age of Shipping – The Classic Merchant Ship 1900–1960*. London: Conway, 1994.
Gardiner, R., and Chumbley, S. (ed.). *Conway's All the World's Fighting Ships 1947–1995*. London: Conway, 1995.
Gibbons, T. *The Complete Encyclopedia of Battleships and Battlecruisers – A Technical Directory of All the World's Capital Ships from 1860 to the Present day*. London: Salamander Books, 1983.
Gibbons, T., ed. *The Encyclopedia of Ships*. Leicester: Silverdale, 2001.
Goodwin, P. *The Ships of Trafalgar – The British, French and Spanish Fleets October 1805*. London: Conway, 2005.
Hadden, A. C. *Canoes of Oceania – Vol. II: The Canoes of Melanesia, Queensland, and New Guinea*. Honolulu: Bernice P. Bishop Museum, 1937.

Hogg, G. *The Hovercraft Story*. London: Abelard-Schuman, 1970.
Hosch, C. R. *Heraldic Coats of Arms on Coins of the World, 1700–1998: Complete Descriptions*. Marietta, GA: Regal Treasures, 1998.
Hosch, C. R. *National Coats of Arms on World Banknotes, c.1800–1997*. Marietta, GA: Regal Treasures, 1997.
Hosch, C. R. *World Gold Proof Sets Since 1900: Complete Descriptions*. Marietta, GA: private issue, 2002.
Hough, R. *Fighting Ships*. London: Michael Joseph, 1969.
Hynds, P. *Worldwide High Speed Ferries*. London: Conway, 1992.
Isaacs, A. (ed.). *The Macmillan Encyclopedia*. London: Macmillan, 1992.
Junge, E. *World Coin Encyclopedia*. New York: William Morrow, 1984.
Kemp, P. (ed.). *The Oxford Companion to Ships and the Sea*. Oxford: Oxford University Press, 1988.
Kludas, A. *Great Passenger Ships of the World* (Volumes 1–5). Cambridge: Patric Stephens, 1972–76.
Koop, G. *Die deutschen Segelschulschiffe*. Koblenz: Bernard & Graefe, 1989.
Landström, B. *The Ship*. Garden City, NY: Doubleday & Company, 1961.
Makins, M. (ed.). *Collins English Dictionary*. Glasgow: HarperCollins, 1991.
Mariners' Museum, The. *A Dictionary of the World's Watercraft – From Aak to Zumbra*. Rochester, Kent: Chatham, 2001.
Marshall, C. (ed.). *The Encyclopedia of Ships*. Leicester: Blitz, 1996.
Miller, Jr., W. H. *Pictorial Encyclopedia of Ocean Liners, 1860–1994*. New York: Dover, 1995.
Morris, R. *Pacific Sail – Four Centuries of Western Ships in the Pacific*. Southampton: Ashford Press, 1987.
Mueller-Reichau, W. *Naves in Nummis – Handbuch der Numisnautik, 1. Teil: Ikonographische Kommentare zu Münzen aus nachantiker Zeit*. Laboe: private issue, 1974.
Munro, C. *Sailing Ships*. London: Pelham, 1973.
Natkiel, R., and Preston, A. *The Weidenfeld Atlas of Maritime History*. London: Weidenfeld and Nicolson, 1986.
Obojski, R. *Ships and Explorers on Coins*. New York: Sterling Publishing Co., 1970.
Paine, L. *Ships of the World, An Historical Encyclopedia*. London: Conway, 1998.
Paxton, J. *Encyclopedia of Russian History – From the Christianization of Kiev to the Break-Up of the U.S.S.R.* Santa Barbara: ABC-Clio, 1993.
Pennington, P. *The Great Explorers*. London: Aldus, 1979.
Pickford, N. *The Atlas of Ship Wreck and Treasure*. London: Dorling Kindersley, 1995.
Preston, A. *An Illustrated History of the Navies of World War II*. London: Hamlyn/Bison, 1976.
Ring, T. (ed.): *International Dictionary of Historic Places*. Chicago: Fitzroy Dearborn, 1995.
Roberts, G. *Do You Know Boats & Ships?* Bournemouth: Pocket Reference Books, 1996.

Schön, G. *Weltmünzkatalog, 19. Jahrhundert*. Munich: Battenberg.
Schön, G. and Schön, G. *Weltmünzkatalog, 20. Jahrhundert, 1900–2006*. Munich: Battenberg, 2006.
Server, D. *Klippers en windjammers – Hoogtepunten uit de geschiedenis van de vierkant getuigde schepen*. Alphen aan de Rijn: Atrium, 2000.
Stuart, R. H. (ed.). *The Pictorial Story of Ships*. London: New English Library, 1977.
Talvio, T. *The Coins and Banknotes of Finland*. Helsinki: Bank of Finland, 1987.
Taylor, K. *A Tribute to the S.S. "VEGA" – The Channel Islands Red Cross Ship (1944–45)*. CISS Publishing, 1996.
Waldman, C., and Wexler, A. *Who Was Who in World Exploration*. New York: Facts on File, 1992.
Winton, J. *An Illustrated History of the Royal Navy*. San Diego: Thunder Bay Press, 2000.

Periodicals

Much of the information in this book is based on articles and news items in issues of 1970 onwards of the periodicals listed below. The articles are too numerous to be detailed here, for which I apologize to their authors.

Canadian Numismatic Journal, The, later *The CN Journal*. Ontario: The Canadian Numismatic Association.
Coin Monthly. Brentwood, England: Numismatic Publishing Co.
E-Sylum, The. Electronic weekly publication of the Numismatic Bibliomania Society.
Flaschenpost. Bremerhaven, Germany: Numisnautic Research Center.
Geldgeschichtliche Nachrichten. Frankfurt am Main, Germany: Gesellschaft für Internationale Geldgeschichte.
Münze, Die. Vienna, Austria: Austrian Mint.
Numismatist, The, later *Numismatist*. Colorado Springs, CO: American Numismatic Association.
Numisnautik. Hamburg, Germany: AG Numisnautik.
Topical Numismatics Society Newsletter, later *Journal of the Topical Numismatics Society*. Long Beach, CA: Topical Numismatics Society.
World Coin News. Iola, WI: Krause Publications.

INDEX